THE MARINES'
LOST
SQUADRON

THE ODYSSEY OF VMF-422

MARK CARLSON

Norad Bruno

(signature)

SUNBURY
PRESS

Mechanicsburg, PA USA

Published by Sunbury Press, Inc.
Mechanicsburg, Pennsylvania

www.sunburypress.com

ISBN: 978-1-62006-747-5 (Trade paperback)
ISBN: 978-1-62006-780-2 (Mobipocket)

Library of Congress Control Number: 2017960989

SECOND SUNBURY PRESS EDITION: June 2018

Product of the United States of America
0 1 1 2 3 5 8 13 21 34 55

Set in Bookman Old Style
Designed by Crystal Devine
Cover by Terry Kennedy
Edited by Erika Hodges

Continue the Enlightenment!

• CONTENTS •

PART THREE: *Semper Fidelis*—Always Faithful, Marine Corps Motto

It was my intent to tell a story involving Second World War military history and aviation in a narrative form that would be comfortable for the average twenty-first century reader. With that goal in mind, many of the contemporary military terms, words, or acronyms are explained in the text. For example, "NAVCAD" is first mentioned as Naval Aviation Cadet, and the long-obsolete Landing Signal Officer is called the "LSO." On the other hand, the ubiquitous life vest known colloquially as the "Mae West" needs little explanation. A glossary of military and contemporary terms is provided for easy reference in the appendices.

Often a word in quoted text or documents may need some clarification. The word "knot," for example. A knot is a unit of speed, based on the nautical mile, which is about 6,070 feet long. One hundred knots are approximately 115 miles per hour. Both terms appear in the text.

Since this event occurred prior to the formation of the Department of Defense, I only refer to the existing command structure of the War Department and Navy Department. Some places had different names in 1944. Tarawa is now the Republic of Kiribati, and the Ellice Islands are the nation of Tuvalu. I have consistently used the original names. Also, service ranks are written as they were then, such as "Lieutenant (jg)" instead of the current "LTJG." Unit designations are given in the manner in use at the time, but are defined for the reader.

Throughout much of the text, I use military dates and the standard 24-hour clock. Therefore, January 24, 1944 is written as 24 January 1944. The only exceptions are for civilian dates. Times are written as "1300 hours," rather than 1:00 p.m. The exceptions are in quoted statements or in a civilian context. "I saw him at one o'clock, on January 24." Often there are references to certain documents or recorded interviews. I referred to them in the first one or two cases to clarify the source. A listing of interviews, articles, letters, transcripts, memos, and other documents and their source will be listed in the bibliography.

I hope the reader will find this narrative informative and comfortable to read.

Mark Carlson

Mark Carlson has written a book that tells a story that has needed telling for seventy years. Known as the "Flintlock Disaster" because it occurred during the buildup to the invasion of the Marshall Islands code named "Operation Flintlock," the ferry flight of Marine Fighter Squadron 422 truly was a disaster that remains relatively unknown to this day. It resulted in the loss of six young Marine Corps aviators and twenty-two brand new F4U Corsairs. Fifteen pilots were ditched at sea to drift in rafts for four days in a huge storm. Only one lucky pilot defied all odds and made it to his destination. As tragic as the details are, Carlson has provided some lighter moments, including the story of the pilot who crash-landed on an island, then spent his time avoiding being married to one of the young daughters of the local chief.

This event should have received a lot of attention, especially from military officials. Any one of the following circumstances should have garnered interest: a general officer directing the squadron commander to fly the mission after denying his requests for an escort; a twenty hour old weather forecast that did not mention that a massive Pacific typhoon was building along their flight path; and the destination airfield not being informed that a flight of twenty-three aircraft were inbound. Any one of these circumstances that created the disaster is unimaginable today and I would submit that they should have been unimaginable in January of 1944!

This true account of the catastrophe has been thoroughly researched and Carlson's writing style will keep you on the edge of your seat from the first chapter to the end of the book. As a combat pilot myself, and one who has flown training flights that I probably should not have attempted, I fully appreciate the tension and apprehension these airmen undoubtedly experienced.

This is a truly spellbinding drama that will be talked about at cocktail parties and in aircrew ready rooms for years to come. Hopefully, it will also be a reminder of why we have procedures in place to keep something like this from happening again.

With best wishes for your reading pleasure,

Robert G. "Thunder" Butcher
Major General, US Marine Corps, Retired

Marine Fighter Squadron 422
The Flying Buccaneers
April 1943 to April 1947
Artwork by James Queen

25 JANUARY 1944

Shortly after noon on Tuesday, 25 January 1944, a calm sunny day over the central Pacific Ocean, twenty-three Marine Corps fighter pilots were suddenly confronted with a fate that none of them had ever imagined. Marine Fighter Squadron 422, known as the Flying Buccaneers, was a brand-new Corsair squadron, having become operational in California only four months earlier. The pilots were young men who came from all over the United States, hailing from big cities and farming towns, from high schools and universities, and from baseball diamonds and race courses. Only three had ever seen combat, but every man was eager to get into the war and destroy the Japanese. Trained at the best naval aviation schools in the country, they were as capable and ready as any group of patriotic Americans who followed the stars and stripes into the war. They were prepared to fight and risk their lives to serve their country. But when the new pilots reached the war zone in the Pacific, they suddenly encountered an enemy that did not carry guns in suicidal Banzai charges. Yet that enemy was just as implacable and deadly.

In 1944, the Second World War was in its fifth year. More than ten million American men and women had gone into uniform in the great crusade to rid the world of tyranny and fascism. Hundreds of transports, tankers, and warships were plying the seas carrying supplies and troops to the far-flung theaters of war across the globe. Occupied Europe was still prostrate under the Nazi boot heel but Hitler's Third Reich was being ground down on three battle fronts. From bases in England and Italy, the US Army Air Force and Royal Air Force were bombing Germany's war industry into rubble in preparation for the still-secret Normandy landing.

In the Pacific during the two years since the devastating attack on Pearl Harbor, the battles of the Coral Sea, Midway, Guadalcanal, and New Guinea had finally turned the tide against Japan. The once-unstoppable Imperial Navy and Army were on the defensive. Whole island groups and nations conquered by the Japanese were liberated and used as stepping stones from which to take the fight ever closer to the enemy homeland. The Gilbert Islands and Tarawa had fallen to the US Navy, Marines, and Army in late 1943. The next targets were two of the most important Japanese bases in the western Pacific, Kwajalein and Eniwetok, in the Marshall Islands. The campaign was code-named "Operation Flintlock."

In preparation for that invasion, VMF-422 took off from Hawkins Field on Tarawa at ten minutes to ten on that warm, clear January morning, bound for a small atoll named Funafuti at the southern end of the Ellice Island chain. It was to be a totally routine ferry flight of just over eight hundred miles to the south-southeast with a stop for refueling at Nanumea. Their Vought F4U-1D Corsairs were brand-new, fully armed, and fueled.

The commander was Major John S. MacLaughlin, a 1937 Annapolis graduate from Collingswood, New Jersey. VMF-422 was his first command. He had a wife and infant son back in California. Among the twenty-three pilots flying behind him was First Lieutenant Mark "Breeze" Syrkin, a New York-born graduate of Ohio State at Columbus. Tall and handsome with dark hair and hazel eyes, Syrkin had earned his nickname from his squadron mates because of his breezy way of charming women. Far behind him in the formation that day was First Lieutenant Robert "Curly" Lehnert, a Long Island native who had majored in chemical engineering at the University of Michigan. Curly had earned his nickname from his severely short Marine haircut.

First Lieutenant Ken Gunderson of Wisconsin, a tall, athletic basketball player was in the lead flight three slots behind MacLaughlin. Like his commander, he was married. First Lieutenant John Hansen was a twenty-one-year-old Iowan who had been an Eagle Scout. He was known for being soft-spoken in a profession dominated by extroverts.

Other Flying Buccaneers were Captains Cloyd Jeans and Charley Hughes, Lieutenants Walter "Jake" Wilson, Chris Lauesen, Sterling "Shou" Price, Royce "Tex" Watson, John "Abe" Lincoln, and Robert "Tiger" Moran. They and their thirteen comrades were well-trained and confident. MacLaughlin, aware this would be the first time his pilots would make a long over-water flight, had requested a navy patrol plane escort from the Marine Air Wing commander, but had been refused. MacLaughlin had no choice, yet he and his flight leaders were not overly concerned. The weather forecast over their route was for scattered clouds and occasional rain squalls. That weather report was twenty-six hours old.

The Flying Buccaneers winged their way south as their sleek Corsairs' engines thrummed out the cadence of power. For the first two hours, the sky was a clear azure blue. Flying at 1,800 feet the placid green ocean beneath their wings was like something from a picture postcard. They saw small islands dotted with palm trees and ringed by pure white beaches, garlanded with turquoise coral reefs. The waves were delicate brush strokes creeping across the calm water.

At ten minutes after noon, the marines saw a line of gray clouds rising over the distant horizon. At first it did not appear threatening, but as they flew closer the line rose into a towering barrier that looked like a gray death shroud.

The new squadron was unknowingly headed right at one of nature's most powerful and dangerous forces: a Pacific typhoon. Extending more than a hundred miles from east to west, the massive storm rose to well above fifty thousand feet. Inside its churning walls was a hellish black maelstrom of hammering rain, one hundred mile per hour winds and virtually zero visibility. The leaden clouds hung less than 250 feet above churning, heaving waves that charged like green mountains covered in gray beards of spray and foam. No one had told them it was there.

With few choices open to him, Major MacLaughlin decided they should fly into what he hoped was only a large rain squall. The huge mass welcomed the squadron into its malevolent embrace. One by one the planes disappeared like tiny insects into the storm. The sun began to fade, and then as if someone had turned off a switch, winked out. The clear blue world of sky and sun turned into a black hell. For the marine pilots, it was the beginning of an ordeal they could never have imagined.

In four days six pilots would be dead, five disappearing without a trace, twenty-two brand-new Corsairs would be on the bottom of the ocean, and seventeen pilots would endure the raging storm in tiny rafts, their lives threatened by man-eating sharks and exposure. It would become the worst non-combat loss of a Marine Corps fighter squadron in the war, and enter history as "The Flintlock Disaster." Yet for the next seventy years, it was virtually ignored and forgotten by all but those who lived through it.

"We knew whose fault it was," Major Mark Syrkin said many years later. "It wasn't Major MacLaughlin's fault. It wasn't even the briefing officer at Tarawa who'd told us the weather all the way to Funafuti was clear with scattered rain squalls. We were thrown into that storm by the orders of one man. We knew exactly who to blame for the disaster."

That man was the commanding officer of the Fourth Marine Base Defense Air Wing on Tarawa, Brigadier General Lewie G. Merritt.

PART ONE

ODYSSEY:
A LONG VOYAGE WITH
MANY CHANGES
OF FORTUNE

• CHAPTER 1 •

MARINE WINGS OF GOLD

In order to understand why those twenty-three young marine pilots were flying their Corsairs over the ocean, it will help to relate their role in the Pacific War. To accomplish this, we will follow the history of Marine Corps aviation. Along the way the reader will meet some of the key figures in the odyssey of VMF-422.

The United States Marine Corps is part of the Navy Department and has many of the same traditions and vocabulary. Marines say "overhead, deck, rack, and head" for ceiling, floor, bunk, and latrines. They respond to orders with "Aye-aye sir." Their emblem is of a globe and eagle surmising an anchor. Marine detachments serve on US warships and guard United States embassies overseas. A common bond links the United States Marine Corps and the United States Navy and this is nowhere more apparent than in aviation. Marine aviators receive the exact same flight training as navy flyers. Their squadron organization is the same, as are the gold wings they wear. Only their uniforms, insignia, and rank structure are different. They fly from land bases and aircraft carrier flight decks. Because of this, they have a pride second to none. To be a navy or marine aviator is to be one of the best, one of the few.

During the Second World War, more than ten thousand marine aviators and 125,000 ground crew served in 145 squadrons. Marine fighter pilots claimed 2,344 enemy planes, while losing 2,500 of their own. From Wake to Midway, from Guadalcanal to Kwajalein, from Iwo Jima to VJ Day, the marines were there.

It began on a warm, late May morning in 1912 when a fresh-faced Marine Second Lieutenant named Alfred Cunningham began his training as a marine aviator at Annapolis, Maryland. Cunningham, who'd been fascinated by flying since witnessing a hot-air balloon ascent in 1903, had joined the marines during the Spanish-American War. While on duty in the Philadelphia Navy Yard, he joined with other aeronautical enthusiasts to promote aviation for the armed forces. With the help of the Aero Club of Philadelphia,

Cunningham gained the support of influential businessmen and in-siders who convinced Major General William Biddle, Commandant of the Marine Corps, to seriously consider an aeronautical branch of the marines. Cunningham was ordered to the Naval Academy at Annapolis for his flight training, despite the fact that the Navy's own aviation branch was less than a year old and consisted of three officers, three mechanics, and three airplanes.

The date that Cunningham reported for duty, 22 May 1912, is considered the birthday of Marine Corps aviation. The US Navy's first aviators, First Lieutenants Theodore G. Ellyson, John H. Tow-ers and John Rodgers, had learned the art of flying from Glenn Curtiss on Coronado Island in San Diego. A Connecticut-born former motorcycle racer, Curtiss was one of the most ambitious pioneers of early flight. He had started training Navy aviators in 1911. At that time, he was in the midst of a bitter patent war with the Wright Brothers, an expensive legal feud that would only end with the American entry into the Great War. In fact, the first plane ever purchased by the United States Navy was a Curtiss A-1 Triad, an amphibian pusher biplane with controls for two pilots. Rodgers, whose family and naval lineage went back to the War of 1812, was also the cousin of Calbraith Perry "Cal" Rodgers, the audacious pilot who attempted the first coast-to-coast flight in a Wright EX called the "Vin Fiz" that same year. These men were in every sense the pioneers and architects of the future of naval aviation. Until the development of the aircraft carrier in the early 1920s, the only role seen for navy aviation was in coastal reconnaissance and defense. Even this was hotly contested by the army, whose own fledgling air arm was seeking to dominate the skies. At the new aviation camp at Annapolis, Ellyson and the others accepted Cunningham into their rarefied ranks and passed their own newly-acquired skills on to the marine officer. He received his actual flight training at the Burgess Airplane Company of Marblehead, Massachusetts and logged a to-tal of two hours and forty minutes. He was then considered ready to solo. On 20 August, Cunningham lifted his tiny Curtiss B-1 open-cockpit seaplane into the balmy summer air over Marblehead.

According to *A History of Marine Corps Aviation* by the Naval Heritage and History Command, Cunningham's first safe landing was due as much to luck as skill. Cunningham stated that just as the gasoline gage stick was indicating about empty, "I got up my nerve and made a good landing. How, I don't know."

Cunningham earned the coveted Wings of Gold and became Naval Aviator Number 5. He was quickly followed by Lieutenants Bernard L. Smith and William McIlvain.

*Lieutenant Alfred Cunningham by a Wright B-1 biplane in
1912. (Official U.S. Marine Corps photo.)*

Over the next several months Cunningham logged more than
four hundred flights and was a tireless promoter of marine aviation. He evaluated several aircraft for military use, and most importantly, how they could best be used. His work soon put him in the
front lines of the struggle to define Marine Corps aviation's role in
future warfare. Besides their traditional job as the advance infantry, marines on the ground and in the air would also be responsible
for the occupation and defense of advanced bases for the fleet, as
defined by the Navy Department in 1911. Cunningham and Smith
disagreed on the primary role of the airplane for the marines. Cunningham was in favor of using planes in total support of any and
all marine operations while Smith felt the Marine Corps, as part of
the navy, should use its aircraft to support combined operations.
As things turned out, both views proved to be correct.

The airplanes of the 1910s were not taken seriously as a weapon
of war. They were slow, woefully underpowered, and fragile. They
had very short range, could carry only small payloads, and for the

most part were considered useless by "old guard" navy and army officers. In the first two decades of the twentieth century, the battleship reigned supreme. Their huge guns were the ultimate projector of power in the same way that the nuclear bomb would be in a later generation. In January 1915, Secretary of the Navy Josephus Daniels made the important decision that all navy and marine aviation cadets would receive the same training in the use of land planes rather than amphibians exclusively. This, to the army's outrage, was a critical move towards giving the Marine Corps the ability to hold and defend land bases and project power.

That same year, Mr. and Mrs. John S. MacLaughlin of 23 Merrick Villa, Collingswood, New Jersey, became the proud parents of a baby boy, John S. MacLaughlin, Jr. A bright and ambitious boy, young John did well in school and had his sights on attending the Naval Academy.

The United States declared war on Germany on 6 April 1917, exactly one day before a new class of cadets graduated from The Citadel in Charleston. One of them was Lewie Griffith Merritt. Born in Ridge Spring, South Carolina in June 1897, Merritt was from an old and fiercely proud southern family. He was eager to join the action in France, but as a new marine second lieutenant he was assigned to counter-guerilla operations in the Dominican Republic from June 1917 to August 1918. It was not until November, just as the war was drawing to a close, that Captain Merritt served as a company commander in France. He saw brief combat with the "Devil Dogs" at Belleau Wood.

The fledgling Marine Aeronautics Company consisted of 34 officers and 330 enlisted men. They were to provide reconnaissance and artillery spotting support using Curtiss HS flying boats. In October 1917, Captain William McIlvain commanded the First Marine Aviation Force which was to use land planes. Ironically, they were trained by the army's aviation school at Hazelhurst Field at Mineola, Long Island. They were trained by civilian instructors in the venerable and trusty Curtiss JN-4 "Jenny."

After further advanced training in Louisiana, they went to Florida where the new unit was fully consolidated, but they were unable to muster the numbers needed for four full squadrons. The United States Navy came to the rescue. Of the 135 pilots that deployed to France in the summer of 1918, more than half had been reserve aviators who transferred to the marines. Four squadrons, designated A, B, C, and D were ready by July when they sailed for France. But when they arrived and set up headquarters at Ardres near the Belgian border, they had no planes to fly. The British-built de Havilland DH-9s ordered by the Navy Department were nowhere to be seen. The resourceful Captain Cunningham managed to work out a deal with the British that provided some DH-4s for their use. In the meantime, he arranged for his pilots to fly missions with Royal Flying Corps squadrons to give them some combat experience.

In October, the marines were ready to begin their own operations. On the fourteenth, they bombed German positions in Belgium and were engaged in a battle with German fighters. Lieutenant Ralph Talbot, one of the navy reserve officers who had transferred to the marines and his gunner, Corporal Robert G. Robinson, fought off several determined attacks by twelve German planes. Robinson was three times wounded but he shot down one adversary and Talbert brought down another. Both men would receive the Medal of Honor.

During their time in France, the marines flew more than fifty-seven bombing missions without fighter escort, shot down four Germans, claimed eight more, and earned thirty decorations.

After contributing to victory in the "War to End All Wars," the marines returned home to great acclaim and glory, but this was to be short-lived as a parsimonious Congress slashed military budgets. The public was convinced there was no longer a need to spend prodigious amounts of money on ships, planes, tanks, and soldiers. Major Cunningham, still devoted to the cause for which he and the others had struggled, gathered up the remnants of the First Aviation Force, which had been disbanded in February 1919, to form two squadrons to support the two Marine Provisional Brigades then garrisoned in the Dominican Republic and Haiti.

Only after determined effort by Cunningham and other dedicated supporters did Congress acquiesce to the need for an expanded marine air branch. The Marine Corps would have a permanent strength of more than 26,000 officers and men, while the aviation branch was set at 1,020 men. The bases at Quantico, Virginia; Parris Island, South Carolina; and San Diego, California incorporated permanent aviation facilities. On 30 October 1920, Marine Commandant Major General John Lejeune approved the aviation table of organization as Expeditionary Force East and Expeditionary Force West. This led to the formation of four squadrons, each of two flights, designated A through H.

The postwar years saw the first baby boom, in which the millions of young men and women who would serve in the Second

World War were born and raised. Among them were Bobby Lehnert of Long Island, Mark Syrkin of New York, Royce Watson of Texas, Sterling Price of Missouri, John Hansen of Iowa, Johnny Lincoln of Boston, Ken Gunderson of Milwaukee, Bobby Moran of Illinois, Tommy Thompson of California, Walter Wilson of Mississippi, Rex Jeans of Joplin, and many others.

The period from 1919 to 1928 was one of the most dynamic in aviation history, seeing a surge in aeronautical technology and flying feats. Some of the most famous airplanes of the era flew for the first time, such as the Ford Trimotor, Armstrong-Whitworth Atlas, Boeing Model 40, Curtiss P-1 Hawk, Keystone Pathfinder, and Ryan M-2. The navy quickly got into the act in May 1919 when four Curtiss-built flying boats called NC (Navy Curtiss) attempted to fly from New York to Lisbon, Portugal. The NC-1 piloted by future admiral Marc Mitscher was forced down in the ocean by lack of visibility, but he and his crew were picked up by a destroyer. The NC-4 took nineteen days with stops in Massachusetts, Newfoundland, and the Azores. Yet it was the first time a heavier-than-air aircraft had crossed the Atlantic.

Two weeks later, two Royal Flying Corps officers, John Alcock and Arthur Whitten Brown, flew a Vickers Vimy bomber from Harbor Grace, Newfoundland to Ireland, completing the first non-stop flight of an airplane across the Atlantic. In 1921, Brigadier General William "Billy" Mitchell, in a spectacular demonstration in Chesapeake Bay, proved that bombers could sink armored battleships. This was a watershed moment in military thought. It indirectly led to the commissioning of the US Navy's first aircraft carrier, USS *Langley,* four years later. The 1941 Japanese attack on Pearl Harbor also had its roots in Mitchell's feat.

In 1925, former Curtiss engineer Chance Vought had purchased full control of the Lewis and Vought Corporation to form Chance Vought Aircraft in Long Island City, New York. Vought would soon be building many planes for the US Navy including the successful VE-7 "Bluebird," which became the first airplane to launch from the USS *Langley.* This was the early genesis of the finest navy fighter ever built, the F4U Corsair.

By this time, Captain Lewie Merritt had served on the staffs of two Marine Corps commandants and had been in command of the marine detachment on the battleship USS *New Mexico* (BB-40). After undergoing aviation training at Pensacola in 1923, he received his wings in January of the following year.

The successful Vought VE-7 "Bluebird" was the forerunner of a long line of warplanes. (Official U.S. Navy photo.)

The marines had not been idle during this period and commanded headlines and support by conducting flights that demonstrated the utility of aircraft to support ground operations as well as maintain peak proficiency. In 1922, a column of four thousand marines had marched from Quantico to Gettysburg, Pennsylvania while three Marine Martin MBT bombers (a torpedo-capable variant of the MB-2 used by Mitchell) flew simulated attack missions in support of the advancing troops. They flew more than five hundred hours and carried cargo and personnel.

Marine Corps aviators competed in several air races around the country. Lieutenant Christian Schilt took second place in the prestigious Schneider Cup seaplane race in 1926, and Major Charles Lutz won first place in the Marine Trophy Race at Anacostia in 1928, flying a Curtiss Hawk.

The most famous aviation event of the roaring twenties was Lindbergh's solo flight from New York to Paris in May of 1927. This single event stimulated public interest in aviation and had no small effect on many young men and women who were inspired to become pilots. Among the huge throngs that lined the sidewalks of New York City as Lindbergh was showered in ticker tape was a six-year-old boy seated on his father's shoulders. His name was Mark Syrkin, who would join the marines and fly in VMF-422. Many years later, while stationed at Eniwetok Atoll in the Marshall Islands, Mark Syrkin would meet and fly with his idol, Lindbergh.

A civil war in Nicaragua again brought the marines into the fray as ground troops struggled to fight the jungle guerillas. Observation Squadrons One and Four were sent to support ground operations. This was a milestone in that it was the first time the tactics that would later be known as "close air support" were employed. For the first time, marine ground and air units worked as a team.

By the time of the Wall Street crash in October 1929, the marines had squadrons based on both US coasts, the Pacific, Nicaragua, and China. They flew the Curtiss F6C-4 biplane fighter, a carrier-capable variant of the trusty P-1 Hawk. Introduced in 1925 the F6C-4 served for the next five years.

Some cutbacks were made to the Table of Organization and Equipment, yet this actually had a beneficial effect. Like the British in 1940, the marines learned to do with what they had, and as a result, were more efficient and imaginative. The reorganization built the Fleet Marine Force (FMF). FMF Aircraft One was based at Quantico and FMF Aircraft Two at San Diego. The Marine VMF (fighter) squadrons were flying the new Grumman F3F-2, the biplane precursor to the tough little Wildcat. They were followed by the Brewster F2A Buffalo, which outperformed the first F4F-1s to emerge from Grumman. The dive bombers flown in the VMSB (Scout-Dive Bomber) squadrons were the Vultee SB2U Vindicator. While these planes would prove woefully obsolete in the first months of the Second World War, they were nearly state-of-the-art in the early 1930s.

By this time, the Navy Department had established the system of squadron and aircraft designations for the navy and marines. (See Appendix A).

A 1934 study of amphibious tactics at Quantico finally established the Landing Force Manual. This was the bible for all subsequent marine amphibious operations. Further refinements in fleet exercises throughout the 1930s finalized the overall concept. When the marines stormed ashore at Guadalcanal, Tarawa, Peleliu, Iwo Jima, and Okinawa, they followed the doctrine laid down at Quantico in 1934. This was no small matter. As stated in the Naval Heritage and History Command essay *A History of Marine Corps Aviation,* "The manual, as a whole, gave recognition to Marine Aviation as an integral and vital element in the execution of the primary mission of the Marine Corps."

Between 1936 and 1940, the number of active pilots did not substantially increase. But as the war clouds loomed ever closer over the Atlantic and Pacific, this was helped by activating the Marine Air Reserve pilots. Yet even this only added a further 100 pilots to the 145 on active service. As seen below, from the period of 1936 to 1945 the Marine Corps' air strength increased over 225 times in pilots and more than 137 times in aircraft/squadrons. The USMC air strength had the highest increase in men and equipment of all branches of the United States armed forces in the Second World War.

Pilots
1936: 145 pilots
1941: 425 pilots (193%)
1945: 10,000 pilots (2,252%)

Support/Ground Personnel
1939: 1,350 men
1945: 125,000 (9,159%)

Air Strength
1936: 160 aircraft, 10-11 squadrons
1941: 204 aircraft, 13 squadrons (27%)
1945: 3,000 aircraft, 145 squadrons (1,370%)
Source: National Museum of the Marine Corps

In July 1941, even as the Japanese were in the advanced stages of planning the Pearl Harbor attack, two Marine Air Wings (MAW) were formed at Quantico and San Diego. An Air Wing generally consisted of three to four Marine Air Groups (MAG), each with at least six fighter, bomber, and observation squadrons. MAG 11 was at Quantico, while San Diego's MAG-21 was based at Marine Corps Air Station (MCAS) Ewa Field on Oahu. Before the end of the year, MCAS Cherry Point in North Carolina replaced Quantico as the home of marine aviation training, a position it holds to this day. MCAS El Toro south of Los Angeles took the lead from San Diego. These changes were influenced by the proximity of the two major ground training bases, Camp Lejeune and Camp Pendleton.

At 0610 hours on 7 December 1941, the carrier HIJMS Akagi's fighters, led by Lieutenant Commander Shigeru Itaya in his gray A6M Zero, #AI-159 took off into the predawn sky. Eight more followed from Akagi, each armed with twin 20mm cannons and twin

7.7mm machine guns. Thirty-four more Zeros were launched from the carriers *Kaga, Hiryu, Soryu, Shokaku,* and *Zuikaku,* followed by torpedo bombers, level bombers, and dive bombers.

The first wave of 183 fighters and bombers swept south over Oahu at 0730 hours. One of the first targets they approached at 0753 was MCAS Ewa Field, less than ten miles from Pearl Harbor. Even before the first of Lieutenant Commander Shigeharu Murata's forty B5N Kate torpedo bombers had banked out of Southeast Loch to begin their attack run on Battleship Row, the bombs were falling on Ewa.

The leading Zeros found forty-nine American planes on the ground that Sunday morning, VMSB-231's Vultee SB2U Vindicator dive bombers and VMF-221's F2A Buffalos.

The Zeros under Lieutenant Commander Kiyokuma Okajima from the *Hiryu* strafed the neat ranks of planes clustered at the center of the tarmac to guard against sabotage, which until that morning was considered the primary threat. The Zeros made at least eight runs at the flight line while the Val dive bombers hammered at the buildings. In less than thirty minutes the entire line of MAG-21's planes was in flames. Not a single US Marine fighter had managed to get into the air, but several officers and men did find machine guns and rifles to shoot back at the attackers. The base commander, Lieutenant Colonel Claude Larkin, was wounded while he directed the defense. One marine private named Merle Thompson shot at Lieutenant Yoshio Shiga's Zero with his Colt 45 while swearing at the top of his lungs.

Also at Ewa that morning was twenty-six-year-old Marine Captain John S. MacLaughlin. Three years after graduating from Annapolis, he had earned his wings at Pensacola and assigned to MAG-21 on Oahu. The sight of black smoke rising from the wreckage undoubtedly angered him as it did every other American that morning.

A new lieutenant named Charley Hughes had just been assigned to VMF-221 under Major Floyd "Red" Parks. It is not known if Hughes and MacLaughlin ever met at Ewa, but their paths would cross again nineteen months later at MCAS Santa Barbara.

Fortunately, forty-four of MAG-21's ninety-two planes had been deployed to other bases prior to 7 December. USS *Enterprise* (CV-6) was returning from Wake Island after delivering a dozen Grumman F4F of VMF-211, while USS *Lexington* (CV-2) was *en route* to Midway with eighteen Vindicators of VMSB-231. These planes would play a small but significant role in the desperate fight at Midway six months later.

A destroyed Marine dive bomber at MCAS Ewa Field after the Pearl Harbor attack. No Marine plane managed to get off the ground. {Official U.S. Marine Corps photo.)

Wake Island was located two thousand miles west of Oahu. It had been, since the mid-1930s, a Pan-American clipper stop between the US and China. The navy had built facilities on Wake for military aircraft, but by the summer of 1941, much work remained to be done. When Major Paul Putnam's twelve VMF-211 F4F-3s launched from *Enterprise* and landed on Wake in August, they realized the only runway was too narrow to allow more than a single plane to take off at a time. Navy and marine pilots always took off in two-plane elements. Likewise, the taxiways were small with no hard revetments to protect the planes. The advance units of the First Marine Defense Battalion went right to work to make the island a stronghold, but time and materials were short. There was no radar, no fueling system, and not even adequate maintenance for the fighters. Fueling had to be done by hand from fifty-five-gallon drums. In retrospect, it is easy to assume that Wake Island was doomed from the start, yet the marines were determined to fight it out to the last.

Wake was hit on 8 December—the atoll is west of the International Date Line—by thirty-six Mitsubishi G3M twin-engine Type 96 land-based bombers, known as "Nell" by the Allies. After taking off from Marcus Island to the west, they made their run from the south under a rain squall and hit the base from 1,500 feet. Four of Putnam's Wildcats were in the air to the north and failed to see or intercept the bombers. When the attack was over, the only undamaged planes were those four Wildcats. The fuel dump had been destroyed as well as the meager repair facilities. More bombers came on 9 and 10 December, but both times the marines hit back, shooting down four bombers. On 11 December, a Japanese task force arrived off the island and prepared for a landing, but the navy began shelling the ships with coastal batteries, sinking a destroyer. The enemy withdrew, whereupon three Wildcats, each carrying two 100lb bombs attacked the force. With the fierce determination that would characterize the Marines during the war, the fighters were credited with sinking another destroyer and damaging two cruisers and a transport. But VMF-211's planes were being whittled down. Another bombing resulted in more damage to the base, with three bombers shot down.

Only by the heroic efforts of the ground crew and pilots were the marines able to keep two F4Fs in the air. On 20 December word arrived of a relief force from Hawaii, but it would be too late. That same day, a Japanese carrier-based aircraft bombed Wake, finally knocking out the last anti-aircraft (AA) guns. Two days later, the last two Wildcats were out of the fight. The remaining aviators took up rifles to defend the beaches for the coming invasion. Wake Island fell to the Japanese on 23 December. "Remember Wake Island" became the marines' battle cry.

The war had begun very badly for Marine Corps aviation.

Four months after Pearl Harbor, the Japanese empire had expanded to encompass nearly the entire western Pacific Ocean. They had captured the US stronghold of the Philippines, the British colonies of Singapore and Malaya, the Dutch East Indies, the Marianas, and Wake Island. They had defeated or destroyed the fleets of four Allied nations and killed or captured half a million Allied troops. They controlled the lives of 150 million people, more than the entire population of the United States. In May of 1942, Japan seemed unstoppable.

Midway Island, 1,200 miles northwest of Oahu was a Pan-Am clipper stop. Midway consisted of two islands, Sand and Eastern, and totaled little more than 2.4 square miles, surrounded by a wide coral reef. A seaplane hangar, hospital, barracks, power house, and a weather station dotted Sand Island, while three runways crossed Eastern. What made Midway of supreme importance was its location. If the Japanese could take the atoll, they could interdict, disrupt, and control all air and sea traffic between Hawaii and other US bases. No matter the cost, Midway had to be held.

VMSB-231's Vindicators and VMF-221's Buffalos arrived on the island shortly after the fall of Wake. They were the first cadre of what was to be a large and legendary build-up. Admiral Chester W. Nimitz, Commander-in-Chief Pacific (CINCPAC) visited the island on 2 May. What he saw convinced him to send whatever he could to bolster the island defenses. Guns, ammunition, and supplies were sent to Midway in an attempt to make the tiny atoll into a fortress. By the end of May, tiny Midway Island had literally disappeared under a veritable hedgehog of barbed wire, entrenchments, coastal and air-defense guns, machine gun posts, and land mines. The runways on Eastern Island, which normally hosted only a few squadrons, were almost invisible under more than a hundred airplanes. The United States Navy had sixteen Consolidated PBY Catalinas, while the army had seven B-17E Flying Fortresses, and four new Martin B-26 Marauders. MAG-22 had nineteen Douglas SBD-2 Dauntless dive bombers, seventeen Vought SB2U-3 Vindicators, seven Grumman F4F-3 Wildcats, and twenty-one Brewster F2A-3 Buffalos. Even six brand-new (and untried) Grumman TBF Avenger torpedo bombers found space on Midway.

The Battle of Midway has been well-documented by other historians, but the marine aviation contribution bears particular examination. The marine pilots, with very few exceptions, were inexperienced and fresh from flight training.

The first attack wave of enemy bombers and fighters was launched from four carriers at 0430 on 4 June and headed southeast to Midway. The 108-plane force was made up of 36 Nakajima B5N "Kate" level/torpedo bombers, 36 Aichi D3A "Val" dive bombers, and 36 A6M5 Zeros for fighter cover. They were at twelve thousand feet, or in pilot jargon, "Angels 12." At 0515, a PBY patrol spotted the four Midway-bound Japanese carriers and their escorts. Ten minutes after the SCR-270B radar post picked up the incoming bombers, the marines were in the air. In command was Major Floyd "Red" Parks in an F2A Buffalo. Parks was a thirty-one-year old Missourian who had attended Annapolis and been given the infamous "Black N" award for serious infractions. To say the least, Parks was not fond of rules, but he graduated in the top ranks in 1934. He joined MAG-22 in San Diego, and was promoted to major in May.

Parks led VMF-221 into the sky and headed north-northwest to intercept the enemy force. His only advantage was in surprise. The Japanese had little experience with radar and weren't expecting an American force to attack. VMF-221's executive officer, Captain Kirk Armistead took twelve Buffalos and a single Wildcat off on a slightly different bearing. The marines knew better than to mix it up with the Zeros, which already had a well-deserved reputation for superb maneuverability at low speeds in a dogfight. They waited at fourteen thousand feet for the enemy to appear below them.

At 0614, Captain John Carey, who led one of the divisions with Parks, spotted the lead Kate high-level bombers and made the now-legendary call, "Tally-ho! Hawks at angels 12!"

Carey's wingman, Captain Marion Carl, who would soon become a famed marine ace, and Lieutenant Clayton Canfield dived on the lead Kates and shot two of them down before the Zeros were on them, as Canfield put it, "Like a swarm of angry hornets."

Captain Armistead, in an F2A had this to say about the battle:

"I was endeavoring to get a position above and ahead of the enemy and come down out of the sun. However, I was unable to reach this point in time. I was at seventeen thousand feet when I started my attack. I made a head-on approach from above at a steep angle and at very high speed. I saw my incendiary bullets travel from a point in front of the leader, up through his plane and back through the planes on the left wing [of the formation]. I continued in my dive, and looking back, saw two or three of those planes falling in flames. After my pull-out, I zoomed back to fourteen thousand feet. I looked back over my shoulder and, about two thousand feet below and behind me, I saw three fighters in column climbing up toward me, which I assumed to be planes of my division. However, they climbed at a very high rate, and a very steep path. When the nearest plane was about five hundred feet below and behind me, I realized that it was a Japanese Zero. I kicked over in a violent Split S and received three 20mm shells, one in the right wing gun, one in the right wing root tank, and one in the top left side of the engine cowling. I also received about twenty 7.7mm rounds which sawed off a portion of the left aileron."

Armistead led the remnants of his force back to Midway where they managed to land after the bombing had ended. Major Parks and all the pilots of his division were killed. But Parks' own death inflamed the ire of every marine who witnessed it. After Parks bailed out of his shattered Buffalo over the atoll's reefs, a Zero pilot strafed him while he hung helplessly in his parachute harness.

The final death toll was fourteen marines dead out of the twenty-five that had taken off to defend Midway. But they had shot down or damaged almost half of the bombers, a remarkable score under the circumstances. One of the pilots who survived that day was Lieutenant Charley Hughes of Oklahoma.

But the marines were not done with the Japanese. Major Loften Henderson took sixteen SBD dive bombers out to hit the Japanese carriers. Following separately was Major Ben Norris with eleven SB2U Vindicators. These last were slow and vulnerable. Captain Wallace Griffin, who trained in the Vindicator at Jacksonville, said, "Those were the worst damn dive bombers we ever had. You had to lower the landing gear to control the dive, and the fabric came off the wings at anything over 150 knots."

Few of VMSB-231's pilots were experienced in the skill of dive bombing, which required diving on a ship target at nearly seventy degrees from ten thousand feet. To make matters worse, the dive bombers had no fighter cover.

Henderson and Norris led them in. Starting from eight thousand feet, the bombers made long, slow glides at the carriers, which were twisting and turning at high speed. Henderson was shot down in the first few minutes, and one by one, eight of his dive bombers spun into the sea.

Norris's Vindicators fared no better, losing three planes. Postwar Japanese records show that two carriers, *Akagi* and *Soryu,* received minor damage. Even though none of the half-dozen Midway-based air attacks inflicted any damage to Admiral Chuichi Ngubo's carriers, they did contribute to what Walter Lord called the "incredible victory" at Midway. By forcing the carriers and their escorts to maneuver wildly and avoid the bombs, they slowed the fleet's advance and timetable, making it possible for the SBD Dauntless dive bombers from USS *Yorktown* and USS *Enterprise* to find them. In one five-minute orgy of destruction, three of Japan's front-line carriers were turned into burning hulks. The fourth suffered the same fate hours later. Most historians agree this was the turning point of the Pacific war. Admiral Nimitz later praised the marines at Midway. "Please accept my sympathy for the losses sustained by your gallant aviation personnel based at Midway. Their sacrifice was not in vain. When the great emergency came, they were ready. They met, unflinchingly, the attack of vastly superior numbers and made the attack ineffective. They struck the first blow at the enemy carriers. They were the spearhead of our great victory. They have written a new and shining page in the annals of the Marine Corps."

With the exception of the Vindicator and Dauntless dive bomber attacks on the Japanese carriers, for the marines, the battle of Midway was primarily defensive. This has never been the marine way. They were trained to be on the offensive, to attack and hold ground. Their chance finally came at a small jungle island in the Solomons called Guadalcanal, a place that would soon be as linked to marine valor as Thermopylae was to the Spartans.

In August 1942, Lewie Merritt, having been promoted to colonel, was assigned to Headquarter Squadron, Marine Aircraft Wings, Pacific, at NAS San Diego (Now NAS North Island). Under the command of General Ross Rowell, Merritt led the Service Group, which oversaw the formation, personnel, and materiel of the Pacific Marine Air units. One of the first to be assembled by Rowell and Merritt was MAW-1 under Brigadier General Roy Geiger, who had been flying for the Marines since 1916. Geiger and the wing were sent to the southwest Pacific.

Japan's overriding aim was to dominate the Pacific from China to Hawaii, and from the Aleutians to Australia. After taking Singapore and Java, the next objective was Australia. They needed a solid foundation from which to launch the campaign on Australia, and this was the Solomon Islands. The Solomons, known as "The Slot," are a long double chain of islands that run like twin dotted lines between Australia and New Guinea to the west and New Caledonia, Fiji, and New Zealand to the east.

General Douglas MacArthur, who had set up his headquarters in Australia after the fall of the Philippines in February, was determined to cut Japan off at the knees with his own attack on New Guinea. Meanwhile, Admiral Nimitz was working on a long-range plan to cut off Japan's vital supply and support from its huge base at Rabaul in New Britain.

By the summer of 1942, the marines were based at Efate in the New Hebrides. Lieutenant Colonel Harold Bauer with MAG-24 set up an airfield with the help of the army. Efate was within land-based air cover of the next two objectives, Tulagi and Guadalcanal. Bauer commanded two squadrons, VMF-212 at Efate, and VMO-251 on Espiritu Santo. The latter used photo reconnaissance F4F-3P Wildcats. Neither squadron was ready to support the 7 August landing of the First Marine Division on Guadalcanal. But VMF-223, commanded by Captain John Smith, received brand-new F4F-4s while VMSB-232 under Major Richard Mangrum was equipped with the new SBD-3 with self-sealing fuel tanks and armor plate for the crew. Among VMF-223's pilots was a twenty-three-year old Second Lieutenant from Joplin, Missouri named Cloyd Rex Jeans.

Both squadrons shipped out from Hawaii aboard the USS *Long Island* and reached the Solomons on 20 August. They launched from the carrier and landed late that day to great applause from

Lieutenant Rex Jeans at left, with other pilots of VMF-223
on Guadalcanal in 1942. (Photo courtesy Andrew Syrkin.)

the ground troops. The other two squadrons of MAG-23, VMF-224, commanded by Captain Robert Galer, and Major Leonard Smith's VMSB-23 left Hawaii on 15 August aboard the aviation transport ferries USS *Kitty Hawk* (APV-1) and USS *Hammondsport* (APV-2), landing on 30 August. They were all under General Geiger's command.

They took the initiative by denying Japan control of the strategic islands, particularly Guadalcanal, code-named Cactus. The Imperial War Ministry had other plans and undertook a massive and protracted effort to push the marines off Guadalcanal. Starting in early September, Japanese bombers arrived almost daily to destroy the airfield and facilities. Two heavy battleships hammered the airfield for nearly twenty-four hours, causing near-total devastation.

The American transports carrying supplies were at great risk. General Alexander Vandergrift, the marine commander on the island, was informed that the transports could not remain unless they could be covered by American aircraft. The Japanese were sending seven thousand troops on transports protected by warships to retake the island, while US forces were even then working to hold and expand the airfield. The marines worked twenty-four hours a day to bring ashore the fuel, spare parts, food, medical supplies, weapons, ammunition, and vehicles to keep the airfield in operation. Every man, from the grunts in rifle pits and machine

```
FMAW-2199
Vella Lavella
5 Jan 44  Photo by:  TSgt. D.Q. White

Marine Ace Major Marion E. Carl, recently
ran his score of Japanese victims to 18½,
making him the Number 4 Marine Ace.
Only Major Joe Foss, Major Gregory
Boyington (both with 26), First Lieutenant
Kenneth Walsh (20) and Lieutenant Colonel
John L. Smith (19) have better records.
Major Carl is on his second trip to the
South Pacific.  He shot down one plane
during the Battle of Midway, 15½ during
the early fighting on Guadalcanal, and
two within the last month.


DEFENSE DEPT. PHOTO (MARINE CORPS)
pd                         69869
```

Major Marion Carl's combat record went back to Midway. By January 1944 he was credited with 28 victories. (Official U.S. Marine Corps photos.)

gun posts, to the radio operators or the mechanic had only one major objective: to keep the Japanese from retaking the all-important airfield.

For the next few months, the Americans on Guadalcanal worked with what equipment could be scrounged. Constant bombing raids caused the destruction and damage of planes on the ground, whereupon new ones were flown in from Efate and Espiritu Santo. Army Air Force fighters and medium bombers, as well as US Navy carrier planes, arrived to beef up the air strength. General Roy Geiger inspired and drove his marine pilots and ground crew, keeping up their morale and fighting spirit, and the soon-to-be legendary "Cactus Air Force" was born. The CAF fought doggedly on from November to February 1943. Bauer's VMF-212 was permanently assigned to the airfield on Guadalcanal which had by then been named Henderson Field for Major Loften Henderson, the commander of VMSB-231, killed at Midway.

Among the score of squadrons was a soon-to-be-famous unit, the "Green Knights," VMF-121, under Major Len Davis. His executive officer was Captain Joe Foss. Foss would soon be as well-known an ace as Eddie Rickenbacker.

In the states, dozens of new squadrons were being organized and fitted out as waves of new aviators graduated from flight training each month. Thousands and thousands of new planes were rolling out of the factories. In early 1943, VMF-124, the first marine unit to be equipped with the new and radical Vought F4U Corsair arrived in the South Pacific. They slowly began to replace the trusty but less-capable Wildcat. The long domination of the A6M Zero was coming to an end. Within three months, all eight marine fighter squadrons in the Solomons were equipped with the Corsair. Instead of having to make do with what they had as at Wake Island, the fighter squadrons were well-trained, well-equipped, and well supported.

Compare this impressive build-up with how Nimitz had to scrape the barrel at Midway only eight months earlier. The long arduous struggle for Guadalcanal, even though no one knew it at the time, was the first step on the road back. From that point on, the marines were no longer purely on the defensive, reacting to enemy moves. By February, the Japanese had been thwarted in a major campaign. Australia, their original goal, was forever out of Tokyo's reach. More than 50 transports and warships, 1,500 aircraft and over 86,000 men littered the sea floor of "Iron Bottom Sound." The fighting went on, driving northward up the slot. Rabaul was bypassed rather than invaded, which cut off a major portion of the Japanese forces in the region.

Those six months at Guadalcanal were, as Field Marshal Carl von Clausewitz would call it, *"Ein wendespunkt der geschichte,"* a turning point in history. The Solomons proved that not only was Marine Corps aviation here to stay, it was a force to be taken seriously. As envisioned by Alfred Cunningham, Bernard Smith, and William McIlvain more than twenty years before, aircraft bearing the name "MARINES" were a major contributor to Allied victory.

CHAPTER 2

REACHING FOR THE SKY

Naval Air Station Pensacola is located far along the west coast of Florida on the great arc that defines the north edge of the Gulf of Mexico. Today NAS Pensacola is the home of the National Naval Aviation Museum and the home station of the US Navy's precision flight demonstration team, the Blue Angels. But Pensacola's history goes back to well before the American Revolution when Spanish explorers were the first to use the excellent harbor. In the 1820s, President John Quincy Adams purchased the land for the building of a large navy yard. The harbor and abundant forests provided the navy with the shelter and materials for building and repairing ships. During the Civil War, the Confederacy controlled Pensacola until 1862 when it was abandoned after the Union capture of New Orleans.

For most of its history the station at Pensacola served the surface fleet, but that changed after the turn of the century with the invention of the airplane. In 1911, Captain Washington Irving Chambers headed a review board that included the pioneering marine aviator Alfred Cunningham. The board convinced Secretary of the Navy Josephus Daniels to include an appropriation for aeronautical development resulting in the commissioning of Naval Aeronautical Station Pensacola.

Several officers interested in the new ventures traveled to San Diego where they learned to fly under the tutelage of Glenn Curtiss. In January 1914, the Navy Department established its pioneering naval aviation training station at Pensacola. The first US Navy airplane to fly over Pensacola rattled into the air in February 1914, just prior to the outbreak of the Great War in Europe. It was a small but significant beginning. By the time the United States entered the war in April 1917, Pensacola had turned out thirty-nine cadets for aviation service. The captains and admirals who commanded the great carrier fleets during the Second World War were among the early fledgling pilots who honed their skills in the humid skies over the Gulf Coast. During the interwar years, the US Army attempted to dominate the air by denying it to the navy. Surprisingly, the most vocal advocate of army air power, General William "Billy" Mitchell gave the rival United States Navy the initial push to develop aviation.

The advent of aircraft carriers with the commissioning of USS *Langley* in 1925 changed the world of military aviation in ways that only became obvious after 1941.

As the only training facility for all naval, marine, and coast guard aviators prior to 1935, Pensacola was inadequate to handle the huge influx of cadets. New facilities were established at Jacksonville, Florida and Corpus Christi, Texas. Two additional satellite fields were built adjacent to Pensacola in late 1942 and early the following year.

By 1943 Pensacola was turning out hundreds of new cadets every month, yet this was still far short of what would be needed as the war progressed.

On 30 April 1943, a new class of naval aviation cadets stood on Pensacola's parade ground. It was a hot and humid day as a weak salt-tinged breeze wafted in to tease the flags that hung limply in the lifeless air. The endless expanse of white concrete tarmac reflected the broiling sun and seared the exposed faces of the ninety-four men who stood in neat ranks.

One of them was Marine Aviation Cadet Mark Warren Syrkin, a handsome twenty-two-year-old from New York. Standing ramrod straight at 5'11" with black hair and hazel eyes, he weighed a solid 175 pounds, the perfect image of a marine officer. In an interview many years later, Syrkin related his decision to become a pilot, "Back in 1927 when I was about six years old my father took me to New York to see the ticker tape parade for Charles Lindbergh. I couldn't see over the hundreds of people so Dad put me on his shoulders and I saw Lindy going by."

As the procession of open cars moved slowly down lower Broadway on June 12, 1927, the famous Lindbergh, in the Mayor's black touring car, waved to the crowd.

Syrkin said, "I yelled and waved like crazy, and I swear he looked right at me. Ever since that day I wanted to be a pilot." But like most young boys he was soon distracted by other interests. "As I got older I discovered sports and girls. We went to Coney Island and Brighton Beach to ride the roller coaster and swim in the ocean."

Syrkin admitted that he even considered becoming a lifeguard after seeing how the girls thronged at the lifeguard towers. "I liked charming the girls and I guess I was pretty good at it. Then I got a baseball scholarship to Ohio State University at Columbus. I wasn't

*Cadet Mark Syrkin during flight training at NAS Pensacola.
(Photo courtesy Andrew Syrkin.)*

sure what I wanted to do. I should have gone into engineering but I chose to major in fine arts."

Syrkin's old dream of becoming a pilot was reborn after Pearl Harbor. He signed up for the Civilian Pilot Training Program in Ohio and qualified for his license. In early 1942, as the newspaper headlines daily related Japan's ever-spreading conquests, he was accepted by the Naval Aviation Cadet (NAVCAD) program. "I was determined to be a marine fighter pilot. Nothing else would be good enough."

For him and many others the ultimate goal, the Holy Grail, as it were, was to earn the Wings of Gold and be called naval aviators. There was a distinct and important difference between pilots and aviators. The army air force had pilots. They could only land on big, safe dry runways while aviators were trained to land their planes on tiny, pitching, wet, and windy carrier flight decks. In other words, aviators were better than mere pilots. For many cadets, the choice of being a navy aviator or taking a reserve commission in the marines was an easy one to make. There was a very strong *esprit de corps* unique to the marines. It alone among the armed services could operate independently in conflicts on land, sea, and in the air. From the outset, the Marine Corps imparted a deep sense of responsibility. Marine training made each man more afraid of letting his buddies down than he was of being hurt or killed.

Not far from where Syrkin stood was John Hansen, another newly graduated marine cadet. Although his family lived in Orlando, Florida, Hansen was born in Des Moines, Iowa in August of 1920. Hansen stood 5'11" tall, weighed 165 pounds, and bore strong Nordic features with dark brown hair and green eyes that harkened from his Aalborg Denmark ancestors.

"John was not the typical jarhead officer," recalled Syrkin with a smile. "He was easygoing and laconic, not like John Wayne or anybody like that. He was very meticulous in everything he did. If he was asked a question, it was a long time before he responded, because he took his time in phrasing the response."

Hansen attended schools in Orlando after the family moved from Iowa during the Depression. When he was thirteen, he won a car in a raffle and caused both amusement and outrage when he drove his prize through the school's halls.

During his teen years he enjoyed going to Daytona Beach to watch the races, which in those days were still held on the hard-packed sand of the beach itself. He attended the University of Florida, but interrupted his education to care for his father, who was dying of stomach cancer. When the Japanese attacked Pearl Harbor, he was determined to do his part and join up. He signed up with a group of students from the university. He then earned his pilot's license through the CPTP, which gave him an advantage when he put in for NAVCAD training in June 1942. Hansen found a home in the rigid and disciplined life of military pilot training. "They stressed fitness and exercise," he said later. "But they weren't fanatics about it. The cadets ran, swam, and boxed. Yet a lot of them smoked like fiends. I never smoked when I was young, but after a few months in combat I picked up the habit."

"John was a real athletic type," said Syrkin of his fellow Pensacola Alumnus. "He loved to fish, and play tennis. He was the best tennis player I ever knew. I later found out he'd been an Eagle Scout and earned pretty much every merit badge there was. I guess he was probably the perfect marine officer. That's not something I was known for," he added with a chuckle.

Hansen was engaged to Mary Shreffler, the president of Alpha Delta Pi Sorority at Iowa State while his mother was the sorority's house mother. When he came home on leave during the war, the sorority girls all wanted to go with Mrs. Hansen to meet the famous marine aviator, but John only had eyes for Mary.

His sister-in-law recalled that "John wanted to be a pilot. All of us back then thought it was glamorous, prestigious. Way better than being a foot soldier. Everything John did was prestigious and above reproach."

With such a pedigree, it was small wonder that John Hansen, the Iowa boy who spoke little but did much received his wings of gold that day and started on what would be a thirty-one-year career in the marines. He saw combat in World War II, Korea, and Vietnam before retiring as a colonel.

At Pensacola, Jacksonville, Corpus Christi, and Chicago, eighteen other future marine aviators were on their own odyssey to the Wings of Gold. Although few of them knew one another during training, they would soon become as close as brothers.

Robert Lehnert's story was typical. His memory of his youth and thirty years of service in the marines showed a remarkable personal honesty and warmth.

"I grew up in a town called Richland Hills, a part of Queens, New York. That's the same town the Marx Brothers came from. I went to a technical high school in Brooklyn because I planned to be an engineer, and there were no good technical high schools in Queens. For the most part I was just like any other Queens kid, but I loved mind games. I often challenged myself to remember the names of all the presidents, or list the entire Periodic Table of Elements. That came in handy when I had lots of time on my hands, like when I was drifting all alone in a life raft in the middle of the Pacific Ocean."

In 1941, Lehnert attended the University of Michigan to study chemical engineering. "Tuition didn't cost much in those days. My first year only cost about $650. I planned to take a year off after that to work to make the money I needed for the next two years. I kept a ledger with all my expenses. In fact, I still have it."

As with thousands of other young Americans, the Pearl Harbor attack changed Lehnert's plans. "That day made me change course. I applied for the NAVCAD program. I thought I'd better hurry because my dad and uncle both flew in the First World War and they had only been in it for about eighteen months and then it was over."

He laughed. "I really thought this war would be over quickly and so I rushed to get into it. Boy was I wrong!"

Lehnert wasn't the only cadet in a hurry. From the age of eight, Sterling Price of St. Louis, Missouri had his heart set on being a naval aviator. "Not just a pilot," he said in a 1998 video interview produced by John Coleman, "but a *naval* aviator. In 1942, they lowered the entrance standards from two years of college to high school graduate. The day after I read that in the paper I was down at the federal building to sign up."

"I became interested in flying when I was a college student in Louisiana," said Royce Watson of west Texas. "I was looking for an elective, and heard about the CPTP. I told one of my instructors and he said, 'Watson, you can't become a pilot. You can't even ride a l'il ol' bull.' So to me, that was a challenge." He signed up, completed the program, and in the spring of 1942 he received a letter. "It said, 'Cadet Watson, welcome aboard the United States Navy. Report to Grand Prairie, Texas for Basic Training on 2 August 1942.' That was one of the best things ever to happen to me."

"I was working for an oil company in Milwaukee when the war came along," recalled Ken Gunderson. "The city started up a civilian pilot program. We were called the Milwaukee Tornado Squadron."

Often a NAVCAD first completed the CPTP with civilian instructors. The CPTP schools were located all over the country and run by aircraft companies, like Ryan, Aeronca, Piper, and Taylorcraft. This was essentially an elimination process, whereby candidates fly simple trainers like the N3N tandem biplane built by the Naval Aircraft Factory of Philadelphia. Painted a bright yellow like all navy trainers, the N3N was dubbed "The Yellow Peril," although the docile Piper J-3 Cub and even the nimble N2S Stearman often claimed the title. This early phase was intended to weed out the unsuitable candidates quickly. If after logging twenty-two hours of flying the cadet failed to measure up, he was "washed out."

Lehnert said, "The US Navy was overstocked with potential cadets so they sent some of us to Chapel Hill in North Carolina for preflight training in May 1942. After that I did my elimination training in NAS New Orleans. Besides learning to fly, that was where I got into boxing. I was a lightweight and later organized matches between squadrons when we were in the Pacific. Then it was on to

Pensacola, where I got my wings. I didn't make it back to college until after the war," he chuckled. "I guess I got kind of sidetracked."

Lieutenant Colonel Dean Caswell is the last living marine ace. In his book, *My Taking Flight,* he relates his own experiences in naval aviation training. While he was not part of the VMF-422 saga, his memories offer a profound insight into the world of flight training.

He had this to say about the elimination process. "Since the expenditure of thousands of dollars to train each applicant was at stake, it was necessary that these young men were actually capable of flying an airplane in combat. Some were not. To be as sure as possible early in the program, the navy contracted with civilian flight schools to determine whether each candidate could proceed or be dropped from the program before a large sum of money was spent or the student killed himself in the effort. In retrospect, basic flying is easy and could be compared to riding a bicycle—almost. Yet, there are those who just cannot put together balance, muscle, and eye coordination, and other elements of machine control."

Caswell continued, "Ground school instructors, both male and female, introduced the students to basic aircraft design, engines, control surfaces, aircraft instruments, and how weather affected flight. We studied radio and Morse code."

Preflight Training was the big step before actually going into the air. Here the cadets learned how to be officers. Caswell wrote, "We stood at attention for twenty minutes to hear the officer in charge give his introductory speech. His message was clear as he said, 'We are here to teach you things an officer should know, and you will learn discipline. But most of all we'll be seeing if you can take it. If you can't take it, now is the time to find out, not when you are out there.' We believed him."

Cadets spent hundreds of hours in classrooms to learn the ways of the military, terminology and traditions, aeronautics, geography, mathematics, science, and history. They ran, swam laps in the pool, did calisthenics, and learned how to box.

"Marching and drill were the daily routine, and not an airplane in sight," Caswell said. "There seemed to be a conviction among military minds that if you can teach a body of men to walk and trot together to the side and around corners without falling all over each other, you will instill essential fighting efficiency among them. Our living conditions were nothing to brag about, but we were fed well and were relatively comfortable."

The NAVCADs passed from preflight to basic/intermediate flight training and finally primary instruction at one of the large training stations, such as Pensacola, Jacksonville, or Corpus Christi. There were at least two classes every month, starting on the first and fifteenth. Each class was given a number.

Commander Dean "Diz" Laird holds the distinction of being the only carrier fighter pilot to have shot down both German and Japanese planes. A career officer with more than eight thousand hours in the air, he saw combat with VF-41 and VF-4, the latter known as the "Red Rippers." Laird served from 1942 to 1971. He described some of his memories of naval aviation training. "I was in Class 4A42," he said in an interview in his Coronado home. "That was the first class in April 1942, starting on 1 April. The second class began two weeks later, 4B42."

In primary training, they flew the Piper J-3 Cub, a small cabin high-wing plane so docile that a cadet really had to work hard to crash it. As stated by one former Northrop test pilot, "It could just barely kill you."

Basic/intermediate flight training put the cadets in the N2S Stearman biplane. Caswell said, "The Stearman, as an airplane, was anything but perilous; it was possibly one of the safest and strongest aircraft ever built. It could be flown through aerobatic maneuvers that probably could disintegrate some fighters, it could be dropped to a landing from twenty feet in the air, and it could be ground-looped with no more damage than a bit of scraped paint. I did some of those things to Stearmans and they always survived."

At around this time they were introduced to an odd-looking contraption that would not have appeared out of place at an amusement park. The Link Trainer was an enclosed cockpit fitted with vestigial wings and a tail. In 1928, Edwin Link, son of a Binghamton, New York organ manufacturer, began work on a pilot trainer. Air suction through fabric bellows and a motor provided the means for the trainer, mounted on a pedestal to pitch, roll, dive, and climb as the student "flew" it. Despite earnest efforts to sell his pilot maker training device to the US military, most of his first sales were to amusement parks. There was very little interest by the flying community in Link's trainer. But in 1934, after a series of tragic accidents while flying the air mail, the Army Air Corps bought six Links to assist in training pilots to fly at night and in bad weather. With supreme irony, Link's largest customer in 1935 was the Imperial Japanese Navy. Eventually the War Department

John Hansen standing at far left of fourth row, in 1942. (Photo courtesy Heidi Hansen.)

realized the Link was the perfect means to train pilots to fly on instruments without the risk of crashing. By 1945, Link had sold 6,271 trainers to the army air force and 1,045 to the Navy Department. The Link was the grandfather of the modern computerized virtual reality flight simulator.

"The first time I saw that thing," said Syrkin of his debut with the so-called Yellow Box, "I said 'You've got to be kidding! That thing belongs on Coney Island. But a few weeks of working with the Link and then flying under a hood taught the skills of flying blind on instruments. Very good training.'"

Further training used the Vultee SNV Valiant monoplane, which had a lot more power and speed than the gentle biplanes. The students were in the air whenever the weather permitted, sometimes flying three times a day.

Laird remembered the SNV with a smile. "We called them Vultee Vibrators, because they shook so much you could hardly see the instruments."

The last plane the fledgling aviators were expected to master was the ubiquitous North American SNJ-5 advanced trainer, what the army air force called the AT-6 Texan. Virtually every military pilot from 1939 to 1953 received their intermediate training in the AT-6 or SNJ. It was a superb trainer, and in a way, was the most important plane ever built for military use. The trainer, which began as the NA-16 in 1937 was built for the US Navy, Army Air Corps, Royal Air Force, and the French, Canadian, and Chinese Air Forces. It would be famous as the most successful and widely-used trainer in history. More than seventeen thousand were produced and hundreds still fly today. They turn up at air shows across the country under private ownership, but they are probably most recognized as playing the role of the Japanese Zero in movies and television shows. The plane had a Pratt & Whitney R-1340 radial engine rated at 550 horsepower, giving a pilot a taste of real power. They had a maximum speed of 205 knots, or about 235 miles per hour and could fly at twenty-one thousand feet for over 750 miles. Yet it was not a real fighter.

Caswell said, "We practiced air-to-air gunnery on towed targets. Another plane had a cable with a colored sleeve at the end. Four to eight planes queued up for a run at it. We came in an 'S-curve' from above the tow plane and took turns. When we saw the sleeve in the crosshairs we opened fire with our .30 caliber wing guns. Every pilot had bullets painted with a different color so we could tell later on who had hit the sleeve."

He went on. "By now, all the cadets had become believers in instrument flying. This included true instrument flying until you felt comfortable in any weather condition. We also learned to navigate using only a plotting board on our knee and the cockpit instruments, judging the direction and speed of the wind from the movement of trees and other growth on land; waves and wave caps on the ocean surface. This method over water had to be learned well, because carrier flying and navigation to a target from a carrier required this ability."

Royce Watson found he not only could fly these planes, he seemed to have a natural knack for it. "I really loved to fly," he said in his languid Texas drawl. "It came as easy as fallin' off a log for me."

Not all cadets were so fortunate. Some washed out, unable to meet the rigid standards, but those who failed to measure up might have been grateful. The brutally Darwinian world of combat was far less forgiving than the instructors at Pensacola. Even during early training when the margin for error was relatively broad, cadets and their planes fell from the sky with alarming frequency. Their fellow cadets soon learned to build a shell of hardness around their feelings. "We could not get worked up over every guy who got himself killed in a crash," John Hansen said. "We'd go nuts if we did that.

Sometimes a cadet died from sheer bad luck, such as a mechanical failure, but more often from just making a stupid mistake."

Flying at more than one hundred knots in a complex aerial maneuver, a young pilot often had only seconds to make a life or death decision, and most had not gained the experience to choose the correct course. Every crash was examined to determine the cause, but most of the time it was chalked up to pilot error. Some men died from not performing a thorough preflight check of the aircraft.

Mark Syrkin said, "I never took any chances with my plane. I took extra care and time to go over every inch of it before I climbed into the cockpit." This was more prudent than it sounds. Every aircraft was flown by scores of cadets each week. Even with regular maintenance, any of a hundred minor mechanical faults could be missed, resulting in an unexpected breakdown during a flight.

Sixteen years before becoming one of the Mercury Seven astronauts, John Glenn was in the early part of his training to become a marine aviator. In his memoirs, Glenn said that he worked hard to eliminate carelessness in his flying habits. Things happened so quickly that the smallest slip could have disastrous results. Glenn checked and rechecked every gadget and switch on his plane before taking off. Flying was intolerant of human error, and he considered being "Check Happy" as good life insurance.

When Syrkin had performed his required maneuvers in the SNJ in late April 1943, he landed with all the skill and precision his instructors had demanded. After jumping down from the wing, he turned to find his flight instructor waiting. "He told me, 'You'll do, Cadet Syrkin. You'll do.'"

Now, more than a year after first entering the NAVCAD program, Syrkin stood among the ninety-seven cadets and eagerly waited to hear his name called. He was sweating, but that was of little consequence. He and his classmates had made it through the difficult months of preflight, primary, basic, and advanced training to earn the right to receive their wings of gold. While the ceremony was attended by crowds of friends and families, the demand of war would not allow the pace of training to abate. As the training station commander made his speech, dozens of N2S Stearman biplanes, Vultee Valiant, and SNJ monoplanes soared over the field, adding the roar of their radial engines to the tumult. Just a few days before, every man in the graduation ceremony had been flying those same planes.

Syrkin's memory of the moment of truth was clear. "They called my name and I snapped to attention and saluted. The captain took

Robert Lehnert climbing into his fighter. (Photo courtesy Colonel Robert Lehnert.)

a pair of gold wings from a tray held by an ensign and pinned them onto my blouse. He shook my hand and congratulated me."

One by one the new aviators were given their wings. Robert Paden Moran, a slim, short twenty-one-year old from Depue, Illinois was back in the line with his own wings. Moran was barely tall enough to qualify for the NAVCAD program, but more than made up for his lack of height with extra spirit and determination.

"We called him Tiger because he was a real feisty fellow," Syrkin said. "He and I got to be good friends. His one great weakness, as far as I could tell, was a fear of deep water. He hated when we practiced ditching in the bay."

The process of selecting who would go on to fly fighters was as much based on the needs of the Navy Department as on a cadet's choice. For instance, Dean Laird, who from the outset had his sights on being a fighter pilot recalled, "When we were going through basic, we were given the choice of VC, which was carriers, VP, for patrol planes, or VOBS, for observation. I only put down two choices, VC and the Army Air Corps." Needless to say, Laird, who had been the highest-scoring cadet in aerial gunnery and who graduated second in his class of ninety-two, was given his first choice.

Considering Laird's success as a fighter pilot in the Atlantic and Pacific, it was the right choice for him. Fighter pilots as a rule were independent and proud to the point of conceit. Unlike the men behind the controls of the big bombers, patrol planes, and transports, a fighter pilot had no one to share the flying with, no one to turn to. He was on his own. It was his hands, feet, eyes, and brain that controlled the fighter from start-up to landing. He made it turn, climb, and dive. When he saw a target, it was his eyes and reflexes that directed a deadly stream of bullets into the enemy.

When the Pensacola graduation ceremony was over, Syrkin, Moran, and Hansen, along with several other men who had their sights on being fighter pilots, received orders to NAS Jacksonville for operational training.

While not as humid as Pensacola, Jacksonville, located on the north Atlantic coast of Florida, was hot with strong winds off the ocean. The smell of swamps and marshes swept in from the coast only to be overwhelmed by the ripe tinge of airplane exhaust, burned rubber, and scorched metal. Everywhere one looked was an immense plain of white concrete, huge hangars, and hundreds of airplanes.

Established as a naval aviation training facility in 1940, Jacksonville had a long and proud history that went back to the First World War, when it had been a US Army base called Camp Joseph E. Johnston, where the army's quartermasters received their training. The needs of billeting and training the entire Quartermaster Corps for the army required a huge facility of more than six hundred buildings. In 1928, the National Guard took over the base and it was named Camp Foster. When the navy acquired the land in October 1940 as a new aviation training station, it grew even more, becoming part of the Jacksonville Navy Complex. The satellite bases included Naval Station Mayport and NAS Cecil Field.

By the time Syrkin and the others arrived in the spring of 1943, NAS Jacksonville was in full swing, turning out hundreds of aviators every month.

Advanced/operational training started on real fighters at Cecil Field, the largest of Jacksonville's facilities. It was commissioned that same year in honor of Henry B. Cecil, who had died in the crash of the US Navy dirigible USS *Akron* in 1933. Cecil Field was used for training the navy's dive bomber pilots, but several fighter pilots learned their trade there. To the dismay of Syrkin and the others, they found themselves looking at a decrepit line of Brewster F2A Buffaloes, the most obsolete monoplane fighters in the navy's inventory.

"It was pretty depressing to think we were going to fly those things," said Hansen. "They looked like fat pigs with wings."

Dean Laird also commented on the careworn fighters he and the others had been expected to fly. "I heard they were brought back from the Pacific. Some had been the survivors of the squadrons mauled at Midway. They had cloth patches over the bullet holes."

The Buffalo, which resembled a fat barrel with short, stubby wings, had been considered advanced when it first entered navy service in 1937. It was the first all-metal monoplane carrier-capable fighter ordered by the United States Navy. It was also purchased by the Belgians, British, and Dutch. The Finnish Air Force used them in their defensive war against the Soviet Union in 1942. Against the clumsy Soviet fighters, they were superior, but when pitted by the US Navy, British, and Dutch against the Mitsubishi A6M Zero, the Buffalo was, as one veteran of the air war commented, "a fat sitting duck."

However, Laird believed the Buffalo was a better fighter than history has painted it. "I don't think the navy knew how to use it," said the veteran with seven kills to his credit. "It wasn't a dogfighter. If it had been used in high-speed diving attacks the way the Flying Tigers used the P-40 Warhawks, then it would have performed better. I found it to be very nimble and easy to fly. It was also the first true fighter we ever flew."

Once they mastered the Buffalo, the marines were checked out on the venerable Grumman F4F Wildcat, the only fighter to have shown real success against the vaunted Japanese Zero. Cactus air force marines had been flying the Wildcat in the Solomon Islands, where they had to be tough and reliable. The US Navy's first ace, Lieutenant Edward "Butch" O'Hare also flew the trusty Wildcat. Among Japanese Zero pilots, it earned a reputation for being easy to hit but hard to kill. Saburo Sakai, Japan's top surviving ace had tried to shoot down a damaged Wildcat with his twin 7.7mm machine guns. He poured more than 250 rounds into his enemy until it was literally shredded, yet he never managed to bring it down.

If the F4F Wildcat had one major weakness in combat, it was in the power-to-weight ratio. At a hefty seven thousand pounds, the F4F was heavy and the Pratt & Whitney R-1830 radial engine put out 1,200 horsepower. This gave the Wildcat a rate of climb at between five hundred to one thousand feet per minute, a serious limitation in combat against the A6M Zero, whose own rate of climb was nearly twice that. In a dogfight, American pilots, knowing that they had more powerful engines, often climbed to escape a pursuing Zero. But as the two adversaries climbed, the Wildcat's greater weight slowed it until the engine was no longer able to overcome the aircraft's weight. At that point, the F4F literally fell out of the sky, whereupon the Zero, whose engine had kept pace, was able to pounce on the helpless American. This flaw was only alleviated by clever cooperative tactics such as the famous "Thach Weave," developed by Commander Jimmy Thach of VF-3.

If Syrkin and the rest had any complaints about the F4F, it centered on the landing gear. After takeoff and before landing, the heavy fuselage-mounted landing gear had to be laboriously hand-cranked with a handle on the inside of the cockpit.

"I hated having to crank the gear up and down like a goddamned car window," Syrkin said. "Thirty-two turns brought the gear up after takeoff, and all the time the plane wobbled like it was on a bumpy road. We'd been told that eventually it got easier, but you could not prove it by me."

John Glenn, who trained in the Wildcat with VMO (later VMF) 155 at MCAS El Centro in California, related an account of a Wildcat pilot coming in for a landing, but forgetting to lower the gear. He slid off the runway on the plane's belly and flipped over in a drainage ditch. When the crash crews arrived they found the pilot, still hanging upside-down in his harness, cranking the landing gear *up* from the fuselage so he could avoid being reprimanded for failing to lower the wheels.

Classroom instruction taught the basics of attacking a moving aerial target from the rear, and the art of setting up a deflection shot from the side, something the army air force rarely did. In the air, they practiced against towed targets and each other. In time, they gained confidence in themselves and their aircraft. Probably the most fun was in strafing ground targets with their machine guns.

"That was a real thrill to have those big Brownings blazing away," recalled Hansen. "But it wasn't like the movies. We only had about thirty seconds of ammunition and we were trained to use it in short bursts. Only John Wayne hosed the ammo in one long burst."

There remained one more major hurdle for them to surmount. In order to be considered true navy aviators, they had to be carrier qualified. Carrier Qualification Training (CQT) took place at Naval Air Station Chicago in Cook County, southwest of the Windy City. Originally named Curtiss Field in 1929, it was the hub of commercial airlines for the Chicago area. In the 1930s, the National Air Races were held at Curtiss Field. Aviation legends like Wiley Post, Jimmy Doolittle, and Charles Lindbergh flew out of Curtiss Field. The navy had been using the Naval Reserve Air Base (NRAB) at Naval Training Base Great Lakes on Lake Michigan. When the size and number of naval aircraft increased in the late 1930s, the Navy Department purchased Curtiss Field. After extensive construction, the new NAS Chicago was dedicated in 1937. During the war, more than nine thousand NAVCADs received their primary flight training at the base, which in 1944 was re-named NAS Glenview.

The "aircraft carriers" assigned to NAS Chicago proved to be antiquated coal-fired side-paddle steamers. The United States Navy converted two of them into USS *Sable* and USS *Wolverine* by adding a five-hundred-foot-long wooden flight deck. The ships were based at the navy pier in Chicago and sailed every day to provide a platform for landing and takeoff training.

"There were a lot of jokes about Mark Twain and riverboat gamblers," recalled Hansen. "We were amazed that the navy used those relics to train carrier pilots."

The conversion of the two paddle-wheeled excursion vessels was a brilliant solution to a serious problem. Unarmed, they were never intended for combat, but they took the role that would otherwise have required the use of one of the precious carriers needed in the Pacific or Atlantic. Thousands of pilots who later fought in the skies over the Pacific earned their qualifications aboard either *Sable* or *Wolverine*. Although the old 7,200-ton ships could barely maintain eighteen knots, or about twenty-one miles per hour, the high winds on Lake Michigan gave the new pilots plenty of headwind to practice their first landings on a flight deck.

They appeared alarmingly tiny when seen from a Wildcat at five thousand feet.

"It grew bigger as I closed in," said Syrkin, "but it was still a very small space to land a plane on."

Lehnert commented, "We heard that the bottom of Lake Michigan was littered with Wildcats and Dauntless dive bombers that had missed the deck."

Lieutenant John Lincoln, whom Syrkin and the others would soon meet, had had to ditch his F4F during an engine failure on approach to USS *Sable* that same month.

Watched by an instructor, the pilots began their approach. From the downwind leg, which was parallel to but in the opposite direction of the ship's course, they banked around and approached on the upwind leg where the ship's wake, a long white streak like a brush stroke on a blue canvas led them in. Streaming from the ship's funnel was a sooty gray ribbon of smoke. This proved to be a useful tool.

Syrkin said, "I remembered what our instructor had said about watching the funnel smoke. It would help us judge the wind over the deck."

The tiny figure of the Landing Signal Officer on the stern guided him in. Every motion of the LSO's orange paddles gave the approaching pilot vital information on his altitude and attitude as he came in at over one hundred knots.

"The trick was to watch the LSO and not the ship. It took a lot of faith to trust a man you'd never met, but he knew better than you did how to bring you in."

As the last few seconds stretched into near infinity and the ship hurtled toward Syrkin's plane, he saw the LSO give the "cut" sign by snapping the right paddle across his chest.

With a surge of relief, he felt the sudden jerk as his tailhook caught the wire and his Wildcat lurched to a halt.

"I felt great that day," he said. "But I was glad when it was over. The only thing we didn't do on those ships was catapult launches. My first time was at Tarawa."

"I did four landings on *Sable* the first day and four on *Wolverine* the second day," said Lehnert. "It was easy."

That was the last hurdle. They were now fully qualified marine aviators. Each received their orders for squadron assignment.

"My orders were to proceed to Los Angeles' Union Station," recalled Syrkin. "Then take a bus to MCAS El Toro, California for squadron assignment no later than 20 July 1943."

He and several others boarded a train in Chicago. For a week, the new pilots watched the miles and states pass by the windows while sailors, soldiers, airmen, and factory workers came and went. Every town seemed to have an army camp or air base. There were naval stations hundreds of miles from the ocean. It was another sign that the nation was at war. "We played cards, talked, wrote letters, and slept from Illinois to California. I never saw so much land in all my life even when I was at Ohio State. But you know it didn't look any different. People worked on farms and walked on the roads. Kids played and waved as we went by. It's a big country."

Every mile brought him and the other new marines closer to war.

CHAPTER 3

THE FLYING BUCCANEERS

Los Angeles' Union Station was a huge stucco edifice on Alameda Street. It was famous for the long-running gag on the Jack Benny radio program where Mel Blanc as the station announcer would call out "Train leaving on Track Five for Anaheim, Asuza and Cuc...": and after a *very* long pause, "...a-mun-ga!"

During the Second World War, Union Station was a beehive of activity twenty-four hours a day. The cavernous halls were like a cathedral. The din of hundreds of footfalls and voices echoed off the tall windows and stone floors. Every bench, chair, and even some of the vast floor space was taken up by sailors, marines, soldiers, and airmen. Some talked or wrote letters, but most grabbed whatever sleep they could before leaving for yet another duty assignment, base, or ship. Many had small printed papers under their hands that stated, "Please wake me at..."

It was no different on a late July 1943 day as the train from Chicago arrived and the weary passengers stepped onto the busy platform. After washing, changing into clean khakis, and wolfing down sandwiches at a lunch counter, the marine aviators boarded a bus to MCAS El Toro, located in Orange County south of Los Angeles. Checking in at the station administration building, they were directed to an office where several marine officers and enlisted men were waiting.

El Toro served as the clearing station for new pilots and enlisted men who had orders for squadron assignments. One new arrival from Jacksonville was Second Lieutenant Andrew Jones, a friend of Bob Lehnert. He was posted to VMF-113 at El Toro. Others received their orders to a new squadron in San Diego. As for Syrkin, Moran, and several others, they were to join VMF-422, a new reserve fighter squadron at MCAS Santa Barbara up the coast north of Los Angeles.

The gray navy bus was packed with marine officers and enlisted men. While most of the officers were strangers, there were a few familiar faces from Pensacola, Jacksonville, or Chicago.

The bus rolled north on Highway 101, a two and three-lane concrete road that ran through endless miles of orange groves, farms,

A view of hangars at Marine Corps Air Station Santa Barbara in the fall of 1943. (Photo courtesy Andrew Syrkin.)

and small towns. The hot July air that blew into the open bus windows was sweet with the aroma of oranges, but on the bus only the pungent cloak of cigarette smoke filled the nostrils.

As the bus passed east of Los Angeles, the famous "HOLLYWOODLAND" sign was clearly visible to the marines and many thought of beautiful movie stars and the Hollywood USO. Once past the city, the highway led up the coast through towns of Spanish colonial stucco and adobe houses.

Marine Corps Air Station Santa Barbara was located on flat farming land outside Goleta. In the early 1930s, it was called Santa Barbara Municipal Airport and no different from hundreds of other small airports of the era. In 1940 the Civil Aeronautics Authority, forerunner of the FAA, chose the site for military use. Several hundred acres were purchased and a large tidal wetland known as the Goleta Slough was filled in to accommodate the enlarged air base. Two crossing runways of six thousand feet and three thousand feet were built with facilities to support marine air operations.

The first planes to use the field were US Army Air Force P-40s for the defense of the coast and Los Angeles area. In the months following Pearl Harbor, the West Coast was in a high state of alert, even near panic, that a Japanese force would attack and invade the mainland. Army units of the Seventh Infantry Division from Fort Ord near Monterrey patrolled the beaches while a civilian air defense system was hastily assembled. The US Army provided antiaircraft guns, some whose origins went back to the First World War, for the defense of San Francisco, Los Angeles, and San Diego.

There were valid reasons to fear an attack as several airfields, key industries, oil refineries, and aircraft plants dotted the Los Angeles region. Lockheed, Douglas, and North American Aviation produced hundreds of new planes a month. The hysteria peaked during February 1942, when the Japanese submarine *I-17* shelled the oil tanks and refinery installations at Elwood near Santa Barbara. It was the first time the US mainland had been attacked by an enemy ship. The very next night, the air raid sirens all around Los Angeles wailed and air raid wardens swarmed over the city to enforce the blackout.

In moments, the gunners of the 37th Coast Artillery, based at Fort MacArthur overlooking San Pedro began hammering their deadly cadence into the night sky. They were quickly joined by gunners and soldiers all over the city. The barrage lasted for over an hour, and more than 1,400 shells were fired. When the blackout was lifted, the streets of San Pedro, Long Beach, Los Angeles, and Hollywood were strewn with thousands of bits of shrapnel, yet no burning Japanese planes were found. The air raid had been another case of what was blithely known as "war nerves." To this day, no solid evidence of what triggered the air raid has ever been proved.

By early 1943, the army air force squadrons relocated to Santa Maria, and in May of that year, the marines arrived at Goleta. Two dive bomber squadrons, VMSB-243 and VMSB-244, equipped with the reliable Douglas SBD-5 Dauntless, began training and flight operations. Both units eventually saw service at Bougainville and the Philippines, earning several decorations for valor.

From May 1943 to late 1945, twenty-four marine fighter, dive bomber, and torpedo bomber squadrons were stationed at MCAS Santa Barbara where more than five hundred officers and nearly 1,300 enlisted men worked and lived. Every time a squadron deployed to the Pacific, another one moved in. Some, like VMF-221, which had been decimated at Midway, were reorganized and reequipped. Major Joe Foss, the Guadalcanal veteran with twenty-five victories and the Medal of Honor commanded a Santa Barbara squadron. One of the units that passed through the station was VMF-214, infamously known as "The Black Sheep," led by former Flying Tiger Major Gregory "Pappy" Boyington.

As ordered by Commander Air Wing, Pacific (COMAIRPAC) in Order No. 062354 in December 1942, US Marine Fighter Squadron Number 422 was formed under the initial command of Captain James K. Dill, USMCR at San Diego. At that time, it existed only on paper, but things moved quickly in wartime. With a cadre of officers

Captain Edwin Fry, who commanded VMF-422 prior to the arrival of Major MacLaughlin. (Photo courtesy Andrew Syrkin.)

and staff, Dill was ordered to move to MCAS Santa Barbara where they arrived and took quarters on 27 January.

Designated as a reserve unit, VMF-422 would be assembled and organized, trained, and deployed as events warranted. Dill and his staff took delivery of the increasing mountain of men and equipment needed for a fighter squadron, and by early April, the infant unit was turned over to Captain Edwin C. Fry, USMCR. Dill was sent to El Toro.

Fry, who was a Santa Barbara resident, had seen combat in the Solomon Islands and had been rotated back to the states for reassignment. His combat experience made him ideally suited for shepherding VMF-422 into shape. But he was not to hold the post of commander for long.

Enter Major John S. MacLaughlin, Jr. There are few men in the VMF-422 story that generate more intrigue and controversy than John MacLaughlin. Strong, easygoing, and intelligent, his life and death have become a *cause célèbre* for military historians. But today there is little to go on but official information and the memories of those who knew him. Born in 1915 in Collingswood, New Jersey, MacLaughlin graduated from Collingswood High School in 1932. He was athletic and able, and graduated from the Naval Academy in 1938, receiving his commission in the Marine Corps. After a year of duty at the Philadelphia Navy Yard, he was sent to NAS Pensacola for flight training. While there he met Naomi Oppenheimer of Atlantic City, New Jersey. They fell in love and married on July 7, 1940. As the war clouds loomed ever closer, he led several flights of fighters from NAS New York (now Floyd Bennett Field) to San Diego, often in poor weather and near-zero visibility. Assigned to Coronado in San Diego, he worked under General Ross E. Rowell, commander of Marine Air Wing, Pacific.

From San Diego, the newly promoted Captain MacLaughlin went to Hawaii. MacLaughlin rose quickly in rank due to his excellent administrative skills. He was at MCAS Ewa on Oahu on 7 December 1941 and witnessed the destruction of every marine plane on the ground. This undoubtedly inflamed his eagerness to get into the fight, and in April he was promoted to major.

Naomi gave birth to their only son, John S. MacLaughlin III on 6 April 1943 at the Coronado Hospital.

So, it was on 17 July 1943 that Major MacLaughlin, with two gleaming gold oak leaves on his collar, accepted his new command. Captain Fry was made the executive officer. Naomi moved to Santa Barbara to be close to her husband.

A typical wartime Marine Corps fighter squadron, with some minor variation, had forty pilots. The pilots were formed into two parts, the lead, or first echelon, of twenty-four, and the rear echelon, of sixteen. More than one pilot would fly a particular aircraft, but the lead echelon would be, to use a football analogy, the "first string." When a pilot in the lead echelon was wounded or for some other reason taken out of the rotation, a pilot from the rear echelon replaced him. This also applied to when men had completed their tours and were sent home. This way a squadron was able to maintain a full complement of qualified pilots as the war progressed.

The ground echelon consisted of officers and enlisted men, usually around 120 in all. They were responsible for administration, supply, and maintenance, among other duties. In a deployment, the lead echelon and their planes traveled by aircraft carrier with their planes while the ground and rear echelon followed on a transport.

In the case of Major MacLaughlin and Fry, the commander led the lead echelon while his exec oversaw the rear. Considering what was to transpire, this may have been a blessing for Captain Edwin Fry.

The first pilots to arrive on station in the late spring had no fighters, instead having to settle for twelve North American SNJ-5 advanced trainers. In June, four Grumman FM-1 Wildcats and a

Major John MacLaughlin, the new commander of VMF-422. (Photo courtesy family of John MacLaughlin.)

single F4U-1 Corsair were delivered from the San Diego Air Depot. The FM-1 was manufactured under license by General Motors after Grumman ceased F4F production in early 1943 for the production of the new F6F Hellcat. The five fighters gave the new pilots a taste for real power and performance, but as more men arrived, each man had less opportunity to fly them. When a pilot came to join 422, he had to take the low slot in the rotation with the SNJs.

The bus from El Toro pulled into the main gate of MCAS Santa Barbara. The marines exited the bus to be greeted by the warm, blossom-scented California air. But as Syrkin recalled, there was a ripe animal smell as well. "I noticed it right away, kind of a stink like from a pig pen. I learned later there was a hog slaughterhouse a few miles away."

Captain Fry came out of the administration building to greet them. He asked to see their orders. One by one the officers presented their papers. Then the enlisted men did the same.

Among them was Corporal Ed Walsh, a seventeen-year old mechanic who had lied about his age to get into the marines. He presented his orders to Fry, who questioned Walsh about whether he was old enough to be out by himself. This caused some laughter among the others.

Walsh, who was remembered by a squadron mate as a very strong-willed young man, replied firmly with "I'm not on my own, I'm a marine."

"We were directed to a room filled with rows of folding chairs and a table at one end," Syrkin remembered. "I guess there were about ten or twelve of us. One fellow came up to me and asked if I'd been at Pensacola. The questioner was Second Lieutenant Walter Wilson, known as Jake. A Mississippian by birth, Jake Wilson had a deep, lazy southern drawl and liked to smoke Camel cigarettes. A graduate of "Ole Miss," he was a staunch Baptist who liked Dixie jazz and played the trombone. He was engaged to a girl back home. Of all the pilots in VMF-422, his story would become the most compelling.

For several minutes, the new pilots talked and introduced themselves to one another. "I felt right at home with them," Syrkin commented. "They were from all over the country."

Then the door opened and four officers dressed in crisply pressed khakis entered. The man in front was of medium height with short brown hair over a narrow face. His eyes were bright and alert. This was Major MacLaughlin. It was the first time Syrkin and the others had met their new squadron commander.

MacLaughlin introduced himself, then pointed to the men who'd come in with him. They were Captains Cloyd Rex Jeans, Charley Hughes, and Edwin Fry.

Captain Jeans was from Joplin, Missouri. The twenty-six-year old had earned his Bachelor of Science degree from Northwestern University in 1940 and joined the US Navy Reserve for his pilot training in May 1941. He later transferred to the marines. He was married to a girl named Patricia. His staff position was Air Operations Officer. Quiet and businesslike, Jeans would prove to be an able and resourceful officer. He had seen combat with VMF-223 at Guadalcanal during the first desperate months, flying patrols alongside Marion Carl and John Smith. He was the closest thing to an ace in the roster, having been credited with four confirmed kills.

The author found a fragment of a clipping from the Joplin *Globe* that gives an intriguing but incomplete account of a battle sometime in late 1942. The date is not given, nor any unit names.

JOPLIN FLYER HELPS BAG JAP PLANES
Lieutenant Cloyd Jeans, remembered in Joplin as Rex Jeans, was among Marine Corps pilots who bagged Japanese

planes during a furious two-day aerial battle recently at Guadalcanal island and which took part in the daring rescue of a detachment of marines who had been given up for dead. The story of Lieutenant Jean's part in the battle was carried recently in the Wichita, Kansas, Evening Eagle and was sent by the United Press.

The battle started when a member of the squadron saw on a desolate beach the word "Help" lettered with...

The clipping ends here. The author was unable to find more from the *Globe* or *Evening Eagle* archives or even from historians at the National Museum of the Marine Corps. It probably happened between August and November of 1942. Even more interesting, Jeans was awarded the Distinguished Flying Cross for his participation.

Charley Hughes, the training and maintenance officer, was an engineer from Oklahoma. He had a ready wit and strong religious beliefs. He too had seen combat, in his case with Red Parks in the ill-fated VMF-221 at Midway

Edwin Fry was the Executive Officer and in command of the rear echelon. Like Jeans, he saw combat at Guadalcanal with the Green Knights of VMF-121 in the Cactus Air Force. The Knights had more aces than any other marine squadron and were credited with over two hundred victories.

MacLaughlin began, "You are all assigned to VMF-422, a reserve unit. We're still assembling the roster. More pilots and enlisted will join us in the next two weeks. We'll eventually have forty pilots. Your quarters have been assigned. Captain Jeans will show you around. Any questions?"

There were several. "One fellow, I remember," continued Syrkin, "was really tall and muscular with blond hair and blue eyes like from a Nazi recruiting poster. He asked the skipper what planes we would be flying. That was a pretty important question and I was glad he'd asked it."

MacLaughlin replied that for the present, VMF-422 had a dozen SNJ-5s, four FM-1s, and a single F4U-1 Corsair, but the Corsair was being flown by every pilot who could get their hands on it so it was often down for maintenance.

This, according to Syrkin did not go over well with the eager pilots who wanted to fly the hottest and best fighters. The Wildcat was virtually obsolete.

"Then he said that we were supposed to get the new Corsairs, but he wasn't sure exactly when."

At that point Charley Hughes affirmed that Wildcats had done very well in the Pacific. At both Midway and Guadalcanal, they had an excellent record of kills against the Japanese. All the navy and marine aces like Marion Carl and Joe Foss swore by the Grumman fighter.

That ended the matter for the moment and MacLaughlin went to each man and asked his name, checking it off the roster on his clipboard. Then he stood at the head of the room and addressed his new pilots. Syrkin remembered the major saying, "Gentlemen, for the next few months we are going to work like hell to make a combat-ready fighter squadron out of a bunch of kids who know nothing at all about each other. I don't care where you come from, what your last name is, if you pray to God or Abraham or Groucho Marx, or even what ball team you cheer for, as of now you are part of VMF-422. That is your team, your god, your home. I expect you to get to know and respect each other. I'm sure some of you think you're better pilots than the others. You wouldn't be marine aviators if you didn't, but you're going to have to work like a team. Every one of you has to learn to respect and trust every other man. I mean trust as in trust with your life. You will learn to work together to the best of your ability. That's what will keep you alive." Then Major MacLaughlin smiled and said, "Welcome to the Flying Buccaneers."

The author encountered conflicting accounts on this matter. The official squadron history, compiled in January 1945 by Major Elmer Wrenn states that it officially became the "Flying Buccaneers" in the fall of 1944 while they were on Engebi in the Marshall Islands. But it also appears that the name and an emblem of a grinning pirate with an eyepatch astride a Corsair had been adopted as early as the fall of 1943. The author found several photos, including one of Ken Gunderson and Chris Lauesen on Midway in November of that year. Lauesen's jacket has a patch bearing the emblem. The appellation was likely a nickname, a way of giving them an identity beyond a number.

Second Lieutenants Earl "Tommy" Thompson, Bill Aycrigg, Robert K. Wilson, Don Walker, Bill Reardon, and Ted Thurnau had also joined VMF-422 on that day. In the officer's mess, they met the men who had arrived earlier. These included John Hansen, John Lincoln, Bob Whalen, Caleb Smick, Ed Farrell, Bob Scott, and Stafford Drake.

"I had been there for a week when this second bunch showed up," recalled John Hansen. "We welcomed the new fellows and got to know them." Hansen described those early days in the squadron, "Right away, just like pilots everywhere, we began to size one another up. We talked and compared notes on where we had come from, how we had done in training, and so on. Almost no one ever really came out and said so, but we all had this 'I'm a better pilot than you' attitude. Especially John Lincoln. We called him Abe of course, even though he came from Massachusetts."

Second Lieutenant John Lincoln was from Boston, smoked Lucky Strikes, and drank bourbon. It was generally agreed he was one of the best natural pilots in the squadron.

Robert "Chick" Whalen was a handsome young Massachusetts Irishman of average build. He was a baseball player and had a ready repertoire of witty jokes. Caleb "Cal" Smick turned out to be a smooth-talking Topeka, Kansas boy with a winning smile and personality. He was the son of a respected Kansas educator.

"Cal was a good swimmer," said Syrkin, "But we didn't know until much later how good he was."

Second Lieutenant Stafford Drake from Wilmette, Illinois sported a neat haircut and perfect white teeth, and Second Lieutenant Edmond Farrell from Louisville, Kentucky was a likable country boy who enjoyed hunting. Bob "Scotty" Scott was from New England and spoke with a pronounced twang like Jimmy Stewart.

Sterling Price proved to be a solidly-built Missourian from Hazelwood. His unique nickname of "Shou" or "Shoe" was due to his having parachuted out of a trainer at Jacksonville. Like another soon-to-be-famous Missourian named Harry Truman, Price was very outspoken and never failed to voice his opinion on everything from politics to women to baseball.

Then there was First Lieutenant Royce "Tex" Watson from west Texas. As much a southerner as Jake Wilson, Watson spoke with a languid drawl. He was as patriotic as any of them, having joined the marines in 1942.

Second Lieutenant Kenneth Gunderson was a twenty-two-year old from Gilmanton, Wisconsin. A graduate of the University of Wisconsin, he played baseball, football, and basketball. When the war started he first joined the navy and then transferred to the marines. He was engaged to a girl in Milwaukee named Verna Hagen. Another second lieutenant was Earl Thompson from Compton, California. He received his flight training in the west, beginning at Love Field near Prescott, Arizona. The blond man whom had first asked about what they'd be flying was Second Lieutenant Chris

Lauesen of Chicago. Handsome and athletic, he was addicted to sports and exercise.

Pennsylvanian Don Walker was considered a good man to have around in a tight spot. His attitude about flying was summed up in a relaxed, "I just get the plane ten feet off the runway and from then on it's on its own." Ted Thurnau, who stood nearly six feet tall, came from Westwood, New Jersey. Bill Aycrigg was from Fairfield, Connecticut, the son of a wealthy Washington, DC businessman, while Bob Wilson was a solid, reliable man from Springfield, Illinois. Bill Reardon was another Massachusetts native.

"We had a lot of fellows named John, Bob and Bill," said Hansen, reflecting on the roster. "Bill Reardon and Chick Whalen got to be buddies, both being Boston Irish. I think I remember some early problems between Gunderson and Syrkin."

"Ken Gunderson and I became rivals, sort of," stated Syrkin. "He was this big, bluff fellow with sandy hair and muscles. He and I were about the same height but he was a lot stronger looking. He was kind of a bully and really rode Tiger Moran. I usually told him, 'Hey why don't you pick on someone your own size?'"

Gunderson, who retired from the LAPD in 1966 and later went to work for Douglas Aircraft, said of Syrkin, "We got along okay for the most part. Supposedly he resented how I was picking on small guys like Tiger Moran. I don't remember that at all. We were like the two big kids on the same block. But if you talk to guys like Curly Lehnert and John Hansen, they say there wasn't much to it. Time has a way of making all this stuff blurry."

The next few days were taken up with paperwork, drawing their equipment and being assigned their quarters in three clapboard barracks. The buildings each had a living area, two bathrooms with showers and separate rooms, each with two double-decker bunk beds and wardrobes.

By the end of the following week, the lead echelon was up to full strength with the arrival of three more pilots, Captain John Rogers, First Lieutenant Robert Lehnert, and a southerner named Jules Flood, Jr.

Rogers was a quiet, thin officer from New Jersey with pale skin and dark blond hair. As one of the three combat veterans, he would take over the post of Training Officer from Hughes.

First Lieutenant Bob Lehnert sported an almost severely short marine haircut. He went by the name of "Curly," as in Curly Howard of the Three Stooges, but Curly Lehnert was no stooge. He was an intelligent, thoughtful, and insightful officer who got along well with everyone he met. He proved to be quick-witted and friendly. His favorite topics beyond flying were science and chemistry. He was the only one of the new pilots who had soloed in a Corsair at Jacksonville before being sent to Santa Barbara.

Second Lieutenant Jules C. Flood, Jr. of Washington, DC was lanky and had driven race cars before the war. He impressed the other pilots with his deft driving of the station jeeps, and was a talented mechanic. He turned out to have the most envied skill for a fighter pilot, perfect hand-eye coordination. He and Lincoln liked the same brand of bourbon and cigarettes.

"Flood and I often flew the same plane," said Lehnert. "He was very picky about it being in perfect running order. He was great with engines."

The Flying Buccaneers had little in common but for their training. All were white, either Protestant or Catholic, other than Syrkin who was Jewish. Their ages ranged from MacLaughlin at twenty-eight down to the youngest at twenty-two. As a rule, they were fit and healthy, standing between 5'4" and 6' in height. Bob Moran was the shortest man in the squadron, while both Thurnau and Watson topped six feet.

All had volunteered and received their wings at Pensacola, Jacksonville or Corpus Christi, Texas. They were city boys or small-town kids. Nearly all had fathers or older relatives who had served in the First World War, and a few had siblings in the military. Most had gone to college while a few had made it into the service through the Civilian Pilot Training Program.

While MacLaughlin was one of the few married men, several were engaged. Ken Gunderson would marry while on leave just before the squadron shipped out to Hawaii.

Major MacLaughlin relied on his officers, staff, and senior NCOs to manage the nuts and bolts of organizing, equipping, and training VMF-422. But even amidst the hectic pace of wartime urgency, there was time for relaxation. On Friday and Saturday nights, after a long day of flying and classroom work, the officers found enticements in the city.

The lights of Los Angeles were an almost irresistible draw to men who had grown up on farms and in small towns. Hollywood was a virtual mecca of beautiful movie stars and the place to be was the Hollywood Canteen, a former livery stable at 1451 Cahuenga Boulevard. Opened in October 1942, it was the brainchild of stars Bette Davis and John Garfield, who would portray a marine blinded at Guadalcanal in 1945's *Pride of the Marines*. The Canteen was open free to all servicemen and women in uniform. Drinks, food, and music were donated by local businesses and entertainers. Hundreds of stars of the silver screen came to entertain the troops, not only out of patriotic fervor but often to boost fading popularity. There were The Andrews Sisters, Abbott & Costello, Marlene Dietrich, Bette Davis, Mary Astor, Don Ameche, Eddie "Rochester" Anderson, Ava Gardner, Judy Garland, Joan Fontaine, Cary Grant, Sidney Greenstreet, Lana Turner, Benny Goodman, Gene Tierney, and every soldier's dream girl, Betty Grable, to name but a few.

"It was a real thrill to have someone like Paulette Goddard serving drinks," recalled one Normandy-bound paratrooper about his visit to the Canteen in 1943. "I just about dropped in my tracks when she even lit my cigarette for me."

Some of the pilots found their way into Hollywood by bus, but due to the huge crowds that thronged the sidewalks, they often had little luck in gaining entrance to the Canteen.

"I didn't expect to see Veronica Lake or Ann Sheridan strolling down the sidewalk," said Syrkin of his only wartime visit to the club. "But I also didn't think we'd have any trouble getting in."

The marines contented themselves with wandering the streets of downtown Hollywood, going into bars and nightclubs for a drink or a dance. They noticed, among the Angelinos, a blasé indifference to the war mixed with a restrained sense of alertness. The latter was borne out if they saw one of the many anti-aircraft guns that had been sited on vacant lots to guard against air attack. But war or no war, Hollywood never slept.

"I did find a couple of nice clubs and danced with girls," said Syrkin, grinning. "They were impressed that I was a marine aviator, and of course I took every advantage of it."

The farming town of Goleta was a quiet place. The bars, movie houses, dance halls, and night clubs were a far cry from the allure of Hollywood, but it was closer.

Corporal Ed Walsh remembered his time off base. "The townspeople were lovely. There was gas rationing and the locals couldn't drive far. A lot of us were privates. The bus used to cost a quarter to go into Santa Barbara. We would go to the gate and people would stop and ask, 'Where are you going? Come with us for dinner.' We went to Goleta and Santa Barbara and the people were very positive to us. The American Women's' Volunteer Service (AWVS) had a storefront down on State Street where all day and into the early evening they had cake and coffee for us. I remember going to a

Sterling "Shou" Price, John Hansen and Bob "Curly" Lehnert in a Los Angeles nightclub while stationed at MCAS Santa Barbara. (Photo courtesy Andrew Syrkin.)

dance or a prom at the high school. A lot of girls were in formal gowns in the gymnasium. We used to go to the El Paso Club to drink zombies. That was the popular drink back then. We rubbed elbows with movie stars. Rosalind Russell was there, she was quite a big star."

The local people purchased, at their own expense, a Jeep or truck, depending on who told the story, and presented it to the air station. It was named "The Spirit of Goleta," and used by the enlisted men as an alternative mode of transportation. "I drove that Jeep a lot," said Walsh. "It was really nice of those folks to do that for us."

Far less glamorous or crowded than Hollywood, Santa Barbara was one of the early California mission towns. Its architecture was pure Spanish colonial, stucco and red tiles roofs, high garden walls, and winding roads. California white oak trees provided shade along sidewalks, while near the beach, tall slender palm trees swayed in the cool Pacific breezes. Beyond the pristine beaches, the surf enticed swimmers and surfers. MacLaughlin, who loved to swim in the ocean, often spent his limited free time snorkeling and exploring the lush underwater kelp forests.

On Saturday nights, the pilots often took the bus into Santa Barbara and spent their evenings in one of the bars that studded the downtown area. Because of wartime gas rationing, traffic was light. The only cars on the roads were built prior to 1942, when US auto manufacturing turned to building the vehicles and aircraft of war. There was no blackout, but dance music drifted from open windows as the marines passed pedestrians who greeted them with smiles and waves.

They often encountered officers from other marine fighter and bomber squadrons based at the air station. As with marines everywhere, there existed a squadron pride that resulted in good-natured jeering and taunts, but according to Lehnert, those encounters rarely escalated beyond verbal heckling. "I never witnessed a real fight like the ones you see in movies. We got along pretty well."

That might not have been the case if the marines encountered any army personnel from Santa Maria, farther up the coast. The enmity between the army and Marine Corps was legendary. This stemmed from a long-standing interservice rivalry. An old joke among US Navy aviators said that the only way to tell if an army squadron was flying in formation was that they were going in the same direction. "There was a lot of friendly rivalry between the army and the marines," said Lehnert, "but not as much as you see in the movies. We did like to heckle the army pilots about their flying."

Hansen said, "The bars we went to usually contained a jukebox, dart board, and a few dozen tables. It wasn't like nowadays with neon beer signs and loud country music. Back in those days a lot of people smoked and the ceiling was almost hidden above this layer of gray haze."

The pilots each had their own preferences for alcohol. Hughes and Fry drank Scotch. Tex Watson and Jake Wilson were solid bourbon drinkers, while Reardon, Whalen, and Aycrigg preferred scotch or Irish whiskey. Nearly all drank beer. Anchor Steam, a strong beer from San Francisco, was popular up and down the coast in the 1940s.

The jukebox ate scores of nickels and constantly erupted with Glenn Miller, Tommy Dorsey, or the Andrews Sisters. In the summer of 1943, a popular single was called "Comin' in on a Wing and a Prayer" by the Song Spinners. Even eight months after the Christmas season had ended, Bing Crosby crooning 'White Christmas' was also a favorite. "It seemed like we never could get that song out of our heads," said Lehnert, "especially when we were far from home."

Talk often turned to where they might be sent, and what kind of fighting they would do. This usually segued into speculation on the commanding officer. Charley Hughes had a high opinion of Major MacLaughlin, as did Jeans and even Fry, who'd had to turn command of VMF-422 over to the Major.

Although the pilots recognized that MacLaughlin had been a graduate of the Naval Academy, his lack of combat experience was a matter of no little concern.

Lehnert commented on this. "The skipper was a great guy. He sometimes came to the bar and drank with us. We could call him "Mac," talk to him, feel comfortable, but we really didn't know him, or how good a leader he'd be in battle." He recalled that his commanding officer had both an easygoing side and a hard-nosed, nononsense side. "He was easy to talk to if you needed to discuss something personal," he said, "but underneath that was a man who put the job and the good of the squadron first, last and always. I liked him as a person and respected him as an officer."

John Hansen agreed. "I remember asking Charley Hughes about Mac. Charley, who'd been at Midway, said Mac was a good leader, very motivated and a fantastic pilot. But we still had to wonder how well he would do when the lead started flying. Mac was determined to make VMF-422 the best marine fighter squadron in the corps, and he also made it known that he would tolerate nothing that made the squadron look bad."

Ken Gunderson, whose own personality was brusque and frank, recalled, "The skipper rode us hard to make us the best. I remember that he once gave a pilot hell for leaving his leader and chasing after an Army P-38 that jumped us. He rode that guy for ages. He drilled it right into us, 'Never, ever leave your leader! Marines do not leave men behind!'"

Charley Hughes told them about his own baptism of fire in VMF-221 at Midway, when he had been with Red Parks. He described swooping down on the Japanese bombers and Zeros north of Midway and seeing so many of their fellow marines falling into the sea. "But he loved the Wildcat," said Hansen. "He and Rex Jeans, who was also at Guadalcanal, swore by it."

"We didn't always talk shop," Lehnert added. "We liked to relax and dance with local girls. MacLaughlin was married and his wife Naomi lived in Santa Barbara. Once in a while Mac brought her into a bar to socialize. We liked her a lot. A very pretty girl from New Jersey. They had a boy, I think he was about four or five months old at the time. It's really sad he never really knew his father."

As the hot days of August passed, the pilots and ground crews molded themselves into a unit. Although there was little actual

interaction between officers and enlisted men, there was a cama-
raderie that transcended rank. Syrkin was a rarity, an officer who
went out of his way to be cordial and friendly to the enlisted men.
He respected the men who worked hard to keep the planes flying
and those who cooked and served the food and did the laundry. In
a short time, Lieutenant Mark Syrkin was the most popular officer
in the squadron. While he wasn't alone in his respect of the enlisted ranks—Lehnert, Hansen, Flood, and a few others were equally
egalitarian towards the ground echelon—he did go out of his way to
do small favors for them, even going so far as to loan them money
or pay a fine if any of his ground crew got into minor trouble with
the local police. This was his character, but also stemmed from his
feeling of being part of something special.

"I thrived on being in a marine fighter squadron," Syrkin said. "I
had reached the pinnacle of my chosen profession. To fly a fighter
plane demanded the best, the most highly skilled pilot."

To be a marine fighter pilot was the very peak of the pyramid, to
paraphrase Tom Wolfe. The marines had reason, after their breth-
ren had finally defeated the Japanese at Guadalcanal and the Solomon Islands, to feel a kinship with the British pilots of the Royal Air
Force who had fought outnumbered against the mighty Luftwaffe.

Only time would tell if the men of VMF-422 would carve their
names in the annals of history.

CHAPTER 4

CORSAIR!

By the middle of August, the squadron roster was complete but there was still much to be done before they were ready to deploy to the Pacific. The pilots spent dozens of hours in grueling classroom instruction learning about fighter tactics, formation flying, instrument flying, and celestial navigation. Instructors drilled them on how to ditch their planes at sea or bail out over the jungle, and most importantly, how to survive. Veterans of the Pacific air war came to give them lectures, including the famous Commander John S. "Jimmy" Thach, inventor of the "Thach Weave." Another was Commander Joseph "Jumping Joe" Clifton, who had commanded two fighter squadrons and now led VF-12, soon to be deployed on the USS *Saratoga*. He had been one of the pilots who tested the Mitsubishi A6M2 Zero that crashed in the Aleutian Islands in June 1942. Virtually intact, the Japanese fighter was tested in San Diego with US markings. Clifton, Fred Trapnell, and other pilots learned the Zero's strengths, and more importantly, where its weaknesses lay. Trapnell eventually went on to become the father of naval flight test at NAS Patuxent River, Maryland.

These men told the neophytes what air combat against the Japanese was really like. But they also told their rapt audiences what would likely happen if any of them were captured.

"It was common knowledge in the military what the Japanese did to prisoners," commented Hansen. "We'd heard stories of how they treated downed pilots by torture and beheading. I know now that a lot of it was propaganda but there was no doubt the Japs were merciless and cruel. We never talked about it among ourselves but there was a sort of grim fatalism that we had better not be taken alive."

They often made two or three flights a day. Eight pilots took off to form up into a flight of two four-plane divisions of two-plane elements. This was the standard unit for a squadron. Every day they took either the SNJs or the few FM-1 Wildcats aloft to practice formation flying or over-water navigation. The wide-open expanses

Vought F4U Corsairs and Grumman FM-1 Wildcats on the tarmac at MCAS Santa Barbara, 1943. (Photo courtesy Andrew Syrkin.)

of sky over the Ventura Channel off the coast provided plenty of air room to apply what they'd learned in the classroom.

Colonel Dean Caswell told the author about his time training with VMF-221, which was stationed at Santa Barbara in early 1944. This was after VMF-422 deployed to the Pacific, but his own experiences would have been familiar to the Flying Buccaneers.

"Santa Barbara was beautiful," recalled the ninety-three-year old Caswell. "The nights were foggy and we flew with the thrill of flying at night. But when we came back from wherever we had been training, San Diego or the desert, the whole coast was often socked in under fog. Believe it or not the only way we managed to land at night, since there were no electronic aids in those days, was to fly out to sea about twenty-five or thirty miles past the fog, until we could see the reflection of our wingtip lights on the water. Then we reversed course and headed back to Highway 101. When we saw the cars, we followed them right to the airfield." He chuckled. "Some of the pilots didn't make it."

Caswell also related that the carrier USS *Ranger* was in San Diego at the time and the marine squadrons flew down there to get further carrier qualification training. "San Diego became as important to us as Santa Barbara because some of us had not undergone CQT. But even when we had launched off the *Ranger* and came back to North Island we had that goddamned fog again. We wrecked about eight planes coming in at night."

The marines of VMF-422 honed their flying skills by doing what was and still is, euphemistically called "flat-hatting," or "flying on the deck." The practice was officially frowned upon, but tolerated. If a pilot crashed or there was damage to private property though, it could mean severe disciplinary action. Few aviators could resist doing it if they could get away with flying under bridges or in extreme cases, "cutting the grass" with their propeller blades.

Another activity that every marine aviator indulged in was dogfighting. This practice was encouraged as it was essential in honing a fighter pilot's skills for combat. Hellcat ace Dean Laird said, "It was highly satisfying to make a perfect pursuit curve and line up a deflection shot or get on his "six," the perfect position for a kill."

First Lieutenant Royce "Tex" Watson was the most aggressive pilot in VMF-422. Sterling Price commented, "Tex Watson was probably the most colorful character in the squadron. He claimed to be the best poker player. You never saw him in a pressed uniform. It always looked like he slept in it. But you put him in an airplane and he was something else. I never saw a better pilot. He could make a fighter do anything. He loved to dogfight and often boasted, "I'm gonna whip your ass when I see you in my sights, boy!"

The marines soon found they weren't the only predators prowling the skies of southern California. The army had several airfields in the Los Angeles area and the San Fernando Valley. Besides preparing for overseas deployment, they had the duty of protecting the region from enemy air attack.

At Santa Maria Army Air Field, squadrons of Lockheed P-38 Lightnings conducted daily patrols and training. The Lightning was already a legend in both the Pacific and Europe. Famed as the plane used to shoot down Admiral Yamamoto in April 1943, P-38s shot down scores of Luftwaffe aircraft over North Africa and the Mediterranean. Its power, speed, long range, and firepower were enough to counter the Me-109's greater maneuverability. The Lightning's unique profile and powerful weaponry earned it the ominous name of "Gabelschwanz teufel," the "Fork-tailed Devil," by the Luftwaffe. There was another name for the P-38. Even with two roaring Allison V-1710 engines, the Lightning was a very quiet plane in flight. German ground troops almost never heard it coming, nicknaming it "Whispering Death."

While the P-38 was ill-suited for dogfighting, it did have the advantage of speed and weight, but only as long as the element of surprise was on their side. The Wildcat could easily turn inside a P-38 at low speeds. But that didn't deter the eager army air force pilots. They flew above fifteen thousand feet, far above the marines' altitude. When they spotted the tiny blue F4Fs coasting along far below them, the P-38s dived like falcons at their prey.

"Charley Hughes told us we might meet some army fighters," said Syrkin. "I was sure I could beat them in a fair fight. But they never fought fair."

The first indication was a sudden "Tally-ho!" over the guard frequency. The dogfight often lasted only seconds, during which the marines suddenly found themselves in the sights of a Lightning's four machine guns and single 20mm cannon. Then, before the marines could use their superior agility, the army planes had dived away, usually accompanied by a cheery "Better luck next time, Jarheads!"

"That happened several times while we were at Santa Barbara," said Hansen. "It really got us riled up but we couldn't do anything about it." Then the retired marine colonel paused and gave a wry smirk, "Not until we got the Corsairs."

Once the lead echelon was complete, the next step was to organize them into a flying unit. As mentioned above, a squadron of twenty-four aircraft was divided into three eight-plane units called flights, each of which consisted of two divisions of four planes. These in turn had two, two-plane elements. A flight was commanded by a captain, while division leaders were first lieutenants. The elements had a leader and wingman.

According to Lehnert, "Mac had it written up on a blackboard. We were Buccaneer Flight. Each flight of eight planes had a color for their call sign. Red, Gold and Green for Flights One, Two and Three. We were to take off in two-plane elements, form up in divisions of four planes each and then into flights. From that point on we usually flew in right echelon formation."

The following list shows the flight formation of VMF-422 from September to December 1943, as Lehnert remembers it. Ken Gunderson, John Hansen, and Mark Syrkin state agreement with this formation structure.

Two officers, First Lieutenant Stafford Drake and Second Lieutenant Edmond Farrell were later killed in a mid-air collision at Midway on 20 November. They were replaced by pilots from the rear echelon, First Lieutenants Jules Flood and Robert Scott.

VMF-422 Formation Call Sign: "Buccaneer Flight"
(WM denotes wingman)
Red Flight
1st Division
Major John MacLaughlin Call Sign: Buccaneer Lead
1st. Lt. Earl Thompson WM Call Sign: Red Two

1st. Lt. Chris Lauesen Call Sign: Red Three
1st. Lt. Ken Gunderson WM Call Sign: Red Four
2nd Division
Capt. Charley Hughes Call Sign: Red Five
1st. Lt. Sterling Price WM Call Sign: Red Six
1st. Lt. Stafford Drake Call Sign: Red Seven (Jules Flood
   after 20 November)
2nd Lt. Edmond Farrell WM Call Sign: Red Eight (Robert
   Scott after 20 November)

Gold Flight
3rd Division
Capt. John Rogers Call Sign: Gold Leader
1st. Lt. Walter Wilson WM Call Sign: Gold Two
1st. Lt. John Hansen Call Sign: Gold Three
1st. Lt. Don Walker WM Call Sign: Gold Four
4th Division
1st. Lt. Mark Syrkin Call Sign: Gold Five
1st. Lt. John Lincoln WM Call Sign: Gold Six
1st. Lt. Robert Whalen Call Sign: Gold Seven
1st. Lt. Royce Watson WM Call Sign: Gold Eight

Green Flight
5th Division
Capt. Cloyd Jeans Call Sign: Green Leader
1st. Lt. Bill Aycrigg WM Call Sign: Green Two
1st. Lt. Robert K. Wilson Call Sign: Green Three
1st.Lt. Robert Moran WM Call Sign: Green Four
6th Division
1st. Lt. Robert Lehnert Call Sign: Green Five
1st. Lt. Ted Thurnau WM Call Sign: Green Six
1st. Lt. Bill Reardon Call Sign: Green Seven
1st. Lt. Caleb Smick WM Call Sign: Green Eight

"We studied the formation so we would know where everyone was by their position and call sign," Lehnert continued. "I was the Second Division leader behind the First Division under Captain Jeans. My call sign was Green Five, with Ted Thurnau as my wingman."

They normally flew in what was known as "echelon" formation, a term derived from a French word meaning ladder rungs. Echelons

A flight of F4U Corsairs in echelon formation. (Official U.S Navy photo.)

were used in infantry and cavalry as far back as the Greco-Persian Wars of 400 BCE.

If one imagines a flock of geese flying in a "V" formation, an echelon would be one of the diagonal lines to either the left or right. Navy and marine squadrons often flew in right echelon, each plane following to the right of and behind the plane ahead.

On 16 August, Major MacLaughlin informed his pilots that they would be receiving their new Corsairs. "An R4D transport will be waiting on the tarmac. We take off at 0700. Take only your flight gear and log. We'll be flying back here with our new planes."

This news was greeted with enthusiasm by the pilots. "We were going to get the new Corsair," Lehnert said. "We had known it for a few days but it was still a wonderful surprise."

NAS San Diego (now NAS North Island) was the birthplace of navy aviation when Glenn Curtiss started his flying school on the Coronado shore of the bay in 1911. Four years later, the Navy Department purchased a huge parcel of land from sugar tycoon J. D. Spreckles. At that time, it was nearly all open fields and scrub brush, a place for the wealthy to ride horses and hunt. A shallow inlet known as the Spanish Bight separated North Coronado from South Coronado and this became the dividing line between the military and civilians on the island. To the south, the distinctive conical red roof of the Hotel del Coronado jutted into the skyline.

Naval Air Station San Diego was commissioned in 1917, just as the United States was entering the Great War. In the early years, the US Navy shared the area with the US Army Signal Corps, which was the parent branch that ran the air service. Later, the Army Air Corps established Rockwell Field. In 1934, the army left and the navy expanded the air field for its exclusive use. To the south was the original base of the US Pacific Fleet prior to its being moved to Pearl Harbor in 1940. Coronado was also home to Naval Station Coronado.

Some notable aviation firsts took place on or over North Island, including the first mid-air refueling. In 1914, a woman named Tiny Broadwick was the first person to successfully use a parachute in southern California when she jumped from a plane piloted by aviation pioneer Glenn L. Martin. Ironically, Martin had instructed some of the men who would one day become America's most dangerous foes during the Second World War. In 1911, he trained six Japanese officers, including Lieutenant Sadayoshi Yamada, who would command the Imperial Japanese Navy Air Arm.

Most notably, when Charles Lindbergh lifted his "Spirit of St. Louis" into the air to begin the first leg of the long journey that would culminate in the historic New York to Paris flight, it was from Rockwell Field on Coronado. Dozens of motion pictures had been filmed on the site, including *Devil Dogs of the Air* (1935), starring Jimmy Cagney and Pat O'Brien, and *Dive Bomber* (1941), starring Errol Flynn and Fred MacMurray. In several of these films, audiences watched navy and marine squadron operations using planes that later went into combat.

During the war, NAS North Island and Naval Station Coronado were the primary staging areas for all major navy, marine, and SeaBee forces headed to the Pacific.

When the lead echelon of Marine Fighter Squadron 422 stepped off the transport, the hot August sun reflected off the white concrete, but a cool breeze from the Pacific beyond Point Loma kept it from becoming oppressive. Situated as it was in the crook of San Diego Bay, the air station afforded a magnificent view of the surrounding city.

Across the bay to the east was downtown San Diego. The stucco bulk of the Santa Fe train depot guarded the long boulevard of Broadway, lined with hotels, office buildings, and bars. The city was bustling with people and traffic, while dozens of fishing boats hung with nets lined the wharves. Just to the north past the runway of the San Diego Airport were the neat pale-yellow buildings and barracks of the Marine Corps Recruit Depot. Hundreds of marine recruits were training on the obstacle course and parade ground. To the west, the rocky arm of Point Loma cradled the harbor entrance in a protective embrace. At the tip was a squat lighthouse that looked like something from a Winslow Homer painting. Patrol boats skittered across the narrow harbor mouth like gray water bugs under the watchful guns of the coastal defense batteries.

The marines boarded a bus to the administration building. Conversation was almost impossible as the air resounded with roaring radial engines.

"Everywhere we looked were dozens of planes of every type," Hansen said. "Dauntless dive bombers, TBM torpedo planes, trainers, fighters, transports, you name it. In those days NAS San Diego never slept. Carriers were coming and going and their air groups were there one day and gone the next."

Curly Lehnert had the distinction of being the only one among VMF-422's pilots who had flown the Corsair during advanced flight training. "When I was at Jacksonville in March, our instructor told us he was going to get the six of us in our flight a check ride in a Corsair. Of course, that was great for us. We all went on to fly them later on. It was one of the first F4Us, with the old 'birdcage' canopy and the bouncing landing gear. The heavy bracing on the canopy made me feel as if I were in a jail cell."

The morning was spent watching a training film on the F4U Corsair. After that they were given copies of the pilots' manual and emergency procedures.

VMF-422 was issued twenty-four brand-new Vought F4U-1D Corsair fighters. The California sun glinted off the smooth navy-blue skin, adorned only by the star and bar national insignia and a white block number.

"I found my plane in a long line near the bay side of the station," recalled Hansen. "They were lined up in numerical order. I don't remember what my number was, but I was next to the plane that Charley Hughes climbed into."

To the marines, the massive two thousand horsepower Pratt & Whitney R-2800 radial engine made the old 1830 on the Wildcat look like a toy. It was a brute-force fighter, made to fly fast, hit hard, and destroy anything the enemy threw at it. Six machine guns poked their black muzzles from the deep sweep of the forty-one-foot inverted gull wings.

A restored F4U-5 Corsair in flight. (Ernie Viskupic, Wingman Photography.)

"I was in love," said Syrkin. "That Corsair was just beautiful."

Few military aircraft of the Second World War have been as revered and legendary as the Corsair. For the last seventy years, warbird buffs have had their favorites, among them the superb North American P-51 Mustang, the trusty Douglas SBD Dauntless dive bomber, or the venerable Boeing B-17 Flying Fortress. Many would give grudging respect to the Grumman Hellcat or mighty Republic P-47 Thunderbolt, but no one will deny that the F4U has earned a place in the pantheon of great warplanes.

The Corsair was undoubtedly an unusual design. There was nothing plebian or even typical in its appearance. The distinctive inverted gull wing looked like a broad letter "W." The long nose in front of the canopy was perfectly circular and angled sharply upward on its landing gear struts, making it look as if it were ready to leap into the sky like a hound on a scent. The rudder and horizontal stabilizers appeared as if they had been added almost as an afterthought.

It was the perfect example of form following function, a synergy of utilitarian engineering. Its job defined the Corsair's unique design. It proved to be the most successful and longest-serving interceptor and fighter-bomber ever developed in the United States, in service with foreign air forces until 1979. More than 12,500 Corsairs in sixteen variants were built in the longest running production of a piston-engine fighter in history, making it the most successful warplane in the world. It was faster and more agile than virtually anything else in the skies over the Pacific. According to official sources, the Corsair had the highest ratio of air-to-air victories of any Allied fighter, eleven to one.

As with many success stories, the Corsair had its share of problems. In fact, when it first entered service in late 1942, the United States Navy didn't even want it.

In 1938, the Navy Department put out a request for single- and twin-engine fighter designs. The RFP dictated high airspeed and low stalling speed, rugged construction, and long range with at least four machine guns. In June, Chance Vought Corporation of Stratford, Connecticut was awarded the contract to build a prototype, the XF4U-1. Vought had a long history of successful planes for the army and navy, including the VE-7 trainer, which in 1923 made the first flight from the newly commissioned USS Langley (CV-1).

Vought's design was radical and underwent several changes and revisions, resulting in a very long development cycle. By the time it was ready for testing in May 1940, the new plane, now named Corsair, possessed the largest wing and most powerful engine of any previous aircraft used by the US Navy. The big Pratt & Whitney R-2800-8 twin-row 18-cylinder radial engine was rated at over two thousand horsepower to drive a thirteen-foot Hamilton-Standard 3-blade Hydromatic propeller.

One of the most common stories about the Corsair concerns its unique inverted gull wings. It has been generally affirmed that when Vought chose to use rearward-retracting landing gear, the limited wing chord (the distance from leading to trailing edge) did not allow for long struts, but a large propeller was needed to get maximum performance from the engine. The inverted gull wing raised the fuselage high enough to provide clearance for the propeller, but there is another, more prosaic reason. The extreme anhedral wing roots intersect the fuselage at exactly ninety degrees. This maximized the airflow into the oil coolers and supercharger intakes.

The Corsair's skin is remarkably smooth and clean, having spot welding instead of rivets. As designed, the Corsair could fly well below one hundred knots without stalling, and was rugged enough to sustain the impact of carrier landings. The gull wing was very difficult to build, particularly with the added complexity of including a robust folding mechanism.

After early test and evaluation flights, the XF4U-1 became the first single-engine fighter to exceed four hundred miles per hour. In full-power dives, the Corsair flew more than 540 miles per hour, but this caused damage to the control surfaces.

There were further problems in spin recovery that required more revisions, so it wasn't until April 1941 that the US Navy ordered 584 F4U-1s. The first production Corsair flew on 24 June 1942, four years after the original contract with Vought had been signed.

But, as with all radical designs, there were some serious teething problems. The F4U-1 was tested for carrier operations on the new *Essex*-Class carrier USS *Bunker Hill,* then on her sea trials. The squadron chosen to fly the new fighter was VF-17, commanded by Captain Tom Blackburn. VF-17 would soon gain fame as the "Jolly Rogers."

The Corsairs tended to bounce alarmingly upon landing, often out of control and missing the arrestor cables. Engines broke off and flaps deployed without warning. Other problems involved hydraulic fluid from the cowl flap actuators spraying onto the windshield, and worst of all, the starboard wing sometimes stalled and dropped without warning during a slow approach to a carrier deck.

To add to Vought's woes, the navy wanted some major changes. The first planes had only four Browning ANM2 .50 caliber machine guns in the outer wing panels, but the navy decided that six guns would be more effective, so Vought had to reduce the wing fuel tanks to accommodate two more guns. A 237-gallon self-sealing tank was installed in the fuselage. This in turn forced the removal of twin .30 caliber cowling machine guns and the cockpit to be moved back more than thirty inches, which consequently caused other major and minor changes.

In September 1942, the United States Navy, after evaluating the F4U-1 on the USS *Sangamon* (CVE-26), chose to pass the Corsair to the Marine Corps. The navy test pilots had called it "The Widowmaker," or the "Ensign Eliminator."

Fortunately, the Grumman F6F Hellcat was there to fill the gap. The F6F proved to be an excellent carrier-based fighter, even if it was not as fast or nimble as the Corsair.

The Marine Corps welcomed the Corsair as a replacement for the well-worn Wildcats. Since the Corps operated chiefly from land bases, the Corsair's teething problems were no concern. The Corsair and the marines were quite literally made for each other. With its incredible speed, rugged design, powerful armament and large bomb capacity, as well as a range of nearly nine hundred miles, the F4U was exactly the right plane for the marines in the Pacific.

The Corsair's baptism of fire was on St. Valentine's Day 1943 when Major William Gise of VMF-124 led his new planes from

Henderson Field on Guadalcanal to escort Consolidated B-24 Liberators to bomb a Japanese base at Kahili. USAAF P-40s and P-38s also accompanied the bombers. The raid was not a success in regard to air-to-air victories, but soon the marines learned how to maximize the advantages of their new mounts. In May, as VMF-422 was being organized in Santa Barbara, Second Lieutenant Ken Walsh of VMF-124 became the first Corsair ace. By the end of the war he would score twenty-one victories.

The first marine fighter squadron to be organized and equipped with Corsairs in the US was Major Loren D. "Doc" Everton's VMF-113 at MCAS El Toro in January 1943. Known later as the "Whistling Devils," VMF-113 played a background but significant role in the story of VMF-422.

After Vought finally cured the F4U's ills, the US Navy accepted the new fighter, which then showed its superiority as a fighter-bomber and kamikaze interceptor. Armed with five-inch rockets, conventional, incendiary and napalm bombs, the Corsairs were highly effective against Japanese positions at Okinawa in the spring of 1945. The US Navy also intended a unique role for the Corsair by forming VFB (Fighter-Bomber) 19a special unit of Air Group 19. These Corsairs were to carry the new and radical "Tiny Tim" solid-fuel rocket, a huge beast more than ten feet long, to be slung under the fuselage. They were intended to be used as "cave busters" in the impending invasion of the Japanese home islands.

Captain Wallace S. "Griff" Griffin, who had volunteered to join VFB-19 in early 1945 after being a Helldiver pilot, was trained to fly the Corsair armed with the big rocket. He talked about the process of launching the huge weapon. "You'd line up on a target at about two hundred knots. A mile out, pull the bomb release. The rocket just fell away. The plane jumped about ten feet from the release of over a thousand pounds. A long lanyard let the rocket clear the propeller, then it pulled loose and the rocket motor ignited."

Griff admitted the launch of the big rocket was awesome. "Just a loud roar over the engine, and all of a sudden was this huge ball of fire and away it went! Scared the hell out of me. I never knew if I hit anything in training. But I knew that if we ever had to really use those things in an attack, we'd never come back."

Until the atom bomb sealed the fate of Japan, Griff and his fellow pilots were dubbed "The American Kamikaze Squadron."

John Hansen described his introduction to the Corsair. "The ground crewman told me he was just about to do a preflight check, so I went along to learn the ropes. You always got the best information from the grunts, not the officers."

After placing his parachute on the deep curve in the wing, Hansen followed the man around as he pointed out various important details of the preflight check. The oleo struts of the landing gear, flaps, control surfaces, and navigation lights were checked off one by one.

At the engine, the mechanic took a grip on the lowest blade of the big propeller and pushed it through a third of a revolution. Then he grabbed the next blade that had come down and did the same thing until the propeller had been through four full revolutions.

"That Pratt & Whitney R-2800 had a lot of compression," Hansen remembered. "It took a lot of work to get the vapor lock out of the cylinders and get the oil moving."

Standing at the starboard wing root, he slung the parachute on, put his right foot on the step built into the inboard wing flap, then heaved himself up and stuck his left foot into a recessed step in the fuselage. He climbed over the sill into the cockpit and then sat down against his parachute pack. The life raft under the parachute doubled as a seat cushion. After pulling the safety harness over his shoulders, he adjusted them to fit.

The new plane's cockpit was set high on the fuselage, well aft of the wing. This gave the pilot a view straight down on either side. It was roomier than any of the trainers they had been flying. Even the tall pilots like Syrkin, Watson, and Gunderson had plenty of leg room.

With feet on the rudder pedals, the knees were about six inches below the instrument panel. The Corsairs were brand-new, like newly minted coins. All the instruments and gauges worked and even the non-skid paint on the rudder pedals was clean and unscuffed.

The ground crewman leaned in and pointed out some of the Corsair's controls and systems.

The big radial engine was a star performer at over thirty-five thousand feet, but few new pilots had ever flown that high for more than a few minutes. The Wildcat's engine petered out at thirty thousand feet.

"It wasn't that different from the other planes I'd flown," said Hansen, "but it was the first one I ever flew that had a two-stage supercharger."

The supercharger was essentially a big vacuum cleaner that inhaled the thin air at high altitudes and forced it into the cylinders to improve combustion. This was one of the most important technological advances the United States had developed before the war, another being high-octane fuel. Together these inventions allowed US aircraft to perform well at extreme altitudes.

"The mechanic pointed out the handle to raise and lower the wings. It was right behind my left elbow. It was a bit hard to reach, but at least it couldn't be bumped accidentally."

That was a hazard on the early Curtiss SB2C Helldivers, which had a T-shaped handle under the edge of the instrument panel. Captain Griffin told the author that he had landed from a routine training flight in Hawaii and after stopping, bumped the handle with his knee. It turned and the wings folded. "It wasn't locked!" He said with a grim smile. "If I'd hit that thing during flight, the wings would fold up and that would have been it."

The author was given a detailed tour of a Corsair cockpit by Rob Patterson, a pilot with the Planes of Fame Air Museum in Chino, California. Patterson, a very experienced pilot pointed out and explained the myriad controls, dials, and switches. "The lower half of the rudder pedals manipulated the rudder," he said, pointing to the rudder bar. "The upper half serves as the brake pedals."

Then he pointed at the instrument panel. "Here you will find the engine and flight gauges. Altimeter, airspeed indicator, magnetic compass, chronometer, artificial horizon, engine temperature, oil pressure readouts, fuel, and manifold pressure gauges."

On a console on the left wall were the throttle, fuel mixture, propeller pitch, and supercharger controls. Against the fuselage on that side were wheels that adjusted the elevator, rudder, and aileron tabs. To the right was another console with the ignition, radio, generator, and electrical systems. "The Corsair cockpit is very well designed," said Patterson. "I'm still impressed with how easy it is to reach the controls."

It is worth noting the Corsair's radio "transmit" key was a button on the end of the throttle handle, so the pilot could press it with his left thumb and not let go of the lever. There were several contemporary air war movies, including *God is My Co-pilot* (1944), starring Dennis Morgan as Colonel Robert L. Scott, which shows Japanese fighter pilots actively engaged in dogfights while using a hand-held microphone to taunt the Americans. Presumably the enemy pilot had his right hand on the control stick, but no hand on the throttle.

In combat, a pilot needed to have his hands on the control stick and throttle at all times. To let go of either in order to make a radio call could lead to disaster. This was equally true in a storm, when

Lieutenant John Hansen flying his Corsair during the squadron's time at MCAS Santa Barbra. (Photo courtesy Heidi Hansen.)

it would be necessary to make instant adjustments to the throttle and fuel mixture controls.

The Corsair had no floor to speak of. About four feet under the pilot's feet and seat, the inner ribs and longirons of the fuselage were visible. If he were to drop anything, it would be virtually impossible to recover, especially in flight.

Rob Patterson told the author that there was one way to get at something dropped while in flight. "Just fly upside-down until it comes back," he laughed.

When Hansen and the others were ready, they went through the start-up procedure. A checklist was printed on a board that slid out from under the edge of the instrument panel. Cowl flaps, full open. Propeller to low pitch, high rpm. Blower on neutral. Mixture control to idle cutoff.

Hansen recalled a Corsair pilot suggesting that he push and pull the mixture lever a few times to help prime the injectors. "It's a good trick when you have a cold engine."

Then it was time to start the engine. The pilot checked to be sure there was no one near the propeller, and then he placed his thumb on a switch on the distribution panel and pushed. A starter cartridge, really a blank shotgun shell, fired with a bang and suddenly the big three-bladed propeller began to turn. With a shuddering roar, the engine pounded to life as blades of blue flame stabbed out of the exhaust under the cowling. In moments, it settled down into the potent snarl of an angry dragon.

The pilot set the fuel mixture to "auto rich" and set the throttle to 700 rpm. From that point on, the F4U was ready to fly.

All that remained was to release the brakes and roll out to the runway, yet this was not as easy as it sounds. Experienced Corsair pilots often commented on learning how to drive the plane on the ground. As a "tail-dragger," the F4U's long nose was very high and it was impossible to see forward. Pilots learned the art of weaving to the left and right, leaning out of the cockpit to see ahead.

"That took some getting used to," Hansen said wryly. "Once you had it lined up on the runway it was no problem, but getting there required very deft throttle, rudder, and brake input."

Major MacLaughlin called on the squadron frequency to move out in two-plane elements. The pilots each went through the same routine. Wings down and locked. Flaps set at thirty degrees. Arresting hook lever in the "up" position. Fuel tank selector on reserve. Rudder tab at six degrees right to counter the torque from the big propeller.

They watched the temperature readings of the cylinder head until they touched 120 degrees and thirty inches of manifold pressure. Then they released the brakes, slid out of their parking slots, and formed into two-plane sections. Major MacLaughlin was first in line with his wingman, Earl Thompson, beside him. They were followed by Chris Lauesen and Ken Gunderson to form the first division. Shepherded by navy ground crew, the Corsairs moved along the tarmac to the runway threshold. The propellers blew the pale gray exhaust in a whirling cloud behind them.

MacLaughlin requested weather information from the tower. After receiving clearance to take off, he and Thompson advanced their throttles. As a wingman, Thompson did not look at the runway, but at his leader and matched his every move. In a sense, the leader "flew" both planes.

The Corsairs' tails lifted at about 110 knots and they felt the increased airflow on the control surfaces through the stick and rudder pedals.

Suddenly the twin planes were airborne and climbed smoothly into the warm southern California sky. Lauesen and Gunderson followed, with Charley Hughes leading the second division right behind them. In neat pairs, the Corsairs took off from NAS San Diego.

It took less than ten minutes for all twenty-four Corsairs to assemble at ten thousand feet and head out at a bearing of 350 degrees at two hundred knots. Far below to their right was the green and beige coastline of California. In a short time, they passed the huge expanse of Camp Pendleton Marine Base where the tiny antlike figures of thousands of marines swarmed onto the beach from landing craft. One day soon the pilots of VMF-422 would be flying cover for those same marines over some unnamed island far out in the Pacific.

They landed at Santa Barbara two hours later and the ground crew admired the new Corsairs. It was commonly said among marine pilots that landing the high-spirited Corsair was like milking a mouse. It was a delicate job.

The official history of VMF-422 was compiled by Major Elmer Wrenn in January 1945. The author used this document as a foundation to establish a timeline for the squadron from May 1943 to December 1944. While it is largely factual, there are a number of small and a few glaring inconsistencies. These will be noted as events progress.

"The pace of training increased as the impending date of departure loomed closer. The working day was lengthened from 0600, when the first flight was airborne, until 1900 when the last one landed. The training consisted of section and division tactics, camera gunnery, touch and go landings, navigation, gunnery, and night flying."

For ground gunnery and bombing practice, they often flew out to China Lake on the Mojave Desert. In the fall of 1943, the Navy Department was still establishing part of the area for what would be known as the Naval Air Weapons Station (NAWS) in November. There, the navy would conduct research, development, and testing of advanced weapons. Physicists and engineers from the California Institute of Technology, known informally as Cal-Tech, would use the station for the design of rockets and missiles, including the little-known but remarkable "Tiny Tim" solid-fuel rocket intended for use in the invasion of the Japanese home islands. In the jet age, China Lake was the birthplace of the famous AIM-9 Sidewinder heat-seeking air-to-air missile.

In the years prior to the station's official establishment, navy, army, and marine squadrons made good use of China Lake's immense expanse of flat, hard-baked, dry lakebed.

The bombing range was a series of broad concentric rings painted on the hard desert floor.

In his memoir, John Glenn stated that they practiced bombing using small bombs containing white smoke charges that allowed them to see where they hit. They mimicked the behavior of real bombs.

Dean Caswell related his memories of bombing practice. "Trying to hit a target of concentric rings was very much like throwing darts. I learned to approach the target in a steep dive, my weight thrown forward against the seat belt. This helped me keep steady as I used the bombsight. The earth rose incredibly fast toward me. I had to bring the concentric rings into my bombsight, jerking the plane over with stick and rudder, holding it dead on the target for an instant while dropping the bomb. The first run or two did not turn out well and the bomb sailed over the target. I got the hang of it in a couple more tries and on my fourth attempt, I put the bomb in the ring. It was a lot more fun than throwing darts."

For ground gunnery, the targets were sometimes broad lines or colored panels laid out at right angles. The fighters were to dive in from five thousand feet and line up on the parallel panel, then open fire when they crossed the perpendicular one. Contrary to what many air war movies portray, it is not easy to hit a stationary point from a fast-moving plane. There was only enough ammo for about thirty seconds of firing, and even a tiny nudge or bump on the controls could send the stream of bullets far from the target.

"I found the Corsair to be more responsive to elevator, rudder, and aileron controls than the Wildcat," said Hansen. "But it moved so quickly that the first time he lined up, the orange stripe was under the blind spot beneath my wings before I could fire."

With practice, the pilots soon learned to anticipate the moment to pull the trigger and hose a stream of shells into the orange panels.

Syrkin said, "It was a fantastic plane. Even with all six guns firing eight hundred rounds per minute, the Corsair hardly shuddered at all."

It is impossible to determine the exact date that Mark Syrkin had his revenge on the Army P-38s but, as related by Lehnert and some entries in Syrkin's flight log, it was probably on or about 25 August, nine days after returning from San Diego.

In the years since, Syrkin had often told the others that he and his division of Lincoln, Watson, and Whalen were flying back from China Lake after gunnery and bombing practice. They were over the San Gabriel Mountains at twenty-eight-thousand feet. "Then Tex said, 'Gold Five, this is Gold Eight. I see some silver planes off to the southwest, course east, about ten thousand below us.' I saw the two P-38s far below. I told my division that we would circle in from the west and come in with the sun behind us." The four blue planes moved in a wide arc until they were facing east. Syrkin kept the two silver, twin-boomed P-38s in sight just past his port wing root. Then he signaled Lincoln by pointing straight down.

With the throttle wide open, the Corsairs dived at nearly four hundred knots as the leftmost Lightning appeared in the gun sight reticle. The wide silver wings filled the outer circle. "Then I keyed my radio and called on the army frequency. I don't remember exactly what I said, but it was something like 'Semper Fi! The marines are here!'"

The army pilots applied power but the Corsairs had a hundred-knot speed advantage and were able to keep them centered in the sights. "They were totally stunned. One asked me where in hell we had come from and I think I told him New York City. I also told them that there was a new sheriff in town and his name was Corsair."

Syrkin wasn't the only marine to get the upper hand on the army but his story is the most often repeated. Staff Sergeant Jack Brouse, who had been the first former VMF-422 marine to tell the author about the Flintlock Disaster, related how he had been an armorer for the Corsairs. "I loaded the ammo when they went off to China Lake to practice gunnery," Brouse said in his deep southern drawl. "The normal load was 2,550 rounds of ball, tracer, and armor-piercing .50 caliber shells in the ammo trays. The four inboard Brownings each took belts of 400 rounds while the two outboard guns were loaded with belts of 375 rounds. I always told those flyboys to be careful. I liked to tell them those bullets were for making holes in enemy planes, not each other. But when Breeze Syrkin came back that day and told us he'd gotten two Army P-38s, I was sure he'd really shot them down!" Brouse laughed at the memory. "He really wanted an army scalp on his belt."

A small crisis struck the squadron in September. It was not mentioned in the squadron history, but was confirmed by Curly Lehnert and Ken Gunderson.

As mentioned above, the pilots practiced touch-and-go landings. This was a useful skill in the event that a pilot was coming in for a landing while the airfield was suddenly under enemy attack, but even the practice had its hazards. Curly Lehnert was working on his landings. It was a hot, dry day and the sun baked the tarmac as he made several perfect touchdowns, then gunned the engine and took off for another go-around.

On his final approach for landing, he was rolling down the runway at eighty knots when the brakes suddenly locked and slammed the Corsair onto its nose. The propeller clattered as it struck the concrete and the F4U flipped forward onto its back. A crash crew, which was always on alert, raced to the scene to find Curly unconscious and hanging upside-down from his harness.

The crew realized they could not get the insensible pilot out until the plane was righted, so a cable from the crash truck winch was attached to the tail wheel. With a grinding, scraping noise, the Corsair was turned over and the bent and shattered canopy hood was pried open. Lehnert showed no signs of injury but the medical corpsman said he might have a concussion.

Lieutenants Chris Lauesen, Ken Gunderson, Jules Flood, and Tiger Moran jogged beside the ambulance as it took Curly to the station sick bay. The doctor quickly examined the pilot and said he would be okay, but needed rest.

Charley Hughes, the maintenance officer, later examined the plane in the main hangar. He and the ground mechanic agreed the accident had been caused by hot brakes. When Lehnert was making his repeated landings, his brakes grew steadily hotter. Finally, they seized up.

Lehnert, recalling the incident, said, "Hughes knew it wasn't my fault. The day was hot and the brakes were just too hot."

The Corsair could be repaired. After ascertaining that there had been no serious damage to the engine, wings, or fuselage, a new propeller would be fitted and the dents hammered out. "Just like any fender-bender on the road today," he said with a laugh. "But it was a problem that might have come out bad for me."

Curly Lehnert was a good pilot, but to crack up a Corsair during his first month wasn't a minor matter. Hughes met with MacLaughlin and discussed the incident with him, but Lehnert didn't hear the details until days later.

"The Skipper was considering having me transferred. The Marine Air Wing Commander wanted ten of our pilots to be sent to MAG-10 in the South Pacific. I didn't want to go but I had little say in it."

Lehnert had some of the highest ratings from Pensacola and Jacksonville. He had achieved eight perfect carrier landings at NAS Chicago. But if he wrecked another fifty-thousand-dollar plane, it would look bad for MacLaughlin. He and Hughes decided that Captain John Rogers would make the decision.

"Charley was a good guy and he was worried that if Mac or he sent me off to MAG-10, the other fellows would resent it. I had a lot of friends in the squadron."

As things turned out, those friends were Curly's salvation. Mark Syrkin, Chris Lauesen, John Hansen, Bob Moran, John Lincoln, and a few others found out about the impending transfer and went to see Rogers. They knew full well what they were doing was against protocol but they convinced the captain to keep Lehnert.

Lehnert awoke in his bed at the station sick bay a day later. "When I learned of the others going to bat for me I felt both surprised and relieved. That crash could really have blown it for me. But I had to be very careful not to wreck any more Corsairs." He shrugged. "As it turned out, I lost one more."

CHAPTER 5

HAWAII AND MIDWAY

On 24 September 1943, the Commander, Fleet Marine Force, Pacific declared VMF-422 operational. They received orders to report to NAB (Naval Amphibious Base) San Diego to embark for overseas duty.

At this time, states the squadron history, the flight officers had an average of seventy-five hours in the Corsair and all had reached the operational stage of training. In addition, four had already flown as combat pilots. The roster consisted of forty-seven officers and 237 enlisted men.

"By that time nearly all of us had been promoted to First Lieutenants," Lehnert said. "We had gained enough flight time and completed the syllabus for fighter squadron training. VMF-422 left the states with a remarkable record of safety. Except for my little mishap, there was not one serious accident in all of the hours that we put in."

On 27 September, MacLaughlin told the lead echelon pilots to pack their sea bags and have them on the Curtiss R5C transport by 0600 the next day. They were to fly the Corsairs down to San Diego where they would be loaded on board the aircraft carrier USS *Bunker Hill*. The rear echelon was to follow a few days later on either a transport or liner. Their destination was MCAS Ewa Field on Oahu.

Ken Gunderson recalled, "I had dated Verna Hagen seven times before I was ordered out to Santa Barbara. We got married in September. Two weeks after that, the squadron got orders to ship out to the Pacific. My new wife and I went down to San Diego and stayed at the Hotel Del Coronado for a couple days. I didn't see her again for over a year."

A day later, the pilots were on the dock at Naval Station San Diego beside the looming gray bulk of the aircraft carrier USS *Bunker Hill*. One by one, the Corsairs, which had been towed over from the air station were hoisted by crane up to the flight deck. From there, with wings folded, they were lowered by elevator to the hangar deck. This was standard procedure when a marine squadron embarked on a carrier. The regular air group flew out to the carrier after it cleared port.

USS Bunker Hill *in 1943. (Official U.S. Navy Photo.)*

USS *Bunker Hill* (CV-17) was the ninth of the *Essex*-Class fleet aircraft carriers, launched at the Fore River Shipyard in Quincy, Massachusetts on the first anniversary of Pearl Harbor. Even at a ponderous twenty-eight thousand tons and 820 feet in length, she was fast and nimble. The class had been designed and built using the hard-won lessons of the early Pacific War. With improved fire-fighting and damage-control systems, weapons, and fuel storage, she was capable of withstanding damage fatal to the older *Lexington* and *Yorktown*-class carriers. For the first time, radar and radio was used to direct the 5.38 caliber turrets, the seventeen Bofors 40mm quad-mounts and more than sixty 20mm guns arrayed in deadly ranks around the flight deck. Her "Sunday Punch" was a powerful air group of thirty-six Hellcats, thirty-six Helldiver dive bombers, and eighteen Avenger torpedo planes.

Once the marines were on board, an ensign showed them around. The Corsairs were stowed at the after end of the immense steel gray cave of the hangar deck. Long rows of lights dotted the high ceiling overhead while the sun cast acres of light on the hard deck through the huge elevator doors. "Even all of our Corsairs looked tiny in there," Hansen admitted. There was a smell hanging in the air, a clinging odor unique to a warship; warm metal, oil, and rubber.

They were given the use of a squadron ready room, located high on the starboard side of the hangar deck. "We were told we could smoke in our room but only when the smoking lamp was lit. That was when the crew was not handling fuel or bombs. It was rather intimidating."

The ensign explained that during battle stations the marines were to go to their "ready room." When asked if there really was any chance of enemy action between the US coast and Hawaii, he explained that Japanese subs patrolled the area and an American carrier was a prime target.

The ship's wardroom was open to the officers of VMF-422, while the enlisted men had the use of the crew's mess and recreation room.

The pilots were assigned quarters near the bow. Each small compartment was about ten feet square with two bunks, two wardrobes, and a small desk. Syrkin recalled his first introduction to junior officer's quarters on a carrier with a wry grin. "They called them 'quarters,' but they looked more like sixteenths to me."

With San Diego in *Bunker Hill's* wake, her escort of four destroyers took stations a few miles off each quarter. Then the air group began to land. The Buccaneers watched with fascination as first the F6F Hellcats landed, followed by the Curtiss Helldivers and last, the big, cumbersome Grumman TBF Avenger torpedo planes. Each plane seemed to drift almost reluctantly towards the flat gray-brown expanse of the flight deck while the tiny fluorescent yellow form of the LSO waved his orange paddles. Then, with shocking suddenness, the huge plane smashed down and surged to a jarring stop as it caught the arrestor cables.

"I watched a lot of carrier landings during my time in the Corps," said Hansen, "but I never got used to the violence of it. Just a controlled crash is all it was."

Few of the squadron's officers and men had ever been out of the country before, and even fewer on a big warship. They tried, mostly without success, to learn their way through a bewildering maze of hatches, ladders, companionways, and narrow steel doors. The overheads were festooned with pipes stenciled with cryptic notations. *Bunker Hill* had more than two thousand compartments and at least fifty miles of corridors. Eventually they located their ready room, their so-called "battle station." The room, which held chairs, a table, blackboard, and status board was about the size of a middle-class suburban living room. It was right beneath two of the starboard-side 5.38" gun mounts. To one side, a small pantry held the standard navy-issue Silex two-burner coffee maker, an icebox, and a cupboard. A black navy steward was available to serve them. In the days before the end of segregation in the US military, stewards were usually black, Hispanic, or Filipino.

"I asked the steward if he could help us find our way around the ship," said Syrkin. "He thought that was a great joke. It would take weeks to learn how to find our way around and we'd be in Pearl in three days."

That was exactly what happened. The *Bunker Hill* slid up the narrow channel past Hospital Point into the wide calm waters of Pearl Harbor on 3 October. After rounding the north end of Ford Island just after 0900 hours, the carrier headed for its mooring. The warm, humid air was redolent with the stink of fuel oil, burned paint, and rotten seaweed. The acrid tinge of acetylene torches was mixed with diesel and radial engine exhaust.

From their vantage point on the flight deck more than sixty feet above the water, the marines watched, spellbound, as the ship moved past the dry docks and anchorages of the navy yard and repair facilities. There was activity everywhere they looked. Launches carrying officers and work boats loaded with sailors crisscrossed the harbor as a constant air patrol droned overhead. A dozen ships, from destroyers to battleships, crowded the slips and docks. Every ship showed the burns and scars of battle as antlike figures of men swarmed over them. Tiny blue-white stars flickered from the acetylene torches as wounded metal was replaced by healthy steel. The massive red-and-white crane towered over the dry dock, turning like a primeval mother dinosaur as it hauled steel plate or engine turbines to the hungry ships below.

Along the eastern shore of Ford Island rested the remains of America's once-mighty battle fleet. At anchorage F7, the shredded, sunken hulk of USS *Arizona* was a bent and forlorn citadel of death. Beneath the filthy water lapping at the gun turrets, 1,177 men lay entombed. But among the drab dark tones of death and defeat, an American flag fluttered from the ship's mast. *Arizona* may have been destroyed but she was still part of the fleet. The capsized *Oklahoma* was again upright while the sunken *West Virginia* had been raised and sent to the states for major repairs. A carrier and battleship lay at anchor forward of *Arizona*.

"I'll never forget what it felt like to see all that destruction and knowing that a lot of American boys had died that day," said Curly Lehnert.

USS *Bunker Hill* was nudged into the anchorages forward of the other carrier. The air wing had been launched while the ship was still approaching the harbor and landed at the air station. This ensured that in an emergency, the air wing could take off, something that would be impossible when the carrier was docked.

Ford Island had been used by both the army and navy since 1919. The army based bombers and observation planes at what was then known as Luke Field, named for First World War ace Frank Luke. The Secretary of War, Newton Baker, divided the island evenly between the two services.

In the late 1930s, the navy contracted to have a deep channel dredged around the island to allow battleships to moor, and the dredged material was used to expand the island from 350 to 441 acres. In 1939, the Army Air Corps transferred to the new Hickam Army Air Field on the main island and Luke Field became NAS Ford Island.

A launch carried the pilots while the Corsairs were loaded aboard barges. Ground crews fueled the fighters for the short hop to MCAS Ewa Field on the western end of Oahu.

Unknown to all but a few senior officers at CINCPAC Headquarters, *Bunker Hill* would not remain in port for long. She was to join up with Admiral Charles Pownall's Task Group Fifty in the western Pacific as part of Operation Galvanic, the huge Allied campaign on the Gilbert and Nauru Islands. There, after three savage days in November, the marines would add another battle ribbon to their standard, bearing a name few had ever heard but none would ever forget: Tarawa.

The beauty of Oahu entranced the new arrivals as they flew in formation west from Ford Island. Visible to the east past the three runways of Hickam Army Air Field, the hotels and offices of Honolulu cradled the deep curve of Waikiki Beach. Beyond that the gray-green promontory of Diamond Head rested like a protective sentinel. Passing under their wings were hundreds of acres of pineapple and sugar cane fields, coffee plantations, and thick green hills. The slopes and craggy escarpments of the Ko'olau Mountains were the most rugged any of them had ever seen. However, to MacLaughlin, Jeans, Rogers and Hughes, the island was familiar.

Marine Corps Air Station Ewa Field (Ewa, pronounced "Evva" meaning "west" or "westward" in Hawaiian), was seven miles west of Pearl Harbor. The base had been established in 1925 as a station for US Navy dirigibles. When the crash of the USS *Macon* ended the US Navy's rigid airship program in 1935, Ewa was made a Marine Corps Air Station. A short dirigible mooring mast still projected

MCAS Ewa Field in 1943. (Official U.S. Marine Corps photo.)

from the windward end of the field. With four runways, it hosted all the marine fighter and dive bomber squadrons intended for the Pacific. On 7 December, Ewa was the first air base to be bombed, and all forty-nine aircraft stationed there were destroyed on the ground. Some scars of the attack still lingered. A few bomb craters spotted the pristine landscape, and here and there were the shells of burned-out buildings. The concrete was pitted in long rows from Japanese strafing.

The field's usefulness to the Navy Department was short-lived. By the beginning of the Korean War, it was apparent that the fields' runways were inadequate for jets. The field was decommissioned in June 1952 and placed under the jurisdiction of NAS Barber's Point. From that point on, all marine air operations were based at MCAS Kaneohe Bay on the eastern shore of Oahu.

"When we landed," Lehnert said, "Mac took us into our ready room. He told us about the base, the island and what we would be doing there."

MacLaughlin explained that Ewa and Midway were essentially advanced training bases. At Ewa, they were part of MAG-21 of the Second Marine Air Wing.

The briefing continued with the news that they would soon be flying out to Midway where they would join MAG-22.

After wrapping up the administrative matters, MacLaughlin said, "We will continue flying and doing formation and gunnery practice until we leave for Midway in ten days. As of now you're free to go. You can get a bus into Pearl City or Honolulu."

"Mac said that the city was patrolled by Army MPs and Navy Shore Patrol," Hansen commented. "He warned us not to fool with them. They did not have a sense of humor and did not like disturbances."

An hour later, after changing into their tropical uniforms, Syrkin, Moran, Lincoln, Hughes, Jake Wilson, and Lehnert walked to the station entrance to catch a bus into Honolulu. Lehnert said, "We passed the swimming pool where about a dozen men and women were swimming, diving, and sunning themselves. The women were nurses based on Ewa. And there was Gunderson and Chris Lauesen. They were showing off to the nurses on the diving board. Those two were certainly the most athletic men in the squadron and had muscular physiques. Kind of like Johnny Weissmuller in the *Tarzan* movies."

Honolulu looked like Santa Barbara but with more palm trees. They walked along Waikiki Boulevard, admiring the stucco houses and lavish hotels. The streets thronged with civilians and servicemen. But unlike Los Angeles, this was Oahu, a place that had actually come under attack. Every few blocks were Army MPs and Navy Shore Patrols.

"We found a nightclub in Honolulu open to military," said Lehnert. "Some had signs saying 'off limits,' some did not. I don't remember the name but it was decorated in a Polynesian motif with fake palm trees and torches. We got drinks and sat down. The band was playing swing music. A few navy officers were on the dance floor."

What made the evening memorable to the officers was the incident that led to Mark Syrkin's infamous nickname.

"I think that was the night Breeze got his nickname," said Lehnert. "That first time in Honolulu really stands out in my memory."

Like a wolf on the prowl, Syrkin began scanning the patrons for a likely target: a single, pretty girl. He spotted one and sauntered over to buy her a drink. What he told her became legend at squadron reunions.

"A lot of fellows back then used the old line about going off on a dangerous mission and that they probably wouldn't come back. But he did it with style. He was really a good-looking man, almost like a movie star. I suppose he got lucky often enough."

Syrkin spent some time with the girl, while the others drank, smoked, and danced. It may have been Jake Wilson who gave Syrkin his famous nickname.

"Jake or someone said, 'There he goes again, shooting the breeze,' and the name stuck." Further considering the memory, Lehnert recalled that there had been "a character in a movie named Breezy or Breeze McLaughlin. I think someone remembered it."

Swing Shift Maisie (1943) starring Ann Sothern was one of a largely-forgotten series of MGM comedies released from 1939 to 1947 about a woman named Maisie Ravier, a pretty ingénue who gets into romantic entanglements. Her co-star was James Craig. His character was named, in a remarkable coincidence, Breezy McLaughlin.

When Syrkin returned to the table where his buddies waited, they kidded him, asking pointed questions about the girl.

He recalled the moment. "They were calling me Breeze.' At first I ignored it, but that name has stuck with me all these years. Actually, that was the funny part of that night," he added.

What Syrkin did not know was that the girl he was wooing was a reporter for a Honolulu paper. His efforts to entice her into bed only resulted in a story in the very next edition of the paper.

Before the consequences of his amorous venture became apparent, another event caused no end of ribbing for another Buccaneer, First Lieutenant John "Abe" Lincoln.

John Hansen was certain it was the same day they landed at Ewa. "We were told we would be issued new equipment. For our sidearms, we were each given the Colt .45 automatic. I think later on we were given a choice of the .38 caliber Police revolver."

Lieutenant John Lincoln was issued the Colt, but said he wasn't familiar with it.

"That turned out to be true," agreed Hansen with a wry grin.

The pilots retired for the night. Their rooms in the officer's quarters each contained two double bunk beds, a table and chair, and four narrow wardrobes.

Curly Lehnert said, "John Hansen and I were in one room. I think Shou Price and Breeze also were assigned that room with us, but I'm not positive. Hansen was sitting on a lower bunk and I was sitting at the desk."

Suddenly there was the sharp bark of a gunshot. Splinters sprayed out of the wall and scattered onto Hansen as he threw himself on the floor.

"We both hit the deck. I didn't know what had happened, but you know it would have been easy to think the worst. Then I saw a ragged hole in the wall just over Hansen's bunk. I pointed at it and his face went real white."

Lehnert then found another hole over where he'd been sitting. The bullet had gone right through the thin wooden walls.

Their door burst open and there stood Lincoln holding a pistol. "He looked at us with this horrified expression and asked us if we were okay."

Unsurprisingly, Hansen also recalled the incident. "I picked myself up off the floor. I asked 'Abe, what in hell are you doing?'"

Lincoln was visibly shaken. He admitted he had been examining the pistol in the next room when it accidently fired.

"He told us he wasn't familiar with the Colt Automatic."

Lehnert said, "Hansen started calling Abe a dummy for messing around with a loaded weapon. Then I looked at the gun and realized the slide was forward and the hammer was cocked. It was ready to fire again. I told Abe to point it at the ceiling and drop the clip and rack the slide."

The chastened Lincoln did as he was told. When he racked the slide back, a live round was ejected from the chamber.

Hansen picked it up. "I faced Abe and said something about getting John Wilkes Booth's ghost to shoot him if he ever did anything that stupid again."

In the way of all close-knit groups, the story of Lincoln's blunder with the pistol swept through VMF-422 like wildfire.

"The next morning a bunch of us were in the ready room when Lincoln came in," said Lehnert. "We started calling him Annie Oakley and Little Sure Shot."

Then Major MacLaughlin entered the room with Jeans right behind him. He wore a look of suppressed anger on his normally placid face. He said, "Gentlemen, we have a couple of very serious matters to discuss. First of all, at no time will any of you carry a loaded firearm unless you are going on a mission. Your sidearms are to be kept unloaded while you are off duty. No exceptions. Is that clear?"

But Lincoln was not the only member of the Flying Buccaneers to be the center of official censure that morning. The morning paper had a story about a marine pilot who had volunteered for a hazardous and suicidal mission. The pilot was not named, but he was based at MCAS Ewa and flew the Corsair. That could only mean VMF-422.

"Mac read the article in the paper to all of us," said Lehnert with a smile. "He kept looking right at Breeze, who was really quiet. We all knew just what it was about." The pilots, including MacLaughlin, chided Syrkin about the incident for days.

"I was totally stunned," Syrkin said. "I had fed her that old line about going on a dangerous mission and possibly not coming back. I never knew she was a reporter."

The squadron received ten pilots to replace the rear echelon members MacLaughlin had had to send to MAG-10 a few weeks before. The "old sweats" helped the new men to fit in and for several days, they did formation flying and gunnery practice off the coast. The Flying Buccaneers were again at full strength, forty pilots and 220 enlisted men.

"One day we were driven out to a place near Pearl," Lehnert said. "We had been told to bring swimming trunks. I supposed it was something to do with ditching, and I was right."

They found themselves at a large swimming pool, being addressed by a navy instructor. A strange contraption that appeared to be the cockpit of an old F4F hung from a cable that stretched across the length of the pool. The marines were going to be given advanced emergency egress training. Although they had all undergone egress training in Florida, it was proving to be inadequate under combat conditions on the open ocean.

During the Battle of Midway, when pilots of USS *Hornet's* VF-8 were forced to ditch after running out of fuel, they had less than thirty seconds before the plane sank. By the time a pilot recovered his senses from the impact, the water was usually up to his neck.

In the summer and fall of 1943, a Massachusetts Institute of Technology engineer and Naval Reserve Ensign named Wilfred Kaneb was working to design a device to simulate the impact of a water landing. Kaneb had been told to show a pilot what it was like to drown, but he was going beyond that. The army air force used a B-24 cockpit that was simply dropped into the water, but Kaneb went one better. His apparatus would slide down a cable and hit the water at about twenty-five miles per hour—a not-inconsiderable speed—and flip over under water. The pilot was to open the canopy, slip out of his harness, climb out, and swim underwater until he was clear of the sinking plane.

The pool at Pearl Harbor contained a crude precursor to Kaneb's dunker which would first be used at Pensacola and Jacksonville in mid-1944. Soon it would gain the name by which it is still known today, the "Dilbert Dunker." A character named Dilbert—in navy parlance, a slow-witted and bumbling pilot—was featured in a series of inspirational posters and pamphlets to show "How NOT to do it."

Major MacLaughlin, an experienced swimmer and diver was the first to be strapped into the bifurcated cockpit. "Mac was that kind of guy," recalled Hansen. "He set the example for the rest of us."

When released, the cockpit slid along the cable, which inclined into the water at the far end. The pilot had only seconds to release his harness and get out before he was fully submerged. "Mac made it look easy," said Hansen. "But it wasn't, not really. That cockpit only went about ten miles an hour along the cable, but you really had to move fast when you hit the water. I mean, in an instant you were sinking. I did what I'd been told and managed to get out. Just barely."

Gunderson said of the training, "The only problem was that I'd forgotten to pull out my life raft. The guys gave me hell for that."

There was one pilot whose experience with the pool had tragic consequences. "Tiger Moran hated deep water," said Curly Lehnert. "Breeze Syrkin and Moran were at Pensacola together and he told me Tiger hated when they had to learn to use the Mae West life vests and life rafts out in the bay."

"Tiger was a tough kid," Syrkin agreed, "but he hated deep water. He had so much trouble getting out that the divers in the water had to help him."

After climbing out of the pool, Moran steadfastly maintained that he would never ditch in the sea or bail out over water. "He said he didn't even plan to get his feet wet." Then Syrkin paused. "Poor kid."

On 15 October, the lead echelon received orders sending them to Midway Island for patrol duty. The island was 1,200 miles northwest of Hawaii, so they would be ferried there by Navy Curtiss R5C transports, more commonly recognized as the Curtiss C-46. They would be flying Corsairs based at Midway.

This news was greeted with disgust by several of the pilots, especially First Lieutenant Jules Flood.

"Flood was great with engines and machines," explained Lehnert. "I knew he wasn't happy about using some old clunker from MAG-22."

Ken Gunderson and Chris Lauesen on Midway in November of 1943. Note that Lauesen's jacket bears the squadron's Pirate emblem. (Photo courtesy Andrew Syrkin.)

As the transport flew northwest, the pilots tried to catch up on their sleep, but that was a flat impossibility in an R5C.

This was the first long-distance over-water flight for the marines. Unlike their training, when they had rarely flown more than a hundred miles from shore, the sea between Oahu and Midway was totally empty and vast. Even from five thousand feet, the view from the tiny windows was less than forty miles.

Ten hours later, the big transport began its descent to Midway. The marines all looked down at the tiny specks of sand and coral that denoted one of the now-legendary battlefields of the war.

Midway's two islands, Sand and Eastern, totaled little more than 2.4 square miles, surrounded by a wide coral reef.

Once they were standing on the Eastern Island runway, the marines took in the sight. The highest point was less than forty feet in elevation. The trade winds swept in from the sea with a cool salt-tinged wind.

They walked over to the narrow tarmac where some gray-painted jeeps waited to take them to the west dock to board a launch.

Along the way, they were entertained by Midway's famous Gooney Birds. From the early days when Pan-American Clipper passengers stopped at Midway in the 1930s, the thousands of nesting and migrating albatrosses were a delight to behold. The black-browed albatross was a large sea bird with a six-foot wingspan. They were extremely dignified and graceful in flight, but upon landing, did so with all the elegance of a car wreck.

"We laughed our heads off watching those big birds crashing on the sand," said Lehnert. "You couldn't believe how clumsy they were. We heard that during the battle the birds hardly paid any attention to the bombs and guns."

The launch took the new arrivals to the old Pan-American Hotel, known locally as the "Gooney Bird Lodge" or "Gooneyville Lodge."

Marine Air Group 22's commander, Colonel Jim Daly, had established a regular routine for new marine squadrons in Hawaii. Each fighter squadron was rotated to Midway for two months of advanced training in what was technically a "war zone," but offered little chance of combat.

The nearest Japanese air units were on Wake Island eight hundred miles to the west, within range of land-based bombers and long-range flying boats.

The following day, after a night's rest at the Lodge, the marines went to Eastern Island to sign out their planes. "We weren't impressed," said Curly Lehnert.

MAG-22 had between twenty and thirty Corsairs, but they were older F4U-1As, the first variant incorporating the improvements dictated by the early tests in September 1942.

They were, according to Lehnert and Hansen, "well-used."

Syrkin remarked, "The Corsairs that we flew at Midway were part of the base defense pool and, while still serviceable, had a lot of hours on them."

After a briefing by one of MAG-22's officers, a routine of flight operations began. They flew pie-shaped searches all around the islands out to two hundred miles which gave them some good practice at over-water flying. On the first flights, an experienced marine pilot accompanied them to show them the ropes. He cautioned the new arrivals about the Pacific's capricious weather. "It can go from flat calm and clear skies to a heavy rain squall and no sky at all in ten minutes," he'd said. "Keep your eyes peeled in all directions at once."

For the most part, the patrols were almost boring. No Japanese planes came near enough to the island to be a threat, much to Tex Watson's frustration. Along with Syrkin, Gunderson, and a few others, Watson was determined to be the first ace in VMF-422.

Each four-plane division was given a segment to patrol. Each segment was like one slice of a pie with twelve pieces. Each slice was 250 miles from the island and covered a 30-degree arc. One patrol might fly out at 360 degrees for 250 miles, then turn to the right until they turned again to fly back at 30 degrees. In this way, the entire 360-degree circle was covered by air search.

Midway had a newer version of the SCR-270 air-search radar that had been so instrumental in the June 1942 battle. VMF-422's pilots practiced interceptions, guided by the orders of a ground control officer who was able to "see" the sky for two hundred miles in all directions. Occasionally an alert was sounded of an unidentified aircraft. The fighter pilots scrambled to get into the air while the airborne patrols were vectored to the intruder, but they never saw a single enemy plane.

"The Japanese were too smart to try and hit us when we had radar," said Lehnert.

Off duty, the officers and enlisted men passed the time by playing baseball, listening to the radio, fishing, or watching the antics of the Gooney Birds. Gunderson and Chris Lauesen usually did athletic activities together. MacLaughlin showed a few others how to snorkel. Together, they explored the colorful and fascinating underwater world in the tropical lagoon. Some took walks on the beach.

Lehnert said, "We had been warned to be careful. There were still a lot of homemade booby traps, mines, and barbed wire entanglements left over from the battle. John Hansen found a large piece of shrapnel from a Japanese bomb and he put it in his sea bag as a souvenir."

"I kept that thing for ages," Hansen said. "But I really don't remember what I did with it."

The days passed without incident, until disaster struck on 20 November. First Lieutenant Stafford Drake was on a training patrol with Second Lieutenant Edmond Farrell as his wingman.

What happened that day over the lagoon is related in the squadron history. As they approached the runway at Eastern Island, Bill Aycrigg, in the second element, suddenly slid over and beneath Farrell's Corsair. Unable to avoid a collision, Aycrigg watched in horror as his propeller tore into the tail of the other plane. Farrell's tail tore away and he, in turn, collided with Drake to his left. The two fighters plummeted into the lagoon three hundred yards offshore as Aycrigg was just able to land with a dead engine. He was nearly frantic with grief and guilt as two launches sped out to

Lieutenants Edmund Farrell and Stafford Drake, who were killed in a mid-air collision over Midway Lagoon in November 1943. (Photos courtesy Andrew Syrkin.)

find Farrell and Drake. Only an oily slick of fuel remained to mark the spot. First Lieutenant Stafford Drake of Wilmette, Illinois and Second Lieutenant Edmond Farrell of Louisville, Kentucky were the first casualties of VMF-422. Drake's body was never recovered.

John Hansen, who had witnessed the crash said, "Bill Aycrigg told us that his left rudder petal had jammed in the down position, forcing him into Farrell's plane."

When Captain Charley Hughes and a MAG-22 officer examined the Corsair, they found a piece of broken cable had caught in the rudder bar track. It had not been Aycrigg's fault, but he continued to blame himself. It was a terrible loss, and the first tragedy suffered by the squadron.

The empty slots in the formation were filled by Lieutenants Jules Flood and Bob Scott.

The same day Drake and Ferrell were killed, the Pacific War entered a new phase. One of the long-range Allied objectives was the capture of the Marianas, Saipan, Tinian, and Guam to provide forward air bases for air strikes on the Japanese home islands. But before the Marianas could be taken, the Allies had to control the major Japanese strongholds of Kwajalein, Majuro, and Eniwetok in the Marshall Islands, and Truk and Ulithi in the Carolines. The former were bases for land-based bombers and fighters, while the latter two were used as anchorages for the bulk of the Imperial Navy and merchant fleet. Taking the Marshalls and Carolines would provide air bases for the forces attacking the Marianas.

Yet even before that day, the United States had to control the Gilbert Islands several hundred miles to the southeast. A string of islands with Japanese airfields and seaplane bases, the Gilberts lay directly astride the American axis of advance from the Solomons to the Marshalls. They were also between the Marshalls and Pearl Harbor.

The main Gilbert atolls of Tarawa, Makin, Apamama, and Nauru had been under Japanese control since being seized from the British in 1941. Tarawa Atoll, now the Republic of Kiribati, nearly straddled the line of 180 degrees longitude, and had a string of tiny coral islets and three larger islands on the ring of a 250-square mile atoll. The main island of Betio, located on the southwestern rim of the atoll was a wide narrow triangle of mostly flat, palm-studded land two miles wide by a half mile deep. An airfield cut directly through the center of the land mass. The island's long north coast faced the lagoon while the southern and western coasts faced the open ocean. A coral reef divided the deep lagoon from the shallows several hundred yards from the beach. The Japanese built a long pier to allow ships to unload beyond the reef while remaining anchored in the lagoon.

Operation Galvanic, first decided upon by CINCPAC, Admiral Chester W. Nimitz, and Chief of Naval Operations Ernest J. King was the first major move in the central Pacific after the Solomon Islands were in Allied control. This was no surprise to the Japanese, who had seen the writing on the wall when Marine Colonel Evans F. Carlson of "Carlson's Raiders" of Midway fame had attacked nearby Makin Island in August 1942.

Since the fall of the Solomons, the Japanese War Ministry recognized the Gilberts' vulnerability. They began a hasty but earnest build-up of troops, weapons, ammunition, and supplies. With nearly a year to prepare, a complex and well-designed defensive network was constructed by an experienced engineer, Rear Admiral Tomanari Saichiro. His plan was to destroy the American landing forces on the water before they reached the beach. To this end he built an interconnected series of pillboxes, gun emplacements, mortar pits, machine gun nests, and communication tunnels connected directly to the island's central command post. Saichiro recognized the danger from American heavy bombers and battleship guns, so he had built several large hardened bunkers to shield his troops until they were needed to fight off the land assault. In July, Tarawa's defense was put under the command of a veteran of the fighting in China, rear Admiral Keiji Shibazaki.

The commander of the Central Pacific Force (later designated the US Fifth Fleet), Vice Admiral Raymond A. Spruance, along with Admiral Richmond K. Turner of the assault force and Marine General Holland M. "Howling Mad" Smith commanded the largest force ever assembled to that point, consisting of six fleet carriers, eleven light and escort carriers, twelve battleships, twelve cruisers, more than sixty destroyers, and thirty-six transports. They had the job of putting thirty-five thousand troops of the Second Marine Division and the US Army's 27th Infantry on shore. The Second Marines were battle-hardened veterans of the savage and desperate fighting on Guadalcanal. They had spent the last several months in New Zealand recuperating, refitting, and replacing their losses from combat and disease.

At the same time, the Army's 27th Infantry Division was preparing for landings on nearby Makin Atoll in the northeast Gilberts for Operation Kourbash. Capturing the Gilberts would provide air bases for the next phase of the Pacific war.

Nanumea and Funafuti, 463 and 820 miles respectively to the south-southeast in the Ellice Islands had been taken by the Allies in the fall. From those two islands, long-range B-24 Liberators of the Seventh Air Force had begun bombing Tarawa in October. From 13 to 19 November, they dropped more than sixty tons of bombs on Betio, code-named "Helen." To keep Japanese forces from interfering with the landings, they also bombed Makin and Mille islands.

Admiral Shibazaki's troops rode out the daily attacks in their shelters, waiting for the main landing that was sure to come.

The initial phase of Operation Galvanic began in the predawn of 20 November with a gun duel between Shibazaki's four eight-inch guns and the huge sixteen-inch broadsides of the battleships USS *Colorado* (BB-45) and USS *Maryland* (BB-46), the latter fully repaired after being damaged at Pearl Harbor. Three thousand tons of heavy battleship shells slammed into Betio. One lucky salvo destroyed Shibazaki's eight-inch ammunition magazine, which erupted in a titanic fireball that was visible for twenty miles. With it went three guns.

During the bombardment, minesweepers with destroyer escorts entered the lagoon to clear it of mines and obstacles for the landing craft to approach the three assault beaches, designated Red Beach One through Three. The south and western end of Betio was a contingency landing site called Green Beach.

From the outset, the landings were virtual shambles. The chief cause of this was a serious miscalculation of neap tide. Neap tide is when the sun, Earth, and moon form right angles, and the sun's gravity counteracts the moon's pull. Normally neap tide at Tarawa was about five feet deep over the reefs, but on the morning of 20 November, it was unusually low at three feet. This was too low to permit the landing craft to cross the reefs into the shallow water leading to the beach.

The LCVP (Landing Craft, Vehicle/Personnel), known colloquially as the Higgins Boat, was what author and historian Stephen Ambrose considered one of the miracles of World War II. The brainchild of Louisiana boat builder Andrew Higgins, and constructed of plywood, the boat could carry thirty-six fully armed troops right onto a beach. At Higgins's yard in New Orleans, near where the National World War II Museum is today, over twenty thousand LCVPs were built, a greater number than any Allied warplane. Higgins Boats participated in nearly every major assault in Europe and the Pacific.

But at Tarawa, they were unable to carry their human cargoes past the reef. They were trapped five hundred yards from their objective. The assault on Betio was the first time the marines encountered serious Japanese resistance to a landing during the war. The 3,600 defenders were well-entrenched, equipped, and determined to fight to the last man.

Even before the heavy guns had ceased their barrage, the Second Marines were moving in as Japanese defenders swarmed out of their shelters and began firing on the first wave. With the Higgins Boats trapped behind the reef, the only craft that continued on were the LVT (Landing Vehicle, Tracked) known as "Alligators." They were vulnerable to large-caliber shells. Those that managed to gain the beach were badly shot up and were unable to crest the log sea wall just in from the tide line. Some tried to go back out to the reef and bring in more troops but were too badly damaged to stay afloat.

The appellation of "Red Beach" was gruesomely appropriate. Within hours, the white sands were crimson with the blood of defenders and attackers.

Despite the fierce opposition, Betio was declared secure at 1330 on 23 November.

Admiral Shibazaki had boasted that it would take a million men one hundred years to conquer Tarawa. Thanks to the American army, navy, and marines, the island was taken in three days by less than thirteen thousand men, but it was a costly victory. Of the twelve thousand marines and sailors who assaulted Betio, 3,100 were casualties. The number of American casualties at Tarawa was comparable to those lost at Guadalcanal. However, that campaign had lasted more than six months; the bulk of marines dead and wounded at Tarawa was incurred in three days. It had been called a "successful disaster" and many lessons had been learned the hard way. General Holland M. Smith, commander of the marine forces, likened the attack to Pickett's ill-fated charge at Gettysburg. More than 3,600 enemy troops had been killed. Only one officer and sixteen enlisted men surrendered.

The attack on Makin Island was by contrast almost a cakewalk, resulting in sixty-six American soldiers being killed. The US Navy's greatest loss occurred with the sinking of the escort carrier USS *Liscome Bay* (CVE-56) by the Japanese submarine I-*175* on 23 November. The sinking cost the lives of 644 officers and men, including the carrier division commander, Admiral Henry Mullinix, and one of the heroes of Pearl Harbor, Navy Cross recipient Doris Miller. The airfield on Tarawa's Buota Island was subsequently named Mullinix Field.

Three flag-rank officers had significant if little-remembered roles in Operation Galvanic. Task Force (TF) 50's carriers were under the command of Rear Admiral Charles Pownall, while the land-based air defenses were led by Rear Admiral John Hoover, who controlled six squadrons of navy patrol planes, PBY Catalinas, PV Venturas, and PB4Y Privateers.

Under Hoover, Marine Brigadier General Lewie Merritt directed Task Group 57.4 Defense and Utility Group in the Ellice Islands to the south of Tarawa, which included the marine fighters, dive bombers, and observation planes.

The overall command of Tarawa Atoll was given to Captain Jackson R. Tate, USN. These four men would play a critical role in the Flintlock Disaster two months later.

The Flying Buccaneers' last night on Midway was 15 December. The elated pilots celebrated by throwing each other into the lagoon from the seaplane pier. It was just a way of sloughing off the excess energy they had accumulated during the last two frustrating months. Six Japanese raids, hundreds of hours on patrol and two dead friends had cemented the men of VMF-422 into a tight cohesive unit. They were ready to go to war. Colonel Daly and the rest of MAG-22 were also ordered back to Ewa on 15 December for overseas assignment. VMF-114 arrived to take their turn in patrolling Midway.

The official VMF-422 history states that the first five flights (thirty-six of forty pilots) flew back to Ewa by transport plane, while the rest traveled by ship, the USS *Gemini* (AP-75) which also carried the remaining ground crews.

"Most of us flew back to Ewa in another R5C," said Hansen. "When we landed we saw our Corsairs. But these were not the ones we'd left behind. They were brand new. I guess Santa Roosevelt gave us a Christmas present."

The Marine Air Depot Hawaiian Area delivered twenty-four of the newest F4U-1D Corsairs to VMF-422. Syrkin was very pleased with his new mount. Chance-Vought F4U-1D Bureau No. 55883 bore a large white block "28" on the fuselage. He had a name painted on the cowling. "I called her *Francey II*, after my mom. Mom had always taken good care of me, so I hoped my new plane would live up to the name."

· CHAPTER 6 ·

THE USS *KALININ BAY*

The deployment orders arrived just a few days after New Year. The lead echelon of twenty-four pilots, plus three in reserve, with three enlisted men and the twenty-four Corsairs were to board the escort carrier USS *Kalinin Bay* for transport to the newly-established base on Tarawa, where they would be part of the Fourth Marine Base Defense Air Wing (MBDAW). The remaining thirteen pilots and eighty enlisted men would board the liner USS *President Monroe* (AP-104) leaving Oahu on 20 January. The ground echelon, spare parts, and tools were to depart Hawaii on 27 January on board two other ships, the *MS Island Mail* and the *SS Cape Isabel*. The intention was that all the air and ground elements would be on hand for operations when the Marshalls had been taken. The rest of Colonel Daly's MAG-22 would also be going to the Gilberts in early February.

From 19 December to 17 January, VMF-422 flew their new Corsairs to gunnery and bombing ranges at NAS Kanului on Maui. In concert with Curtiss SB2C Helldiver dive bombers and Grumman TBF Avenger Torpedo planes, they participated in mock coordinated attacks on simulated bases, airfields, and ships. They had been issued new flight equipment and packed their personal gear for the voyage to the war.

"That was a heady moment," recalled Hansen. "After all those months, we were about to go to war. I don't mind admitting I was very anxious. I guess we all were. But no one showed it."

They flew to NAS Ford Island, where the Corsairs were again barged out to the ship that would carry them west. But unlike the imposing majesty of the *Bunker Hill*, the USS *Kalinin Bay* was almost miniscule.

Lehnert said, "It wasn't much bigger than those paddle-wheelers I landed on at NAS Chicago."

USS *Kalinin Bay* (CVE-68), like *Liscome Bay*, was one of the fifty *Casablanca*-class escort or "Jeep" carriers built by the Henry Kaiser shipyards in Vancouver, Washington. Launched on 15 October—coincidentally the same day VMF-422 shipped out to Hawaii—she was fitted out and commissioned six weeks later, a remarkably

USS Kalinin Bay *heading into San Diego with battle damage in late November 1944. (Official U.S. Navy photo.)*

short time. Her commander was C. R. Brown, USN-R. The small carriers had earned a dubious reputation for being virtually defenseless and christened "Kaiser Coffins." The designation CVE, which actually stood for "Carrier, Heavier than air, Escort," was derided as meaning "Combustible, Vulnerable and Expendable."

Despite this, the Escort Carriers were very effective in providing air cover for the unarmed transports, tankers, and cargo ships that daily crossed the Atlantic and Pacific. They obviated the need to divert the big, fast fleet carriers from major fleet operations.

At 510 feet long, the small carrier was only able to transport twenty-seven planes. VMF-422's Corsairs were tied down on the aft hangar deck, wings folded. "They were really packed in there," said Lehnert. "You couldn't get a dime in between them. Those navy boys really knew their stuff."

Kalinin Bay was small but her interior spaces were very efficiently designed to make maximum use of the limited space. The Flying Buccaneers were berthed in the junior officer's quarters, cramped cubicles right next to the forward engine room. The heat often became intolerable. Many chose to take their mattresses up to the flight deck and sleep under the wing of a plane. With the steady breeze from the bow, it was much more pleasant to sleep out in the open. The pilots took every advantage of the leisure time before they arrived in the war zone. They spent their time writing letters home, reading, sunning on the flight deck, and playing volleyball on the forward elevator.

In the wardroom, talk often turned to what they might expect when they reached their destination. Only MacLaughlin had been briefed on what they would do when they arrived at Tarawa, but beyond that, he knew almost nothing. He informed his men that their Corsairs would be taken up to the flight deck to be catapulted off the ship.

Mark "Breeze" Syrkin had the dubious honor of being the first to be catapulted off the ship. The catapult officer had never launched a real airplane before. (Photo courtesy Andrew Syrkin.)

This was no small matter to many of the marines, particularly Syrkin. He had never catapulted off a carrier deck. "I admit it was kind of scary," he said. "I didn't say anything to the other fellows. I went up to the flight deck to look at the catapult. I found a young ensign and machinist's mate looking at it."

Syrkin asked several questions about the procedure, but was horrified to see the young officer referring to a printed book for the answers. "He was reading from the damned catapult manual! I asked him how many planes he'd launched, and he said that he had never actually done it with a real airplane."

The officer explained that while the *Kalinin Bay* was undergoing sea trials, he had tested the catapult by "launching" concrete blocks. "He said that the only difference was that the blocks were supposed to go into the water," Syrkin recalled with a twisted smile. "That didn't exactly make me feel any more confident. But he seemed to know what he was doing."

As Syrkin went down the ladder to the hangar deck he saw that his plane, number twenty-eight, was the farthest forward. "Mine would be the first plane to be taken up to the flight deck. I'd be the first one launched."

Sterling Price also remembered the neophyte catapult officer. "I asked him what kind of experience he had and he said, 'I've shot dead weights.' I didn't think much of that name."

Five days after leaving Hawaii, the USS *Kalinin Bay* and her escorts entered the forward area off Tarawa Atoll in the Gilbert Islands. Several of the marine pilots were on the flight deck, watching as the tiny green lumps of coral atolls and lush palm islets passed in the distance. The air was heavy and humid, tinged with the scent of salt water and tropical foliage.

"We were surprised that the islands we passed were just these little lumps of sand and brush poking out of the water," said Hansen. "There were dozens of them but only a few were even as big as Midway."

"I'm not sure what we thought we'd see," Syrkin said. "I sort of expected it to be like in the movies, with white sand beaches and native girls. But all we saw was palm trees."

At 0530 hours, the ship's P.A. system called "all marine pilots, man your planes." After donning flight gear and shouldering their bags, the pilots climbed the ladders and emerged on the flat expanse of the flight deck. There they found *Kalinin Bay's* plane handlers bringing the Corsairs up from below and fueling them. As Syrkin feared, his plane was at the head of the pack. He climbed onto *Francey II's* starboard wing and put his parachute on the seat. After settling in, he pulled on his harness.

A plane captain made the motion for him to start the engine and lower the wings. Syrkin had been told to put the flaps to thirty degrees and set the elevator tabs at two degrees up.

Four plane handlers pushed the Corsair to the single catapult. The end of the narrow flight deck loomed ever closer. Syrkin thought it looked like the edge of the world. A destroyer was keeping pace off the carrier's port quarter to pick up any pilots that hit the water. But there was always the danger that the ship would run him over first.

The fighter plane was nudged into position over the catapult shuttle, a blunt hook poking out of the rail. A Y-shaped bridle was fitted to the lugs by each of the F4U's landing gear struts while an alligator clamp was attached to the tail wheel. The latter would hold the plane in place as the pilot ran the engine at full throttle.

Syrkin viewed the procedure with interest. "I knew the other fellows were watching me. It was like being the only guy in the ring at Madison Square Garden."

It was 0730 hours. The young catapult officer was holding a small orange flag and whipping it in circles over his head. That was the signal for full throttle. *Francey's* R-2800 roared like a caged tiger.

"Marine Special," flown by Chris Lauesen is launched from the USS Kalinin Bay on the morning of 24 January. (Official U.S. Navy photo.)

Syrkin put his head against the headrest and snapped the "ready to launch" salute to the officer, who whipped the orange flag down. With a banshee scream, the steam catapult yanked the Corsair down the rail to the end of the deck at ninety knots. "That was some ride," Syrkin said. "It felt like I'd been kicked in the butt by King Kong."

But suddenly, the Corsair dropped like a stone towards the water racing by below. Syrkin fought the controls and managed to climb. In a minute, the tiny shape of the *Kalinin Bay* was far behind him. He raised the gear and flaps and began to orbit off the ship's port side at two thousand feet while the others were launched and joined him. Bill Aycrigg was next, followed by Jules Flood and Charley Hughes. Aycrigg's plane, whose elevator tab had been set too low, pitched upward alarmingly until he was able to regain control. Flood's launch was nearly perfect, as was Hughes's.

The second flight was composed of Chris Lauesen, Tex Watson, Shou Price, and Bob Scott.

The ship's photographer caught Lauesen's plane with the name "Marine Special" painted on the cowling.

There is a discrepancy on a US Navy Missing Aircrew report from 1944. Lauesen's Corsair is listed as an F4U-1A, Bureau No. 18015.

But on the *Kalinin Bay's* official launch roster for Monday, 24 January, he is in Plane 16, No. 17933. No. 18015 was flown by John Lincoln. It is entirely possible that Lincoln and Lauesen switched planes after landing at Tarawa, but it is more likely an error in the aircrew report.

MacLaughlin led the third flight with Jake Wilson, Curly Lehnert, and Ken Gunderson. The fourth flight of four off the ship was Chick Whalen, Cal Smick, Bill Reardon, and Abe Lincoln. They were followed by John Hansen, Bob Wilson, John Rogers, and Earl Thompson. The last group to launch was led by Tiger Moran, Rex Jeans, Ted Thurnau, and Don Walker. When all twenty-four planes were assembled, a blinker light on *Kalinin Bay's* bridge flashed the letter "N," and MacLaughlin led them to Tarawa. It was 0930 hours.

Tarawa and Makin Atolls were the staging areas for the next major phase of the Pacific War: Operation

Four of the Flying Buccaneers shortly before being deployed to Tarawa. Left to right: Robert "Chick" Whalen, Jake Wilson, Royce "Tex" Watson and John Hansen. (Photo courtesy Andrew Syrkin.)

Flintlock and the neutralization and capture of the main atolls of the Marshalls, six hundred miles to the northwest. Flintlock's hammer was the mighty US Fifth Fleet under Vice Admiral Raymond A. Spruance, one of the victors at Midway and Guadalcanal. The Fifth Fleet had four task groups consisting of six fleet carriers, six light carriers, eight battleships, a flotilla of heavy cruisers, light cruisers, and over a hundred destroyers. Accompanying this mighty armada were scores of tankers, ammunition ships, transports, hospital ships, and repair vessels. Hundreds of specialized amphibious craft were ready to play their role. Most had only existed on the drawing board three years earlier, such as Landing Ship Tank (LST), Landing Ship Dock, (LSD), Landing Craft Tank (LCT), Landing Vehicle Tracked (LVT), and the ubiquitous Higgins boats. The US Navy and Marines had learned their lessons after the debacle of Tarawa.

Rear Admiral Charles Pownall commanded Task Force 50. An Annapolis graduate, Pownall had been awarded the Navy Cross for action as the captain of a patrol vessel against U-boats in the First World War. Prior to the Japanese attack on Pearl Harbor, he commanded USS *Enterprise*.

In the months leading up to the invasion of Tarawa, he led Task Force 50, the fast carrier force, consisting of Task Groups 50.1, 50.2, 50.3 and 50.4, with ten fleet and light aircraft carriers. Together with the battleships, cruisers, and destroyers, this was a formidable armada.

But by January 1944, Charles Pownall was also an officer with some undesirable official baggage. Critics in Pearl Harbor said that he lacked aggressiveness. During raids on Minami Torishima, known to the United States as Marcus Island in August 1943, Avengers from USS *Yorktown* (CV-10) Torpedo 5 bombed Japanese defenses on the island. One plane failed to return. As commander of TF 50, Pownall bore the ultimate responsibility for his air crews. Air searches were conducted by planes from the cruiser division and Avengers from VT-5, but no trace of the missing airmen was found. Word began circulating around Pearl Harbor that Pownall had deliberately refused to send TF 50's ships to find the downed aviators. Even though the rumors were later found to be untrue, they had their effect. Nimitz had been considering relieving Pownall of command and sending him to the West Coast. In the end, Pownall was replaced by the avuncular Rear Admiral Marc Mitscher. Mitscher's naval aviation career went back to the NC-1 in 1919. His name would soon become synonymous with fast carrier forces in the Pacific.

Spruance intervened on Pownall's behalf and he was given the title of Commander, Air Force Pacific Fleet (ComAirPacFor) under Spruance. It was essentially the end of the admiral's combat career. But during Flintlock, he still had some authority over the ground-based air assets in the Gilberts that were to support the invasion. This of course included the marine fighter squadrons.

On 31 January, Spruance's four carrier groups were scheduled to begin sustained air attacks on the Marshalls. One group was to hit Kwajalein, another, Maloelap, the third the twin islands of Roi and Namur, and the fourth, Wotje. This generous dispersal of forces illustrates how far the United States Navy had come since Midway. Their job was to neutralize enemy air units on the surrounding islands, while the fleet's heavy guns shelled the Japanese defenses on Kwajalein and Majuro. Their primary objective was the anchorages at both islands. The amphibious assault would carry seven army and marine regiments, totaling over twenty-one thousand men onto the beaches to take the island by direct assault. The successful completion of Flintlock would be followed by Operation Catchpole, targeting Eniwetok and Engebi Atolls.

The ground-based air defense of Operation Flintlock was given to Rear Admiral John H. Hoover, whose command ship, USS *Curtiss*, was anchored in Tarawa Lagoon. Hoover, known as "Genial John" in contrast to his acerbic demeanor, was a former submarine officer who changed to aviation in the late 1920s. Hoover was not popular with his men. Admiral John Towers, the senior air officer in the Pacific called Hoover "an enigma." He was physically fit and a competent commander with a reputation for being aggressive. As in Galvanic, he commanded Task Force 57, the Air Defense Forces, and land-based air units. He bore the ultimate responsibility for the disposition of all marine squadrons for Flintlock. On air bases throughout the Gilberts and Ellice Islands were hundreds of marine fighters and dive bombers, two USAAF heavy bomb groups, and six squadrons of navy patrol planes, about 350 in all. Back in December, Admiral Nimitz told Hoover that his job was to use his air assets to reduce the Japanese air strength on Wotje, Roi-Namur, Maloelap, and Jaluit. Nimitz expected the B-24 Liberators of the 11th and 30th Bomb Groups based in the Gilbert and Ellice Islands to do decisive damage to the enemy facilities, but this proved to be unrealistic. Enemy anti-aircraft artillery and fighters were extremely effective. During one daylight mission over Maloelap and Wotje, three B-24s were shot down. Hoover then turned to night missions, leading to a decrease in bombing accuracy. The main Japanese air bases were still in operation as Flintlock drew nearer.

Marine Brigadier General Lewie G. Merritt was the commander of the Fourth Marine Air Base Defense Wing on Betio. Merritt had had a successful if unusual career in the marines after graduating from the Citadel on the eve of the US declaration of war on Germany in 1917. Merritt earned his wings almost exactly twenty years before in January 1924. He became one of the first marine aviators to complete carrier qualification training and was very involved in developing marine air combat doctrine. He commanded one of the two air units in Haiti in the early 1920s and later attended George Washington University for a law degree in 1928. After working for the navy's judicial branch, in the Judge Advocate General's (JAG) office in Washington, D.C., Merritt returned to line service. In 1941, he attended the US Army Air Corps Tactical School, after which he became commander for Air, Fleet Marine Force, Pacific. In this capacity, he formed Marine Air Wing Two in Hawaii and played a role in increasing the air assets on Midway and Wake Island. A promotion to Brigadier General in January 1942 led to an assignment as air attaché to the American Embassy in London. This was followed by a tour of duty in North Africa where he observed how the British Eighth Army utilized Sir Arthur Cunningham's air forces. Merritt was nearly killed when his RAF Wellington bomber was shot down by German anti-aircraft guns. He managed to reach British lines and returned to Washington to report his findings. Then, the marines sent him to the Pacific. In the summer of 1943, he commanded the Fourth MBDAW in New Britain. From there, he oversaw marine air operations in the Gilbert Island Campaign until mid-January when he arrived on Betio to oversee the marine air forces in the Gilbert and Ellice Islands.

Tarawa's commander was a respected navy officer, Captain Jackson R. Tate, a career aviator whose flying went back to the 1920s. He had competed in the National Air Races, been a member of an aerobatic team called "The Nine High Hats," and was involved in developing carrier tactics.

CHAPTER 7

TARAWA

Tarawa Atoll slid into view over the horizon as the Corsairs winged their way west. The low sun dappled the waves as the thin necklace of islands ringing the lagoon passed under their wings. The lagoon had a channel to the southwest large enough for ships to enter. From the air, Betio resembled a seahorse lying on its back. It barely rose more than ten feet above sea level and had little natural fresh water. Betio was code named Helen, while nearby Buota was code named Ella. Connected between Ella and Helen by concrete and wood causeways was Bairiki, code-named Cora, the main command base and home to Acorn 14. Acorn 14 was the Construction Battalion (SeaBee) Unit that installed the SCR-270 radar, and expanded the airfield and facilities after the island had been secured. Tarawa's palm trees were stripped bare and burned black, looking like bristles on a hog's back. The airfield's intersecting runways dominated the center of the small island while dozens of ships, barges, and landing craft dotted the water and beaches. It looked too small to have been the center of so much attention.

"You never saw so many men, trucks, bulldozers, Jeeps, tanks, airplanes, Quonset huts, and tents in one place," recalled Lehnert. "I don't know why the island didn't sink under all the weight."

Hawkins Field was named for Marine Lieutenant William Dean Hawkins who was killed during the fighting. He had posthumously received the Medal of Honor. The first air units to occupy the newly expanded airfield were B-25 Mitchells of the 41st Bomb Group and B-24 Liberators of the 11th Bomb Group of the Seventh Air Force. It was soon apparent the runway wasn't long enough for the big planes and they were moved to Mullinix Field on Buota Island.

Hawkins' runway and ramp were newly built and showed few of the skid marks and oil stains that characterized airfields all over the world. But there were places where hasty patches had been poured into shell and bomb craters.

Major John S. MacLaughlin landed at 0950, followed in two-plane elements by his pilots. They were directed to hardstands

Hawkins Field on Betio Island, Tarawa in mid-1944. (Official U.S. Navy photo.)

along the secondary runway. As the marines climbed down from their planes, the first thing they noticed was a putrid smell. It wafted over the island on the warm tropical breeze and invaded their nostrils like the reek from a burned slaughterhouse. When they asked what the stink was, an officer who introduced himself as Colonel Lawrence Burke explained that hundreds of Japanese corpses still lay unburied in bunkers and rifle pits.

MacLaughlin shook hands with Burke, whom he had known in California and Hawaii. Burke informed the new arrivals that he was operations officer for the Fourth Marine Base Defense Air Wing under Brigadier General Merritt, whom MacLaughlin had also known.

"Mac told us to see that the ground crews took care of our planes," recalled Hansen. "Rex Jeans talked with him and Colonel Burke. I guess that's when we first heard about this flight to Funafuti. We would be briefed later that day. In the meantime, we were to take care of any maintenance for our planes. I heard Rex ask about new wheels for some of our planes, but I really can't recall what that was about."

There is ample evidence that Colonel Burke told MacLaughlin that General Merritt had orders from Admiral Hoover to send VMF-422 to Funafuti as soon as possible, which meant that very afternoon. When MacLaughlin asked about the preparations for the flight, Burke said he "would make all the arrangements." By this he presumably meant obtaining weather, navigation, and radio data and to have the field Combat Area Service Unit, or CASU, ground crews fuel the Corsairs. It also presupposed that Burke, being familiar with the island commander's policies, would have the flight cleared for takeoff.

As they were talking, a gray navy Jeep drove up and a marine officer stepped out. He introduced himself as Lieutenant Colonel John Stage of Admiral Hoover's staff on the USS *Curtiss*. Stage asked if there were anything he could do to help MacLaughlin to prepare for the flight, but Burke insisted that he would take care of all the details.

In a later statement, Stage recalled those first few minutes along the runway on Hawkins Field. "Burke said that General Merritt desired that the squadron clear Tarawa as soon as possible, preferably that afternoon. I asked if an escort had been arranged. Burke replied no, and that General Merritt did not desire that the flight should have an escort. I strongly recommended that the flight be held over at least until the following day so that the pilots could be properly briefed and prepared and urged that an escort be obtained, even if the general had to be talked into it. I mentioned bad weather in the Ellice Islands which had been reported by Colonel McQuade, Commanding Officer of CENCATS (Central Pacific Combat Air Transport Service) who had flown up from Funafuti the previous day, and called attention to the fact that the pilots of VMF-422 had had little chance to learn anything about these islands and this area. Colonel Burke replied by saying that he knew that General Merritt was anxious to have the squadron leave as soon as possible and that he definitely did not intend to provide an escort. However, he did say that he would do his best to see that an escort was obtained and that the squadron was fully prepared in every way for the movement. Later in the day I saw Colonel Burke again and at that time plans for the movement were in the same status as during our first conversation."

Colonel Stage was in a position to know about such matters. A 1938 graduate of Pensacola, he had flown nearly every type of navy aircraft, including the F4U, amassing over 2400 hours in the air.

What MacLaughlin thought about this conversation is not recorded, but he certainly took note of Stage's mention of bad weather and his urging of an escort. However, he had no reason to doubt that Burke would see that everything was done properly.

After all, Burke was under orders to see that VMF-422 reached its destination.

The question of an escort is the key to the Flintlock Disaster. As will be seen, it was standard US Navy policy to provide a multi-engine patrol plane escort for fighter and bomber squadrons on long ferry flights, even outside the war zone. The patrol plane crew would not only have an experienced navigator, but would be familiar with the region and local weather conditions. This was accepted practice all over the Pacific from Pearl Harbor to Midway, and from the Solomons to Australia.

On 10 January VMF-113, under Major Loren "Doc" Everton, a Guadalcanal veteran, had been given an escort to Funafuti, even after being denied one by Merritt. A week prior to that, a US Navy fighter squadron, VF-12, under the famous Commander Joseph C. "Jumping Joe" Clifton requested and was given an escort for the same route. Clifton was a highly experienced and skilled commander, yet even he insisted on having an escort on the eight-hundred-mile flight. In his case, he did not have to request one from Merritt, but from the base operations officer, Commander A. W. Wheelock.

Stage later said, "I believe that it is currently accepted that single seaters proceeding over water for considerable distances should be escorted by a multi-engine airplane with complete radio and navigational equipment."

Earlier that morning the Assistant Air Operations Officer on Tarawa, Major Theodore Brewster, had asked Burke about VMF-422. Brewster's normal duties when a new squadron arrived on the island was to meet them and after determining their orders, to provide them with the full use of the base facilities, which included weather and navigational information. Burke told him that VMF-422, being under the command of the Fourth MBDAW would be taken care of by Burke himself. Brewster apparently believed this relieved him of all responsibility for assisting MacLaughlin. It also meant that VMF-422's flight did not come to the official attention of the normal base chain of command or air operations.

Burke led the squadron commander to the search headquarters tent near Hawkins Field. During their conversation, MacLaughlin asked Burke about an escort plane to Funafuti. MacLaughlin was well aware that few of his pilots had much experience with long, over-water navigation. Burke told him it was impossible to obtain an escort as it was contrary to the general's policy for flights of this nature.

According to Burke's later testimony, MacLaughlin accepted this without comment and "appeared to be confident in his pilots' ability to make the flight." However, that was before MacLaughlin learned about the adverse conditions they would be facing.

Burke and MacLaughlin settled themselves in the small office of Captain Alan Campbell, USMC, Assistant Operations Officer for the Fourth MBDAW and Burke's immediate subordinate.

Picking up the phone, Burke called the base Air Operations Officer, Lieutenant George Sandlin, and asked him to come over to give MacLaughlin a briefing on tower frequencies and radio call contact information for the bases between Tarawa and Funafuti. He also told Campbell to see to the weather report. Burke evidently wanted Sandlin and Campbell to carry out the job he himself had pledged to do. It appears that the Fourth MBDAW Chief of Staff did no more than delegate various duties to his subordinates. Even though Burke made sure MacLaughlin was provided with virtually all the necessary information he would need, he completely dropped the ball in one vital respect: he did not keep the base operations office informed of the impending flight. This would have dire consequences.

Sandlin arrived to find the three marine officers discussing the flight. Sandlin, an efficient and conscientious young naval officer, provided a list of radio range frequencies, emergency frequencies, tower frequencies, and base voice codes.

MacLaughlin asked about maps and charts. Sandlin said he would provide the maps VMF-422 would need. He also informed MacLaughlin that he could find everything at the command post, including intelligence reports.

Campbell handed MacLaughlin a mimeographed page of radio aids for the Ellice Islands. This document, which was later entered into evidence as "Exhibit 4" listed several islands in the region, including Funafuti, Nanumea, Nukufetau, and Apamama and their code names.

The list was dated 17 December 1943 and had been altered since then. For example, Apamama had the name "Chungking" crossed out and "Lilac" written by hand. However, the all-important call signs for Nanumea and Funafuti were not included on the list. At some point MacLaughlin may have been verbally informed that Nanumea's call sign was "Rocky Base" and Funafuti was "Lone Star."

Yet an incomplete list could lead to serious problems in an emergency. Without knowing what base used what call sign, a pilot would have no way of knowing who he was in communication with.

As for weather reports, Captain Campbell said he would contact the *Curtiss* and request an update from Lieutenant Commander James Shilson, the senior aerological officer on Hoover's staff.

Captain Richard C. Pennington, commander of Marine Utility Squadron (VMJ) 353, arrived in the tent about this time. Besides being familiar with the local weather and navigation, he was also the pilot of General Merritt's personal R4D. Pennington told MacLaughlin what kind of weather VMF-422 could expect on the flight to Funafuti. In his later testimony Pennington said, "I told the Major that the weather from Tarawa as far as Nanumea had been fairly good, but that from Nanumea to Funafuti it had been stormy with rain squalls and high cumulus clouds."

As the hot equatorial sun reached its zenith, the other pilots of VMF-422 went to the field mess hall for lunch. While they ate sandwiches and drank coffee, seated on boxes and benches under the stubs of palm trees, they watched the unceasing activity on the island. They chatted about the war and what their first combat assignment would be like. They fully expected to go into action very soon.

Shortly after noon, the phone rang in the aerological office on the USS *Curtiss*. Lieutenant Shilson took the call from Captain Campbell for an updated weather report for the area between Tarawa and Funafuti, to be delivered no later than 1300 hours. Shilson and his team of eight officers and enlisted men compiled what were known as synoptic reports from various bases and ships in the region. These reports were assembled every six hours and sent to the bases under Hoover's command.

The most recent report was phoned in to the headquarters of Fourth MBDAW on Betio while MacLaughlin was in the search headquarters tent. The report, which was primarily based on figures collected at 0600 that morning, predicted mostly clear skies between Tarawa and Nanumea, with rain squalls, cumulous clouds, and winds between Nanumea and Funafuti. But Shilson had also been hearing of what he later described as a "front" lying near Nanumea. It had apparently been "sitting there" for some days but there was little solid information and no reason to assume it was anything more than a local storm front and therefore did not mention it in the report.

Back in the search headquarters tent, the question of an escort evidently did not come up again that afternoon. Lieutenant Sandlin was aware that it should have been provided for such a long flight by single-engine fighters; however, he later admitted that he felt his job was only to give MacLaughlin whatever he needed and to ascertain whether or not conditions were safe for the flight. Being subordinate to Burke and Merritt, he did not have the authority to bring up or question the wisdom of not having an escort.

Campbell discussed the peculiarities of local weather with MacLaughlin. According to Campbell's later testimony, "I advised him not to try and dive out of any rain storms that appeared to go from a cloud all the way to the water because I understood they did go right into the water and he might dive into the water in an effort to get below the storm."

At some point MacLaughlin had been told of VMF-113 and VF-12's earlier flights to Funafuti. Whether or not he was also told that both squadron commanders had insisted on having an escort can only be guessed. In light of subsequent events, it is unlikely Burke mentioned the matter.

The meeting broke up. MacLaughlin, more than likely dazed by all the information he was given in such a short time, went to the mess hall. While in the chow line, he again bumped into Campbell, who asked when VMF-422 would take off, but MacLaughlin didn't know. This illustrated how badly he had been served by Colonel Burke, who was supposedly taking care of everything.

The pilots met up with their commander sometime around 1700 hours. He informed them that they would spend the night aboard a ship in the lagoon. There they would be briefed on their mission. Captain Jeans and Captain Rogers both asked about an escort, to which MacLaughlin replied with what Burke told him. To those who heard this conversation, the three officers were not happy about this. Jeans later said, "He [MacLaughlin] was not too pleased about going without an escort. I knew the major fairly well but he was a difficult man to figure out. But by just his actions, he didn't appear to be too happy about the whole prospect."

It was not the end of the matter. Three more times Jeans, Rogers, and Hughes urged their commander to push harder for an escort the following day.

They walked down to the island's main dock. It jutted far out into the blue lagoon. Landing craft and gray-painted boats of every description were tied along the dock. The placid lagoon was dotted with other craft, some riding at anchor, others mere skeletons, burned out or blasted apart. The SeaBees had more important things to do than dismantle and remove them. A launch was waiting for the marines and they climbed in. As they moved out to the lagoon, fighters passed overhead in unceasing patrols, seaplanes took off and landed on the water, and the air was filled with the never-ceasing drone of demolition and construction.

The launch was steering towards a small ship. It was painted the regulation navy gray, but there was no hiding that it had once been a luxury yacht.

The USS *Southern Seas* was built as *SS Lyndonia* in 1920 in Morris Heights, New York for wealthy publisher Cyrus Curtis. After Curtis died in 1933, Pan-American Airways purchased the yacht and remodeled her as the *SS Southern Seas,* a floating hotel and passenger transport between Nomea and Australia. When the war began, the US Army bought her for one dollar. Driven by two diesel engines, the two-hundred-foot yacht could travel for three thousand miles at sixteen knots.

Serving as a small transport and cargo carrier, *Southern Seas* sailed around the Coral Sea until being grounded near New Caledonia. The US Navy recovered the yacht and commissioned her as a patrol yacht, PY-32. She was called a "quartering ship," and had twenty luxury staterooms, some of which were divided into smaller berths for junior officers and crew.

After supper, the marines assembled for a briefing in the main salon. MacLaughlin began by outlining Operation Flintlock, the massive joint navy, army, and marine effort to invade and take the Marshall Islands. This was the first time most of the marines heard the code name.

MacLaughlin used an easel bearing a large chart of the Gilbert, Ellice, and Marshall Islands. Tarawa was in the center, surrounded by small islets and reefs. Running in a long string roughly south-southeast from Tarawa were the small atolls of the Ellice Islands, ending at Funafuti. Six hundred miles to the northwest were the Marshall Islands, which encompassed the Japanese strongholds of Kwajalein, Majuro, Eniwetok, Wotje, and Engebi. The Marshalls had an interesting history. Once a German colony, they were given to Japan by the now-defunct League of Nations after the end of the First World War. The South Pacific Mandate gave Japan all German-held islands north of the equator. They were considered part of the empire. The Japanese had been fortifying the islands and many of the surrounding atolls since the mid-1920s. Admiral Halsey and other carrier task forces had been attacking and harassing the enemy in the Marshalls since February 1942, but with little lasting effect.

"Here," MacLaughlin said, pointing at a group of islands, "are our first objectives, Kwajalein and Majuro Atolls. They are the main

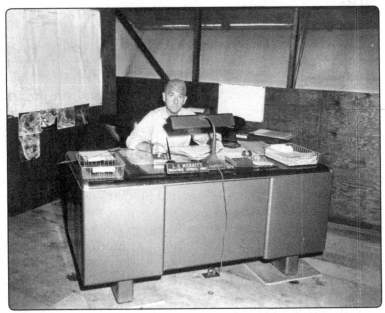

General Lewie Merritt at his headquarters sometime in 1943. For the campaigns on Tarawa and the Marshalls, Merritt had overall control of some of the Marine and Navy air units. (Photo courtesy The Citadel.)

Japanese army and navy bases in the Marshalls. It is the job of Task Group 57.2 to destroy the enemy forces when the invasion is underway."

But to the chagrin of his pilots, MacLaughlin explained that they were not going to participate in the initial assault. VMF-422 was to fly south to Funafuti, where they would be out of range of Japanese bombers. Hawkins Field had no hard revetments for the Corsairs. A surprise air attack could easily destroy the entire squadron. Therefore, Rear Admiral Hoover of the air defense forces for Task Group 57.2 directed Merritt to send VMF-422 and all other marine fighter and bomber squadrons to Funafuti until Kwajalein and Majuro have been secured.

"That was kind of hard to take," Hansen commented. "We had been training for years to get here and the first thing they wanted us to do was hide in a safe corner."

Syrkin recalled feeling a similar resentment. "I was stunned. But Mac didn't bat an eye, neither did Charley or Rex. They knew how the game was played."

MacLaughlin informed them that there was already another marine Corsair squadron on Funafuti, "Doc" Everton's VMF-113.

Curly Lehnert was happy to hear this. "I had gotten to know a pilot named Andy Jones at Jacksonville," he said. "Jones had joined VMF-113 at El Toro and he would be at Funafuti when we arrived."

MacLaughlin continued with navigation and radio information. "We will be flying to Funafuti via Nanumea. The total distance is 820 nautical miles. The first leg to Nanumea is 463 miles. Takeoff at 0930, course, 155 degrees, altitude between fifteen hundred and two thousand feet, airspeed two hundred knots. Figure fuel burn at 55 gallons per hour. Our Corsairs will be filled with 439 gallons of fuel, which will get us to Nanumea with 211 gallons, or enough for another three hours and fifteen minutes. ETA for Nanumea is 1225 hours. Depending on weather, ETA Funafuti will be 1500 hours."

Maps were distributed. According to Lieutenant Bob Scott, these were small charts showing the Gilbert Group from Tarawa to Nanumea. Other charts displayed the route from Nanumea to Funafuti with the Ellice Islands, each one bearing tongue-twisting names like Niutao, Nukufetau, Fangaua, Nukulaelae, Nanumanga, and Niulakita. The charts each pilot had on his "knee board" showed little more than the rough layout of the islands along their route. There was little chance of using them for serious navigation.

The senior officers, MacLaughlin, Jeans, Hughes, and Rogers carried detailed charts of the Gilberts and Ellice Islands.

For the most part, the Flying Buccaneers would navigate by the old "dead reckoning" method. By knowing their heading and airspeed, judging the wind by the waves, and keeping an eye on the time, it was not difficult to fly to a specific destination. But as with all non-absolutes, dead reckoning had its share of caveats. Good visibility and predictable weather were a major factor in reaching safety.

"We each carried a Mark 3A plotting board," said Scott. "We were told that every pilot was to navigate and track the lead plane all the way down. We were to fly by sight as well as navigating along the string of islands. Our first stop would be Nanumea. On the flight from Tarawa to Nanumea we expected fair weather and visibility until we got close to Nanumea. As the visibility was poor, we would ease over towards these islands so as to keep a check. Our plan of position in flight was to fly more or less abeam of the leader in a slight "V" so that all planes could be seen by the leader at all times. The division leader would report to the flight leader approximately every twenty minutes the condition of the division."

Hansen admitted he had felt better about the impending flight after hearing that. "I was sure we could do it but eight hundred miles over open water was a long way. As far as I knew, none of us, other than perhaps Hughes or Jeans had ever flown that far over water. Mac told us what kind of weather we could expect on the way to Nanumea and Funafuti. He said it was mostly clear with about three-tenths cloud cover at twelve hundred feet with scattered cumulus from two thousand to seven thousand feet. They expected us to run into some small rain squalls and variable winds about a hundred miles northwest of Nanumea, but nothing to worry about."

In the event that they encountered bad weather of the type predicted, they were to fly around it until they could take up the original heading. At no time, according to any statements made later, was the possibility of turning back ever discussed.

Curly Lehnert remembers the briefing. "Mac was telling us all this stuff and we wrote it down. It was a lot to absorb, but I don't think any of us ever really thought we'd get into trouble. Mac was too good an officer to lead us astray. He said, 'We're flying a straight line along a string of island landmarks. As long as we see them, we're on course. Since we're so close to the equator, our magnetic compasses are more reliable.'"

During the war, hundreds of pilots had been complaining of erratic compass readings that occurred without warning. The Navy Department ordered an investigation and learned that any kind of anomaly in the aircraft's electrical system or outside interference such as the kind encountered in thunderstorms could often cause the compass to swing as much as 120 degrees off its heading.

The F4Us' radio equipment consisted of a 233A VHF transmitter and receiver, a ZB receiver, a 6000-9000 kilocycle (now kilohertz or kHz) receiver, a 200-500 kilocycle receiver, and a transmitter which was set on 6970 kilocycles. It was planned to communicate with the operations towers of the various fields in the Ellice Islands on 6970 kilocycles, which according to the communication plan, all of them monitored. It was also the primary channel to talk between the planes.

Scott said, "The major gave us army radio aid sheets. These charts had alternate airports available along the route. Our sets were to be on 6970, which I believe was the only one we could contact the towers of these fields with."

The squadron also had an alternate frequency, 6210 kilocycles, for plane-to-plane voice communication. Under ideal conditions the effective range of transmission or receipt was around five hundred miles. However, VHF Frequencies over 5000 kilocycles were often affected by atmospheric interference and were only effective when not obscured by bad weather or the Earth's curvature.

There was another concern, which would later become a serious issue for VMF-422. When listening in on one frequency for tower communication and another for squadron voice calls, the chances of missing an important transmission were compounded.

"We had the ZB sets in the planes but they were not calibrated," Scott said. "They have a channel set with seven channels on it, but there was no "coffee grinder" knob for the pilot to adjust. It was set up internally."

The ZB Scott referred to was primarily used by carrier-based aircraft to home in on their ship after a mission.

The primary means of radio navigation available to the marines was known colloquially as the "radio range." These used lower frequencies between 190 to 535 kilocycles and were less affected by poor weather. On an air base, an array of antennas broadcast in four 90-degree quadrants the Morse Code dot-dash letter "A" and the dash-dot "N" on a frequency specific to each base. To illustrate using a clock face, the two quadrants from twelve to three and from six to nine, as it were, might be "N" while the other two quadrants would be "A." As a pilot neared his destination, he might hear the dash-dot "N," and he would alter his course until he heard the dot-dash "A." After adjusting his heading back and forth, he would hear the two letters as a continuous tone as he came in "on the beam." This simple but effective system, known as the Low-Frequency Range (LFR) or Four-Course Radio Range had been established in the United States during the 1930s when the volume of air mail, commercial, and military air traffic grew to unprecedented numbers. The old system of using lighted beacons to help pilots find airports was only effective on clear nights. In bad weather, pilots often ran out of fuel or crashed, unable to find a field. Radio ranges were eventually set up at four hundred locations around the continental United States. Radio range navigation made modern air travel possible, but electrical storms could cause the signal to be lost or turn to static, making it difficult to follow the beam.

While LFR worked well, it did hinge on two critical factors: The pilot had to know which frequency to tune in and which quadrants were "A" and which were "N."

MacLaughlin was not told that the radio aids data were incomplete, and not all the call signs for the bases were listed. Unfortunately, the marines were unaware of this as the briefing ended. While a few remained to examine the maps and charts, the others went out on deck to smoke or talk. The air was warm as salt and palm-scented breezes wafted over the black water of the lagoon. The night sky over Tarawa Atoll was a deep indigo blue as the Milky Way spanned directly over them like a star-spangled river. To the east, a new moon rose over the distant reefs. Then they went to bed. The next day would be a busy one.

At 0600 on Tuesday, 25 January 1944, the marine pilots were jolted from sleep when the ship's P.A. speakers blared out "Reveille." Grumbling and muttering they climbed out of the racks in the junior officer's quarters and began to dress. They wore khaki one-piece flight suits over skivvies and a white t-shirt. A leather shoulder belt held the holstered sidearm, either the powerful Colt .45 automatic or the Smith & Wesson .38 revolver. Strapped to one leg was a marine combat knife. They wore high-sided brown shoes and carried a flight helmet, goggles, Mae West life preserver, and web belt with a canteen.

Breakfast was typical navy chow, powdered eggs and cold bacon served with toast and ersatz marmalade. They ate ravenously, knowing they had a long day ahead. Syrkin recalled downing at least four cups of strong navy coffee.

The same launch that had brought them out the day before was waiting at the ladder. MacLaughlin led them down to the launch and said there would be one more briefing at Hawkins Field before takeoff. Meanwhile, they were to go and do preflight checks of their Corsairs.

The CASU crews were busy fueling and arming the fighters when the marines arrived. One by one they carefully checked their planes, asking about the fuel, oil, and other important maintenance details.

The Aerological Officer on Betio, Lieutenant (jg) William Snell, telephoned the weather report to the Command Post at 0830 hours. It stated:

Tarawa to Funafuti, three-tenths to five-tenths low clouds, increasing to six-tenths to eight-tenths below four degrees south. Light to moderate rain showers below four degrees south. Base of cumulus 1,200 to 1,800 feet lowering to 800 feet in showers. Tops 8,000 to 12,000 feet in southern half of route. Visibility eight to twelve miles in northern half, six to eight miles reduced to two miles or less in showers in southern half of route. Winds northwesterly twelve to sixteen knots shifting to northwest to west below four degrees south. Flying conditions undesirable in showers.

It was essentially the same as the report MacLaughlin had been given by Campbell the previous day. But what it did not reveal was that it was based on data that had been received at 1800 hours on 24 January, fourteen hours before. Furthermore, the 1800 report was no more than a repeat of the 0600 report, now twenty-six hours old.

MacLaughlin reviewed the updated weather report tacked to the command post bulletin board. What he did in the time between 0900 and 1000 hours needs some examination. He talked to Lieutenant Sandlin again and asked about navigational charts. These were different from maps as they had bearings, distances, and radio navigation information on them. Sandlin gave MacLaughlin the charts he requested.

Next, MacLaughlin was met by Major Theodore Brewster, the Air Operations Officer for Hawkins Field and Commander A. W. Wheelock, the Base Operations Officer. During this time MacLaughlin busied himself with last-minute details of the flight, but it was apparent that some matters were not covered. For one thing, he never filed a flight plan for VMF-422's move to Nanumea and Funafuti. This was supposed to be required procedure for all flights that were not routine local post-maintenance check flights. Every pilot or squadron commander was to file a flight plan after having received his orders and all his weather, radio, and navigation information. No flight was to be allowed to leave the field without direct clearance from either the Air Operations Officer or the Base Operations Officer. Until a flight plan was filed and reviewed, no aircraft could leave the field.

The reason for such stringent procedures went back to mid-November. As soon as the smoke cleared after the island had been secured, fighters, bombers, patrol planes, and transports came and went almost at will, often without a flight plan or being cleared to take off. It was literally no way to run a railroad. On 27 December, Admiral Hoover sent a dispatch to Captain Tate, the Island commander, that air operations on the islands of Hawkins and Mullinix Fields were a full-time job and that Tate was to assign officers specifically for the duties of air operations and base operations to assure that no flights could come and go without being properly cleared.

Under great pressure, Tate then supervised a "house cleaning" of the base operations. But as late as 20 January, the matter had not been resolved. It was still too easy for a flight to leave without the knowledge or consent of Tate, Wheelock, or Brewster.

MacLaughlin, who had been dealing more or less with Colonel Burke, was apparently never told he had to file a flight plan with the air operations office. He may have assumed, with some justification, that Burke took care of his movement orders. While we might feel some reluctance to point a finger of blame at MacLaughlin, it cannot be denied that he should have made an effort to make sure his flight was on the Hawkins Field schedule. In his defense, he was probably distracted by his not having been given an escort, the old weather report, and the impending flight itself. In any case, while he was with Brewster at the command post, the clearance for VMF-422 had neither been applied for, nor obtained. Brewster did not know when the marines were due to take off and might easily have assumed that it was an open question. If MacLaughlin had known to file a flight plan as directed by both Hoover and Tate, or if Colonel Burke had done as he had promised, the flight would have come to the attention of Commander Wheelock, who knew all long-distance flights were, *if practicable*, to have an escort. He would likely have inquired about this to MacLaughlin, and after being informed that Merritt had denied the escort, told him that it was fully within the authority of the base or island commander to provide an escort. Additionally, the filed plan and approval would result in an official departure report being sent to both Nanumea and Funafuti.

This is what should have been done. However, in his later testimony, Brewster stated that he drove MacLaughlin to the revetment near the tower and next to the squadron's Corsairs where the major gave his pilots their final briefing.

Brewster was charged with making sure no plane left the field without official clearance, but he failed to do so even when the marines were suited up and preparing to leave. He later said he had expected MacLaughlin to return to either the tower or the command post and file a plan. Brewster was sorely mistaken. At virtually every level, someone either failed to do his job or was unaware that VMF-422 was about to leave for Funafuti without an escort and without proper clearance. Sandlin, who did know VMF-422 was due to fly to Funafuti sometime that day, spent the morning in his underground post and never saw the preflight preparations. By the time he emerged for lunch, the marines had been in the air for two hours.

At 0925, the last briefing ended with MacLaughlin returning to the command post tent to check for any new information on the weather. Having been urged by Jeans, Hughes, and Rogers, he sought out Colonel Burke to request an escort.

Mark Syrkin said, "I needed to walk off the coffee I'd had on the yacht. I decided to go and find the head. Lieutenant Price went with me."

The marines walked along a dirt road where Jeeps and trucks roared by in clouds of dust and sand. They passed the command post tent, a large open-sided structure where enlisted men and officers worked at desks and phones.

Outside, they found MacLaughlin talking with Colonel Burke.

"From what I heard," Syrkin recalled, "Charley and Rex had convinced Mac that we needed a PV Ventura to fly with us. They were concerned about the eight-hundred-mile flight over open water. To tell the truth," he admitted, "I was too. That was a long way to go for a first mission, even a ferry flight."

When MacLaughlin mentioned VMF-113, Burke responded by saying that he had authorized that escort, but had been dressed down for it.

It's hard to imagine a senior officer admitting that he had been verbally disciplined by his superior. It can be assumed Burke felt some guilt over not being able to repeat his earlier actions on behalf of VMF-422 and finally agreed to ask the general. He led MacLaughlin into the tent.

In the 1998 video, Sterling Price explained what he saw. "Suddenly I heard someone yelling at the top of his lungs, 'I told you colonel, the answer is no! How many times do you need to be told? No escort. You did it on your own last week and I chewed you out for it. Do we have some sort of hearing problem here?'"

Syrkin added, "Then Merritt said, '422 can make the flight to Funafuti on their own. I don't want to use any antisubmarine patrol planes for an unnecessary escort. Now get the hell out of here or I'll ship your ass back to the states!' He was really shouting."

A minute later MacLaughlin emerged alone. He looked at his men around him and shrugged. "You heard the man," he said. Then he collected his gear and walked to the flight line.

Merritt's contention that he did not want to give up any planes from anti-submarine patrols makes little sense. There had been a greater threat of Japanese warships in the area in December to January when he was still allowing escorts than there was in late January when he chose to stop the practice.

Lehnert, who heard about this when Price and the others returned said, "I can't believe even now that there wasn't a basic operation plan in place at Tarawa. Even if Merritt had a valid reason for not wanting to give up one of his patrol planes for us, he didn't even have any planes on alert in case of an emergency. Nothing like a PBY on standby at Tarawa, Nanumea, or Funafuti."

Noted historian and author Robert Sherrod wrote about VMF-422 in his landmark book, *The History of Marine Aviation in World War II*. The pertinent entry stated that if Major MacLaughlin requested an escort plane, a Lockheed P2V with a navigator, would have been provided to keep the fighters safe on the flight south. But the formal request was not made. When the squadron left, it had no escort.

Furthermore, an article entitled *The Mystery of VMF-422* by M. W. Emmet refers to this by stating that the island operations officer knew that no escort aircraft had been requested. Had it been, it would have been provided.

Every surviving 422 pilot considered these accounts both false and insulting. "I first read Sherrod's book after it came out," said Lehnert. "I was angered. He got it totally wrong. But even worse it gets General Merritt off the hook by saying Mac never formally requested the escort. It made Mac seem negligent."

Syrkin was in agreement. "Robert Sherrod never talked to any of us, nor did he even read the official Board of Inquiry report. I heard Merritt yell at Burke when Mac made the request."

Moreover, General Merritt's actions that morning were in direct contravention of Navy Department policy. There was little, if any, room for modification or change when a squadron was sent into combat. A marine fighter squadron's job was to be the hammer, so to speak, with the marines on the ground as the anvil. Their job was basically to provide air cover and support to the ground troops. They were flying artillery and kept enemy fighters from interfering, but they were valuable tactical assets, and thus were to be intact and ready until they were needed. While an air wing commander had some discretion in the disposition of his units, he still had to follow Navy Department policy. This system was well-established when VMF-422 arrived on Betio on 24 January; however, by then there had been a significant change in relationship between Hoover and Merritt concerning their official duties. This deserves some examination as it may have had a direct effect on what happened to the squadron.

During the research for this book, the author examined the orders of battle for Galvanic and Flintlock. An order of battle lists the hierarchy of all the commanders, task forces, ships, squadrons, and units in a given campaign. A study of the two documents revealed an interesting anomaly. Before and during Operation Galvanic, Hoover had commanded all marine and army air assets in the pre-invasion phase, including the navy patrol planes. Under Hoover's command, Merritt led the Ellice Islands Defense and Utility Group as well as the Fourth MBDAW, comprising of ninety fighters, more than seventy scout bombers, twenty-four observation planes, and twelve transports

Merritt's fighters and bombers played virtually no role in the pre-invasion of Tarawa or its aftermath, but by December, one particular responsibility of the two officers reversed. Hoover still retained overall command of the army and marine air units, but he now had direct control of the fighter and bomber squadrons, while Merritt was given the search and patrol group. In other words, on the eve of Flintlock Merritt no longer directly controlled the attack groups, i.e. fighters and bombers. Instead, his overall job was to support Hoover's disposition of the marine fighter squadrons. His primary duty was to send his eight squadrons of PBY Catalinas, PV Venturas, PBM Mariners, and PB4Y-1 Liberators on search and rescue and anti-submarine patrol. For an ambitious and aggressive combat officer like Merritt, this was close to a demotion, and there is little doubt he resented having the fighters taken from him. That was how matters stood in late January when VMF-422 arrived on Tarawa for their flight to Funafuti.

With supreme irony, Merritt the marine was expected to commit his navy patrol planes to protect a navy admiral's marine fighters, the very same fighters he himself had recently commanded.

While there is no solid proof that this was the "last straw," consider that when Merritt had been Commander, Marine Air, Hawaiian Area, he routinely approved escorts for any long-distance flight by single-engine aircraft.

Who ordered the change? The prime suspect would be Hoover, who was also an ambitious, combat-minded officer, but it may have been the commander of Task Force 50, Admiral Pownall. Pownall was later shown to be highly critical of Merritt in the aftermath of the disaster.

Merritt's outburst at Colonel Burke probably had another effect. Cowed, Burke failed to inform MacLaughlin that there was another option. The island's commander, Captain Jackson Tate, had the overriding authority to release a patrol plane for escort duty over Merritt's orders. Major MacLaughlin was never told this.

PART TWO

EX COMMUNI PERICULO FRATERNITAS—FROM COMMON PERIL, BROTHERHOOD

CHAPTER 8

TAKEOFF

The twenty-four new F4U-1D Corsairs were fully fueled, armed, and ready.

One by one the Buccaneers waved or shook hands and climbed into their planes.

Curly Lehnert remembered an amusing incident. "I had two canteens of water on my belt," he said. "But the plastic cap on one got cracked and when I climbed up on the wings the water spilled all over my leg. I hoisted myself into the cockpit, and then the mechanic taps on the side of my plane and hands up a full canteen. I was really touched that he'd gone out of his way to get me another one." Lehnert smiled. "He saved my life, even though we didn't know it then."

The pilots sat on their parachute with the one-man life raft underneath. Together they served as a seat cushion, but were far from comfortable.

Syrkin wriggled into his parachute harness and made sure the life raft strap was strapped to it. Once his helmet was on, he plugged in the microphone and headset line. He heard the radio voice of MacLaughlin. "Check in and start engines."

The pilots went through their startup procedures until one by one the Corsairs roared to life. The engines were cold, but in less than a minute they were running smoothly.

All but one. First Lieutenant Bob Scott, the last man in MacLaughlin's Red Flight, had starter trouble.

"All the carrier aircraft at that time were equipped with shotgun shell starters," explained Syrkin, "and were not as dependable as the electrical type that replaced them later on. Scotty was out of luck."

Scott, who had been in the rear echelon until the crash that killed Drake and Farrell, was not happy to be left behind. He watched as his buddies moved out, waving as they passed. Soon his Corsair was the only one left on the field.

The twenty-three F4Us took their positions at the runway threshold. To avoid broadcasting flight information to the enemy, the standard procedure was to signal the tower by flashing landing lights. When the tower showed a green light, it was the indicator to go. A wind sock and anemometer provided visual information on wind direction and speed. It was from the east at ten knots.

Radioman Second Class James Allison had been on duty in the Hawkins tower since 0600 that morning. Next to him was a navy lieutenant with the unlikely name of Seebury Waring, the Field Operations Officer. Waring oversaw the tower and the movement of aircraft on the field, while Allison manned the radio and tower signals. Waring had been on the field the previous day just before VMF-422 left the carrier and was informed of its imminent arrival by Colonel Burke. Waring had little room for twenty-four Corsairs, but he was able to squeeze them in. He also learned the squadron was bound for Funafuti that very day or the next.

After spending the morning of 25 January dealing with fuel reports, Waring climbed up the ladder into the tower at 0915 hours. He took his place at the windows overlooking the runways to see the marine pilots climbing into their Corsairs. By 0940, the marines were queuing up for takeoff.

Captain Tate's 20 January directive, as prompted by the 27 December written orders from Hoover, stated that no aircraft or flight would be allowed to take off without the knowledge and approval of the island operations officer or the Hawkins air operations officer. But as with many aspects of the VMF-422 drama, this was not the case on 25 January.

As matters stood on that day, the tower did not actually require a written authorization from the air command post. Having been told by Burke that he would "take care of everything," Waring reasonably assumed that a flight plan had been filed and approved by the chain of command. In a dramatic illustration of how easily the normal running of a military organization could go awry, Waring gave Radioman Allison the order to flash the green light to the Corsairs.

Allison, who also assumed that any aircraft that had gotten as far as to be fueled and ready to leave the field had obtained clearance, hit the switch that flashed a bright green lamp extending from the tower's side.

MacLaughlin saw the light and called his pilots. "Buccaneer lead to Buccaneer flight, follow and rendezvous at 1,200 feet at five miles, over."

Sergeant Leon Furgatch, one of the VMF-422 mechanics, had been ferried over from the *Kalinin Bay* the previous afternoon. He was there to see his squadron take off. "Major MacLaughlin had

Curly Lehnert in flight gear. Note pistol and web belt.
(Photo courtesy Colonel Robert Lehnert.)

his canopy open. He turned to look back at the trailing planes and gave a 'thumbs up.' He closed the canopy, released the brakes, and vaulted into the clear blue sky."

Sergeant Furgatch was the last man on the ground to see MacLaughlin alive.

At exactly 0947 hours, the blue Corsairs began their takeoff rolls. In pairs, with Major MacLaughlin and Thompson in the lead, they lifted off, followed by Chris Lauesen and Ken Gunderson. Red Flight was followed by Gold Flight, with Green Flight last to depart.

It took ten minutes, and just before 1000 hours, VMF-422 was climbing through a hazy overcast and broke out into bright sunlight at 1,500 feet. Captain Hughes, after realizing that Scott had still not joined up, circled back to land. He learned that the Corsair's starter would not work, and climbed back into his own plane.

Interestingly, when Scott later gave his testimony to the Board of Inquiry, he did not seem to remember that Hughes had landed to check on him. He assumed the plane, Number 6, had landed to tighten a loose gas filler cap. Lieutenant Waring in the tower later stated that it was F4U Number 28 that landed. That Corsair was flown by Mark Syrkin, who never mentioned returning to Hawkins for six minutes. In either case, at 1005 hours Hughes rejoined the rest of the marines. They were on their way.

Back in the Hawkins tower, Radioman Allison confirmed from Waring that the flight was on its way to Funafuti. In another example of the poor communication over the flight, Waring had not been told of the stopover at Nanumea. Allison called Lieutenant Sandlin in the air command post to inform him that VMF-422 had taken off and its destination was Funafuti. At approximately 1030 hours Sandlin sent a departure report, Dispatch # 252159 to Funafuti. No dispatch was sent to Nanumea. At no point did anyone inform the Hawkins Field Operations Officer or the island commander of the marines' departure.

"I looked down and saw Betio far behind us," said Lehnert. "It looked like a beehive from the air. Ahead was a very big ocean."

"It was really nice flying weather," said Hansen. "Far to the south I saw some small cumulous clouds. They made dark shadows on the ocean. But otherwise it was perfectly clear." The squadron slid into a "V" formation of Red Flight in a left echelon, with Gold and Green in a longer right echelon.

Since they were flying in a war zone, MacLaughlin cautioned them to keep their eyes open for enemy planes. At once every pilot began what was known as "quartering the sky," by focusing out to the horizon and back in sections, starting with the port side. They also maintained a vigil on the small rear-view mirrors fitted on the canopy frame.

For the first hour, the marines flew in bright sunshine and clear skies. Every so often they passed lush islands ringed by pure white beaches, garlanded with turquoise coral reefs. The breakers looked like pearl necklaces. From their altitude, the low swells were delicate brush strokes following long white lines creeping forward to the reefs and beaches. The Corsairs' mighty Pratt & Whitney engines pounded out the cadence of power as the miles passed below them.

Each pilot checked off the islands on their plotting boards. At 1130 hours, MacLaughlin ordered the squadron to spread out. According to Lehnert, who remembered it clearly, Red Flight spread out laterally in a wide left echelon, followed by Gold Flight with about a hundred feet separating them. Then his own Green Flight took its place in a right echelon off the last plane in Gold Flight, that of Tex Watson. This put VMF-422 into a wider formation and provided a greater field of view.

They passed the small island of Tabiteuea, their last checkpoint before Nanumea.

At 1135 hours, one of the pilots called on the squadron channel that he saw an aircraft approaching from the south.

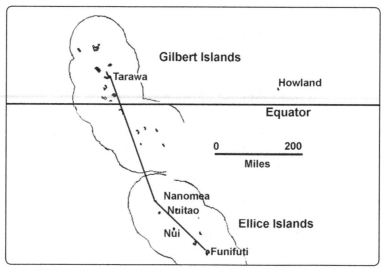

Map of Gilbert and Ellice Islands. VMF-422's course took them southeast to Nanumea and Funafuti at bottom right of map. (From the collection of the Naval History and Heritage Command.)

The lone plane turned out to be a navy Douglas R4D transport bound for Tarawa. The big plane did not call them but did waggle its wings as it passed ten miles away.

A few minutes later they approached the equator at zero degrees latitude. "I have to admit," said Syrkin with an abashed grin, "I think I expected to see a big yellow line on the ocean when we crossed the equator."

John Hansen recalls, "Charley Hughes called us on the squadron channel and said we were now exalted Shellbacks in King Neptune's Reign, or something like that. But it was sort of exciting. We were now in the South Pacific Ocean. Just like that."

The region they were entering is today called the South Pacific Convergence Zone (SPCZ). It runs within a wide band from the Solomon Islands through Fiji to Samoa and Tonga. The low-pressure convergence along this band commonly results in persistent clouds, rain, thunderstorms, tropical storms, and typhoons. These massive vortices begin with the most prosaic and innocent of origins. In the northern hemisphere, January is winter, but after crossing the equator, it is comparable to mid-summer. An area of warm humid air will rise from the surface of the ocean like an immense bubble. Colder air will rush in to fill the void. Under the influence of the Earth's rotation, known as the Coriolis Force, this mass of rising warm air and wet cold air begins to revolve around its vertical axis, giving birth to a depression that can evolve into a tropical storm, and finally a cyclone.

For much of history, Pacific cyclonic storms were called typhoons. Today, however, they are categorized by their location. North of the equator and west of the international date line at 180° longitude, they are still called typhoons. In the region south of the equator, they are known as cyclones. Cyclones spin clockwise and move southeast while typhoons spin counter-clockwise and generally travel northwest. They vary in size, but the largest and most dangerous may be three hundred miles in diameter. Other than tsunami caused by undersea quakes, they are the most powerful and destructive forces that the sea can breed. A typhoon destroyed most of Kublai Khan's two invasion fleets in the thirteenth century, giving rise to the legend of the Kamikaze, or "Divine Wind."

Professor Gary Barnes is the Chairman of the University of Hawaii's Atmospheric Sciences Department. A "hurricane chaser," Professor Barnes has been studying hurricanes, typhoons, and tropical storms for more than forty years. He is the author and co-author of several noted papers and monographs. Barnes explained the origins, development, and characteristics of these powerful storms by describing the basic force inherent in a cyclone. "When the wind on the north of a low-pressure zone is coming from the west, and on the south is coming from the east, you have what is known as 'vorticity,'" he explained. "This creates a spin around a vertical axis. The vorticity of a cyclone behaves the same way as a spinning figure skater. When she has her arms out straight she revolves slowly, but as she pulls them in she spins more rapidly. A storm might begin with winds of twenty knots but as it conserves the angular momentum the winds can easily reach eighty or ninety knots."

From the relatively mild winds at the center of the cyclone, known as the "eye," the winds increase in velocity. Ten to thirty nautical miles farther out can become violent tempests of 150 knots or more in the eye wall. Hundreds of miles from the eye, torrential rains and gale force winds are still possible.

The very winds that characterize a cyclone add to its power and fury, allowing it to feed upon itself, becoming ever more violent. These same powerful, low-altitude air currents give birth to and move the deadly mountainous waves that radiate out from the storm's center. Outside the eye wall are wide zones of strong winds and rain squalls.

When asked about how the United States Navy could fail to notice a cyclone, Professor Barnes said, "It's amazing how ignorant the navy was about storms in World War Two. A system can spin up to moderate intensity in as little as twenty-four hours, but more often takes thirty-six to forty-eight hours. Given a lack of weather stations within an area four to five degrees in latitude, even a [fully developed] beast could easily hide in there."

It was not a new problem, nor was it the last time the US Navy had serious difficulty in detecting and tracking major typhoons. In December 1944, a huge typhoon code named "Cobra" scattered and savaged Admiral Halsey's Third Fleet in the Philippine Sea, sinking three destroyers and costing the lives of 790 sailors. The winds reached 148 knots in this storm but the fleet's aerologists failed to provide adequate warning. This was the typhoon depicted in Herman Wouk's novel, *The Caine Mutiny*.

At the Board of Inquiry, Rear Admiral Frederick Sherman, Commander of Task Group 38.3 testified, "Without meaning any particular prejudice to some of our present-day aerologists, I'm inclined to think they have been brought up to depend on a lot of readings they get from other stations. I think they are much weaker than the older officers at judging the weather. I think they should be taught to judge the weather on what they actually see."

This may have been the case during the days prior to 25 January in the Gilbert Islands. Even as the aerologists on *Curtiss* were updating their weather reports, a cyclone of great size and strength had been born and was waiting to engulf the unwary marines into its deadly embrace.

Eighty miles ahead of VMF-422 was Nanumea Atoll. It was less than two square miles in size, just one of a few hummocks of dry land on the circumference of a three-mile-wide lagoon. Nanumea was the base of the USAAF's 30th Heavy Bomb Group, consisting of Consolidated B-24 Liberators. The bomb group had arrived on the island in January and immediately began flying missions to destroy Japanese air bases in the Marshalls.

Now Nanumea was under siege. Beginning at 1030 hours, the island was increasingly lashed by high winds and torrential rains that cut visibility down to what was known as an "instrument level," meaning that it would be impossible to fly using Visual Flight Rules (VFR). The weather grew worse as noon approached.

"Cyclones generally don't form within three or four degrees of the equator, said Barnes. "Nanumea is at five degrees south latitude.

The cyclone [eye] may have been west-southwest of Nanumea, moving east, so its northern quadrant would lash at the island."

This describes exactly what was happening at Nanumea after 1030 hours. While they were not hit by the main force of the cyclone, the wind and rain coupled with near-zero visibility would have been enough to close the base for several hours.

In the Quonset hut that served as the 17th Headquarters squadron operations post, the barometer was falling alarmingly. The group commander, Lieutenant Colonel John F. Payne, who had been told by the base aerological officer of the approaching storm had already ordered the airfield to be shut down. Payne was a career US Army Air Force officer who took care of his base, planes, and crews. By 1130 hours, trucks had been driven into hangars, fuel pipes were sealed, and loose gear was stowed. The first harbingers of what was to come were the increasing swells coming in from the west. By 1200 hours, the distant cyclone was already driving huge waves onto the narrow beaches. Palm trees swayed, and their fronds whipped and snapped in the wind.

Payne checked the air operations schedule to find out if any planes were due to land at Nanumea. None were on the list because air operations at Hawkins Field had not informed them of VMF-422's impending arrival. Standard operating procedure was to broadcast a warning that the airfield was being shut down and for all nearby aircraft to steer clear or return to their own base. VMF-422 was listening in on 6970 kilocycles, but they apparently never heard this broadcast. This may have been due to interference from the storm, or the squadron was not close enough to pick it up. In either case, the problem of voice radio communication would soon make a bad situation far worse.

The sequence and timing of events over the next six hours has been extrapolated from personal accounts, interviews, transcripts, exhibits, and the official squadron history. The most accurate chronology is taken from the transcript and exhibits of the Naval Board of Inquiry held from 27 January to 10 February, but all times given must be considered approximate. As any experienced police investigator knows, eyewitness testimony is highly subjective and often inaccurate. No two witnesses to the same event will agree. It is up to the investigator to piece together the chronology based on fact and reason. This is what the author has attempted to do here.

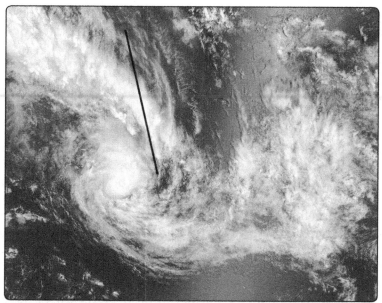

A satellite image of Tropical Cyclone Haley in February 2013. Note the rain bands arcing away from the revolving eye wall. They were often a hundred miles in length. (Courtesy Professor Gary Barnes, University of Hawaii, Atmospheric Sciences Department.)

At approximately 1205 hours, both Captain Jeans and Captain Hughes announced they had the Nanumea radio range and recommended a course change to starboard. Major MacLaughlin agreed and the squadron turned to 180 degrees, directly south.

VMF-422 was half an hour from Nanumea when MacLaughlin and the other lead pilots first noticed a wispy lacework of high-altitude cirrus and stratus clouds ahead of them, looking like thin white fingers reaching into the heavens.

"It looked like a long, curving line of gray clouds," recalled Syrkin. "It seemed to stretch in an arc from the west all the way down to the southeast. I really didn't know what it was. I wasn't in the least bit worried, not then. I'd flown through cloud banks before."

Hansen wasn't overly concerned. "It was really impressive to look at."

Below, the lazy low waves pushed by the trade winds had given way to long deep swells that seemed to be running away from the distant tempest. As they drew closer, the cloud rose ever higher.

Sterling Price described it as being "like a solid curtain. I mean it was *black*, and as wide as you could see and as high as you could see."

Jeans later said, "My impression was we would have scattered showers all over the horizon but nothing covering a large area like we ran into."

They had been briefed about rain squalls and showers, but this was clearly no local rain squall. Then, as if they had passed through an invisible boundary, the Buccaneers suddenly found themselves fighting to keep formation. The wind came from the west and forced them to struggle against the gusts hammering at their Corsairs. Then they passed through zones of wind-whipped rain. Syrkin recalled thinking, "Goddamn, what in hell am I doing here? The wind just kept battering at my controls so I was nearly standing on my right rudder pedal to keep flying straight. It was like riding a bucking bronco."

"We were just being slammed," Curly Lehnert said. "I had a hell of a time keeping my place in formation. It only got worse the closer we came to that storm."

It was 1220 hours. The water that had been so blue and placid below their wings turned a dark gunmetal gray. Whitecaps and long beards of spray crested the increasingly turbulent sea. Along the line where the boiling clouds met the sea was a foaming, heaving mass of gray and green waves. The winds battering them increased in velocity. This prompted MacLaughlin to order a change in altitude to five thousand feet. Even as the Corsairs climbed, there seemed to be no end to the soaring wall of dark cloud ahead. The violent west wind abated slightly, so they were able to maintain formation. The view outside their canopies was totally dominated by the immense wall of angry gray thunderheads. During advanced flight training, aviators were given little practical information on tropical storms and typhoons. The rule of thumb was "if you see one ahead of you, turn back."

· CHAPTER 9 ·

IN THE BELLY OF THE BEAST

Major John MacLaughlin was faced with a true dilemma. He could turn the squadron around and head back to Tarawa. They had enough fuel, but this would make him look ineffectual in the eyes of his superiors if he ran from bad weather and failed to accomplish his mission. Although Major John S. MacLaughlin was far from a vain officer who put his career ahead of the lives of his men, he was not going to turn back unless it grew too hazardous.

The second choice was to attempt to fly around the storm, which he assumed was a front or line squall. This option was full of unknown factors, such as how far the storm extended. They might well run short of or even out of fuel trying to find their way around the rainstorm. The only other choice, which he discussed with Jeans and Hughes, was to fly directly into the storm and try to find their destination. Nanumea, according to Captain Jeans was close, less than sixty miles, and on the other side of the storm front. Their frequent use of the word "front" demonstrated that the marines were completely ignorant of what they were really facing. Even Hughes, who recognized the cloud bank as a tropical storm did not realize that it was in fact a fully developed cyclone of great size and strength. After all, there was no mention of any major storm on the latest weather report.

Time was growing critical. Every mile south was a mile farther from Tarawa and a mile closer to Nanumea and Funafuti.

MacLaughlin, for his part, may have recalled what Captain Campbell had told him about not attempting to fly under a storm, since the cloud bank often descended all the way to the surface of the sea. His first decision was to climb and get over the storm.

But it quickly grew apparent that it would be impossible to fly over the storm.

"Prior to the war," Professor Barnes commented, "it was believed by some that cyclones only reached to about five thousand feet. But in reality, they peaked at fifty thousand feet or more."

Captain Charley Hughes, who was following the Nanumea radio range as they entered the cyclone. (Photo courtesy Andrew Syrkin.)

In a 1985 magazine interview, Charley Hughes stated, "Mac asked me what I thought about flying over what was now a solid wall from horizon to horizon. I told him we could never climb over the tops above forty thousand feet. We'd better go under. He replied that he agreed and *we* started an on-course descent. As we approached the front, I tuned in the Nanumea radio range and found we were on the left edge of the beam. I closed my chart board, stowed it, and started worrying about getting twenty-three fighters into a strange field in that kind of rain without losing half of them."

MacLaughlin began trying to reach Nanumea on 6970 kilocycles. But his calls went unanswered. As MacLaughlin repeatedly called for assistance, no one heard him but his own pilots.

Hughes said, "We were told to use a VHF frequency [6970] which Nanumea and Funafuti monitored, but it turned out that this frequency was monitored only when they were notified that it should be used. Of course, as we learned later, no one told Nanumea we were coming."

Then MacLaughlin called on the squadron frequency of 6210 kilocycles, "Buccaneer Lead to Buccaneer Flight, we are going to enter the storm front and try to get beneath it. Stay tucked in close. It will be dark in there."

John Hansen recalled that transmission. "The skipper was doing the only thing he could. We had to find Nanumea. He was in command and we followed him. The other fellows acknowledged the order, but it was getting pretty hard to hear on the VHF radios. There was a lot of static. I tried to tune it in without much luck. I sometimes heard only bits and pieces of words." It was apparent that the storm was beginning to play havoc with their radios.

Having no other choice, the Flying Buccaneers gripped their controls and drove into the huge mass as it welcomed them into its malevolent embrace. One by one the Corsairs disappeared like tiny insects into the storm. Far above, the sun was a pale disk of yellow-white, surrounded by a thin halo of water vapor. Then, as if someone had turned off a switch, the cold sun winked out. The clear blue world of sky and sun turned into a black hell. It was 1218 hours.

If the reader were to visualize a circular spiral with a hole in the center and a dozen long streamers peeling back from a rotating center, it will illustrate the structure of a Pacific cyclone. The "hole" is the eye, and the disk surrounding it is the eye wall. As it rotates clockwise, the arms of the pinwheel likewise turn. For a large cyclone, these arms, also called rain bands, can be a hundred miles in length and ten to fifteen miles thick. VMF-422's course was taking them into the storm at an oblique angle rather than directly into it. In other words, they did not penetrate the main storm perpendicularly, instead flying into and along the length of one or more of the arms.

Barnes agrees that this is likely to be what happened and helps explain what the marines found themselves in. How big the cyclone was is a matter of speculation. According to Professor Barnes, the region of gale force winds often grew to more than two hundred miles in diameter. The distance between Nanumea and Funafuti is 376 miles. If we accept the two-hundred-mile diameter benchmark, the storm could easily move eastward between the two main islands with more than 150 miles to spare. Weather reports from Nanumea show that the storm's northern edge passed almost over the island, while Nukufetau, two hundred miles to the south, and Funafuti only experienced rain squalls and high winds.

The point where the marines entered the storm was likely on the northeastern quadrant, where the violent winds moved almost due south. From that moment, they were virtually at the capricious mercy of a Pacific cyclone.

Yet the worst part of their ordeal was still to come.

"I thought it had been hard to fly straight before we flew into that monster," said Syrkin. "But this was a lot worse. My stick and rudder pedals felt as if they were alive. I looked outside my canopy at the other planes. They were twisting and leaping like broncos."

Syrkin wasn't alone. Hansen, Lehnert, and Gunderson all recalled experiencing the same thing. Visibility was almost zero as they fought their way down through a boiling dark gray world. Then they entered a zone of torrential rain. Solid sheets of water hammered on the Corsairs as they fought through the wind. In an instant, the view outside Syrkin's windshield turned to a spattering wet blur. He squinted, but could see nothing ahead but water.

"It looked like someone was aiming a fire hose at me." Syrkin snapped his head back and forth to see outside. The world beyond his canopy was all roiling black clouds and wind-driven rain. His left wingtip was just barely in sight. "The white star looked like it was illuminated by a 15-watt bulb."

Such conditions, according to Barnes, are common in large Pacific cyclones. "The gale-force rain is often strong enough to strip paint off the wings of a plane."

Hurricane Irma, which savaged Florida and the Caribbean in September 2017, had sustained winds of over 150 knots, which, according to the Saffir-Simpson Scale, made it a Category Five hurricane. The National Hurricane Center in Miami, Florida calls any storm with sustained winds of more than 130 knots a "Major Hurricane."

Syrkin managed to catch sight of Lieutenant Don Walker's right wing in the distance, but to his own right, there was no sign of Abe Lincoln or the rest of his division.

The radio voices of the pilots were nearly indistinguishable.

At this point Price's compass spun out of control. "It spun like a top," he said. "I couldn't read it. I had no idea which way we were going."

While there would be few electrical disturbances in a cyclone, it is possible that the driving rain leaked into Price's wiring and caused a short circuit.

This probably also gave Tex Watson a far worse problem to deal with: fire.

"Here I was," he said in his slow drawl, "a country boy right off the plains from west Texas, flying a brand-new Corsair over the dark, deep Pacific Ocean. Lost. We had been in this driving rain storm, I guess it was a hurricane, and all at once I smelled smoke. I could smell melted Bakelite, and that was an indication that my radios were burning. I turned them off and the smoke was getting pretty bad, so I cracked the hood and the smoke cleared. When

*Lieutenant Royce "Tex" Watson had serious radio
problems in the storm. (Photo courtesy Andrew Syrkin.)*

you're flying at two hundred knots, that rain that comes in really
smarts. In a burning aircraft, lost in that storm, that was the most
terrifying moment in my entire life."

The fire soon died out and he was able to restart his radio.

The marines flashed their navigation lights to help each other
stay in formation, but it was a losing battle. The noise of the battering rain on Curly Lehnert's airframe was loud enough to drown out
the engine. "I began to think, 'Oh, hell, what if all that water snuffs
out the engine?'"

This became a serious concern for Chris Lauesen, flying as section leader behind MacLaughlin. He called to say his engine was
running very rough. His voice came through the static, saying that
he was losing manifold pressure and power. He tried closing the
cowl flaps to cut down the rain, but his engine was still cutting out.

Jules Flood, the former race car driver and the best natural mechanic in VMF-422 suggested Lauesen should set his fuel mixture

to "auto rich." This would help the engine burn better. It took Flood several tries to make himself understood. Lauesen said that the fix helped, but it also meant his engine would be burning fuel at a furious rate.

Then at around 1230, the rain slackened off, and as if a heavy blanket was being lifted, the boiling clouds rose above them. The Corsairs had broken through the cloud base. Below, the ocean's surface looked like something out of a Hollywood movie. The waves were like charging dark green mountain ranges, nearly fifty feet high and capped in plumes of white, wind-driven spray. Overhead the roiling cloud layer hung like a solid ceiling.

They had been within the storm for about eighteen minutes, but Jeans was sure it had been over an hour, an example of how rational people can have their time perceptions distorted in a crisis.

The three groups were no longer in a tight formation. According to Curly Lehnert, who was leading the last division in Green Flight far to the rear, MacLaughlin's Red Flight was far ahead with Gold Flight still trailing on the right. Green Flight was overlapping Gold Flight's left rear by a few hundred feet. The lead planes were highest, with the following divisions and sections at progressively lower altitudes. Lehnert said that his plane was picking up spray from the waves right under him.

Hansen said, "My altimeter read 190 feet. That cloud deck was fifty feet over my head and the ocean was only one hundred and fifty feet under me."

Syrkin had an even more harrowing memory. "When we came out under the storm I saw that my instruments read two hundred feet *below* sea level. I sure wasn't going to go any lower than that."

The fact that the base of the cloud layer was as low as 250 feet from the ocean bears consideration. Professor Barnes said, "For a cloud base to be that low, which is very rare, you need cooler air and a lot of moisture. They were probably within seventy-five miles of the storm center, given the very low cloud base."

The Buccaneers were on a course of 135 degrees, or southeast. Ironically, they were almost on top of their destination, but totally unable to see it. In addition, the closer a plane is to a radio range transmitter, the harder it is to line up a bearing. It was literally a case of not being able to see the forest for the trees.

Jeans and Hughes, who had been watching the radio range, were very busy keeping formation as they stayed with their squadron commander.

"We had broken out of the storm finally after going through several quadrants of the beam," Hughes recalled later. "I got lost entirely and had to work the beam problem from scratch in order to become oriented."

Meanwhile, on Nanumea the storm continued to lash at the base. In the radio room, the operators peered into the small round screens of the SCR-270 radar sets. Since 1229 they had been watching a series of contacts, the first of which was plotted at 000 degrees, or directly north of the island at nineteen miles. They followed the contact as it moved south along a track to the east. At that moment VMF-422 was deep into the storm, still descending from five thousand feet.

As noted, Nanumea had not been sent a copy of the departure report from Lieutenant Sandlin, and it was assumed the unidentified contacts were B-24 bombers headed to Funafuti.

From 1229 to 1242, the radar operator estimated that the target was moving southeast "pretty fast," which again supported the idea that they were B-24s. This seemingly lax attitude was not unusual under the circumstances. They had no way of knowing that a disaster was in the making.

At 1242, the contact faded. At that moment VMF-422 was breaking out of the base of the cyclone. The radar used in World War II was highly susceptible to atmospheric interference from rain and thick clouds. Once the marines reached 250 feet, they were too low for the radar to detect in the storm.

A few minutes after emerging from the clouds, MacLaughlin made a sudden and unexpected ninety-degree turn to port, taking up a rough heading to the northeast. Exactly why he did this can never be certain, but a ninety-degree turn was just what a pilot would make when attempting to locate one of the legs of a radio range.

MacLaughlin would not have made such a radical course change without announcing it beforehand, but no one in VMF-422 ever heard a word over the radio. In any case, his sudden maneuver wreaked havoc on the formation.

Hughes stated, "My division was following MacLaughlin's lead division. He suddenly went into a left bank of about forty-five degrees. He continued to turn in that fashion. Captain Jeans got caught in there and had to take his flight right through my division. I pulled away out to the side to give him room and never did get

Captain John Rogers was among the group separated from the main formation after emerging from the bottom of the storm. (Photo courtesy Andrew Syrkin.)

close to MacLaughlin's plane again as Jeans' plane was between me and the major. Rogers was flying on me, so when I pulled up, he had to pull up also. Apparently he lost contact at this time and climbed to get clear of the formation."

The consequences of this unexpected turn were deadly. Syrkin, leading the second division in Gold Flight, saw the black shape of Rogers's Corsair suddenly climb and vanish. Jake Wilson, John Hansen, and Don Walker went with Gold Leader. Syrkin, Abe Lincoln, Chick Whalen, and Tex Watson, being farther back, were able to stay clear of the melee and managed to follow MacLaughlin and Hughes.

"I called Rogers several times," said Syrkin. "But all I heard was static. They were gone, vanished into the storm, just like that."

In the transcript of a 1980 oral history for the Defense Department, retired Colonel John Hansen described what happened. "We went down to about two hundred feet over the water, continued on course for a while until, what would've been our arrival time at Nanumea. Then Major MacLaughlin appeared to start searching for the island. He started making turns at low altitude with the twenty-three airplanes. That's when everything began to come apart. I don't know, of course, what his thought might have been. Whether he had his navigation facilities going or any kind of a fix, I don't know. The flight began to come apart when he started making the turns. When you have a large number of airplanes, to make a turn, even at [high] altitude you just slide. You try not to advance throttle just to stay in position on the outside of a turn. You just slide to the inside, and it requires very little throttle change to maintain your position. But at two hundred feet, and it raining very hard, it was very difficult to stay in position. Consequently, the pilots were going full throttle to stay on the outside and going completely power off to stay on the inside and we just couldn't stay in formation."

When asked by the interviewer if the other planes were still in visual contact, Hansen replied, "Nah, you couldn't see all the airplanes in the flight. You could see the ones, maybe the three or four that you were with, and you just had to stay with your leader and hope that he was staying with his own leader."

Less than three minutes after his first turn, MacLaughlin banked sharply to the right, resuming the original heading. Again, the marines struggled to stay with him.

According to the survivors, it was roughly 1240 hours when they broke out of the storm wall into relatively clear skies. The seas below were still being whipped and churned by the wind and about a thousand feet overhead hung a solid layer of overcast. But at least they were out of the storm... or so the marines believed.

As mentioned earlier, they were likely flying obliquely through one or more of the outer spiral arms or rain bands of the cyclone. What they found themselves in may have been the "clear" region between two of these. Ahead was another arm and beyond that, probably another. Each was as deadly as the first. There is no way to be absolutely certain, but the facts and observations support such a conclusion.

Captain Rex Jeans called for the pilots to report in. It was then that the full scope of the evolving disaster became clear.

Captain John Rogers and Lieutenants John Hansen, Jake Wilson, Don Walker, Earl Thompson, and Bob Moran failed to check in. The squadron had entered the storm with twenty-three pilots. Six were now missing.

Hopes were suddenly raised when Don Walker called in. He said that he was alone but had John Hansen on another frequency. Hansen was unable to get through on 6970 and was asking for assistance.

Jeans asked where they were. Walker explained that he, Hansen, and Jake Wilson had followed Rogers up and re-entered the cloud base. They had climbed in a desperate attempt to get out of the storm. They quickly lost sight of each other.

"My Flight Leader, Captain John Rogers, his wingman, (Don Wilson) and me lost the formation right away," said Hansen. "Rogers did not maintain his contact. The three of us headed up in a climb. We lost Wilson somewhere around probably five thousand to seven thousand feet in this climb when he fell out of the formation. I stayed with Rogers up to somewhere around ten or eleven thousand feet, and I lost him. I did continue on up to somewhere in the neighborhood of thirteen thousand feet without climbing on top. I could hear some of the conversation still going on. I could tell they hadn't found the island and that most of the planes were still together down there somewhere."

When Hansen had broken out of the cloud at thirteen thousand feet he found himself all alone. He tried calling on 6970. When it became apparent that frequency was unable to penetrate the thousands of feet of cloud below him, he tried calling on 6210. This time he was lucky and reached Don Walker, who was also alone. Walker, in turn had called Jeans.

Hansen asked for the Funafuti radio range, which Jeans passed on to him via Walker, who was then able to rejoin the main formation. The good news was that two of the six lost pilots were accounted for, but Rogers, Thompson, Wilson, and Moran were missing.

CHAPTER 10

THE FIRST TO FALL

The marines now faced a new problem. They had almost certainly passed Nanumea. The problem was: by how much and in what direction? Going back the way they came was clearly out of the question. With no visual references, such as the sun, it was impossible to determine their location. World War II fighter pilots were not given extensive training in Instrument Flying Rules (IFR). While they could take off, fly, and even land on instruments, the challenges of long-range instrument navigation posed real difficulties. For VMF-422, the presence of a major tropical cyclone was almost a quantum leap into the unknown.

They were in a loose formation where orphans from divisions and sections latched onto whomever was closest. Thus, Lieutenants John Lincoln and Jules Flood found themselves flying on MacLaughlin's starboard wing.

At 1240 hours, Jeans, who was on the far left, called to say he saw something on the water that might have been an island.

"He said it was off to port, about ten miles away," said Price, who was near Jeans. "I looked down but there was just too much haze. We were in the open but that big storm front was right behind us and curved south on our port side."

A few minutes later Jeans called again to say he saw three small vessels, which he quickly identified as navy landing craft. He also spotted a larger vessel, possibly a transport, tied to a dock or pier, but he was unable to see the island itself because of the clouds passing over it.

Jeans said he was sure it was Nui Atoll. While it was the first solid land they had seen since entering the cyclone, it was not a haven for them. Nui had no airfield. A landing there would cause the loss of or at least damage to eighteen brand-new Corsairs. That would mean a Board of Inquiry at the very least.

Although their situation was serious, it was not yet grave. They weren't in any immediate danger. As long as they had fuel to reach their destination, there was no reason to ditch. And if, in fact, the island had been Nui, then they had already covered,

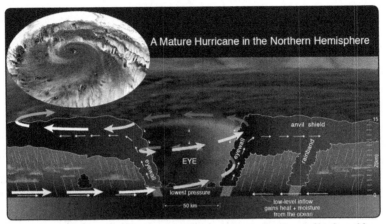

A lateral diagram of a typical Pacific cyclone, showing regions of high and low pressure. (Courtesy Professor Gary Barnes, University of Hawaii, Atmospheric Sciences Department.)

albeit unintentionally, 128 miles, or a third of the distance between Nanumea and Funafuti.

This seems extreme, but Professor Gary Barnes made it clear that once the Corsairs entered the cyclone they could easily have been pushed a hundred miles south. "At an airspeed of two hundred knots, or roughly one hundred yards per second, even a fifty-knot tailwind would add fifty yards per second to that speed. But I'm sure faulty navigation was also a factor."

They first entered the cyclone at 1220 and emerged twenty minutes later, then another five minutes passed until Jeans saw the island. In that time, they apparently traveled about 140 miles at approximately 320 knots, almost double their indicated airspeed. Again, there is no way to confirm this. The visual evidence that Jeans saw landing craft and a dock on the island supports the assumption that they had reached Nui Atoll.

MacLaughlin, whose radio had been unusually quiet up to this point, now called in. He had just gotten the Funafuti radio range and would take them in. That was welcome news. With any luck, the missing pilots would soon join up and the Buccaneers could continue to Funafuti, a bit wiser but no worse for the wear.

As mentioned, the author made use of the official squadron history, compiled by Major Elmer Wrenn in 1945. While helpful, the document offered an often contradictory note in both detail and chronology. "At 1245 hours, Major MacLaughlin radioed that he had made contact with the Funafuti beam and that they would proceed there. He also informed the pilots that they were between Nanumea and Funafuti. As the storm increased in violence, the flight again reported navigational difficulty."

There are three inconsistencies in this. The time of 1245 hours was little more than five minutes after they had emerged from the storm base and just about the time they reached the relatively clear zone. During this time they were not subject to the fury of the rain and wind. MacLaughlin could not have been able to determine their location, only the approximate direction to Funafuti. In order to determine their position, he would also have had to be on the Nanumea radio range, which was not the case. Lastly, there is no mention of the island Jeans had seen.

To add more confusion to the issue, Charley Hughes later made an extraordinary statement regarding the point when they first emerged from the storm. "On our starboard side there were two ships anchored and three boats. We were at Nanumea. I anticipated circling until the island cleared and then landing. Instead, we flew past the ships, turned to port and flew off on a southerly heading. In about twenty minutes we flew over an atoll."

Hughes' statement, while sincere, must be taken with a grain of salt. He gives the impression that they emerged from the storm flying southwest, and then turned to port, or south. He said the first island was Nanumea. It is true that it would indeed be on their starboard side and very close. One of the early radar plots on Nanumea had a contact within nineteen miles to the northeast, moving south.

Yet even in his testimony to the Board of Inquiry, Hughes never mentioned seeing this island, nor did he say he had seen Nanumea after emerging from the storm. The interview in which he made this statement took place more than forty years after the fact, and Hughes, then in his mid-sixties, could have been confused. He never referred to this first island in any official account during the war. Still it is intriguing, and if true, the mysterious island, to use a Jules Verne title, might have been their goal, Nanumea. We will never know for sure, and the enigma will remain in the growing list of peculiarities of the Flintlock Disaster.

Syrkin said, "We passed over Nui Island but it had no landing field. Mac indicated that he now had his bearings and he was setting a course directly for Funafuti."

"I heard Mac's orders," said Lehnert. "I didn't question them, but I sure felt kind of lonely when that little island disappeared behind us."

A few minutes later their luck took a turn for the worse. Lieutenant Chris Lauesen, the blond Chicago athlete who had enjoyed playing sports with Ken Gunderson, called in to say his engine had just cut out. He had tried to restart, but it was soon apparent that whatever had caused problems in the storm had killed his engine. Lauesen was about to ditch his new Corsair in the heaving seas below.

The official history has this occurring at 1235 hours, but based on survivor accounts, it was closer to 1250. In other words, it claims that Lauesen's engine died before they even emerged from the storm, which was clearly not the case. Also, it occurred only after they passed the island.

"I was hanging on to the rear of the formation when Chris called his Mayday," said Lehnert. "I felt totally helpless. We were not out of the storm by a long shot. I watched as his plane fell away from the formation and dropped towards the ocean."

First Lieutenant Ken Gunderson, still holding position as Lauesen's wingman, said, "Chris was a fellow Swede. He was my best friend. I stayed with him as he slid down. We were at one thousand feet, just below the overcast. Chris had his canopy open and I saw him moving around in the cockpit. But it was frustrating as hell to just watch him go down like that. I heard the skipper calling on the radio of our position, but I knew that was no help. Other than that little island about thirty miles back we had no idea where we were."

Lehnert had a similar opinion. "We were told that if any of us had to go down, the rest would plot the location on our plotting boards and report it to the base. But that presupposes that a base would be listening in on the standard frequency, which they were not."

Lauesen kept up a running dialogue as his plane fell helplessly towards the heaving gray-green waves. "I've got my harness as tight as it will go," he said. Then with a terrifying roar that was instantly cut off, the transmission ended.

"His plane stabbed right into a huge wave like an arrow," said Gunderson. "One second he hit with this big white splash, the next second he was gone. Just like that."

Gunderson circled the spot where his leader had gone in, but for several moments there was no sign of Chris Lauesen. "I was flying right over the spot and I kept waiting for him to pop out of the water with his life raft."

Lieutenant Chris Lauesen was forced to ditch after his engine cut out in the storm. (Photo courtesy Andrew Syrkin.)

The squadron circled back to add their eyes to the search for their downed friend. Then Gunderson called, "I see him! He's up. There, he's waving. Chris is okay."

Ordered by MacLaughlin to form up, Gunderson waggled his wings and took his place in the formation as it continued south.

Lehnert, because of his slot far at the rear, was still flying north as he passed over the swimming man. He saw what Gunderson hadn't. Lauesen had failed to retrieve his life raft when the Corsair sank. He released his dye marker and a spreading yellow-green stain began to suffuse the water around him. His only salvation, and a fragile one at that was his Mae West life preserver. In those mountainous seas, he had virtually no chance of surviving.

"He looked so small against that vast surface," said Lehnert, recalling the scene seventy years later. "He disappeared for a moment, and then re-emerged on the other side of the wave. Then he was deep in a valley between huge crests. I called Mac and said

Far to the south of where VMF-422 was struggling for their lives, the tiny atoll of Funafuti lay in clear weather. The navy and army personnel there were unaware that the squadron was coming. (Official U.S. Navy photo.)

that we had to stay with him. But Mac nixed that and said we had to move on. They would notify Air-Sea Rescue of Chris' location."

This must have been the supreme irony for the pilots who had witnessed General Merritt's tirade on Tarawa. The Air-Sea Rescue squadrons in the Gilberts and Ellice Islands were under his command.

Lehnert refused to give up. "You mean we're just going to leave him?" With no other choice the marines flew south, now down to seventeen pilots. Worse was to come.

CHAPTER 11

LOST

A gloom that had little to do with the weather settled into the Flying Buccaneers as they flew south. MacLaughlin was far ahead, driving towards the distant goal of Funafuti and safety. Six of their own had been left behind, soon to become seven.

Still circling the struggling form of Chris Lauesen, Curly Lehnert came to a decision. "I wasn't going to leave Chris behind. I don't remember if I said anything in the radio but I must have. I guess what I did could be considered violating orders, or insubordination, but I didn't worry about that for a second."

In moments, Curly was all alone in the sky. He was determined to stay with Lauesen until rescue planes or boats arrived. If he was lucky, he could rejoin the squadron or at the very least, ditch by the rescue craft or fly to Nui and ditch there.

First Lieutenant Robert "Curly" Lehnert of New York was in a race against time and the elements. He was determined to win and if at all possible, save Lauesen.

Circling at five hundred feet, he kept an eye on the tiny figure of his squadron mate. His left wingtip was always pointed at Lauesen. Checking his fuel and instruments, he guessed he had nearly three hours of fuel left, and the big Pratt & Whitney R-2800 was running perfectly. Every thirty minutes, he climbed to eight thousand feet to broadcast his estimated position and situation. Sooner or later the base at Nanumea would pick up his transmissions. He'd stay as long as it took.

"I did get in touch with Rocky Base, but I did not know who they were because we did not have that on our list of call signs. I tried to tell them my position but they never seemed to get me on their radar."

If indeed Lehnert was some thirty to fifty miles south of Nui, he was far out of radar range of Nanumea. As he maintained his lonely and frustrating vigil, Curly was soon faced with an even more serious problem. They had, for a time, managed to outrun the storm, but it was still coming, approaching with a slow, relentless menace like a moving mountain of angry wind and torrential rain. He

*The air base at Nanumea in 1944. The planes in the distance are single-engine
scout planes attached to the 17th Headquarters Squadron. (Official U.S. Navy
photo.)*

described it as being surrounded by solid cloud banks in all directions. Time would run out before his fuel.

"Chris waved to let me know he was still alive and kicking. I
knew he couldn't last forever,"

Sometime after 1430 hours, Lehnert saw the boiling wall of
clouds moving closer from the northwest. Once it overtook him, he
would not be able to see Lauesen. Even worse, he would himself be
in great danger, and no one knew where he was.

No one knows how long it was before Lehnert's absence was
noticed as the sixteen remaining marines continued south. They
quickly found their route blocked by another storm front. They had
no other option but to go through it. With MacLaughlin leading,
they drove into it. As before, the sun disappeared and they found
themselves in a chaotic world of roiling gray clouds and violent
winds. They struggled to stay in visual contact but it was a losing
battle.

The official VMF-422 history states "Some elements of the formation were compelled to fly full throttle to maintain contact with
the flight leaders as the latter maintained normal cruising speed.
However, the density and violence of the storm prevented flying

standard formation, resulting in maneuvers at full throttle one instant and retarded throttle the next. Several pilots soon reported being low on fuel. Those who maintained good formation had sufficient gas to have possibly reached Funafuti."

That second storm front was a watershed moment in the odyssey of VMF-422. Prior to entering it, they had been reasonably sure of finding and landing on Funafuti, but it was increasingly obvious to Jeans that their chances of reaching safety were quickly evaporating. For the first time, their survival was in doubt.

At that point, around 1300 hours, MacLaughlin lost the Funafuti radio beam. This was no small concern, but the reason is unclear even to this day. In the John Coleman video, Sterling Price said that the transmitters on Funafuti had been turned off for maintenance. "No one had told them we were coming. They didn't think anyone was up there during this storm. They had turned it on, then did some calibration and turned it off."

Price, speaking from the hindsight of nearly fifty years, believed this to be true. However, there are two reasons to doubt it. First, the base at Funafuti, not being in the path of the storm, would not likely have turned off their LFR transmitters. Patrol aircraft and transports were always coming and going. Second, as will be seen, the fact that John Hansen did catch the Funafuti radio range and followed it in, landing at about 1430 hours, proves that the transmitters were operating. It is more likely that MacLaughlin lost the beam in the storm or that it had been interrupted in some way.

Captain Jeans tried to call Major MacLaughlin. On this point, the squadron history states: "Failing to contact the Commanding Officer by radio, Captain Jeans flew across his [MacLaughlin's] bow and secured the Major's attention. In the ensuing transmission, it was decided that Captain Jeans would lead the flight back to Nui, which had been previously sighted. At this time the flight was on a heading of 180 degrees and indicating 180 knots."

The extreme measures Jeans had to make to get his commander's attention—he even fired his guns—dramatically illustrates how bad their radio reception had become.

Syrkin said, "Rex suggested we should go back. We had no idea how far or in what direction the storm was pushing us. We could have been far east of Nui and headed for the empty ocean."

MacLaughlin agreed that Jeans, who said he had the course back to the island, should take over and lead the squadron. This was a very serious decision.

For a squadron commander to willingly turn over control of his unit was considered a court martial offense. There is still a debate among interested historians as to whether Major MacLaughlin actually meant to turn over command to his executive officer or if he was merely telling Jeans to lead the squadron back to Nui. We will never know.

Jeans ordered the squadron to make a 180-degree turn to port, but the intermittent radio reception forced him to repeat the call several times before the other pilots acknowledged the order. For several minutes, they flew on the new heading of 005, looking for the open air beyond the storm front. This time they were bucking severe headwinds and progress was slow. Jeans called for a forty-five-degree turn to the left onto a heading of 320. At last the marines emerged from the storm. It was just as before, with wind-whipped clouds and spray over a heaving grey sea.

Jeans and Hughes had begun to reconsolidate the formation when they discovered that MacLaughlin was not among them. Also missing were John Lincoln and Jules Flood.

Hughes called their commander, but there was no reply on either 6970 or 6210 kilocycles.

A minute later Lincoln came on the air. He and Flood had turned and were coming back. But Major MacLaughlin was not with them.

Lincoln later explained what had happened back in the storm. He and Flood were flying on MacLaughlin's starboard wing when Jeans' order came over the radio. The three Corsairs turned back to the north.

But when Jeans made the forty-five-degree turn, MacLaughlin did not follow. With Lincoln and Flood hanging on his wing, he flew on, widening the distance between them and the larger group.

For the rest of his life, John Lincoln would be unable to forget what he had seen. "I looked over at Mac. He was staring straight ahead, as if unaware of anything around him. He flew straight on as if in a trance. I tried to stay with him. He was just off my left wing. I flew as close as I dared. He had a hand on his earphones. It looked like he was trying to hear something and just stared straight ahead. I waved, waggled my wings, and even fired my guns. He never even looked in my direction. I didn't know what else to do. Flood and I turned and went after the others. I never saw Mac again."

Again, the official history's version only adds to the mystery. "As the flight circled in and out of rain squalls, Major MacLaughlin was observed to fly a course tangent to the rest of the flight. Lieutenants J. C. Flood and J. W. Lincoln, who had been flying wing on him, climbed to sixteen thousand feet in an effort to keep both the major and the flight in view, but he disappeared in the thick overcast and was not sighted again."

The last statement left the impression that the three pilots were flying in the clear, as Lincoln and Flood climbed to sixteen thousand feet in an effort to keep both MacLaughlin and the main group in view. Actually their climb was ordered by Jeans some time later, and it was to turn on their emergency IFF, not to keep MacLaughlin in sight.

As described by Lincoln, MacLaughlin simply failed to make the forty-five-degree turn and flew into oblivion.

Whatever the exact details, MacLaughlin's loss was a terrible blow to the marines' morale. Now eight men were missing, a third of the number that had left Tarawa on that warm sunny morning less than six hours before.

To lose their commander under such conditions was tantamount to a crushing defeat in battle. Even as they tried to come to grips with the situation, it was obvious to all that they were in grave danger.

The command of VMF-422 now rested on the shoulders of Captain Cloyd Rex Jeans, a twenty-five-year-old career marine aviator from Joplin, Missouri.

Jeans' first order was to reconsolidate the formation. This turned out to be difficult as they fought their way north against the cyclone's winds. They flew at five hundred feet at 180 knots to conserve fuel. Other than the solid overcast, the air was relatively clear, but long after Jeans had calculated that they should have reached Nui there was no sign of the island.

"We flew back and forth around where Rex said Nui should be," recalled Syrkin, who was acting as Gold Flight Leader. "But that damned island was nowhere to be seen. We just didn't know where the hell we were."

The squadron history says, "Captain Jeans then climbed to twelve thousand feet, making square searches. Two pilots were instructed to climb to seventeen thousand feet and do the same but no bearing could be had."

This may be related to what Price said about the radio range being turned off, but the absence of data is not conclusive.

Then someone, possibly Jeans—although he never admitted it – called on the radio and asked, "Does anyone have any suggestions?"

Tex Watson, whose radio was again working, heard this question. "Then someone said, 'Yeah, let's turn east. That's always lucky.' I knew definitely that we were lost."

Instead Jeans ordered Lincoln and Flood to climb to sixteen thousand feet and turn on their emergency IFF transmitters. This was done around 1255.

On Nanumea, the radar operators had been following, with little success or comprehension, several widely scattered contacts. They had no idea who was out there in that storm. Between 1258 and 1340 hours, at least four separate contacts and IFF signals appeared on the screens, all located northeast to east of the island. By 1340, they all disappeared.

The first was an emergency IFF signal picked up at 070 degrees, distance forty-five miles, about east-northeast of the island.

The contacts were almost certainly the planes separated from the main formation under the storm: Rogers, Thompson, Moran, or Wilson. What can be certain is that the IFF signals were not from Lincoln or Flood, who were out of range far to the south beyond Nui Atoll.

But there was one contact that appeared to be at least eighty miles south of Nanumea, which drew their attention.

Upon first receiving the emergency signal, Colonel Payne ordered the radio operators to make every effort to contact the aircraft. He still did not know who they were, but they were in trouble. The radio operators went from channel to channel trying to contact the planes. But the same poor radio reception that had plagued the marines wreaked havoc on their own radios. That changed at 1418 hours when they made voice radio contact with one of the pilots.

Jeans was leading his men north, driving hard towards Nui, when shortly after 1440 hours a voice broke in on the squadron frequency. Lieutenant Robert "Tiger" Moran had been separated from the formation during the confused maneuvers under the first storm front. He had been missing for two hours. The aviators' spirits immediately lifted to hear his voice, but that was nothing compared to what Moran had to tell them. He was in radio contact with Nanumea and they apparently had VMF-422 on radar.

The exact circumstances of Moran's miraculous delivery can only be surmised. He had somehow emerged from the storm front far to the east of the advancing cyclone. All alone in the stormy but empty sky, Moran had tried to reach someone on the radio for over an hour without success. At some time between 1350 and 1420 Nanumea managed to establish voice contact with Moran on 6970 kilocycles. Their call sign was "Rocky Base." But Moran, like the others in the squadron, had no way of knowing if "Rocky Base" was Nanumea, Apamama, Nukufetau, or even Funafuti.

The written report from the Nanumea Fighter Director Officer stated that "Moran [said he] was over an island and did not want to leave it. We asked him to describe the island. His description as logged is as follows: 'Island C-shaped. Coral reef encircled it. Oblong shaped with lagoon in the center. S.W. corner has many grass huts. Indian village. A series of small islands within a reef.' One officer thought that Moran was describing Vaitupu."

Lieutenant Robert K. Wilson was flying as leader to Bob "Tiger" Moran in Green Flight behind Captain Rex Jeans. (Photo courtesy Andrew Syrkin.)

Vaitupu, the largest atoll in the present nation of Tuvalu, is far to the east, past the Dateline on nearly the same latitude as Nui. However, Vaitupu was too far east to be the island Moran was seeing. Moran said he thought it was Nui, but was told that Nui did not have an RDF, or Radio Direction Finder to help bring the marines in.

With some urgency Moran then explained that he was very low on fuel and needed a place to land. Nanumea did not have a fix on him but suggested he fly to Nui Atoll.

At the same time that Moran was talking with Nanumea, Captain John Rogers also made brief contact. Rogers had not been seen nor heard from since breaking away from the main formation under the storm at 1240 hours. His transmissions were heard on Nanumea, but not by Moran or Jeans. He did say, "For God's sake, can't anyone hear me?" None of the Buccaneers did. There was so much radio chatter that all of Rogers' calls were drowned out. Tragically, that was the last ever heard from him.

Still trying to get a grip on the rapidly evolving situation, Nanumea told Moran that their radar showed an unidentified contact to the south. The range and number was uncertain, but they assumed it had to be the rest of the squadron. They asked if Moran could contact the rest of VMF-422, but it was nearly 1440 hours before his voice came through on the squadron radios.

Moran relayed what Nanumea told him. Jeans was not able to contact the base directly, a situation similar to what had happened with Don Walker and John Hansen.

Through Moran, Nanumea directed Jeans to turn almost directly northwest on a heading of 290 degrees for eighty miles.

But another question emerged. What island would the course change take them to? Nanumea did not make this clear. They were still being hammered by the northern edge of the cyclone. The only safe haven for the marines, other than Nukufetau or Funafuti, was Nui or Niutao, neither of which had an airfield. If Nanumea had spotted one of the lone planes and not the main formation, the course change to 290 degrees was worthless.

Then around 1450 the radar plots disappeared from the screens. In an attempt to obtain another radar fix, the base directed Moran to tell the others to climb above ten thousand feet with their emergency IFF turned on, but again the radio gremlins struck and the message never got through.

The matter quickly became moot when, at 1505, Moran called Jeans to say that his engine was cutting out. His fuel tanks were empty.

Moran was over Nui Atoll. With the rest of the squadron listening, Jeans told Moran to fly as close to the island as possible and ditch in the surf. Nui not only had friendly natives, but a small navy facility.

Syrkin remembered what happened next. "Tiger said he didn't want to try ditching in the surf. He was going to bail out over the island. I knew what that was all about. All through training, Tiger Moran had hated to practice ditching. He could swim, but didn't like deep water. Rex told him it was a lot safer to ditch his Corsair in the shallow surf than to try and land on the small island after bailing out."

First Lieutenant Robert Moran respectfully disobeyed Captain Jeans' orders to ditch. He was confident he would be able to come down on dry land in his parachute.

Jeans and Hughes tried threats and reasoning, but Moran refused to budge.

"I felt so goddamned helpless," said Syrkin, gritting his teeth at the memory. "There was nothing we could do. Tiger had made up his mind. I just hoped he was lucky."

Moran's last call was drowned out by a roar as he jettisoned his canopy hood. A few moments later there was only silence.

Led by Jeans, VMF-422 flew northwest, hoping that the radar station on Nanumea hadn't been wrong about their location. But fate was rapidly stacking the odds against them. They had each left Tarawa with 439 gallons of fuel, enough to fly to Funafuti via Nanumea with a healthy reserve.

But that reasonable claim presupposed a straight flight with few deviations, not wandering aimlessly for hours in fierce cross winds. Like Moran, they were nearly out of fuel.

Jeans asked each pilot to report his fuel state. One by one, they called in. Syrkin turned out to have the most fuel, thanks to his conservative mixture settings after takeoff. His gauges read eighty gallons. The rest averaged forty gallons, with Bill Aycrigg on the low end with less than thirty. Unless they found an island very quickly, most of them would be forced to ditch. Jeans conferred with Hughes and made his decision, one that would earn him approbation and respect.

"Rex said there was not much chance of finding an island in time," said Syrkin. "If what Moran told us about the Nanumea radar plot was accurate, we'd never reach there before we started running out of gas. Rex said that when the first one of us ran dry and had to ditch, we would all ditch as well."

This was one of the most difficult choices a squadron leader could be faced with. To sacrifice some pilots and planes and try to save the others, or to lose all the planes in order to save all the pilots. Captain Rex Jeans was committing the fifteen remaining pilots to ditching their Corsairs, regardless of how much fuel they might have, in order to keep them together.

"That storm was still coming," Syrkin continued. "If we each kept on flying until we ran out of gas, we'd be scattered all over the ocean. I admit I didn't like it then, but I think Rex made exactly the right decision."

From that point on, the Flying Buccaneers would literally sink or swim together.

· CHAPTER 12 ·

FATE AND FATALITY

At 1250 hours, First Lieutenant John Hansen's Corsair broke out to clear skies and hazy sunlight at thirteen thousand feet. He found himself all alone in between two towering canyon walls of roiling white and gray clouds. Far above on either side, the cirrus clouds rose into the hazy gray sky. He was far from out of the storm. Here the winds were strong but not as fierce as what they had fought far below in the storm.

Hansen had followed Captain John Rogers and Lieutenant Jake Wilson in the confusion of MacLaughlin's maneuverings. With his engine roaring at full power, Hansen climbed ever higher into the belly of the cyclone. He had not heard any radio command from MacLaughlin or any of the division leaders, but his job was to follow Rogers.

He lost sight of Wilson around five thousand feet, and his own wingman, Lieutenant Don Walker was nowhere to be seen.

In the 1980 oral history transcript, Colonel Hansen described his thoughts and actions. "I stayed with the flight leader up to somewhere around ten thousand or eleven thousand feet, and then I lost him. I continued on up to somewhere in the neighborhood of thirteen thousand feet without climbing on top. I could hear some of the conversation still going on down with the larger flight. I could tell they hadn't found the island and that most of the planes were still together down there."

Hansen's radio was apparently picking up some of the transmissions from the main formation as they were attempting to assess their situation.

Hansen admitted he never considered going back down to look for Nanumea, but his first action was to contact the squadron. Due to the constant interference and distance, Hansen was unable to reach either MacLaughlin or Rogers. "The only person I could raise at that stage was my wingman (Walker) who had lost me and stayed with the big formation. I asked him if he could get me the Funafuti radio frequencies. He, in turn, called the squadron commander. I

Lieutenant Don Walker was the only pilot able to establish radio contact with John Hansen after the squadron was scattered in the storm. (Photo courtesy Andrew Syrkin.)

couldn't talk to the squadron commander directly. Simply a radio strength problem, I think."

Lieutenant Don Walker, Gold Four in Rogers' flight, was in contact with Captain Jeans, who gave him the radio range information Hansen needed.

Hansen snatched a pen from his breast pocket and leaned toward the plotting board poking out from under the instrument panel. He hastily jotted down the numbers.

Armed with the frequency for the Funafuti Radio Range, Hansen told Walker to let MacLaughlin know he was going to try and reach the island. He took up a course directly south, or 180 degrees magnetic. This was an audacious move as he had no clear idea of where he was, other than in the general vicinity of Nanumea.

Around him the towering canyon walls of turbulent clouds rose and twisted, but his luck held and, at approximately 1330hours he found himself leaving the cyclone behind. Over his right shoulder Hansen watched the angry churning wall of cloud diminish. It seemed to be pursuing him.

The ocean was empty as far as he could see. He pulled back on the stick to gain altitude, but every dark spot on the horizon was just the shadow of another cloud.

As the cyclone fell farther behind, his receiver suddenly began chattering with the sound of Morse code, a faint, almost pale sound, like a cheap guitar string. Hansen turned up the volume on his receiver. Then he heard it clearly. Dot-dash, dot dash...

Within a minute the faint beeping was stronger. Dot-dash, dot-dash, dot-dash.

With steady pressure on the left rudder pedal, Hansen turned the Corsair to the southeast and was rewarded with a stronger signal. But this time the chirping beeps changed to the Morse letter 'N,' dash-dot, dash-dot...

He made a slow course change back southwest. He caught the Morse 'A,' and one more nudge to southeast made the two letters chatter over each other in a steady tone.

Hansen smiled at the memory. "That was the first time I had flown one of these radio ranges, other than a Link Trainer back in Pensacola. I frankly just blundered down it [the beam]. There was no skill involved. It was good enough to get me close to Funafuti."

At 1420 hours, far ahead of the F4U's long nose, Hansen saw another dark shadow on the ocean. But this one wasn't a cloud. It was the atoll and island of Funafuti, their original destination. John Hansen wasn't one to question fate. After crossing the reefs and lagoon he saw the island's long central runway. It was lined with dozens of aircraft from big B-24 Liberator bombers to PBY Catalinas and farther away rows of F4U Corsairs.

"I guess there were about three or four other squadrons on Funafuti. At first, I tried 6970, but of course that didn't work. I decided to just land."

Hansen lined the nose of the Corsair on the runway and lowered his landing gear and flaps. He touched down lightly, slowing to taxi speed as he turned towards the control tower.

When his fighter came to a stop, Hansen switched off the engine and fuel pumps. A glance at the fuel gauge showed just under eighty gallons remaining. He was very lucky.

John Hansen had been in the air for almost exactly four and a half hours. He reached up and slid back the hood. A few streams of icy water spilled in on him. It had collected in the canopy tracks during the storm.

"A ground crewman ran up to my plane and asked me who I was. I was kind of surprised he didn't know I was from VMF-422. But when I climbed down this officer, a major came over. He said he was the air operations officer for the Eleventh Bomb Group. This major asked me who I was and what squadron I was from. I don't mind saying I was pretty upset that he had no idea we were coming."

The Eleventh Heavy Bomb Group had been sent to Funafuti the previous summer. Admiral Hoover sent them on missions to bomb Tarawa and the surrounding Japanese bases in the Gilberts in support of Operation Galvanic, and to the Marshalls for the impending Operation Flintlock. At present the group consisted of two dozen B-24 Liberators under Colonel William Holzapfel Jr. As ordered by Hoover, Funafuti served as the safe staging area for the Fourth MB-DAW's fighters and bombers. But despite other navy and marine fighter squadrons having already arrived from Tarawa in the last few weeks, no one on Funafuti had been alerted about VMF-422.

The major led Hansen into the operations building. He asked several questions about their time of takeoff and route. "That was the first time they knew there was any flight in the air. They asked me what frequency we were using. I told them." Hansen's face showed evident bitterness. "They said, 'We're not using those.'"

There can be little doubt that John Hansen's unexpected arrival on Funafuti caused some considerable amount of official bedlam. Using the cable telephone line, the operations officer called Tarawa and learned that VMF-422 had indeed left Hawkins Field at 1000 hours and had been expected at Nanumea at 1230. The Funafuti command post received the departure report, but for reasons that are still unclear, it was not read until after Hansen landed. As for Nanumea, they did not get the departure report until they specifically asked for it. According to testimony from Colonel Payne, it wasn't received until *eight hours* after VMF-422 went missing, or about 2200 hours. (Author's italics)

Within minutes the Funafuti radio room began calling VMF-422 on 6970 kilocycles.

A call went out to Nanumea, Nukufetau, and other island bases in the Gilberts and Ellice Islands to do likewise. A serious effort was made to find the missing marine pilots. However, it was too little, too late. While they waited for word, the major asked Hansen how many planes were out there and if he had any idea where they might be. The marine told him what he could. "I had no idea where Mac and the other fellows were. The last I saw of them they were flying in every direction under that storm."

While Hansen paced in the base office, the phone rang. The major picked it up and told Hansen that Nanumea was in radio and radar contact with Lieutenant Robert Moran and giving him the vector to Nui. It was not a coincidence. It was the call from Funafuti that had alerted Colonel Payne of the missing marine squadron and what frequency they were using.

"That was great news," Hansen said. "I didn't know that Tiger was on his own up until then, but I was sure he would be okay. Then the major added that Nanumea radar had other planes on their screens and were in contact with them through Tiger Moran."

For the next several minutes they waited for some word that VMF-422 was headed for a safe airfield, but their hopes were quickly dashed when Moran ran out of fuel. There went the only link between Nanumea and the Flying Buccaneers.

"I asked the major about sending out an air search. He quashed that right off. The typhoon was passing to the north of Funafuti, right in the area where my buddies were. It would be suicide to send some of those big Catalinas into that storm. I could tell he really wanted to find the fellows, but a search would have to wait until the typhoon passed."

Colonel John Hansen paused in his narrative. "I felt pretty low. I thought I'd used up all of 422's luck."

First Lieutenant Robert "Tiger" Moran approached the tiny island of Nui. From five thousand feet, it looked no different from any of a hundred other coral and sand atolls he'd seen since the day before, but this one spelled safety. The Corsair dropped slowly as it slid over the coral reefs that ringed the atolls twenty-one islands. The largest, at 1.7 square miles, was Fenua Tapu, Moran's intended goal. Fenua Tapu was mostly covered with palm trees, sand, and crop land with about fifty small huts and structures. Far away on the other side of the lagoon were a few small buildings and a short pier where some landing craft were moored.

At 1505 hours, Nui was about to be overtaken by the next storm front from the west, with winds of eighty or ninety knots whipping the palm trees and thatched roofs.

Moran was aiming for the widest part of Fenua Tapu, a very small target from five thousand feet, particularly when parachuting out of a Corsair traveling at 150 knots. He approached from the east into the wind to slow his ground speed.

Some of what happened to Moran has been related by the islanders who witnessed it. Moran jettisoned his canopy hood and stood up to bail out. He stepped on to the starboard wing and let himself fall behind the wing.

Fighter pilots who bailed out had to be careful to avoid being struck by the horizontal stabilizer, which was like a deadly steel blade. For Moran, Lady Luck failed him. The starboard stabilizer struck him a violent blow across the upper back.

As he fell, dazed, he was just able to pull the "D" ring of his parachute. The huge silk canopy blossomed over him. He drifted down

Lieutenant Bob "Tiger" Moran, who managed to establish contact between VMF-422 and Nanumea. His luck ran out with his fuel. (Photo courtesy Andrew Syrkin.)

over the island, but fate was merciless. The winds pushed him back the way he'd come. In moments Moran was drifting out over the surf on the eastern end of the island. Dozens of islanders ran that way only to see him fall limply into the raging water a hundred yards offshore.

Moran, still stunned from hitting the Corsair's tail, must have tried to inflate his Mae West, but the collapsed parachute's shroud lines enveloped him in a deadly embrace. He was unable to claw his way to the surface.

By the time the natives reached him, First Lieutenant Robert Paden "Tiger" Moran, twenty-two, of Depue, Illinois was dead. The shortest pilot in the squadron, the man who hated deep water, had died from inhaling sea water. He had also suffered a broken back, which in itself would probably have been fatal.

The islanders carried the dead marine aviator to their church and cleaned him up. He was given a Christian burial. The United States Navy would arrange to recover his body later.

CHAPTER 13

THEN THERE WERE THIRTEEN

Time ran out for the fifteen marines at 1530 hours when First Lieutenant Bill Aycrigg of Fairfield, Connecticut reported that he was out of fuel. That call sent a wave of despair and determination through the others as they prepared to carry out Captain Jeans' orders. The seriousness of what they were about to do could not be minimized. For the last six hours, they had been in control of their aircraft, and to a certain extent, their destinies. But the moment the marines were cast adrift in tiny rubber life rafts scores, if not hundreds, of miles from land, they were totally at the mercy of the sea.

"Buccaneer Flight, this is Green Leader," Jeans said into the radio. "We stay together. The wind is from the northwest so make your approach from the southeast between the swells. Circle and ditch as close together as you can. Try and stay in sight of the others. Over."

The marines watched as Aycrigg's corsair slid closer and closer to the heaving green swells. For the moment the sea was behaving, but that would not last.

"All we had to do was look west and see that damned storm coming at us again," said Gunderson. "It looked just like when we first saw it at noon."

Bill Aycrigg had jettisoned his canopy and turned to line up parallel with the mountainous swells. Then a titanic cape of white spray erupted from the dark gray-green surface as the sea was ripped open. The fighter skipped and bounced twice before coming to a jarring stop. As one, the marines spoke out loud, "Get out!"

The tiny figure clambered from the cockpit. The wings and half the fuselage were already under water. In five seconds it was gone. The foaming white smear was erased by the relentless waves. As Jeans led the others over the spot where their fellow pilot had ditched they saw him swimming in his Mae West with the spreading yellow stain of the dye marker around him.

Major Wrenn's official account states that Aycrigg did retrieve his life raft and had climbed into it, but none of the survivors agree.

Lieutenant Ken Gunderson, who witnessed the ditching of his close friend Chris Lauesen. (Photo courtesy Sandi Lynde.)

The last any of them saw of Aycrigg he had only his Mae West to keep him afloat.

Just then First Lieutenant Ted Thurnau of Westwood, New Jersey said his own engine had quit. In a minute Thurnau's Corsair slipped into the water several miles east of Aycrigg. Jeans kept the others circling in between the two downed pilots. Lieutenant Bill Reardon passed over Thurnau and reported that he had made it into his life raft.

"Things were stacking up fast," said Gunderson. "Ted was way east of us when he had to go down. I think it was like seven miles or so. Rex said that the pilots with the most remaining fuel would ditch last."

This was a sound decision. In the event that someone was out searching for them or had them on radar, the still-flying Corsairs would be easier to locate.

One by one, the marines began the procedure to ditch in the open ocean. Although they had all practiced it, that had been in a pool or calm, sheltered bay under the watchful eyes of instructors.

Captain Jeans said he would be the first to ditch. He had done well in the pool at Pearl Harbor and wanted to set a good example for his men. Jeans lined up his approach just as Aycrigg had and cut his engine and the propeller coasted to a stop. With the nose high, his tail carved a white slice into the sea. In a moment, he too was down and hauling himself onto the sinking wing. Jeans inflated his yellow life raft and climbed in. He waved as the twelve planes roared over.

"He made it look pretty easy," remembered Syrkin. "A piece of cake."

Lieutenant Don Walker of Pennsylvania was next, followed by Royce "Tex" Watson of Texas, Bob "Chick" Whalen of Boston, Caleb "Cal" Smick of Kansas, and Bill Reardon, also from Boston. Walker did just as he'd been trained and managed to get into his raft without even getting his head wet. Watson was not so lucky. In the Coleman video, he said, "I had the raft inflated and tried to climb into it. But there was this lanyard from the Mae West to the raft, and I had put a knot in it so I had only about that much,"– he held his hands about eighteen inches apart—"of lanyard. Every time I tried to climb into the raft the lanyard stopped me and I fell back into the water. I was drowning. I was swallowing water. I said to the Good Lord, 'I need some help.' Then I pulled the tab on the Mae West and it inflated and I popped right up. Then I got into the raft."

Disaster struck when Chick Whalen emerged from his sinking plane without his life raft. His tiny form thrashed in the heaving swells. He was at least three hundred yards from the nearest man. What no one realized at the time was that Whalen had scrambled from his sinking plane and suddenly felt like he was going under. He was desperate to get to the surface and the heavy, wet flight suit was weighing him down. But instead of inflating his Mae West, he pulled it off, followed by his shoes and clothing. When he came to the surface, he was totally naked.

Both Cal Smick's and Bill Reardon's Corsairs sank like stones, but they too emerged and climbed into their rafts. Lieutenant Robert K. Wilson of Springfield, Illinois was the next to ditch. He came down about a hundred yards from the others, and began paddling to join them.

Ken Gunderson made his approach. "If you ever ditch a plane in the ocean," he said in the video interview, "don't do what I did.

I did everything wrong. I didn't jettison my hood, I didn't have my shoulder straps on. I hit the water. Then I jumped overboard without inflating my Mae West. Then I tried to get my Mae West open, I couldn't find the toggle. So I went for the raft, and I tried to find the CO_2 bottle but couldn't find it. I kept reaching for it, but I guess I kept stopping before I reached it and went the other way." Gunderson chuckled ruefully. "All this time I'm swimming with all my gear on and swallowing sea water. I finally got it open and climbed on. I never realized how fast a fighter could sink. One second you're slapping down with a huge white wave spraying over you, the next second the plane is just gone with bubbles coming up."

Next was Jules Flood, the Washington, DC native, who characteristically made a perfect ditching and egress. Bostonian John Lincoln, the last man to see MacLaughlin alive, brought his Corsair down without trouble. "I had some previous experience," he explained. "Because I had an engine go out on me over the Great Lakes. I touched down, stepped onto the wing. Deployed my raft and didn't even get my feet wet."

Lincoln was in his raft, looking for the others, when he heard someone calling to him. "I thought I heard someone, and when I was up on one of the crests, I could see a head bobbing on the water. I pulled out the hand paddles. Those rafts had these little paddles you slipped over your hands, and paddled over to this guy. It turned out to be Chick Whalen." Lincoln shook his head. "I don't know how he survived, he had no clothes, no life vest, and no raft. He was just bobbing in the water. I got him into my raft without turning over."

Lincoln gave the shivering Whalen his t-shirt then began paddling to join the others. They used police whistles to find one another in the heaving waves. Trying to move the raft with the added weight of a second man quickly exhausted Lincoln. At that point Don Walker appeared in his own raft, and Whalen was transferred.

Three pilots remained in the air. Captain Charley Hughes and Lieutenants Mark "Breeze" Syrkin and Sterling "Shou" Price. Hughes had been monitoring the radio and sending calls to Air-Sea Rescue with their estimated location.

First Lieutenant Mark Warren "Breeze" Syrkin of New York had his ditching carefully planned. "I cut my parachute leg straps to free the raft package." He had already untied his shoes and hung them around his neck as the instructor at Pearl Harbor had told them. Then he made a broad sweeping turn around the men in the water and wrapped his right index finger on the trigger for his machine guns. He squeezed the trigger and all six of his wing-mounted .50 caliber Browning machine guns began hammering out a steady stream of bullets. Yellow tracers arced far into the distance.

"I could only imagine the looks on the other fellows' faces as I flew over them with all guns blazing." Thirty-three seconds later the guns went silent. "I was at least two hundred pounds lighter. I wanted my plane to float as long as possible." He lined up his approach and chose the spot to touch down. After cutting his engine and lowering his flaps, he pulled the two pins to jettison the canopy. It fell away in a loud clatter. He watched the glistening water pass him in a blur as he held the nose up as long as possible. The wind roared into the open cockpit. The harness was cinched so tight he could hardly breathe. Then, a sudden sharp tug seemed to grab at the Corsair. It let go, then another one literally pulled it into the water. For a single endless second, the only thing Syrkin saw was a huge plume of white seawater cascading over his Corsair and into the cockpit. When he was sure the plane had stopped, he slapped open the harness release and stood up. Solid green water was pouring over the sill. He pulled the parachute and life raft pack from the seat.

"Then I heard this weird hissing sound. I was climbing out when I saw these plumes of steam coming from the wings. My guns were almost red-hot."

Tossing the raft into the water, he followed. With an abrupt gurgle, *Francey II,* his prized Vought F4U-1D Corsair, sank and disappeared. Her last flight would take her to the bottom of the Pacific Ocean, seventeen thousand feet below.

Holding on to his raft, Syrkin tried to see if any of the others were close by. The swells were like green mountain ridges that passed under him, and for a few seconds at a time he could see for several hundred feet in all directions. But there was no sign of any of his fellow marines.

The water was cool, but not cold. Then the tiny sound of police whistles drifted past him.

"We had whistles attached to our life preservers," Syrkin explained. "I figured they were coming from the west. I kept looking that way every time I crested a wave."

The strong wind drove spray and solid sheets of seawater into his face every time he looked west. He yanked out the safety pin that secured the handle for the raft's carbon dioxide bottle. With a satisfying "Pop!" the bright yellow rubber boat expanded and floated on the water.

Syrkin tried to climb into the raft, but it was a great deal more difficult in the heaving ocean than it had been in a calm swimming pool. After two failed attempts, which only resulted in the raft nearly being overturned, he realized he had lost the shoes he had tied around his neck. "I finally decided to take off my flight suit. It was weighing me down. I put it in the raft along with my helmet and goggles. Then I tried again. This time I managed to get in." He chuckled at the memory. "That was one tight fit for a big fellow like me."

With the slight height advantage afforded by the raft, Syrkin looked for the fourteen other men he knew to be nearby, but he only heard the whistles. He began to paddle into the wind, which quickly exhausted him. "I didn't have any choice," he said. "There was just no way to make any real progress by hand paddling. I tipped myself over the side and put the lanyard on my wrist. Then I began kicking."

Sterling Price was next to last. "I put my flaps down and slowed down as much as I could," said the St. Louis native of his ditching. "I dragged the tail in the water for a little ways, but the moment that big engine caught the water, I mean, it was BAM! It was like hitting a brick wall. I was in and out of that plane in an instant, and in my raft by the time the tail went under."

Price related an amusing anecdote. "The CO_2 bottle on the raft has a safety pin on it. You pull the pin out and turn the handle to inflate the raft. But I just grabbed that handle and twisted that safety pin right off. Later on, after we reached safety, I tried to do that again." He grinned. "I could not put a dent in that safety pin. I guess adrenaline made me do it in the water."

Last to set down was Charley Hughes, the engineer from Oklahoma. Price was in the water when the Corsair came in. "I saw Charley coming down and he was only about twenty or thirty feet from me and I wondered if he could see me in the water. Then he went right by, he landed only about fifty feet from me."

Hughes joined up with Price, then Tex Watson appeared.

"I found Charley Hughes in his raft," recalled Tex Watson. "I saluted him and said, 'Lieutenant Watson requests permission to rejoin the Fleet Marine Force Pacific, sir!' Charley just nodded and waved me in. He said, 'Permission granted. Join up, shut up and behave yourself.'"

Don Walker then arrived, carrying Whalen, followed by Lincoln. Others soon straggled in. A wave crest lifted Syrkin and he saw a small cluster of rafts about fifty yards away. His kicks had a renewed vigor as he drew closer. Then his foot hit something solid underwater. He turned his head, wondering what it was. With an icy shock he saw a dark gray triangular fin slicing the water past him.

"It scared the holy hell out of me. I threw myself back into that raft like I had wings."

Syrkin was close to the small group that included Hughes and Watson, who was grinning at him. "The son-of-a-bitch was smiling at me. He shouted, 'Hey Breeze. Come on over! Someone wants to interview you! Can I have your autograph?'"

"I was still shaking from seeing that big shark so close, but I had to laugh. I shook his hand. God, I was glad to see him."

Over the next half hour more of the downed aviators joined up. Guided by shouts and whistles, the small group was joined by Bob Wilson and Flood. Cal Smick and Bill Reardon had managed to find each other and with their combined efforts, were able to paddle from almost a quarter mile away. Rex Jeans was the next to appear.

Ken Gunderson was wheezing, but he doggedly kept paddling until Flood went out to help him. He looked pale and sick, in marked contrast to his normally ruddy complexion. He explained that he had swallowed a lot of sea water when his plane sank. Hughes told him to drink as much fresh water as he could. Whalen, who was clad only in a t-shirt, looked as bad as Gunderson. By 1745, the only men still unaccounted for were Ted Thurnau and Bill Aycrigg, the first to ditch. It was nearing 1800 hours and the light was fading. Hughes suggested they fire their pistols a few times, hoping one of the other pilots might do the same. For the next several minutes Jeans fired his Colt automatic into the air, after which they all strained their ears to listen for an answering shot. None came.

Captain Hughes described some of his memories of the hours after the ditching. "All together we wound up with thirteen men in *twelve* rafts, but Aycrigg and Thurnau were not present. According to my log, the flight lasted six hours, so we splashed at 1600." As darkness fell over the Pacific, the downed marines took stock of their situation. Apart from Whalen, they each had a full set of survival gear. The standard basic survival gear for fighter pilots was mainly contained in the AN-R-2B one-man parachute package. The raft had a lanyard to hook it to the inflatable Mae West life vest.

The vest had a dye pack, police whistle, and signal mirror. The mirror, about the size of a paperback novel had a hole in it that allowed the user to aim it while signaling a ship or plane. Shark repellent was not yet available but would become standard after the summer of 1944.

The Goodyear-manufactured one-man inflatable rubber life raft was little larger than a baby's bassinet and less than a foot high. It looked too small to hold a grown man. But it held a veritable cornucopia of survival gear. Wrapped inside a rubberized tarp, yellow on one side and black on the other, was a raft repair kit and pump, two hand paddles, and a combination sea anchor and water bucket for bailing. The tarp would shield a man from the blazing sun, and

After the disappearance of Major MacLaughlin, command of VMF-422 fell on the shoulders of Captain Rex Jeans. He made the critical decision that the rest of the pilots should ditch together. (Photo courtesy Andrew Syrkin.)

when a patrolling Japanese plane was nearby, the black side helped hide him from prying eyes. The survival kit contained two cans of water, a waxed box with pemmican, chocolate, malted milk tablets, and sun block. A small packet held fishing line and hooks. The most important item was the flare pistol, manufactured by Very, which looked like a cartoon gun with a wide barrel. Some pilots also carried small flare launchers about the size of a thick felt pen for quick use.

In addition to their combat knives, they each carried a pistol. However, the Colt automatics were almost useless. Unlike the Smith & Wesson revolvers, the Colts soon rusted shut after being immersed in salt water. They were going to need all their gear for what was coming.

To the west, a dark gray rain squall drew closer. It was one of the many peripheral storms that accompanied the cyclone. While they did not have the power and fury of the main vortex, the squalls possessed winds and rain of gale force. The air grew cold as the light faded from the sky. The winds picked up and rain hammered at the tiny flotilla like millions of icy knives. Their first night as castaways had begun.

CHAPTER 14

THE NATIVES OF NIUTAO

Time had also run out for First Lieutenant Robert "Curly" Lehnert of Queens, New York. After two hours of circling the swimming Chris Lauesen, he realized rescue wasn't going to arrive before he ran out of fuel. With no idea where the rest of the squadron had gone, and having had no luck in reaching Nanumea, he had to make a decision.

The sun was nearly down past the scudding cloud banks to the west. Below his circling Corsair, swells streaked with whitecaps passed in unending ranks. A water landing would not be difficult. But Chris Lauesen, floating in his Mae West presented a serious complication. If Lehnert's aim or timing was off, he could end up hundreds of yards away from the swimming man, too far away to find him in the dark.

"I made my choice," said Lehnert. "I'd have to bail out as close over Chris as possible. If I could keep him in sight, then we could share my raft."

Lehnert checked to assure that the life raft's casing was connected to the parachute pack straps. Pulling the canopy latch, he slid it all the way back. A howling cold wind and the roar of the engine filled the cockpit. He banked down to about two thousand feet, judging the wind direction from the spray off the wave crests.

"I wanted to jump just downwind of Lauesen so my forward momentum and the wind would cancel each other out," he explained. "I lowered my landing gear and flaps, and slowed to about eighty knots."

Keeping an eye on his altitude, he undid the safety straps. Another look forward confirmed that he was aimed right at Lauesen. Then he stood up and threw his right leg over the sill and felt for the inset step. The slipstream tore at his clothes and parachute pack, but he managed to get his foot into the step in the flap. He looked straight down and saw the yellow dye smear with the tiny waving figure pass under him. Curly threw himself off the wing, ducking to miss the blade of the horizontal stabilizer. Tumbling in the roiled air he yanked the ripcord and felt the satisfying jerk as the parachute filled with air above him.

As he fell closer to the mountainous waves his field of vision decreased. The swells created deep shadows in the valleys. Lehnert snapped his head around, looking desperately for any sign of the man in the water. He only had seconds before he hit and he had to know what direction to swim.

"I thought I saw him for just a second, but then he was gone. It was getting dark and the waves were just too high."

Like a heavy sack of potatoes, Curly hit the water and was immediately submerged up to his head. "The water was cool, but not cold."

Yanking the tab on his Mae West he popped to the surface. He wormed out of the parachute harness, pulling the life raft from the straps. "I found myself floating over the parachute and I tried to push it away. But a parachute in the water is like a giant jellyfish, it's almost alive. It has a tendency to wrap itself around you. I gave it a big shove and got away from it. When I thought I was clear, I got the raft inflated. I said out loud, 'Bob, get into the goddamned raft right now.'" Lehnert grinned. "I sometimes talked to myself in those days. Anyway, it was a lot harder to get into that raft than it had been in training. I first tried simultaneously pushing down on the tubular rim of the raft while trying to get my feet and body into it. But when I finally got in, a bunch of seawater had come in too. I was sitting in about six inches of water. I said, 'Not your best performance, Bob.'"

Now he had a higher vantage point to search for his squadron mate. The sun had disappeared behind a storm front, and the sky overhead gave him little light. As far as he could see were towering swells of green water. One minute the raft was carried high on one crest, only to be hidden deep in a dark gully the next.

Lehnert yelled, "Chris! Chris! Can you see me? Where are you?" He listened and then yelled again. Every time he was raised on a crest he sat as high as he could and looked desperately for the tiny figure. "I was really frantic," Lehnert remembered. "I kept nearly tipping the raft over as I turned. But I never saw him."

An hour after he'd jumped out of his Corsair, Curly felt a wave of cold despair. He'd failed. Lauesen was alone somewhere out in the gloom. He couldn't last long. With the coming of night on the storm-tossed ocean, the marine aviator found himself all alone.

"To this day I still wonder if I could have done something different," he said. "I felt absolutely miserable. Chris had been depending on me and I let him down."

Despite his despair, Curly knew his first duty was to survive. In addition to the raft's survival gear, he had two full canteens of water.

"That ground crewman back on Tarawa had given me an extra canteen," Lehnert said with a smile. "He never knew how important that water would be to me."

He had also held on to his Very flare pistol and had a few red flare cartridges in his flight suit pocket, and managed to retain his shoes and helmet.

"I had everything I needed. All I wanted was some luck."

With the sun gone the air grew chilly, then cold. Lehnert pulled the small canvas bucket out of the raft's storage compartment to bail out the water, then retrieved the large rubberized tarp and pulled it over him so his body heat would warm the space inside.

"At training they showed us how to let the bucket trail in the water to act as a sea anchor," he explained. "That kept me from drifting like a leaf on a windy pond."

From that point on, all he could do was wait. Even though he was exhausted, sleep was nearly impossible, so Lehnert tried to work out his position. He knew that Lauesen had ditched somewhere south of Nui, probably no more than fifty miles from the island. He was in a well-traveled area and once the cyclone passed, the search would find him.

"Except for losing Chris, I felt pretty confident. I was sure I'd be found and maybe they'd find Chris too. I kept thinking, 'If Eddie Rickenbacker could do it, so could I.'"

Captain Eddie Rickenbacker, America's highest-scoring ace of the First World War, was, after Charles Lindbergh and Jimmy Doolittle, the nation's most famous aviator. Rickenbacker had never been far from the public spotlight. He helped found Eastern Air Lines and bought the Indianapolis Speedway. The former war ace had also been a defense witness in the celebrated court-martial of General Billy Mitchell. Although the outspoken Rickenbacker had been critical of some of President Roosevelt's policies, he became a civilian advisor and inspector to the United States Army Air Corps. General Henry H. "Hap" Arnold sent Rickenbacker to more than forty Air Corps bases in the United States and England, where he spoke to and motivated the men who were preparing to assault the might of the Axis Powers. By the request of the President, he boarded a Boeing B-17D Flying Fortress bound for Australia to see General Douglas MacArthur. On 21 October 1942, due to a faulty navigational instrument, the bomber flew far off course and ran out of fuel in the South Pacific.

The newspapers and radio reported that Captain Eddie was dead at sea and the nation added his name to the list to be mourned, but the intrepid pilot who had more than once cheated death was still very much alive and determined to stay that way. Rickenbacker and the other crewmen had made it into the bomber's life raft. He was a genius at keeping up morale. Their food ran out after three days, but the fortuitous arrival of a seagull, which the old ace managed to catch, helped them survive. For twenty-four days in blazing sun, little rain, and near starvation, they hung on until they were found by a US Navy OS2U-3 Kingfisher float plane. The downed aviators were taken to the island of Nukufetau, not far from Funafuti.

"Rickenbacker's rescue was front-page news all over the country," said Lehnert. "I was in flight training and I read about it in *LIFE* magazine. So I figured, 'If Captain Eddie could last twenty-four days on a raft, so can I.'"

A stormy night had fallen. Visible in the torn rents of the clouds, a new moon cast a flat blue-gray illumination over the restless black water.

Hours passed without a change. Curly tried to get some sleep, but only managed short catnaps. Every time he dozed off, the sudden thought that he'd heard something or worse, missed hearing something, jolted him awake. But a few hours before dawn he drifted off to a restless sleep from exhaustion and the ceaseless rocking motion of the tiny raft.

The sun was low in the sky when Lieutenant Jake Wilson awoke to find himself lying on a bed in a small room. He had no idea where he was or how he'd gotten there. He checked his watch to find that it was 1645 hours. He looked around the room. It seemed to be some kind of hut with bare plaster walls and wooden beams supporting a plank ceiling. Feeling dizzy, he realized his head was bandaged. He was lying on a thick cotton mattress and several brightly woven mats. Just then he heard a male voice asking how he felt. The man was speaking English with a British accent. Wilson guessed he was probably on an island where the natives spoke English. But how had he gotten there? Of all the marines of VMF-422, it is the story of First Lieutenant Walter "Jake" Wilson, the trombone player from Mississippi that generates the most interest and awe. Wilson's personal odyssey has been the subject of amazement, envy, disbelief, and respect.

After the war, Wilson wrote down his recollections of what happened to him after following Captain John Rogers back into the storm. Trying not to lose sight of Rogers' wing, he climbed farther

Mississippian Jake Wilson found himself stranded on an island with friendly girls who wanted to marry him. (Photo courtesy Andrew Syrkin.)

into the storm's underside. Somewhere after passing five thousand feet—based on Hansen's account—Wilson lost sight of Rogers. After finding himself alone, Wilson dove to miss the storm. He flew close to the water, and soon lost all contact with the rest of the squadron. He tried his radio but, at first, failed to reach anyone. Visibility was poor and Wilson had no way of knowing where he was.

The following statements are compiled from his inquiry testimony and his own writings, as well as an interview he gave to *Leatherneck Magazine*. He said, "I first thought about flying a reciprocal course and try to get back up to Tarawa or some of these chains of islands. I flew about 329 degrees for about fifteen minutes. The storm was getting worse. I turned around and flew 149 until my gasoline was about ready to give out." Wilson's initial heading was roughly northeast, but without a known starting point, this had little value. He flew on, straining to see any sign of land. "There was only one thing I could do, keep flying and trust in God. Those hours flying alone over the Pacific were the longest of my life. I was flying on fumes. I knew it would be a matter of minutes and my engine would conk out." Wilson admitted feeling some self-reproach for his hasty choice. "Perhaps I should have gone in another direction. Maybe I should have turned when I had that hunch to fly straight."

He did finally manage to reach Don Walker who told him that Jeans suggested Jake fly a course of 156 degrees. He said, "I flew for a long time. Then the engine sputtered."

Despite his random wandering, Jake Wilson found safety almost exactly where he had started. According to his testimony, he saw another rain squall ahead, but beneath it appeared to be an island. "The storm was so bad I flew right down to the water and almost hit the palm trees. I pulled on my goggles and opened the canopy. I saw the island but no sign of native huts or anything. I turned and went over it again and saw a red-topped church and native huts all around it. The storm was so bad, everyone was in their houses."

In his magazine interview, he had a different story to tell, but the passage of nearly fifty years probably had much to do with that. "I was passing through a cloud bank when I saw something dark pass my wing. I looked down and saw sand below. I just missed a palm tree. Below was a tiny island with a village, church, and a wide beach. I circled it about five or six times looking for a place to land. The wind was blowing right along the beach and when I made my first approach a lot of little native boys ran along the beach. I came around once more. I kept up the power over the water, slid in with my wheels up and skidded in. Not a scratch on the cowling. It wasn't a bad landing. I thought I was home free, but the plane came to an abrupt stop. I had loosened my safety belt and pitched into the instrument panel. I was dazed and bleeding from a gash on the head."

The F4U Corsair's instrument panel has a wide metal shade flange right in front of the pilot's head. Despite his injury, Wilson knew he had to get out of the plane. "I managed to climb out of the cockpit and fell into the water. I heard some shouts. I looked up, and I saw a crowd running toward me. I couldn't tell if they were natives or Japanese. If they were natives, I had no way of knowing if they were friendly. I pulled out my pistol and waved it at them. One of the leaders rushed into the surf and shouted to me in broken English. He said, 'Friend! American! God's man! We God's man too!'"

"I was wading to shore when I plunged into a deep hole in the coral bottom," Wilson continued. "Before I could surface, an old man, whom I later learned was the chief, grabbed me and lifted me into his arms. Then I passed out."

That was how Jake Wilson found himself in the small hut lying on a mattress. He was in the home of the village leader. The downed marine aviator had, against all odds and with unbelievable luck, found the tiny island of Niutao, eighty-four miles east-southeast of Nanumea. Niutao was the very last inhabited island for several hundred miles.

How he managed to find it after nearly three hours of wandering aimlessly through rain squalls and storm clouds is a miracle.

More commonly called a reef island than an atoll, Niutao was a mile-long oval of sand, coral, and rock. Now part of the Nation of Tuvalu, during the war it had a population of less than five hundred people living in three villages, the largest of which was Kulia. The islanders were Protestant Christian. They spoke English and the language of the Marshall Islands. For the most part they subsisted on fish, vegetables, coconuts, breadfruit, and livestock. While Niutao's three small islands had not been occupied by the Japanese, they had often visited or "raided," as one contemporary account by a missionary stated.

Wilson spent the next hour being tended by a British-trained village doctor. He did not know the extent of his injuries. "I pointed to my head. The doctor insisted on wrapping me with a white cloth until I resembled a man who'd broken every bone in his body."

Jake Wilson could not have stumbled on a more congenial and charitable community. The people were industrious and generous to a fault, as he was soon to discover.

"It seemed that everyone on the atoll had heard about me. The chief wanted to protect me from too much enthusiasm. He gave me a bodyguard of four native police. The natives gave me gifts of coconuts and chickens, and I felt obligated to respond to every group with an inspiring speech. I told them how we were going to save them from the Japanese, and I made up some other stuff."

When he asked if there was a way to inform the Navy that he was on the island, he was told there was a wireless station on the island. Someone would contact Nanumea.

This particular point adds more questions than it answers. A native outrigger could sail from Niutao to Nanumea in less than two days. If Jake Wilson had been able to contact Nanumea as early as the morning of 26 January, then it stands to reason that Nanumea would send a plane to pick him up immediately. But as we shall see, that did not happen.

In the meantime, he had no choice but to enjoy the local hospitality. Jake Wilson, a small-town boy from Mississippi, was about to experience the fantasy of every red-blooded American man who was headed for the Pacific: to be shipwrecked on an island with beautiful friendly native girls.

After night fell, the chief, who Wilson learned had been elected by his people, invited him to a banquet in his honor. While Wilson sat on a colorful woven mat, musicians played and singers vocalized. Islanders brought him chicken, fish, mutton, fruit, coconut, breadfruit, and other delicacies. Then a young girl clad in colorful clothes began to dance in front of him. She was followed by another, and then another. They seemed to be putting on a performance just for their American friend. "All the young girls there were pretty and danced just for me. I sat watching them go through their rhythmic motions. It was really nice to watch."

Wilson was enjoying the show when the chief leaned over and informed him he was attending his own betrothal party. He told the American pilot to choose a wife from among the young women who were dancing for him.

"I was stunned. The chief told me I must pick a wife. Heck, I wasn't ready to get married, so I didn't appreciate the honor. The last girl danced and it was time for me to choose."

Wilson was in a bind. He had no intention of marrying a native girl, no matter how pretty or sincere she might be. He had to fend off the matrimonial advances of an entire community.

"The natives had been kind to me and I didn't want to hurt their feelings. So I kept mum. I racked my brain for a way out. I rubbed my head and then it hit me. After a bit, I put on my own show. I groaned and held my head. This startled the chief, and he looked at me with concern. I told him I was having a relapse from the injury. I apologized and said I was too dizzy to pick a wife. The chief was very considerate of my health, but the son-of-a-gun outfoxed me. He told me he would postpone the wedding until the next night. So I was still in a jam."

"Leave it to Jake to fall out of the sky and land in a haystack," laughed Curly Lehnert. "He was the luckiest of all of us. I still can't believe it after all these years. But Jake was kind of straight-laced. He was from the Deep South, with old Baptist beliefs. He might have been offered something we all dreamed of, but I doubt he was

The destroyer USS Hobby *was sent to pick up Wilson from Niutao, then resumed the search for the rest of the downed aviators. (Official U.S. Navy photo.)*

happy about it. Now, if it had been Breeze Syrkin who had landed there, I bet he would have taken every advantage of what was being offered him."

Somewhere far to the southwest, Breeze Syrkin and the other twelve pilots rode out the rough weather. While it wasn't as violent as the storm they'd flown through, it was still a struggle to keep all the rafts together in the dark as the wind and waves passed under them in ceaseless ranks. Each man constantly checked the lanyard that lashed him to the next raft. Even in the tropics, the air at night often dropped to below forty degrees. The pilots shivered and shook in their wet clothes. Chick Whalen was even worse off, having only his underwear. They pulled the tarps over themselves to conserve body heat.

Charley Hughes said, "That night was rather quiet, until some rain showers came over, which gave us drinking water without using our own supply."

The weary pilots caught the fresh rainwater in their buckets. They had been told that exposure and dehydration were the two things that killed most men stranded at sea. The hours passed, the rain and wind came and went. All they could do was ride it out until daylight.

"It was a long, long night," said Syrkin. "I remember wondering about Tiger and Curly and the others. I was pretty sure they would be fine. After all, they weren't in a little bitty raft far out in the open ocean in a storm."

When Curly awoke, a pale purple and pink dawn was rising ahead of him. The squall had passed, but a thick gray overcast promised more rain. From the direction of the dawn, he determined which way was east. He wanted to go north, towards either Nui or Nanumea. But the wind was from the north, while the swells that rolled in weighty majesty were coming from the northeast. In order to move in that direction, he would have to paddle against the swells and across the wind.

"I was starved. The last thing I'd eaten was breakfast on the yacht the morning before. In the raft rations I found pemmican, chocolate, and malted milk tablets. There were two cans of water, too. I tried the pemmican first. It looked like old shoe leather and was about as easy to eat, but not bad tasting. I washed it down with water from my canteen and had some malt tablets and a bite of chocolate. It was cold and hard, like a brick. But no chocolate ever tasted better to this hungry marine."

Lehnert used the daylight to look for his missing squadron mate, but First Lieutenant Christian Lauesen was nowhere to be seen. Lehnert had disobeyed orders and risked his own life to stay with him, but his gamble had failed.

"I was pretty upset," Lehnert said miserably. "I kept calling out until my throat was raw, but I never saw him again."

All that night, while the marines were struggling to remain afloat and alive, the midnight oil had been burning on Tarawa. It was apparent that an entire squadron had disappeared in circumstances that could very well have cost the lives of every man. Although John Hansen was safe on Funafuti, he was only one of twenty-three men, and their fates were not known. Rear Admiral John Hoover, commander of TG 57.2 and Commander, Central Pacific Air Force, took the initiative and ordered that a formal Board of Inquiry (often called an investigation) into the disappearance and possible loss of VMF-422 be immediately convened aboard his flagship, the USS *Curtiss*.

· CHAPTER 15 ·

ORDEALS

As dawn rose on 26 January, the thirteen marines surveyed their surroundings. It wasn't much to look at. As far as they could see, the horizon was blocked by cloud banks and dark rain squalls. The ocean's surface was a series of long, low swells that never seemed to end. To the west, another high rampart of clouds cut across the ocean from northwest to southeast.

"That first dawn we took stock of ourselves." Gunderson said. "We inventoried our rations and gear. Except for Whalen, we were pretty well set. Rex and Charley discussed what we were going to do."

Jeans said the pilots should shift Whalen from one raft to another every six hours. No one protested. They each gave the sick man water from their canteens to flush the seawater from his system. Price helped Whalen into the next raft in the line, that of Bill Reardon.

"Having those two Boston Irish in the same raft gave us something to laugh about," said Syrkin. "They began speaking in this awful brogue like something from a radio show."

Although he had not been present, Curly Lehnert related a story he'd been told about Whalen and Reardon. "They were both in the same raft, and I guess there were a few inches of cold seawater in it. Then Whalen said, 'Bill darlin' I have some bad news for ya." Reardon says, 'Chick, m'lad, what is it?' Whalen says, 'I'm afraid I have to pee. I'm ever so sorry, truly I am.' Then Reardon says in the low voice, 'That's okay, Chick m'lad, it'll warm the water.'"

Ethnic antics aside, the pilots never took their eyes from the horizon or the sky. A few times someone called out that he had seen an aircraft, but it always turned out to be an illusion or a bird. They had been told in Pearl that if they saw seagulls at dusk, to try and follow which way they flew. The birds were probably headed for land.

They discussed their chances of being found and where they were, but aside from some rough guesses based on Jeans' own attempts while still flying, they could only assume they were somewhere about thirty to fifty miles south or southeast of Nui, or

A museum display of the one-man life raft used by the Navy and Marines shows how small and vulnerable they were. yet they proved to be extremely useful and saved countless lives. (Photo courtesy Andrew Syrkin.)

halfway between Nanumea and Funafuti. In fact, they might have been less than thirty miles from Lehnert's location.

Even today, it is difficult, if not impossible to pinpoint the site of the ditching as they were under the influence of a phenomenon known as the "Leeway Effect," which determined how far a person could drift at sea. It depended on ocean currents, wind, and how much of a man's body was exposed. For instance, for men such as Chris Lauesen or Bill Aycrigg who had only their life preservers, most of their body mass was underwater. In this case, the ocean current had more effect on them than the wind. It is likely they were pushed by the currents, which according to Professor Barnes, moved generally south-southwest at a steady one to two miles per hour.

Conversely, for the men on rafts, who were essentially out of the water, the wind was the driving force. Even with the normal prevailing five-knot winds from the northwest and north, they could easily have drifted as far as twenty or thirty miles in twenty-four hours. As an example, Eddie Rickenbacker's raft was estimated to have drifted over 1,400 miles in three weeks. Louis Zamperini's now-famous forty-seven day raft ordeal in *Unbroken*, took him and his companion more than 2,400 miles, from southwest of Hawaii to the Marshall Islands.

For the men of VMF-422, the winds were much stronger. How fast they were being pushed is pure guesswork. Of course, the meteorological offices on both Nanumea and Funafuti kept records of the weather, but they had little accurate data for the 360 miles distance between the two islands.

As the morning passed, the air grew warmer. The wind and spray was a constant irritant and the salt spray began to affect their eyes. The sun, while it brought welcome relief from the cold, had its own special torture for the men in the rafts.

Their eyes were at the mercy of the sun's unshielded glare, both from the sky and reflected in millions of searing spots on the water. Constant winds drove salt spray into and under the eyelids until soon even closing their eyes failed to help. They still saw the sun as if they were staring into it. When this continued for days, the sensitive tissues of the corneas grew inflamed and sore until even blinking was torture, a condition known as photophobia, or light sensitivity. The only relief was to pour cool, fresh water over the eyes and covering the face with makeshift blindfolds. But this solution held its own twisted peril, when the only way to detect a distant airplane was by sight.

Yet even this paled in comparison to another peril that lurked just below the rolling waves. Sometime during the late morning, Lieutenant Price shouted that he saw a shark's fin next to his raft. The marines looked to see a large, dark grayish-brown triangle sliding past. The carnivorous fish was clearly visible in the water. It was at least ten feet long, and had wide pectoral fins like the wings of a fighter plane. Its eyes were black, soulless orbs that watched them as it swam by.

"It was scary as hell," admitted Syrkin. "I spent a lot of my youth at Coney Island swimming in the ocean, but I never saw anything like that big shark."

The shark was joined by another and they began a slow patrol around the rafts. Soon a third shark appeared. This one was even bigger than the other two and had a large piece missing from its fin. For a time, the stranded marines could only watch the three predators. Occasionally one bumped into a raft, making the man in it grunt or call out. But, in the way of Americans, humor soon took over the fear of being eaten by the sharks.

"We named them," continued Syrkin. "I don't remember which was which exactly, but the biggest one with the nick on his fin was Oscar. The other two were Leroy and Herbert. We joked about seafood or going swimming, stuff like that. But it was really kind of scary. Those fish were out to eat us."

The sun was well up when Curly Lehnert began paddling north. The raft contained two small paddles that slipped over the hands.

Former race car driver Jules Flood was considered the best natural mechanic in the squadron. He performed a perfect ditching in the heaving seas. (Photo courtesy Andrew Syrkin.)

As described by one aviator, they were each "about the size of a Gideon Bible and just as useful for paddling."

It was difficult and slow going, but soon Curly developed a rhythm. He paddled for half an hour, then stopped to rest. As far as he could tell he had made absolutely no progress at all. Nothing had changed. The sea was still an endless panorama of long heaving swells and occasional rain showers. He had plenty of water, but when it rained he caught and drank it, thus conserving his supply. By noon the sun had broken through the overcast. It was straight overhead, a blazing white orb that seared his eyes and baked his skin. Again the ever-bountiful raft provided what he needed in the form of a tube of sun block.

"I was about to set off again but when I put my hand on the side of the raft, I was surprised at how hot and taut it was. It was like a pneumatic tire. Usually the rubber was firm, but this was different. I wondered about this until I realized that the sun's heat had made the carbon dioxide in the raft's compartments expand."

Lehnert was worried that it might burst or spring a leak. There was a small tube with a valve poking out of the inner side of the raft. Pulling it out, Curly turned the valve and carefully vented off some of the carbon dioxide gas until the rubber skin softened.

"I could blow more air into the tube when the air temperature dropped. And I did have a repair kit if I needed it. I told myself that if I made it home alive, I'd write a letter of thanks to Goodyear."

Every so often a seagull circled the man on the raft. "I watched them fly past, but I didn't try to catch one. I figured it was impossible.

But one time, while I was resting with my eyes closed, I felt this weight on my head. I knew immediately that it was a gull. I felt his webbed feet trying to get a grip on my flight helmet. I was surprised at how heavy it was. So I made a grab for it."

Lehnert was too slow and the gull flew away with an indignant squawk. "I remembered that Eddie Rickenbacker had caught a seagull by moving very slow until the last moment, so that's what I did."

Curly waited patiently, and sure enough, another gull landed on his head. This time he was ready and had his hands up closer to his head. Moving very slowly, he reached closer and made a lightning fast grab. In a second he had the gull trapped in both hands.

"But that damned bird squawked and flapped and kicked like mad," he said. "I had to turn my head away to keep from having my eyes pecked out. Finally I just let go and decided I wasn't hungry enough yet."

The wind rose an hour later, promising the arrival of another rain squall. Trying to keep the wind from blowing the spray and waves into the raft, Curly experimented with leaning over to keep the high side into the wind. The sea anchor was deployed so he wasn't worried about being blown in the wrong direction. The temperature dropped alarmingly until he was shivering in his wet flight suit. Leaning even more gave him a small measure of shelter from the icy winds. Then, without any warning, the raft flipped over and Curly found himself in the cold water. His precious link to life was several feet away. With a frenzied grab he managed to catch the sea anchor line and pull the raft towards him. A minute later he was back in, breathing heavily and soaked to the skin.

"That was close," Lehnert said with a grin. "One moment I was fine, the next, I was swimming for my life."

Two of the downed aviators, Christian Lauesen, who had been the first to ditch after emerging from the storm, and Bill Aycrigg, the first to ditch on the desperate search for Nui were adrift in life preservers. What happened to these two men is a matter of conjecture. At least their specific fates are. How they spent their last days and hours is not difficult to surmise.

From the time they found themselves floating in the Mae Wests, they were at the mercy of the sea and weather. It is possible they had full canteens of water, but these would have been as much a hindrance as a benefit. Every pound of extra weight, such as shoes or a pistol would drag them lower into the water. The best move would be to drink the water as soon as possible and use the empty canteen as a float, then use the cup for collecting rain water. A human can live far longer without food than without fresh water. The seawater they drifted in was, in fact, deadly.

Seawater is a complex witches' potion containing more than seventy-five percent sodium chloride and other caustic elements like magnesium, potassium, boric acid, and sulfates. In fact, long exposure to seawater is almost as corrosive as a mild acid bath. For a man drifting in the teeth of a storm, it was nearly impossible to avoid swallowing seawater as waves fell over them or spray was forced into their mouths by the wind.

Almost immediately, the potassium would begin working its way into the bloodstream, breaking down the structure of the red blood cells. This started an insidious chain reaction that included pulmonary edema, reducing the oxygen content, and literally slow drowning. One by one, the body's complex mechanisms that depended on stable biochemical reactions shut down. Without large amounts of fresh water, it was impossible to reverse the degeneration.

Their other enemy was the cold. In January, the water in the region near the Ellice Islands was usually around eighty degrees Fahrenheit. While this was not cold, it was still about fifteen degrees below normal core body temperature. As they hung in their life preservers, Lauesen and Aycrigg's body temperature dropped, resulting in hypothermia. Several variables affected how fast they would lose heat, such as body fat and clothing. The more, the better. On average they would lose about one degree Fahrenheit for every hour, particularly at night when the air temperature often dropped below forty degrees. As the air grew colder, they would shiver, and then shake violently. This was the body's way of generating heat, but it also consumed quadruple the amount of oxygen and energy. By the time hypothermia had reduced their core temperature to below ninety-three degrees, they would find it difficult to speak or think clearly and became apathetic. At ninety degrees the kidneys shut down, resulting in blood poisoning. Soon the heartbeat grew irregular. When the sun rose again, they might have regained some vitality, but as the hours passed without sleep, shelter, food, water, or any relief, they would drift into listlessness, unconsciousness, and finally, death.

This is undoubtedly what happened to First Lieutenants Christian Lauesen of Chicago and William Aycrigg of Connecticut.

Eventually their life preservers filled with water and their bodies sank into the cold sea. Their deaths were surely heartbreaking and lonely.

First Lieutenant Ted Thurnau, who ditched his Corsair right after Aycrigg, was alone in his raft. As noted, he was at least seven miles from the main group, which put him below their horizon. He too was subject to the winds and waves, but there was little chance he would drift closer to his fellow Buccaneers. In any event, Thurnau, who never had the opportunity to record his experiences after the ditching, endured the squalls, searched the skies for planes and did his best to survive.

On Niutao, Jake Wilson was looking out the window of the hut the chief had provided for his use. The islanders, after their night of revelry, were at their daily work of tending their gardens and goats. It reminded him of home. Almost. The braless girls and palm trees dispelled any notion that he was back in Mississippi. Wilson was hung on the horns of a dilemma. Clearly, he could not marry one of the many young women offered to him, but he also could not risk offending the generous natives. He owed them his life, yet until word was sent to an Allied base, he was stuck on the island.

With nothing else to do, he decided to go out to his Corsair and see if there was anything he could salvage from it. As soon as he left the hut, four young men in their twenties flanked him and walked alongside. These were members of the island police force. The air was warm and fragrant with the scent of flowers as he walked along the lane through the village. A few palm fronds and other debris from the storm were scattered on the ground. As he walked, the villagers smiled at him and a few came out of their huts to press warm loaves of bread into his hands.

Jake Wilson saw his Corsair in the surf just beyond a reef. He described it as being underwater right up to the cockpit sill. The wings were completely hidden in the surging breakers. The plane would be almost impossible to spot from the air.

There was nothing to be salvaged from it, but Wilson had one duty to perform. He had to destroy the IFF transponder, a device that would be of great value to the Japanese. He leaned in to hit the detonator switch but nothing happened. "I removed the seat and let the armor plate down and found that the cord to the charge had not been hooked up. I connected it and set it off."

After Wilson returned to the village, he was given a present. "The chief had returned my pistol, which was a surprise," he said, but the Colt automatic was rusted beyond use.

The day passed as Wilson tried to think of a way out of his predicament. As soon as the sun set, he would be the guest of honor at another banquet and expected to choose a bride.

There was no other recourse than to repeat his earlier performance. To make it look good, he made sure the villagers saw him holding his head as if in pain. "It was all I had."

The feast was even more elaborate than the one the previous night. Wilson ate his fill of pork, fish, and chicken. He also sampled a local palm wine. He admitted it had almost the same kick as Mississippi moonshine.

All through the feast, the girls danced for him. He continued to feign dizziness and pain, but appeared to be interested in the girls. He said it would be a hard choice and he wanted to take his time. The chief seemed mollified, but it was apparent he expected his American guest to make a choice soon.

As the revelry continued, Wilson wondered if his buddies in VMF-422 were in as big a fix as he.

It was now 1700 hours on 26 January, twenty-four hours since they'd ditched. What remained of the dim sunlight faded over the small band of men in the rafts. The heaving sea went dark and even the whitecaps and spray kicked up by the rising winds were only a lighter shade of gray. It appeared as if the sun was being turned down by a giant rheostat. The New Moon was completely hidden behind the overcast.

By the time darkness fell, the wind had increased. It was not as violent as it had been the day before, but a squall was obviously on the way.

Jeanes issued orders. The raft lanyards were inadequate to keep them tied together in a real gale, so they were each to take the spool of fishing line in the raft survival kits and twist it into strong twine.

"He had us link the rafts in a big circle," said Syrkin. "That way if a line broke, there would be no rafts lost. If the lines broke, we'd hold hands."

The squall, one of several that accompanied a large cyclone like a flock of chicks to a mother hen, struck shortly after dark. With no light to see by, not even starlight, the Marines could only wait it out. They were kept busy by bailing out the seawater and checking the improvised lashings. Some cords broke or worked themselves loose. The pilots held hands to keep together. The constant rubbing and chafing on skin softened by immersion in seawater caused abrasions and bleeding.

The hours dragged by as the squall passed and the wind faded. The weary pilots caught their breath and made hasty repairs.

Syrkin continued, "We managed to tie the rafts back into a circle after the seas calmed down and we got a little rest. The rest didn't last long."

Within the hour another storm swept over them. "It was pretty hairy. One moment you would be on the crest of a wave and the next moment you would be thirty feet below in a trough. It went on all night long. I kept baling and checking my lead to Abe Lincoln's raft. I was exhausted. The air got a lot colder as if it had come from the North Pole."

Only by desperately holding hands were they able to stay together. No one had to remind them to keep their tarps tied down to keep the water from flooding the rafts. There was no thought of catching the rain; it was almost all seawater and spray. The wind drove it at them from all sides as the rafts swayed, dipped, pitched, and heaved.

Price said, "The weather was nasty and we held hands to keep from tearing the rafts apart. We took the shock in our arms. The weather was rough. The back side of the storm was passing over us. The waves were fifty feet high and every single one looked like it was going to come right down on us."

The tiny band was tossed and pitched, lifted high and dropped sickeningly into another black abyss. Groans and wheezes came from the darkness as one or another man succumbed to the fury of the insane weather.

"It reminded me of the roller coaster at Coney Island. Or maybe those little bumper cars. Every time my raft rolled or moved, it bumped into either Lincoln or Reardon and bounced off. With the endless swells rising and falling, it was like being in a hotel elevator run by a deranged operator. Up and down, down and up."

Price said laconically, "You know they say there aren't any atheists in foxholes? Well, there aren't any in a raft in a storm either!"

Hughes encapsulated that night in his account. "Shortly after nightfall, the wind started rising and developed into a full gale. The swells were mountainous with nothing but foam and spray at the crests and three to four-foot waves on the slopes. The rafts would climb up the leading slope of a swell, dive through the spray at the crest, and go skidding down the back slope. The load on the ties was very great, we therefore held hands to ease the load on the ties. Even so, breaks occurred three times during the night. We managed to repair each break. Sometime around midnight the wind died down. About two hours later, the wind was back in full force, but from the opposite direction. So then we knew. A tropical front backed up by a typhoon, what jolly fun."

At some point, a desperate frivolity took over when Don Walker began to sing "Oh, it ain't gonna rain no more, no more..."

Walker's baritone thundered through the darkness and soon others joined in the nonsense verses. "A bum sat by the sewer . . . and by the sewer he died. And at the coroner's inquest, they called it 'sewer side.' Oh, it ain't gonna rain no more..."

Then they belted out a loud and spirited rendition of "How Dry I Am," with the accompaniment of the howling wind, followed by "Don't Sit Under the Apple Tree," then "God Bless America," and the "Marine Corps Hymn." Often their words were lost among the gales of wet wind, but it only made them sing harder. Soon their voices died out from having to sing so loud.

"It was crazy as hell," Syrkin said. "I can't explain it but I felt great after that. I thought 'If I have to be out here, I couldn't ask for better company.'"

The night dragged on hour by torturous hour. It might have seemed to take forever, but the constant need to be alert and hold hands was a blessing. It made the time pass more swiftly.

The wind and rain were beginning to slack off when the marines realized they could see. Instead of being utterly black, the sky was a mottled dark gray and blue. Far in the distance, a pale purple line rose like a halo over the crenulated black horizon. The purple became mauve, then pink, and finally orange. The bow of the sun appeared with a cold brilliance over the tortured sea, and winds toyed with the water, creating long white cat's claws on the surface. The night's raging tempest had ended at last.

Jeans took the roll. All thirteen marines were accounted for. No one had been lost during the dark and stormy night. They took stock of their situation. Except for the lightening sky and diminishing wind and rain, all was as it had been the evening before.

As the hours passed, the pilots were often quiet as their minds turned to thoughts of home and family. They wondered what their wives and girlfriends were doing, and if anyone had reported the missing squadron. Emotions ran the gamut from fear and worry,

Lieutenant Mark "Breeze" Syrkin endured the long hours and days of surviving on the tiny rafts with his fellow marine aviators. (Photo courtesy Andrew Syrkin.)

hope and despair, anger and acceptance, bitterness and cheerfulness, to anxiety and confidence. Rex Jeanes, now in command, was most concerned with their location and how to find land. There was little chance of being spotted by a navy ship, as the bulk of the fleet was far to the north queueing up for Flintlock, slated to begin in a few days. Another factor was the cyclone. Once it had been reported, all warships and transports would have been diverted far from the path of the storm.

But there was always a chance. Jeans knew that several navy patrol squadrons were based on Funafuti and Nanumea, as well as Tarawa, and once the cyclone had passed, their planes would be out scouring the ocean for the missing marines.

One of Jeans' orders had concerned signaling search planes. As mentioned, the marines had signal mirrors, Very flare pistols, small flare cartridges, and dye markers. By far the most visible from the air was the dye marker, which spread out in a fluorescent yellow stain in a wide area. As long as the current and raft moved together, the dye marker remained more or less close by. To assure this, the group kept some of the canvas sea anchors deployed.

There were only twelve dye packets among them, so only one was used at a time. That way, the small group of rafts remained within the penumbra of the dye. Every marine had a specific job when an aircraft was spotted. Some would fire their flare pistols while others used the mirrors.

Syrkin said, "We never stopped looking for search planes. I had my part of the sky to look at, and Tex Watson had his and so on. We had hand mirrors and flare pistols ready. Rex had drilled it into us exactly who would use what to get a plane's attention so we didn't blow everything off in one go. He really had it all figured out."

Jeans' primary job was to keep them alive and safe until rescue arrived. For this, he was confident. They had everything they needed to survive.

Except for the gentle wind and lapping of waves on the rafts, it was quiet throughout the early morning.

Then Cal Smick fell into the water.

"We were all turning and looking at the sky," said Syrkin, "and those rafts were very unstable. It didn't take any effort at all to turn them over. Suddenly there was this big splash, and Cal Smick was in the water, bobbing a few feet from his raft. I don't remember who was closest, but he yelled to Cal that one of the sharks was heading for him." According to the other pilots who witnessed it, Smick yelled in fear and thrashed his way back to the raft. With a violent flurry of flailing arms and legs, he literally flew out of the water and fell into his small craft. The tiny boat tipped and Smick fell into the water on the other side. Again he thrashed and threw himself into the raft, but this time he managed to stay in by clutching its straps in a grip of icy terror.

The sharks, robbed of their easy meal, bumped the side of the raft and passed on. Smick was wheezing and gasping, but unhurt.

"Then he started to laugh," Syrkin said. "I swear he was laughing like a crazy man. And in a minute, we were all laughing. Charley Hughes said, 'He actually walked on water! Did you see that? It's a miracle!'"

Hughes' written account is similar, but he had the incident occurring during the night, which seems odd in that there was absolutely no light to see by. "Sometime during the night Caleb Smick gave a demonstration of water walking when he got dumped out of his raft. One of our 'pet' sharks was under him at the time which motivated him to run very fast. In a cloud of foam, Caleb rose from the water, went across his raft, turned around and stayed in the raft on the second pass. In spite of his undoubted fast foot work, I still suspect him of using some jet assist."

CHAPTER 16

SHARK BAIT

By dawn on the morning of 27 January, Curly Lehnert had gotten through the night. He'd had to endure the edge of a storm that passed to the south, but even so, it had tossed him and the raft about like a toy in a bathtub. As the sun rose, he tried to escape the heat by pulling the tarp over him, but all it did was to trap the heat.

The hours passed slowly. To relieve the pain in his swollen eyes, he splashed water on his face. Water wasn't a problem. He'd managed to fill the bucket twice during the intermittent rains and poured the contents into his empty canteen.

"Around noon on Thursday the twenty-seventh, I was so hot from the sun that I decided to take a chance on a quick swim," he said. "I didn't see any sharks, I guessed it was safe. I didn't hear about the sharks that were swimming around my buddies until later." He grinned. "If I had known, I might not have gone for a swim."

Carefully, after making sure the lanyard was secure around his wrist, Curly put a leg over the side. In a minute the cold Pacific water was like an icy shroud. But "it felt wonderful. I only stayed in the water for about five minutes."

Lehnert hoisted himself back into the raft, and in minutes the sun had dried him off. The quick dip had refreshed him.

Pulling the ration box out of the raft stores he began chewing on a strip of pemmican. "As long as the rains kept coming, I had all the water I needed," he said.

The hours passed slowly. Once, he was sure he'd seen an airplane flying several miles away, but it had disappeared before he could get a flare out and ready. From that moment on, he resolved to keep the big Very pistol close at hand, but also kept two of the smaller flare launchers in his shirt pocket. He wasn't about to miss an opportunity to signal a passing plane again.

After the giddy hysteria over Smick's miraculous escape from the sharks, the marines again had to face reality. At least three big sharks were circling the small flotilla. The carnivorous fish were not going to go away. One way or another, they were determined to get their free meal.

"One of the sharks, I don't know which, came out of the water near us and we saw its mouth," said Ken Gunderson. "It had all these gleaming white teeth. Then Abe Lincoln said he was going to try and shoot one of the sharks."

Lincoln had a revolver. He had changed from the Colt automatic after the near-disastrous shooting incident back at Ewa Field in October.

The big fish was just under the surface less than ten feet away. Lincoln aimed to keep the shark in his sights, but he failed to notice that Ken Gunderson was only a few feet away.

"I was watching the shark passing my raft," Gunderson continued. "Then BANG! I felt the muzzle blast right by my cheek. The crazy bastard had nearly shot my ear off! I swung around and belted him a good one."

But Lincoln had missed and the big shark slid with weighty disdain into the dark green water.

Watson passed the time fishing, but every time he got a bite, one of the sharks made a beeline for his catch.

"He lost at least three fish to the sharks," Syrkin remembered. "He was really angry at them."

Finally Watson was able to haul in a fish that weighed at least three pounds. He used his combat knife to cut the fish into strips and laid them on the side of the raft to dry in the sun. At one point, according to Syrkin, he dropped one slice in the water and Leroy, the smallest of the three sharks nabbed it in a flash.

"Charley said he would try shooting one. He asked me to hold his raft steady so he could get on his knees. I bent over and held his raft close to mine."

Hughes managed to get into a higher kneeling position as he looked for the shark. The dark gray body of the nearest fish was only twenty feet away. Watson tried to entice the shark by dangling a slice of fish in the water. The jiggling bait did the trick, and the predator moved closer. Suddenly the shark's broad, dull back broke the surface.

Hughes' gun barked once, then twice. Two neat holes were punched into the shark's leathery back just behind the gill slits. With a violent twist, its sickle-shaped tail thrashed and drove it deep under the water.

Lieutenant John "Abe" Lincoln, who had accidentally fired his pistol at Hansen in Hawaii, tried to shoot one of the sharks menacing the rafts. (Photo courtesy Andrew Syrkin.)

"Leroy took off like a shot," Syrkin said. "And right behind him was Herbert and Oscar. That was the last we saw of them for a while. But they eventually came back."

Every six hours, Whalen moved into another raft. Syrkin took him that afternoon. "It was a very tight fit with the two of us in there," he said. "I'm a big guy but at least Chick was only about 140 pounds. He kept apologizing for being a burden, but I told him to shut up. I knew he would do the same for me. He was in really bad shape. Without anything but his skivvies on, he was badly sunburned. I kept the tarp over him as much as possible. But the sun beat down on us and it was like a furnace underneath the tarp. I really felt bad for the guy."

Back on Tarawa, the missing squadron was the subject of official concern. By order of Admiral John Hoover, Commander Air Forces, Central Pacific, an official investigation into the disappearance and possible loss of Marine Fighter Squadron 422 had begun that morning.

Under the Uniform Code of Military Justice (UCMJ), the Navy Department decreed that whenever there was loss of life, a ship, or aircraft, an inquiry was convened to investigate. As defined by the Navy Judge Advocate General (JAG) Manual for Courts-Martial, a Court or Board of Inquiry is not a court as the term is commonly used today. Rather, it is a panel of officers who are directed by a convening authority to conduct an investigation. They are charged with examining and inquiring into an incident and offering opinions and recommendations about the incident. It could loosely be compared to a civilian grand jury, empowered to subpoena and question witnesses and examine documents to determine the circumstances leading up to the loss. Their job was to learn who was responsible, determine if any offense had been committed, and if warranted, to fix blame. A board's findings might suggest operational changes to prevent a recurrence of the loss, and in some cases, recommend disciplinary action against, or the court martial of any officers or enlisted men they considered responsible. For this, Boards of Inquiry were often called "Captain Breakers," as they could end a career with a few well-chosen words.

The VMF-422 investigation was conducted behind closed doors in the wardroom of the USS *Curtiss*. Four senior officers made up the board. The *Curtiss'* commander, Captain Scott E. Peck, was the senior member. He was joined by an experienced Marine aviator, Lieutenant Colonel John W. Stage of Hoover's staff, and navy Commander James C. Lang. The board recorder was Lieutenant Commander Elmer N. Buddress. His role was to examine the witnesses, enter evidence, and make recommendations to the other members. Two navy yeomen, Harold F. Oliver and Dalton T. Shaw, served as clerks and reporters.

At 0930 hours, the wardroom doors were closed and the official investigation into the loss of VMF-422 began.

The first witness was the only pilot who had not taken off on the morning of 25 January, First Lieutenant Bob Scott.

Wearing his tropical khakis, he took his place on the wooden chair facing the four taciturn, high-ranking board members. Commander Buddress began by asking Scott his name, rank, and duty

Rear Admiral Hoover's flagship, The seaplane tender USS Curtiss. *(Official U.S. Navy photo.)*

station. It was the beginning of what would amount to fifty-six thousand words and 177 pages of testimony over the next twelve days.

On Niutao, Jake Wilson was going to have to endure another feast in his honor. The islanders were just as cordial and friendly as ever. They showed no signs of tiring in their sincere efforts to make him happy. But he knew time was running out. He had to either get off the island or risk insulting them by not choosing a wife from one of the dozen pretty girls who had danced for him. Wilson had to find a way out of the matrimonial noose being strung around his neck.

It was early afternoon on 27 January, his third day on Niutao when he heard a few of the islanders talking in loud, excited voices. They were pointing at the sky to the west. He looked that way and saw what had excited them.

It was an airplane. A big one. The thin line of its wings grew more distinct and resolved itself into a four-engine bomber. He recognized it as a Consolidated B-24 Liberator.

The big bomber flew directly at the island, the thrum of its engines increasing in volume. Wilson ran out on the road, waving a blanket over his head. The huge plane swept by at less than a thousand feet, flying along the length of the small island while Wilson ran out to the beach next to his plane. The bomber turned and came in even lower, directly overhead. It was apparent that the crew had seen the Corsair in the surf.

In his narrative, Wilson stated that "an Army B-24" found him. While he cannot be faulted for this assumption, he was probably in error. The US Army Air Force had two B-24 groups operating in the region, the Eleventh on Funafuti and the 30th on Nanumea. Their job was to bomb Japanese installations in the Marshalls in preparation for Flintlock. They were not used for search and rescue missions. The route between the Ellice Islands and Kwajalein was far west of Niutao. Furthermore, their normal cruising altitude of fifteen thousand feet would make spotting a half sunken Corsair in the surf virtually impossible.

Wilson did not mention the bomber's paint scheme. Army bombers were olive drab, while navy planes were blue. Both services often painted the undersides gray, so misidentification would not have been difficult. It was far more likely that the plane that spotted Wilson's Corsair was a US Navy PB4Y-1 of VB-108 out of Funafuti. The PB4Y-1 was the navy designation for the B-24. The PB4Ys were on regular anti-submarine patrol in the area to protect Allied shipping to and from the invasion staging areas. The search for the missing marines had been on since the morning of 26 January, but for some reason, the word of a crashed Corsair on Niutao did not trigger a search of that island until the following day. It is also curious that Nanumea, with a full squadron of Douglas Dauntless scout planes apparently did not send any out to search for the missing marines.

In any event, the bomber had seen the ditched Corsair and radioed a report of the sighting back to its home base. This started a chain reaction that began to move ships, including two destroyers, into the search for VMF-422's survivors.

A few hours later another bomber approached the island. Not being a seaplane, it could only fly over the island. But this one had a surprise in store for the stranded Wilson. As it came over, he realized the cavernous bomb bay was open. The instant it passed the center of Niutao, a rain of boxes fell out. Suspended under small parachutes, they drifted slowly to earth until they landed in a field.

Wilson helped the islanders pry open the boxes, which contained canned food, cigarettes, candy bars, gum, medical supplies, and other useful household items.

"The gifts enabled me to repay the natives' hospitality," Wilson wrote.

One box had an envelope taped to the lid and Wilson found it contained a letter addressed to "The pilot of the Corsair ditched on Niutao." It stated that a destroyer would be arriving the following day to pick him up.

That was the turning point for Walter "Jake" Wilson. He had been saved.

The cyclone had passed north of Funafuti by the afternoon of 27 January. A light breeze was blowing sand and dust off the single runway. John Hansen, who had spent the last seventy-two hours waiting, hoping, and praying was informed that a plane had spotted a Corsair in the surf of Niutao Island. There was no information on whose plane it was, but it was obviously one of the missing VMF-422 fighters.

The sun had dipped close to the horizon behind Curly Lehnert. Thumping the raft sides with his hand, he felt safe in adding some air to the floatation chambers. He pulled the short hose from where it protruded from the raft's inner wall and opened the valve. Then he began to blow hard into the hose. After several minutes, he stopped and closed the valve.

"I was bored," Lehnert admitted. "With my eyes hurting it was torture to look for airplanes. I spent a minute looking, and then closed my eyes. I passed the time with mental exercises. I tried to remember every student in my chemical engineering class at the University of Michigan. Then I tried to recite all the elements of the Periodic Table, or every state capital in alphabetical order. Anything to keep my mind busy."

After a time, Lehnert realized the sky was getting dark. With the coming of twilight, he was able to open his eyes fully. The sky overhead and to the west was a brilliant artist's canvas of reds, pinks, oranges, and violets. Far overhead, the first stars were twinkling in the fading indigo blue dome. "It was really pretty. I just wished I wasn't seeing it all alone."

That night was relatively quiet. The rain squalls of the previous night and day had lessened in strength. The stranded marines were able to sleep in their bobbing little rafts.

The morning of Friday 28 January broke with a calm sea and solid overcast. The thirteen pilots were sore and tired. The constant contact of skin softened from the water against the rough canvas and rubber in the rafts had resulted in blisters and raw sores. They were all sunburned. Their eyes were mere slits, while their lips had swollen and split open.

The hours dragged by with agonizing slowness. Then, around mid-morning, the lethargy was broken when a flock of seagulls flew close and made several noisy circles around the men.

Gunderson said, "I think it was Don Walker who was going to try and shoot one but Tex Watson told him it was impossible. Then one gull just lands on Charley's raft. He made a grab for it and caught it and broke its neck."

The other birds squawked and cawed at the murder of one of their own, but Hughes began to pluck and dismember the carcass.

"He gave us each some meat from the gull," said Gunderson, "but it was the most godawful tasting stuff in the world. It smelled like dead fish. I managed to get a bit down and took a swig of water."

"I did take time out [from fishing] to flip a sinker on a fish line over a gooney bird's wing," recalled Hughes. "It wound around his wing several times. I then pulled him in and wrung his neck."

Hughes had called it a "gooney bird," the common term for an albatross, but he probably meant a seagull. An albatross would have been far too big to handle in the raft.

They cleaned the bird for food and used the entrails for bait.

"The men at the back of the line tried the bird first. The snide comments about the taste of my bird would break a saint's heart."

CHAPTER 17

EYES IN THE SKY

The atoll of Funafuti rested like a sand and coral jewel in the center of an eleven-mile-wide azure lagoon. The thirty-three islands and islets that make up the atoll are now the capital of the modern nation of Tuvalu. The five-thousand-foot airstrip was built for the USAAF in 1943 and was equipped with a control tower, administration building, hangars, and repair facilities.

In late January, the island was literally buried in army, navy and marine aircraft. In addition to the home-based Eleventh Bomb Group, there was a squadron of PBY Catalinas, another of PB4Y-1 Liberators, and several army, navy and marine fighter and dive bomber squadrons. A number of big transports cycled on and off the island every day. Except for the heavy bombers and patrol planes, they were all on Funafuti at Admiral Hoover's orders to await their role in Operation Flintlock. These included the Corsairs of VMF-113 and the F6F Hellcats of VF-12, although the latter was actually assigned to USS *Saratoga* and TG 58.4. The only missing squadron was VMF-422.

Navy Patrol Squadron (VP) Fifty-three was based on Funafuti, but their regular tender was the USS *Curtiss*, still at Tarawa. The seaplane tender USS *Mackinac* (AVP-13) was on duty at the island of Nukufetau, fifty-seven miles north of Funafuti. The squadron had twelve new Consolidated PBY-5A Catalinas under Lieutenant Commander David Perry.

In a July 2013 article in *EAA Warbirds* magazine, the author had this to say about the PBY Catalina.

"Some warbirds have made their mark on history, such as the lumbering Consolidated PBY Catalina flying boat. Known with backhanded affection as 'Dumbo' or 'Cat,' PBYs served with every branch of the United States Armed Services, including the army. They saw action in all the theaters of the war. They were workhorses, trucks, buses, and ambulances."

The origins of the PBY began in the 1930s when the United States had its eyes on the tens of thousands of islands in the vast Pacific.

Consolidated designed the XP3Y with a parasol wing mounted on a central pylon supported by external struts. Retractable pontoons extended from the wingtips. The new plane was all-metal and surprisingly durable. The hull was wide and very stable on water, with the "step" which helped it to break the surface tension on takeoff. Powered by two Pratt & Whitney R-1830 800 horsepower radial engines, the XP3Y flew for the first time on 28 March 1935.

The Catalina was nearly as large as a Boeing B-17. But unlike the Fortress, it was equipped for a modicum of comfort for long missions over water. The hull had a small galley, bunk space, and even an actual sit-down toilet, a true luxury in Second World War combat planes. Almost 4,100 Catalinas were built for service between June 1937 and May 1945. The later models were true amphibians, able to land on both water and runways.

In their role as patrol aircraft, Catalinas participated in some of the most notable naval engagements of the war. One of the Catalina's most famous feats helped to shape the course of the Battle of the North Atlantic. In May 1941, the Royal Navy was in a desperate hunt for the German battleship *Bismarck* after the huge ship had broken into the vast Atlantic. The *Bismarck* could destroy convoys with impunity and the Royal Navy had no idea where it was.

The Germans were sure they were free and clear to go where they pleased, but then a tiny shape appeared in the skies to the west of the *Bismarck*, staying just under the clouds. It was an RAF Coastal Command PBY. A day later the *Bismarck* was on the bottom of the ocean and the myth of the battleship's invincibility was shattered forever.

Just over a year later, on the other side of the world, the US Navy was still reeling from the attack on Pearl Harbor and struggling to assemble a force to fight the huge Japanese carriers headed for Midway Island.

A wide search scoured the ocean to the west and north of the island, looking for the first sign of the Japanese invasion force. The plane that found them was a PBY.

When the war in the southwest Pacific moved north after the Solomons Campaign, there were still plenty of Japanese strongholds in the area. The Japanese were forced to move troops, fuel, and supplies by night to avoid roving air and sea patrols. But the US Navy found a new use for the PBY. By painting them flat black and adding Magnetic Anomaly Detectors (MAD), the "Black Cats" special patrol squadrons went hunting at night. During the day, the PBY's 135 knot speed and huge size made them prey for attack from Japanese fighters, but at night they were virtually invulnerable. Using radar altimeters, the Black Cats prowled far into enemy-held waters looking for convoys and unescorted ships. The Black Cats dropped bombs, torpedoes, mines, and depth charges on ship and land targets, including the big base at Rabaul. Through the summer of 1943 until early 1944, Black Cats sank more than one hundred thousand tons of enemy shipping and put at least ten warships out of action. Very little of the Pacific was out of reach of the Cat's claws.

But it was in the role of search and rescue that the Catalina was most revered. When ships sank and planes ditched, the world changed for their crews. Suddenly instead of being in control, they found themselves alone and wondering if they'd see another dawn. The chronicles of the war are full of heroic and tragic sagas of men drifting for days and weeks under the blazing sun on the trackless uncaring sea. For many, rescue was only a dream. Just hearing the distant drone of two aircraft engines quickened the beats of hearts weary with fatigue and despair. It gave the tired, dehydrated men the hope that they must have felt slipping away day after day in the vast, merciless crucible of the Pacific war."

Ensign George Davidson was a twenty-eight-year old Louisiana native. Solidly built at 5'6" in height, his arms were muscular from hundreds of hours manhandling the lumbering Catalina flying boats in endless square search patterns all over the Ellice and Gilbert Islands on anti-submarine patrols.

On the morning of 28 January, he was in the operations room of VP-53's hangar, reading over his orders for the day. Not surprisingly, he was to fly his PBY-5A on another anti-submarine patrol west of Funafuti.

He had little faith that they would even find, let alone sink, a Japanese submarine. Since the loss of their bases in the region, the Japanese Navy had withdrawn to Kwajalein, Majuro, and to Truk Lagoon in the Carolines.

Patrol Squadron Fifty-Three had flown from Hawaii, arriving on 8 November, just before the invasion of Tarawa. Since then, they had been on dozens of raids on Japanese shipping and earned battle stars for conspicuous service. As part of the Ellice Defense and Utility Group, VP-53 and VB-108 patrolled the entire southern Gilberts and Ellice Islands. General Merritt, while he may have resented losing command of the fighters and bombers, was not

The Consolidated PBY Catalina flying boat, the workhorse of the U.S. Navy during the Second World War. Fulfilling a number of roles from ambulances to patrol bombers they were a welcome sight to downed aviators and shipwrecked sailors. (Official U.S. Navy photo.)

foolhardy enough to risk hundreds of ships and thousands of men by failing to mount a continuous patrol for enemy submarines.

His determination to adhere rigidly to this policy is borne out by the orders issued to VP-53 on the morning of 28 January. Merritt undoubtedly learned of the missing marine squadron after reading the first two reports from Nanumea and Funafuti on the afternoon of 25 January. He probably called in Colonel Burke and his meteorological officer to confirm the report of a major cyclone in the region south of Nanumea.

What was said at this meeting can only be surmised. Colonel Burke certainly had mixed emotions upon hearing that VMF-422 was reported missing in the storm, but it is doubtful that he had the courage to remind Merritt of his two requests for an escort. Merritt, for his part, probably never mentioned it.

In any event, Merritt did issue orders that the patrol squadrons on Funafuti, Nanumea, and Nukufetau were to begin an extensive air search as soon as the weather permitted, but he still insisted that all regular anti-submarine patrols be maintained.

This is why Davidson had orders to conduct a routine anti-submarine patrol west of Funafuti. Although a religious man, he was also a pilot and often relied on luck when flying in the war zone. There was always a chance that fate would put an enemy vessel in his sights. His plane was armed with four Mark 3 420 lb. depth charges in addition to the three .30 caliber and two .50 caliber machine guns.

Davidson had been briefed on the missing marine squadron, but his assigned patrol area west and south of Funafuti was far from where the main search was being conducted.

After driving out to the flight line along the main runway, Davidson and his crew chief ran a preflight check of the big flying boat as it was being refueled from a truck. Two aviation ordnance men were fitting depth charges to the wing racks. The PBY-5A was the latest version of the Catalina. It had retractable tricycle landing gear, a major improvement over the earlier model, which could not use runways due to the "beach wheels" that needed to be fitted to the plane by hand before it could be run up a ramp onto land for servicing.

With a 104-foot wingspan, the 67-foot long airplane flew nearly 190 knots and carried enough fuel to fly over 2,500 miles. That was quite enough for Davidson, who always felt like his arms were about to fall off after a ten-hour patrol. He climbed into the main hatch in the side of the fuselage under the wing. His crew of sailors and chiefs greeted him as he made his way into the cramped control cabin. Ensign Davidson was popular among both enlisted and officers in VP-53. A PBY's crew normally consisted of two pilots, a bow turret gunner, ventral gunner, two waist gunners, navigator, radio operator, radar operator, and crew chief. The latter was often a career chief petty officer.

Once seated in the left-hand seat, Davidson and his co-pilot, Lieutenant(jg) Howard began preparing to take off. When the ground crew signaled they were done loading, he began the process of starting the engines.

The ten-ton plane shuddered as the twin radial engines roared to life just eight feet over his head. He had already put on his headset which helped to attenuate, but not eliminate, the noise. He called the crew stations and they checked in that all hatches were secured.

The pilot released the brakes and began taxiing the big plane out to the runway. Land takeoffs were preferred for a fully-loaded PBY, since the drag from a water takeoff would use up too much fuel. The PBY taxied to the south end of the runway, passing scores of bombers, fighters, and transports. To the Louisiana-born Davidson, it seemed as if every single navy, marine, and army plane was on Funafuti.

Ahead of him, another Catalina was starting its takeoff roll. That was Lieutenant Herbert Shivley, who had been assigned to the search for the missing marine pilots. Davidson sincerely wished them luck.

When he received clearance from the tower, Davidson pushed the twin throttle controls to maximum and held the big plane on the centerline of the runway while his co-pilot sounded off the speed. At ninety knots, the Catalina's graceful Davis wing caught the warm tropical air and the plane lifted off. The noisy thrum of the landing gear ceased, to be replaced by the one-hundred-knot slipstream outside. The indigo blue of the lagoon passed beneath their wings. Once the thin white circlet of coral reef was behind them, the ocean turned a dark teal, then green.

The big flying boat banked left and flew west to begin another ten-hour anti-submarine patrol.

As soon as the rising sun emerged from the clouds, Rex Jeans began a serious attempt to calculate their position. Armed only with his trusty Boy Scout compass, his wristwatch, and a note pad and pencil, he made observations and jotted down notes. For the first time, he was able to ascertain the direction and speed of the prevailing winds, and equally important, those of the current. He determined that both ran in a south-southwesterly direction. The cyclone, moreover, had moved east and turned in a clockwise direction. He had no clear idea of wind velocity in the storm, but it was logical to assume that they had been pushed south and east while under its influence. The sighting of Nui after they emerged from the storm three days earlier was an important clue that supported this. Further calculations included the time, direction, and distance they had flown after sighting the island. After a time, during which his fellow marines watched the skies, he made an announcement.

"Rex told us where he thought we were," said Syrkin. "I don't know how he figured it out, but he was pretty sure of himself. So he up and says, 'I have us about seventy miles west of Funafuti.'"

As it turned out, he was remarkably close. Jeans said that they were going to try to reach the island on their own by paddling.

The job before the marines on that late morning of 28 January would be no easy task, even for men who were physically fit and in the prime of youthful vigor. With a steady two-knot wind out of the north-northeast, and a parallel current, they would have to paddle at nearly right angles to those relentless forces. They decided to tie the rafts in a line. Half of the men would paddle for thirty minutes while the others maintained a watch for planes and ships. Every half hour they would switch roles. The other challenge was to keep the rafts moving together. With both wind and current opposing them, the towed rafts would tend to move south on their own.

In his own account, Charley Hughes commented, "Rex announced that he had our ditching spot located. We held a prayer meeting over it and decided on the best target to steer for." Hughes also referred to using a sail for this task. "Unfortunately for me, I was the only one who could hold a straight course with a sail. It is a very taxing job, but except for a couple of short periods when someone else led us in circles, I held us on course all day." This self-aggrandizing statement is difficult to reconcile with the accounts of other VMF-422 survivors, none of whom mention using a sail. Ken Gunderson, the last survivor of the thirteen marines in this group, has no memory of any sail being used. Furthermore, the one-man rafts supplied with the AN-R-2B parachute packs did not have sails. The only thing that might have served in that regard was the tarp, which was about five feet square. But there was no way to erect it, and to hold it upright would have been a futile and exhausting exercise. Using a square sail to move at right angles to the prevailing winds would have been almost impossible.

Curly Lehnert affirmed that the rafts did not contain a sail. "I suppose they might have found a way to erect the tarp, but I don't think it could have worked very well."

Hughes, with the few exceptions already noted, did provide accurate and clear accounts of the disaster, but why he related this particular story can only be guessed.

Slowly the small string of rafts followed in Jeans' wake. They had no way of telling how much progress they made, nor even if they were paddling just to stay in one place. But with their dogged determination to beat the odds and live, the marines pressed on, headed southeast.

In the VMF-422 history, Syrkin was quoted as saying, "We saw several blue-faced boobies. Whoever said that seeing a blue-faced booby is an indication that you're sixty miles from land certainly had never been in our position." Syrkin was probably referring to the blue-footed booby, a common sea bird that ranges all over the islands of the Central Pacific.

Jake Wilson was on the beach, staring at the western horizon as a tiny gray shape resolved itself into the form of a destroyer. It was the USS *Hobby* (DD-610), a *Bristol*-Class destroyer. At 1,600 tons and 348 feet long, she had been launched at the Bethlehem Shipbuilding Corporation in San Francisco in June 1942. Like the men of VMF-422, *Hobby* was new to the Pacific, having spent the first year of the war on convoy duty between the East Coast and the Mediterranean. She had been credited with damaging a German U-boat. *Hobby* was then reassigned to patrol the waters around New Guinea. On 27 January, Destroyer Division 38, which included the *Hobby*, USS *Gillespie*, USS *Welles*, and USS *Kalk* received orders

*Destroyers of Division 38 in Norfolk in late December 1943. From left to right:
USS* Welles, *USS* Gillespie, *USS* Hobby, *and USS* Kalk. *Shortly after this
photo was taken, the division sailed for the Pacific.(Official U.S. Navy photo.)*

to sail at best speed northeast to participate in the search for a
missing marine fighter squadron. On the way, *Hobby's* commander, Captain George Washington Pressey received a directive from
Funafuti that one of the missing marine aviators was on Niutao.
Immediately a course was set for the island.

The destroyer turned and sailed parallel to the outer reef. Then
it stopped and dropped anchor. A few minutes later, a white launch
was lowered. The destroyer's rails were lined with sailors, many of
whom must have wondered at the sanity of a man who would leave
an island full of beautiful native girls.

The launch slowed as it approached the beach and two sailors
tossed out a line, which Wilson caught as a junior officer jumped
down.

After Wilson identified himself, the officer said they could leave
right away. The ship had to rejoin the search.

Wilson bid goodbye to his new friends and shook hands with
the chief and doctor. While he was glad to be going back to join his
buddies, he admitted that life on Niutao had been one of the most
pleasant times he had ever known. The navy officer commented
to Wilson about the experience of being the only white man on an
island of beautiful women.

"Like the man said," Wilson replied dryly, "War is hell."

Curly Lehnert was resting with his head on the rubber side of the raft. The sun was high and hot. It was just another hour on the empty ocean. Then he noticed a bird soaring on the breeze far to the east. But the longer he watched it, the greater his interest grew. With a heart-stopping jolt, he realized it was an airplane!

"I saw that plane moving in my direction at about three thousand feet at least twenty miles away," he recalled. "The high wing and broad tail told him it was a PBY Catalina flying boat. I pointed my Very flare pistol at the sky and pulled the trigger."

The wide-barreled pistol barked as the thick flare shot upward and exploded in a spray of bright red stars that were easily visible even in broad daylight.

"I reloaded it and watched every move that plane made. I also deployed my dye marker." In seconds the chemical stain turned the dark green water a bright yellow.

"I guessed the plane was on a box search pattern and might turn at any moment. But it did not turn. Instead it came right at me. I said, 'That guy is flying right up my ass.'"

The noise of the big plane grew in volume. Just before it flew over him, he fired his second flare. The red streak went past the PBY's port wing as it flew over with a rush of wind and noise. Then the big plane waggled its wings.

"I had to keep from jumping up and down in my raft when I knew they had seen me."

The PBY's pilot, Lieutenant Herbert Shivley of VP-53 judged the wind and began to descend until the wide, graceful boat-shaped hull and wingtip pontoons cleaved the green water in triple fans of white spray. The pitch of the engines changed as it slowed. After making another turn, the Catalina drifted to a stop about fifty feet from the downed Marine. A hatch opened on the side of the fuselage and a crewman leaned out.

"He asked me if I could make it over to them, and I said I could. I felt great and made it in a few minutes."

As Lehnert reached the side of the rocking aircraft, the crewman pointed at the engines. "He told me to keep my head down. Those propellers were whirling only a few feet over me."

Lehnert laughed at the next memory. "Then I saw a name painted on the side of the plane under the cockpit. It said, 'Available Jones.' I started laughing. I said, 'If I had to be rescued by a character from 'Little Abner,' why couldn't it have been Daisy Mae?'"

A favorite regular in Al Capp's popular syndicated 'Li'l Abner' comic strip, Available Jones was known for his constant entrepreneurialism. He sold everything and would do anything—for a price.

"I half expected the crewman to demand a 'small gratuity,' as Available Jones was always doing in the comics."

The marine climbed through the hatch with the man helping. "I thought I was fine, but as soon as my feet hit the metal deck I almost fell over. The crewman helped me sit down on a bench by the blister window. He told me to get out of my wet flight suit and he put a blanket around me. He asked who I was and I told him, 'Lehnert, Robert, First Lieutenant, Marine Corps. VMF-422.'"

Lehnert then asked if anyone had found Chris Lauesen, but no one had. The crewman went to tell Lieutenant Shivley that another marine was out there in a life preserver.

The newly rescued marine aviator was both elated and saddened. He could not stop thinking he'd let his buddy down. All he could do was hope that patrol planes found him.

"The crew chief said they found me about 118 miles northwest of Funafuti. That was a serious shock. That meant I had drifted close to two hundred miles since Tuesday afternoon. Then I asked how they had found me. The crew chief said it was easy. My yellow raft, tarp, and dye marker made me stand out like a dandelion on a blue blanket."

The PBY's engines' roar increased and the big flying boat turned into the wind. In a few minutes, Curly Lehnert was again airborne, headed for Funafuti. "I was sure going to be late, but better late than never."

During the flight, Curly was given hot coffee and fresh island fruit. "Those PBY boys really had it good. They even had a galley and a real, honest-to-god head." Lehnert then asked if a photographer would be waiting on the island and if he could clean up before they landed. The crew looked at their passenger with bemused expressions. "I told them that Eddie Rickenbacker had been photographed by *LIFE* when he got to Funafuti." He laughed. "They didn't think a photographer would be waiting for me. I felt just a bit silly, but I was glad to be alive."

When he was told that John Hansen had landed on the island on Tuesday, Curly felt a wave of hope that the rest of the squadron would be okay. But his hopes fell when he was informed that so far, only Hansen and one other man on Niutao had been found.

An hour later, the big flying boat banked in the final approach to Funafuti. Curly looked out the side blister window at the long runway that cut like a white scar through the center of the narrow island. Then the wheels touched down. He had made it to Funafuti at last. As the plane slowed to a stop by the hangar, Curly saw a Jeep drive up. In the passenger seat was John Hansen.

"Hansen came over to the hatch when I climbed out," said Lehnert. "I looked like hell and here he was in neat khakis."

Lehnert was taken to the base infirmary where the medical officer proclaimed him to be healthy, only suffering from exposure and sunburn. The commander of VP-53, Lieutenant Commander David Perry questioned him about where the rest of VMF-422 might be. Lehnert told him where he and Lauesen had ditched and described the wind and currents. Perry informed them about the death of Lieutenant Robert Moran. This was the first confirmed fatality among the Flying Buccaneers.

Meanwhile, on USS *Curtiss* the investigation continued into its second day. By this time several witnesses had been called, including Lieutenant Colonel John Stage of Hoover's staff. Stage, who had talked to MacLaughlin in Campbell's office on Tarawa on the morning of 24 January, was not only called as a witness, he was also a member of the board, which was unusual but not unprecedented. As an experienced marine aviator, he was able to provide his expertise to the board. More importantly, he was intimately familiar with many of the factors that contributed to the disaster. On the stand, Stage related his conversations with MacLaughlin and Colonel Burke. He testified that he had strongly urged that VMF-422 remain on Tarawa until the next day so that they could be fully prepared, and also that an escort be provided.

Stage was followed by General Merritt and Colonel Burke. This will be further discussed in Chapter 19. By the time the board adjourned at 1600 hours, two events had come to light. Lieutenant Robert Lehnert had been found alive northwest of Funafuti, and Lieutenant Walter Wilson had been picked up from Niutao. It was inevitable that they would be called in to testify. But a far greater event was about to happen.

The thirteen stranded pilots continued their weary task of paddling as the air grew colder and the wind increased. It was blowing south-southwest, but a low cloud bank was overtaking them from the west.

Whalen was transferred to Lincoln's raft. Both being from Boston, the two men were on good terms. Despite being even more sore and burned than the others, Whalen still had his sense of humor and joked about his poker winnings from Syrkin.

But just as the transfer began, Lincoln stopped and turned his head to the east. A frown came over his sunburned face. "Do you hear that?"

No one heard anything, but Lincoln cupped his hands to his ears. Then he pointed, "There! A plane!"

All heads turned as if on one neck. Then they heard the distant drone of a multi-engine aircraft. They pointed at the tiny shape on the horizon. It appeared to be flying south, but then it turned west, almost towards them.

Jeans had drilled into them what to do. Tex Watson and Don Walker pulled out flare launchers, while Price released his dye marker. Hughes and Flood had their revolvers out and all the others held up their mirrors. The plane seemed to grow larger with agonizing slowness and finally resolved itself into the familiar shape of a PBY Catalina.

Tex Watson remembered the moment. "It was the happiest time of my life when that PBY saw us. Everybody had been praying that it would not miss us and it was the answer to our prayers."

• CHAPTER 18 •

RESCUE AND REUNION

Ensign George Davidson's crew had been on patrol for over seven hours, with three more to go before they could return to Funafuti. The patrol had been, as with so many others, a totally fruitless effort. Not one Japanese submarine or ship had been sighted. The only craft on the ocean were native outriggers. They were flying south on the outer quadrant of their assigned search sector. From the bow and waist positions, the crew squinted into the low sun for any sign of a periscope or ship's wake. Far to the west, the sky was eclipsed by low-hanging rain squalls.

Davidson's arms were tired. The sun was low in the sky to his right past the co-pilot's shoulder. Just after 1600 hours, the right waist gunner called in to say he had seen something on the water to the west. Davidson's co-pilot, Lieutenant (jg) Howard said that he saw it too. After banking right, they flew closer and slowed their airspeed. From 1,500 feet, the sun's reflection was a broad shimmering cape of dazzling brightness.

But then they saw several small dark shapes speckling the bright avenue of water ahead. Not a single object, but many. It could have been floating wreckage, but they drew closer and realized they were seeing a small group of rafts. With a start, Davidson realized he had found the missing marines.

Two red streaks rocketed up and exploded into bright red stars past his port wing. The crew called out that there were men in the rafts. Banking to the left, he started to circle the small flotilla of yellow rafts. Davidson told his radio operator to call Funafuti and report their position and what they had found. He wanted instructions.

While it may seem obvious that his duty was to land and rescue the downed marines, Davidson also had a responsibility to his crew. If he had to set down on the water, he would imperil them and his plane. The PBY was designed to set down on the water, but only when the sea's surface was calm in good weather conditions. Being a 5A with retractable landing gear, the Catalina had large recesses in the hull for the wheels. These were very vulnerable. If the hull should strike a wave or swell at an oblique angle in a landing, the

VP-53 pilot George Davidson was ordered to search for Japanese ships and submarines west of Funafuti on 28 January. Instead, he found the missing Marines. (Photo courtesy Barbara Davidson.)

seams and rivets in the landing gear wells could split open, flooding the plane. This happened often enough for the Navy Department to issue orders that a PBY should not set down on the open ocean except in cases of where lives might otherwise be lost. When the heavy cruiser USS *Indianapolis* was torpedoed by the *I-68* in July 1945, more than 1,100 men were left adrift in the open ocean between Leyte and Tinian. After five days, a PBY found one group of men and landed, but the landing had sprung rivets and seams. The Catalina's crew was able to pick up over fifty sailors until a ship arrived. Too badly damaged to recover, it was sunk by gunfire.

Davidson waited for orders, but he did see that a large rain squall was coming from the west, pushing heavy swells before it. Time was running out.

The reply from Funafuti was short and ambiguous. In the 1998 video, Davidson said, "The sea was getting pretty rough, so I sent my position and asked for instructions. They said, 'That's up to you, if you think you can do it.' So I circled them for a time, there was a storm coming. I dropped flares so I could land close enough to them but not land on them."

After judging his approach, Davidson extended the wingtip floats and came down. "But then I saw that the waves were higher than I had anticipated. So I tried to turn and run with the waves." The big PBY touched down on the water, sending twin capes of white spray off to either side. The boat-shaped bow smashed into a wave. Titanic gouts of spray engulfed the plane until it burst out and continued on. What happened next was witnessed by all the marines, but few were in agreement as to exactly when it occurred. Another wave loomed over the bow and the flying boat smashed into it, burying the entire fuselage. For several seconds the plane was lost in a mountain of green water. Like an immense dog it shook itself off, rocking in the wake of the swell.

Davidson said, "As I came in, a huge wave swept right over the plane and tore off my right engine. We came out with only one on the wing. I radioed in that I was able to land but I could probably not take off again."

In an instant, the Catalina was no longer a graceful airplane, but a big, lumbering crippled boat rocking alarmingly in the heavy swells.

It took three tries to get within twenty feet of the rafts. With steady pressure on the left engine he was able to turn the big plane until its nose was pointed into the wind. The waist blisters and the main hatchway were opened and the crew threw weighted lines out to the men in the water. After more than seventy hours in the rafts, the castaways were exhausted and unable to use their legs. They held on to the line and each other as they were pulled in.

"We had the hatches open," Davidson said. "But it was very difficult to get these men inside that way. The plane was bobbing like a cork, and these men in the water were also bobbing like corks. When the plane went up, the men in the raft went down. It was very hard to get them in."

But one by one the survivors were pulled to the flying boat. When Jeans touched the wet metal hull, a pair of beefy arms reached down and lifted him inside.

Syrkin said of his own moment of rescue, "That Dumbo looked as big as a freight train. I tried to grab hold of the handles by the hatch but it was rolling and pitching ten feet at a time. One second the hatch was right next to me and an instant later it was ten feet above me." The massive curve of the riveted hull seemed ready to crush him. He tried to hold on but then a wave pushed him back.

"I felt hands on my shoulders and they pulled me in. I fell onto that cold, wet deck. It was hard as hell but I sure didn't mind."

Robert Wilson said, "I thought I was in pretty good shape after being in the water but when I entered the P-Boat (PBY) and tried standing on my feet, I fell flat on my face."

An hour after landing the sun was gone and the low clouds had turned the sea into a churning mass of wind and rain. Eight Flying Buccaneers had been rescued. Then in the way that fate can suddenly turn malevolent, the line to the next raft broke. In seconds the wind had taken hold and five rafts were lost in the churning, black night.

Davidson was working the throttle to keep the PBY's head into the wind when he heard the shouting behind him. He realized what had happened, and his first move was to turn on the PBY's landing and navigation lights. The powerful beams stabbed out into the stormy night.

Using his remaining engine, Davidson followed his crew chief's directions to find the missing rafts. He prayed out loud that they would save those marines.

The PBY's crew was leaning out of the big open waist blister window, shining big six-volt flashlights into the dark. But the rain cut visibility down to only a few yards. Their shouts were lost in the wildly rolling plane.

An hour passed without the missing men being sighted, then two. Davidson refused to give up. Then one crewman saw a tiny green flare in the distance. After the PBY moved closer, he spotted something yellow in the light from the plane's landing lights. He shouted that he found them.

Keeping his eye on the tiny figures in the rafts, Davidson managed to bring the PBY closer and again the line was tossed. At last the five men were helped into the plane. Charley Hughes was the last aboard.

Lincoln said, "You talk about a higher power or a supreme being, I gotta believe that someone had something to do with the rescue of these fellows because that PBY circled for an hour and a half in flat out darkness. And he found them. It was a miracle. We were all lying on the floor of that PBY and it was just heaven."

Now Davidson was faced with another problem. The radioman had told him that a destroyer was headed their way but it would not arrive until 2100, nearly three hours away.

"The landing did rupture the hull," he remembered. "We were taking on water." With one engine gone, the added weight of thirteen men, the water in the hull, and the heaving seas, taking off was a flat impossibility.

They would have to stay afloat and alive until the ship arrived.

The marines were all wrapped in blankets and being given hot coffee from the PBY's small galley. Davidson kept his single engine running to provide some measure of control, as well as to keep the electrical generators running. A sea anchor had been deployed to keep the plane as close to their reported position as possible. The crew had two new duties, to care for their marine guests and to keep the plane afloat. They pulled off deck plates under the radio compartment and began to bail out the water coming in from the split seams.

At least ten to twelve buckets an hour were entering the hull. It wasn't critical, but they could not afford to let the water gain on them. Syrkin said, "We all started bailing while the destroyer homed in on our radio signals."

By 1900 hours, the squall abated and the skies began to clear. The PBY rocked more gently, a relief to the seasick marines.

Davidson turned the controls over to his co-pilot and went back to greet his guests. He was touched by their gratitude. When Jeans asked where they had been found, his answer surprised them. Their location had been 8 degrees, fifty-five minutes south latitude and 177 degrees, fifteen minutes east longitude. This put them nearly 134 miles southwest of Funafuti.

When they asked about how this was possible, Davidson informed them that what they had flown into on Tuesday was in fact a full-blown Pacific typhoon. This was both a shock and a catharsis for the marines. Now they understood what had happened, but not why.

This is worth further examination. The cyclone, by this time, had continued east after threading the needle's eye between Nanumea and Funafuti. The pilots had ditched in the path of the eyewall. From the moment they were in the rafts, the marines were at the mercy of the vortex's powerful forces and pushed first south, then southwest, and, as the cyclone passed, west-southwest. In short, they rode an immense spinning carousel. By the night of 27 January, only the surrounding rain squalls hammered at them in the wake of the retreating storm; then the prevailing winds had their say. As stated by Professor Barnes, the winds in the region blew south-southwest at five knots. Five knots of wind for twenty-four to thirty-six hours could easily push the band of rafts like leaves on a pond. Their sea anchors would not have made much difference as the currents moved in nearly the same direction. This explains how, after seventy hours on the rafts, the Buccaneers ended up more than two hundred miles from where they had ditched.

At 2030 hours, the radioman said that the destroyer USS *Hobby* was calling and had the PBY on radar. All at once the crew began peering out into the darkness.

"We saw searchlights sweeping the water far off," Syrkin recalled.

According to Captain Jeans in his later testimony, "It was after dark before the destroyer could get to us. Meanwhile we spotted some flares which had been shot up in our vicinity, evidently by someone in another raft."

These flares were almost certainly from Ted Thurnau, still adrift in his own raft. But as far as can be determined, the sighting was forgotten in the excitement of the impending rescue.

The distant warship came into view like a ghost. All her deck lights were ablaze. USS *Hobby* slowed and came to a stop windward of the damaged Catalina. From the water she looked huge, but her main deck was barely higher than the PBY's wing.

"She looked like the *Queen Mary* to me," said a grinning Syrkin.

Sailors tossed lines down and the PBY was tied up. Chick Whalen was the first to be hauled up in a sling. He was followed by Jeans, who saluted the ensign on the stern before stepping onto the broad afterdeck. He was met by Commander George Pressey, who welcomed him on board. Then the officer asked about the health of the men. Jeans explained that Whalen was worst off, but they were all suffering from nausea, lacerations, dehydration, severe sunburn, and exposure.

Among the sailors who watched the survivors of VMF-422 come on board was Electrician's Mate First Class Dwight Edmisten, Jr. He wrote an entry into his personal journal that night. "28 January, picked up 14 (sic) marine fighter pilots in rafts after being adrift for three days."

As the others climbed up the ladder to the deck, Jeans introduced them to the *Hobby*'s skipper. He also asked if any other men from VMF-422 had been found. Pressey surprised them by saying that Lieutenant Walter Wilson was on board. This was welcome news. He told a crewman to lead the marines down to the ship's sick bay for treatment.

Davidson then climbed to the deck and explained that his PBY was taking on water. "I asked the captain if it could be towed back to Funafuti. He said he would try."

In the ship's cramped sick bay, the marines were stripped of their salt-caked and frayed flight suits, examined by a pharmacist's mate, and given fresh clothes. Except for Whalen, they were in good shape, only requiring some salve for burns and sores.

An hour later they entered the officer's wardroom to find Jake Wilson waiting for them. Handshakes and back-slapping ensued and soon the thirteen marines were seated around the green baize-covered table, enjoying a meal of meat, soup, vegetables, and bread.

Wilson regaled them with his adventures on Niutao, which elicited wide eyes and open mouths.

"That was some tale he told us," said Syrkin. "That lucky bastard."

Commander Pressey entered. He informed the marines that John Hansen and Bob Lehnert were on Funafuti, but Bob Moran was dead on Nui.

"Tiger was dead," Syrkin said of his friend. "He should have listened to Jeans about not bailing out. But that's the way it goes. I was glad to hear that Curly and John were okay. That only left MacLaughlin, Rogers, Thompson, Lauesen, Aycrigg, and Thurnau. We could still hope."

The *Hobby* was steaming east towards Funafuti. Commander Pressey radioed that they had fourteen survivors from VMF-422 on board.

But the night's drama was not yet over. Davidson's PBY was being towed behind the destroyer like a dog on a two-hundred-yard leash. It was not going to float much longer. The towline bridle broke and the Catalina was left adrift in the black sea.

Pressey found Davidson on the fantail watching his plane disappear in the distance. "He told me that it would have to be sunk. I asked him if he could find it again and he said they could."

Using her radar, the *Hobby* made a wide circle until the small shape of the sinking flying boat was four hundred yards away, barely silhouetted against the predawn gloom. A voice barked from the ship's speakers. "Battle stations, guns!" Crewmen ran for the twin turrets and in moments, the two after 5" guns rotated out to port. "Commence firing!"

Both after turrets fired. A few of the marines were on the after deck, watching. They felt their clothing ripple from the concussion of the yellow-white blasts. A pair of thin waterspouts erupted from the sea near the PBY.

"Short! Fifty left!" The P.A. announced.

Again the guns roared and this time a bright yellow flash marked a hit. The Catalina's wing was torn away. A third salvo struck the hull and in less than a minute the airplane slipped under the churning waves.

Some VMF-422 pilots were pragmatic, while others felt sorrow. That plane and its crew had saved their lives.

"You know," Syrkin said, "I used to think those Catalinas were the ugliest airplanes I'd ever seen. But I changed my mind. They're the most beautiful airplane in the world."

The surviving pilots of VMF-422 assembled after the USS Hobby delivered them to Funafuti. Six of the original flight of twenty-three pilots had died. (Photo courtesy Andrew Syrkin.)

A bright, cool day greeted the *Hobby* as it entered the lagoon at Funafuti at 1130 on Saturday. A launch came out from the dock to ferry them to the island. They were met on the dock by Major Elmer Wrenn, who had just arrived on the island. He informed Jeans that until Major MacLaughlin was found, he, Jeans, would remain in nominal command of VMF-422. At some point Wrenn would probably take command.

But he had good news. Lieutenant Ted Thurnau had just been picked up by the destroyer USS *Welles*. Thurnau, who had ditched too far from the others to join up, had been found about five miles north of where the main group had been rescued.

Major Elmer A. Wrenn, USMC, of Greensboro, North Carolina was an experienced marine fighter squadron officer, having had been the executive officer of VMF-225 at Ewa in Hawaii.

In the squadron history, he is described as being "held in high esteem by all squadron personnel. In stature, Major Wrenn represents the ideal marine. Just under six feet tall and weighing 185 pounds, he presents a picture of a well-conditioned field officer. As an undergraduate at the University of North Carolina, he was outstanding in football and track earning varsity letters as a member of outstanding teams. He was admitted into the Marine Corps in 1938 and was granted a commission as a second lieutenant of the line. In this capacity he served aboard the battleship USS *California* and later underwent flight training at Pensacola. In the early days of the war, he served with VMSB-151 then stationed at Samoa."

This reads like the cover letter for a job application, and was written by Wrenn himself. Nevertheless, the major was an experienced officer who would be given command of VMF-422 on 2 February, and see it through the rest of 1944.

When the marines entered the main building, they were asked what they would like to drink. Syrkin had his answer ready. "I told them, 'A big glass of cold pineapple juice.'"

Waiting for them were Curly Lehnert and John Hansen. The latter looked fit and healthy, as opposed to Lehnert, who bore the same traces of his time on the raft as the others. The two men greeted their buddies warmly. With the exception of Thurnau, who was expected later that afternoon, all the living members of VMF-422 were accounted for.

On the USS *Curtiss*, the board had just convened when the Hobby's report came in. The official transcript does not mention this, but there is little doubt that the board acted at once, making sure that the survivors who were physically capable would to be flown back to Tarawa as witnesses.

At the Command Post at Hawkins Field, the same report reached General Merritt's office, probably read first by Colonel Burke. This had to have been a tense moment for both officers, but there is no record of what they said or thought. While they were certainly relieved that most of the squadron had survived, they might well have felt apprehension, lest the revelation of how poorly they had handled the flight preparations come to light.

Jeans was informed by Major Wrenn that each of his men were to be examined by the base doctor and then meet with a clerk to give their statements. It dawned on the marines that while their life-and-death ordeal had ended, another one was about to begin. The following day, Sunday, 30 January, they were to be flown on a C-47 back to Hawkins Field. There they were to be made available as witnesses for the Navy Board of Inquiry into the loss of VMF-422. What they felt about going back to the very island they had left only four days earlier after such trials and tribulations is not hard to guess. They felt frustrated, cheated, and angry, but overshadowing this was a deep sense of loss and failure. But for some, such

John Hansen and "Tex" Watson after reaching Funafuti. (Photo courtesy Andrew Syrkin.)

as Sterling Price, John Hansen, and Mark Syrkin, a desire to see justice done.

The flight back to Tarawa was a melancholy one for the survivors. Thirty-six hours of searching by navy aircraft and ships had turned up no trace of MacLaughlin, Rogers, Thompson, Aycrigg, or Lauesen. The marines were silent as they flew north over the same course they had themselves flown only five days earlier with such disastrous results. They were fed, rested, and physically recovered. Only Whalen remained on Funafuti, ensconced in the island infirmary under a doctor's care. He had suffered most, not only physically, but mentally and emotionally. Robert Whalen would never be the same again after his personal ordeal on the rafts.

As the miles passed under the C-47's wings, the Flying Buccaneers each wondered about what was to come. They mourned their losses. Bill Aycrigg and Chris Lauesen were almost certainly dead, having had only their Mae West life preservers. As for MacLaughlin, Rogers, and Thompson, there was no way to know what had happened to them until they were found. If they were found.

After landing, the survivors were taken back to the yacht *Southern Seas*, where they would remain for the time being. The waiting ended on Monday, 31 January, exactly one week after they had first landed on Tarawa. To many of the survivors, it seemed almost a lifetime ago.

PART THREE

SEMPER FIDELIS—
ALWAYS FAITHFUL, MARINE
CORPS MOTTO

CHAPTER 19

TESTIMONY VS. TRUTH

USS *Curtiss* (AV-4) was launched in April 1940 in Camden, New Jersey. At 520 feet long and 8,400 tons, the seaplane tender was capable of supporting, repairing, and replenishing squadrons of PBYs or other flying boats. After working on fleet exercises in the Caribbean, she sailed for Pearl Harbor in May 1941. As war grew inevitable, she ferried aviators, mechanics, and equipment to Wake Island. When the Japanese attacked Pearl Harbor, the *Curtiss* was moored northwest of Ford Island with the other seaplane tenders. At 0839, her crew sighted a periscope. It was the type A midget submarine *I-22A*, piloted by Lieutenant Naoji Iwasa. The sub had been launched from the *I-16* and had managed to enter the harbor and reach the anchorages north of Ford Island before being spotted.

The sighting was relayed to the destroyer USS *Monaghan* (DD-354), which was moving south towards the harbor mouth. Realizing the *Curtiss* had spotted an enemy submarine inside the harbor, the *Monaghan's* captain turned his ship to attack the sub. The submarine fired both of its torpedoes. The torpedo meant for the *Curtiss* missed, instead striking the shore of Ford Island. *Curtiss* fired on the partially surfaced sub with her five-inch guns.

Monaghan drove right at the submarine and managed to graze it. The sub sank. When later raised, it was determined that one of the five-inch shells from *Curtiss* had decapitated Iwasa in the conning tower. During the second wave attack, an Aichi D3A Val piloted by Lieutenant Imori Suzuki of the *Akagi* was hit by fire from at least four ships and crashed into the *Curtiss's* number one crane, where it set fires all over the deck. Another Val dropped a bomb on the ship, which detonated below decks, setting fires in the hangar and handling room. But the sturdy *Curtiss* gave as good as she got, shooting down two planes and putting out the fires. Coincidentally, *Monaghan* would be lost in the typhoon of December 1944 with the loss of all but six of her crew.

After repairs in San Diego, *Curtiss* returned to Hawaii and in the fall sailed for the war zone. According to Commander David Bruhn in his book, *Eyes of the Fleet: The US Navy's Seaplane Tenders and*

USS Curtiss *on fire after a Japanese dive bomber crashed into the afterdeck during the Pearl Harbor attack. (Official U.S. Navy photo.)*

Patrol Aircraft in World War II, "The *Curtiss* left Pearl Harbor at 0645 on the morning of 31 October 1943 bound for Funafuti to support the planned invasion of Tarawa. The *Curtiss* was the flagship of Task Force 57 under Rear Admiral John H. Hoover, commander Air Central Pacific. She remained anchored in Funafuti lagoon with anti-submarine net protection and communication cables to shore."

After the fall of Tarawa, she sailed to that island for her role in the planning of Operation Flintlock. In early February, *Curtiss* was visited by several high-ranking officers and members of the Navy Department. Commander Bruhn provided a partial list to the author. These included CINCPAC Chester W. Nimitz, Admirals John McCain, John Towers, Charles Lockwood (Commander, Submarines, Pacific), and the Undersecretary of the Navy, James Forrestal.

Whether these men were involved in the investigation being conducted on the ship is not known, but considering the high level of official interest it would soon generate, it is likely they were aware of it.

As mentioned, the board had started its investigation on 27 January as the downed Marines of VMF-422 were emerging from the second stormy night. What follows is taken directly from the official transcript and exhibits of the investigation, provided to the author through the Freedom of Information Act (FOIA) from the Office of the Judge Advocate General at the Washington Navy Yard. Some statements have been edited for brevity but what follows is essentially verbatim. It retains the text as in the original typewritten transcript, but some punctuation and misspellings were corrected. The board recorder was Lieutenant Elmer Buddress.

The first witness called was First Lieutenant Robert Scott. While he had not actually been on the ill-fated flight, he did provide valuable information on what had been planned. His testimony established the squadron's history and training and described their arrival at Tarawa.

In response to question, Scott then told the board about the 24 and 25 January briefings and the flight plan. He detailed the route, weather information, navigation aids, and radio range data. In effect, Scott was helping the members determine what had been done and said, and equally important, what had not. He was asked about the escort. To three different questions, he answered that an escort was not going to be provided. He did not know if MacLaughlin or any other officer had formally requested one. He was asked seventy-nine questions in all and then excused. Scott would certainly have been worried about his squadron mates, and may have wondered about the questions he had been asked.

From this point on, the board focused on specific matters, such as the weather report, navigation and radio range information, radio call signs and frequencies, and most significantly, the lack of an escort. More factors that contributed to the disaster would soon emerge.

The next witness was Commander James R. Lee, USN, the operations officer on Hoover's staff. Lee was asked to outline what he knew of Hoover's plans for VMF-422 and how it was to fly to Funafuti. For the first time, the name of Brigadier General Merritt was spoken in the investigation. Lee explained that Merritt was to make arrangements to prepare the squadron for the flight. Prompted by Scott's testimony, the board then asked Lee about what had been done in regard to an escort.

Recorder: "Do you know of any established policy or practice which would make it advisable to escort aircraft of this type on long inter-island flights?"

Lee: "It has been the practice for over a year to escort single-engine aircraft making long flights over water. This practice originated

in the South Pacific when they were having many losses flying between Espiritu Santo and Guadalcanal under the poor
weather conditions encountered at certain times of the year."

Lee was replaced at the stand by Lieutenant Colonel John
Stage, the marine aviator on the board. With his extensive experience, Stage was an excellent witness. He described his meeting
with MacLaughlin on 24 January and what information he was
able to provide. Then Stage was asked about escorts.

Stage: "On January 24, I called the Fourth Wing operations office
by telephone and the duty officer informed me that Colonel
Burke, the operations officer, was making full arrangements.
The duty officer did not know in detail what the arrangements
were, but stated that Colonel Burke was in full charge. The following morning I went ashore on the ten o'clock boat and met
Colonel Burke on Hawkins Field. Several of the F4U planes
had already landed and Colonel Burke was conversing with
the pilots. I asked him if arrangements for the movement to
Funafuti were made and if we on Admiral Hoover's staff could
be of any possible assistance. He said that the Fourth Wing
was making all arrangements, that General Merritt desired
that the squadron clear Tarawa as soon as possible, preferably
that afternoon. I asked if an escort had been arranged. Colonel
Burke replied, 'No,' and that General Merritt did not desire
that the flight should have an escort. I strongly recommended
that the flight be held over at least until the following day so
that the pilots could be properly briefed and prepared, and
urged that an escort be obtained, even if the general had to be
talked into it. I mentioned bad weather in the Ellice Islands
which had been reported by Colonel McQuade, commanding
officer of CENCATS who had flown up from Funafuti the previous day and called attention to the fact that the pilots of
VMF-422 had had little chance to learn anything about these
islands and this area. Colonel Burke replied to my advice that
he felt the same way about all these matters but that he knew
that General Merritt was anxious to have the squadron leave
as soon as possible and that he definitely did not intend to
provide an escort. He added that he would do his best to see
that an escort was obtained and that the squadron was fully
prepared in every way for the movement. Later in the day I saw
Colonel Burke again and at that time, plans for the movement

were in the same status as during our first conversation."

Recorder: "You stated that you advised Colonel Burke that the flight should be held over so that the pilots could be properly briefed and prepared?"

Stage: "Yes."

Recorder: "Do you mean to imply that if the pilots took off as scheduled they would not be properly briefed and prepared for that flight?"

Stage: "That is the inference. My opinion was that the squadron should stay aboard Tarawa at least a day for purposes of getting acquainted with these islands and this part of the ocean."

Recorder: "Is it the practice to send fighters over long distance ocean areas such as from Tarawa to Funafuti?"

Stage: "Yes, this has been done frequently in the Pacific campaigns."

Recorder: "In your opinion, is [it] sound practice to send fighters on long flights over water unescorted?"

Stage: "No, I believe that it is currently accepted that single seaters proceeding over water for considerable distances should be escorted by a multi-engine airplane with complete radio and navigational equipment."

For the first time, the investigation had a possible reason for the disaster. Both Lee and Stage had made it clear that a multi-engine escort plane was virtually imperative for long over-water flights by single-engine aircraft.

On the second day, with Colonel Stage back with the board, Brigadier General Lewie G. Merritt was called in and sworn. The general was dressed in his Class A uniform with three rows of ribbons and decorations for his service since 1917. Prominent on his chest were his wings of gold.

General Merritt was not a tall man, being described by VMF-113 pilot Andrew Jones as a "banty little rooster." Nevertheless, he stood ramrod straight with his dark, penetrating eyes glowering out from under thick brows. As a former JAG lawyer, Merritt knew exactly what the board could and could not do. He understood the limits of their power and reach. The board was up against one of the most cunning of creatures, a southern democrat lawyer with political ambition.

After questioning Merritt about his current duty station, Buddress asked him to describe his role in the disposition of VMF-422 for the flight to Funafuti. Merritt said the orders had come from

*Admiral John Hoover, who ordered the investigation into
the loss of VMF-422. (Official U.S. Navy photo.)*

Admiral Hoover and that he, Merritt, had directed Colonel Burke,
his operations officer, to see to the preparations for the flight.

Merritt displayed a true gift for skirting the issue. Throughout
his replies, he avoided ever making a definite statement that could
be used against him.

> Recorder: "Tell the board what you know of the preparations and
> arrangements that were made for this flight."
>
> Merritt: "I know nothing except what I had told you. I gave orders
> to Colonel Burke. A squadron commander should be able to
> take the squadron from place to place. This was a seasoned
> squadron given to me that had been together for something
> over a year. The squadron commander was an experienced
> pilot."
>
> Recorder: "Do you know who briefed the squadron for this flight?"
>
> Merritt: "No, I don't."

Recorder: "General, would you say that the flight from Tarawa to
Funafuti by single engine planes is unusually long?"

Merritt: "Yes, it is unusually long. However, via Nanumea where
the squadron expected to land, I consider it a very reasonable
flight well within the range of the plane and with considerable
reserve in gas."

Recorder: "Do you consider a flight from Tarawa to Funafuti in
single engine planes a hazardous flight?"

Merritt: "No, I do not consider it any more hazardous than any
type of over-water flight. After all, there is a certain element
of hazard in any type of flight. However, that is a chance we
all have to take. We all understand, presumably, and quite
willingly do so. I do not consider it any more hazardous than
any other over water flight with the single engine plane. To me
this was a perfectly normal flight such as would be expected
any day in this area. After all no squadron can expect to be
assigned forever to one spot and stay over just one locality."

The commander of the Fourth MBDAW was careful in his replies
by admitting the flight from Tarawa to Funafuti was unusually long
but not particularly hazardous, but he also tried to redirect the
question by saying that a squadron should be ready, at any point,
to make hazardous flights, at any time. But this was not true. A
marine fighter squadron was not usually trained for long over-water
navigation. Merritt undoubtedly knew this.

Recorder: "The hazard of flying is relative, is it not General?"

Merritt: "Yes, almost everything, I am told, is relative."

Recorder: "Is it not true that the two principle elements of risk in
long distance over water flying are weather and navigational
risk?"

Merritt: "Yes, those are two, two of the main risks, I shouldn't say
all of them by any means."

Recorder: "From your knowledge of local weather conditions in this
area, would you say that a flight of single engine planes from
Tarawa to Funafuti is more or less hazardous than similar
length of flight in the Hawaiian area?"

Merritt: "No, I would not consider it more so."

Then Buddress led Merritt into the subject the board was most
interested in, that of an escort. However, the canny marine general
refused to take the bait.

Recorder: "Are there any special safe guards or precautions that might be applied in flights of this type in this area?"

Merritt: "Well, of course the best safe guard that I can offer is a well experienced, efficient, and capable squadron commander. An individual who knows over water flying, checks his data, and goes into conditions as they are generally found. Once being certain the leader is competent, I think it is impossible to go very much farther. Because there you run into conditions attempting to control a flight leader in the air after he gets away from the base. Certainly all these conditions in this particular case were present. I consider the radio aids in the area quite efficient and they are of the same general type found at home over the United States. The squadron was supposed to have been checked out through the operations section of the field from which it took flight, and as is invariably the case, no operations officer should clear the flight until all necessary conditions are known by the pilots. However, I felt that I was taking extra precaution in having Captain Pennington talk to the squadron commander. I really felt that it was not a prerogative of mine and that it would have been unwarranted interference to have gone much further into the matter of commanding the squadron from a regularly organized navy field."

If the reader was able to find their way through this labyrinthine diatribe, it is obvious that Merritt shifted the burden of responsibility on three scapegoats. MacLaughlin, the Hawkins Field Air Operations staff, and his own subordinate, Burke.

Buddress, refusing to be sidetracked, continued to press. "Is there any other accepted method besides radio for safeguarding single engine planes on long over-water hops?"

Merritt: "There is none that I can think of at the moment."

The board members, prompted by Lee and Stage, probably raised their eyebrows at this.

Recorder: "Have you considered the practice of escorting single engine planes on such a flight?"

Merritt: "Yes. However, I have always taken the attitude that in the case of a squadron under the command of a competent squadron commander, that he must be able, in time of war, to take a squadron from one point to another. In the case of single

planes or in smaller numbers of planes not under the command of an older and more seasoned pilot, it has always been
my practice to send a navigation plane along with them but not
in the case of squadron formations, as I have never considered
it necessary and it has never been my belief that this was a
general practice. I must say, however, that I would have no particular objection to it, but as I mentioned before, in the case of
a complete squadron, well organized and under the competent
leadership of its commander, I consider it unnecessary."

This last was clearly intended to again shift the blame. While
he said he accepted the utility of an escort, it was only for squadrons that were *not* led by a competent commander. In other words,
MacLaughlin should have been able to make the flight without it.
But this approach carried its own risks for Merritt. As commander
of the air wing, he should have been aware of VMF-422's lack of
long over-water flight training. He was also blaming a man who was
certainly dead. Also note that Merritt admitted not having any ob-
jections to an escort. Whether the board believed him at that point
is not clear. However, the next question may have been intended to
force some kind of strong reaction from Merritt.

Recorder: "Is your policy on that point unchanged by the fate of
this last flight of VMF-422?"
Merritt: "Do I infer in the question that this is an indication that
the flight was lost as a result of not having an escort?"
Recorder: "There is no implication, but am merely seeking facts. I
have formed no opinion."

The transcript does not describe what Merritt's physical reaction had been, but there is little doubt he took offense. One can
almost see the narrowed eyes and furrowed brow. It may be noted
that he did not say ". . . lost as a result of *me not providing* an escort?" Merritt kept his distance from the cause of the disaster.
He continued. "My opinion as to the loss of this flight lies along
different lines. In speaking of a policy in the first place, I do not control this flight from this field. The extent of my authority in this matter was in ordering one of my squadrons from one point to another.
As I stated, the flight cleared through a regular organized navy field."
General Merritt went into his verbal dance to avoid ever being pinned down by a definite statement. He continued. "I have no
particular set policy in such matters, I think each case has to be

judged on its own merits. In the first place, in a case of this sort based on my own experience, it is my opinion that it would have been utterly impossible for a squadron to have remained with any escort if weather conditions were anything like, from what I understand, the squadron unexpectedly encountered."

The board members, as intelligent and experienced military officers, undoubtedly realized that they were watching a master of circumlocution.

> Recorder: "In regard to this particular flight, did you consider ordering an escort for the flight?"
>
> Merritt: "I would not consider it. Colonel Burke asked if I considered it necessary. I stated that I did not. Colonel Burke told me the squadron commander asked if he would have one and was told that none had been planned. The squadron commander seemed perfectly satisfied with the decision."

By this time, the shrewd Merritt may have realized that his hard-headed obstinacy did not look good before the board. He then attempted to shift the focus of the questioning. "If I might continue, if you want my opinion, the matter of escort had nothing whatsoever to do with the loss of this flight. I feel that it is a question of getting insufficient weather information and encountering unforeseen weather conditions. This next statement is entirely hearsay, but I understand that the flight was plotted on the Nanumea screen to within seven miles of the field; what more could an escort plane have done?"

Merritt's sudden *non sequitur* must have raised a few eyebrows. Not only was it totally out of context, it did not explain nor excuse his stand on escorts. It is interesting that Merritt already knew how close VMF-422 had come to Nanumea, indicating that he had made inquiries on that subject. Even the board did not yet have that information.

Buddress returned the questioning to the critical issue.

> Recorder: "On previous flights of this character, have escorts been provided?"
>
> Merritt: "No. At least the ones of my unit have not been so provided. As far as any orders and instructions went for other flights under my command, they have been cleared exactly the same way as VMF-422."

As we know, with VMF-113 and VF-12 an escort was requested and provided, even over Merritt's policy. In contrast to what both Lee and Stage had said, Merritt never admitted that an escort was necessary or warranted in the case of VMF-422. It may be noted that VMF-113 and VF-12, both of which had combat veteran commanders, did receive escorts, whereas VMF-422 under MacLaughlin on his first combat tour, was left to fly the mission alone. This in itself patently contradicted Merritt's assertion that he did not need to provide an escort for competent commanders, but would do so for less experienced ones. It will be recalled that prior to Flintlock, Merritt was relieved of command of the fighter and bomber squadrons by Admiral Hoover. While the exact date is uncertain, it likely occurred in late December, possibly early January. Bearing in mind that VF-12 arrived on Tarawa around 5 January and VMF-113 five days later and were both provided with escorts, this supports the conclusion that Merritt was still equivocal about the matter. By the time VMF-422 arrived, he had made up his mind that no other squadrons under Hoover's command would be provided with escorts. Yet he was careful not to say this to the board.

With his last answers, he had shifted the blame to the two factors that were the hardest to prove otherwise, the weather and the competence of the squadron commander. Weather forecasting, as everyone even today knows, is an inexact science. It was easy to point to a poorly executed weather report as the cause of the disaster. Since MacLaughlin was not present to defend himself, Merritt was on safe ground, even though he might have ruffled the board's feathers at the implication. Unless there was concrete proof that the loss of VMF-422 was directly due to the lack of escort, he had no reason to fear being held liable. Having cast the gauntlet before the board, he left the stand, confident and unrepentant.

Merritt was followed to the stand by Colonel Lawrence Burke. There is of course no way to know if the two men discussed their testimony prior to being called, but Burke may well have felt as if he were walking into the lion's den. Considering Merritt's acerbic demeanor, it is unlikely that Merritt even gave Burke, his personal scapegoat, any support at all.

Burke, like his superior, had a lot to lose if it was determined that his actions had been a primary cause of the disaster. Where Merritt was verbose and long-winded, Burke's replies were short to the point of insolence. Burke hedged his statements and took little responsibility for what happened.

Recorder: "What orders did you issue in regard to the disposition of this squadron after it arrived here?"

Burke: "None."

Recorder: "Did you carry out your general's orders?"

Burke: "I did."

Recorder: "How did you carry them out?"

Burke: "Verbally by direct contact with the squadron commander."

Recorder: "Did you consider that your duty in regard to the movement of this squadron to Funafuti had been completely discharged upon revealing the general's orders to the squadron commander?"

Burke: "I did."

Recorder: "As operations officer, you believe you had no responsibility toward this squadron for the preparation of this flight?"

Burke: "Absolutely none."

These flat responses must have prompted the recorder to be more direct.

Recorder: "Explain to the board the chain of command and the particular officers with whom this squadron commander would come in contact in arranging his flight from Tarawa, if you know."

Burke: "I can only give you my idea of what I think should have happened. I don't know all the officers concerned who run the station over there."

Recorder: "Do you know what arrangements were made by the squadron commander in preparation for this flight?"

Burke: "In detail, no, because I was not present. I remained with the squadron commander after I had delivered the general's orders, talked with him for approximately forty-five minutes or an hour. I then left him. That was the day before the flight and did not see him again."

Burke was giving this testimony before Colonel Stage, who had also witnessed how Burke had made arrangements with other officers, such as Campbell, Pennington, Sandlin, Shilson, and Stage himself, to name a few. For someone who claimed "not to know all the officers who run the station," Burke had assembled a team of qualified officers with little trouble. He also stated that he had only been with MacLaughlin for forty-five minutes, but it was actually closer to three hours. Again, Burke was careful with his replies.

Recorder: "Did the squadron commander ask you for any particular services while he was based at Tarawa, in preparation for this flight to Funafuti?"

Burke: "After I had talked with Major MacLaughlin as I have previously described, I asked him how he felt about making the flight and he said in effect that he would like to have an escort. Other than that, I don't think he made any direct request to me, as I had already previously advised him where he could get any information he needed to plan his flight."

Recorder: "Did the squadron commander state any reasons for his request for an escort or did he make a bare request?"

Burke: "He did not make a straight request. To the best of my recollection, he stated that he would have liked to have an escort. He did not directly ask me the direct question, could he have an escort."

Recorder: "Did you relay the squadron commander's desire for an escort to General Merritt?"

Burke: "No."

Colonel Burke was on very thin ice with this reply, as he was well aware that MacLaughlin had formally requested an escort from him. He may have been hoping that no one witnessed the incident.

Recorder: "Have you experienced similar situations where General Merritt has refused an escort on similar flights?"

Burke: "No."

This reply seems to have caused some confusion, as the recorder asked for clarification.

Recorder: "Upon what do you base your statement that the use of an escort on a flight like this was contrary to General Merritt's policy?"

Burke: "I had discussed the subject of escorts with General Merritt after a previous fighting squadron had left here and the general stated that he did not wish me to discuss the subject any further with him."

From this point on, Burke was laying out the defense that he was merely following orders as they stood on the morning of 25 January, but he had just flatly contradicted Merritt's claim that he had "no particular set policy concerning escorts."

Recorder: "What were the circumstances of that prior flight when the escort question arose?"

Burke: "At that time, without having discussed the matter with the general, I arranged for an escort as it had been my previous custom in the Hawaiian Area."

Recorder: "What were the details of that prior transfer when the question of escort arose before?"

Burke: "A PV plane escorted that flight from Helen [Betio] to Nanumea, I believe, and from Nanumea to Funafuti. The squadron was reporting in the same manner as VMF-422."

Recorder: "What is your understanding as to the general practice in the Marine Corps of escorts for over-water flights?"

Burke: "My understanding was that they will or will not be furnished in accordance with the senior officer who commands the unit."

Recorder: "Do you know of any well-defined policy in regard to use of escorts for long distance ocean flights?"

Burke: "I know of no such policy in this combat area."

Recorder: "You stated that on a previous occasion when a fighting squadron had left here for Funafuti you had arranged an escort. What was the number of that squadron?"

Burke: "VMF-113."

Recorder: "What were that squadron's orders?"

Burke: "To the best of my knowledge, they were similar orders to the ones received by Major MacLaughlin."

Recorder: "How did you obtain the escort for that squadron?"

Burke: "I either called or had an assistant call, I believe, VB-142 or 144 and asked them if they had a plane available they could furnish for this purpose."

What Burke was saying at this juncture is that even though he "was not aware of any set policy in this combat area" to provide an escort, he did so anyway. He was also going against his commanding officer's set policy. The board had apparently noted the inconsistencies.

Recorder: "In answer to a previous question, you stated that the general had directed you not to discuss escorts with him any further. How do you explain that?"

Burke: "It was his directive and I don't know how to explain it other than it was a directive with which I complied. I don't fully understand your previous question."

It can be assumed that Burke was beginning to feel cornered by the questions, which had to be hitting too close to the mark. After an hour, and replying to forty-three questions, Colonel Burke left the stand.

Regarding the testimony of Merritt and Burke, there is an account of how VMF-113 was provided with an escort.

Former VMF-113 pilot Andrew Jones wrote *The Corsair Years* after the war. He related a conversation regarding the escort between his commander and General Merritt

"I was within earshot of "Doc," Major Everton, talking with General Merritt. Doc was pointing at a Lockheed PV-1 and insisting it lead us through possible storms on the flight to Funafuti."

The twin-engine plane, with its full range of navigational equipment was suitable for fighter escort missions, but Merritt denied Everton's request, saying he needed it on Tarawa.

"Then we won't go," Jones remembered his commander replying to the general.

"It might cost you your command," countered Merritt.

"Okay, sir," Everton said, "But I won't take my squadron seven hundred miles across the equator without it."

With neither officer willing to change his position, they entered the command post tent. "Ten minutes later Doc came out and gave us a 'thumbs-up.' We had our escort plane."

Soon VMF-113 was in the air, escorted by the PV-1, and reached Funafuti safely.

This does not tally with what Burke and the official record states. It may be that Everton, while out of sight of Jones, insisted that Burke call Captain Tate, the island commander, to demand an escort. In other words, he went over Merritt's head. In that case, it can be assumed the general resented having to back down, and when Burke asked on behalf of VMF-422, flatly refused the request.

Over the next three days, a parade of witnesses sat before the board. The eight officers that were called after Burke were:

1. Major Theodore Brewster, USMC-R, Air Operations, Hawkins Field
2. Lt. Commander James Shilson, USN, Aerological Officer, TF 57
3. Lt. (jg) William Snell, Aerological Officer, Acorn 14, Hawkins Field

4. Lieutenant George Sandlin, USN-R, Assistant Air Operations, Acorn 14, Hawkins Field
5. Captain Alan B. Campbell, USMC-R, Assistant Air Operations Officer, Fourth MBDAW
6. Commander A. W. Wheelock, USN, Base Operations officer, Tarawa
7. Captain Jackson R Tate, USN, Island Commander Tarawa
8. Lieutenant Seebury Waring, USN-R, Field Facilities officer, Hawkins Field

To these officers, the board asked questions about the weather reports, navigation, radio ranges, and frequencies, but in time, the primary issue seemed to become the manner of how VMF-422 had managed to leave the island without filing a flight plan. The board may have felt that Colonel Burke had been responsible for the breakdown in communication between the Fourth MBDAW and the air command post.

The matter of the escort continued to rear its head for the next two witnesses. When the board questioned Lieutenant George Sandlin, the assistant air operations officer on Hawkins Field, they asked, "Do you consider that the responsibility of the air operations officer is to supply an escort if one is needed, if one is requested?"

Sandlin: "Whether or not it is the responsibility, we would make every attempt to get one. We would see that the escort was provided from whoever might be responsible for providing the escort."

The next witness, the base operations officer, Commander A. W. Wheelock was firm in his conviction that he had not known or received any orders about VMF-422's flight to Funafuti.

Recorder: "On January 24 and 25, was any request made to you for an escort for a flight of VMF-422?"
Wheelock: "No. Furthermore, we received no orders from higher authority to send VMF-422 anywhere."
Recorder: "When did you first learn that VMF-422 was under orders to leave Tarawa for Funafuti?"
Wheelock: "I have never received any notification that they were under orders to leave Tarawa for Funafuti."
The next question further cemented the value of providing escorts.
Recorder: "Did you ever have any conversation with any officer of

the Fourth Marine Air Wing in regard to the use of escorts on flights from Tarawa?"

Wheelock: "No. In this connection, Major Brewster had handled two previous flights to Funafuti of VF (fighter) squadrons, one navy and one marine. One of these flights was flying to Funafuti, [and] which, like VMF-422, had arrived on a carrier. Both of these flights were provided escorts and were carried out without difficulty."

Recorder: "Do you consider that the escort should be provided only on the request or upon the express desire of the flight leader of the single seater flight, or should it be ordered, or should he be normally required to use such an escort?"

Wheelock: "He should be normally required to use such an escort except on strikes, of course."

Captain Jackson Tate, island commander at Tarawa was then questioned about his orders regarding command and control over air operations. He too was asked about his opinion of using escorts.

Recorder: "Do you consider it normal and advisable for a single seater squadron to have a multi-engine escort when it proceeds over water for a considerable distance?"

Tate: "I think it is highly desirable to have an escort, a multi-engine escort, over long stretches of water."

After the last witness left the stand on Sunday, the board adjourned for the day. The next witnesses would be the survivors of VMF-422.

CHAPTER 20

CAUSES AND EFFECTS

On Monday, 31 January, Captains Cloyd Jeans and Charles Hughes, accompanied by First Lieutenants John Hansen, Robert Lehnert, Walter Wilson, and Jules Flood were in the launch to the *Curtiss*. They were each dressed in new khakis, but these failed to mask their red skin and abrasions. Upon reaching the flagship, they climbed the ladder to the main deck, where a navy quartermaster in whites met them. After signing in, they were led through the ship's workshops to another ladder. The ship smelled of steel, paint, and oil. When they finally found themselves in "officer's country," the quartermaster pointed to a bench along a passageway wall. It was 0930 hours. A few minutes later, three navy and one marine officer passed them and entered the ship's wardroom. The door was closed and a marine corporal with a holstered pistol was stationed at the door. At 0945, a navy yeoman stepped out. "Captain Cloyd R. Jeans, please present yourself."

The room that greeted Jeans was about forty feet square, painted light green. The deck was tiled in tan linoleum. The usual long tables were gone, replaced by one table covered in dark green cloth across the far end before two open portholes and an American flag. Another table was stacked with files, folders, maps, and rolled charts. Yeoman Oliver was seated at the stenotype machine.

A single hard, wooden chair was positioned in the exact center of the room in front of the long table. Jeans was sworn in and became the fourteenth witness in the investigation of the loss of VMF-422. This was the first opportunity the board had to question someone who had actually been on the ill-fated flight.

Buddress began. "Are you the senior surviving pilot of VMF-422?"

Jeans: "I am." He was asked to submit a list of the pilots and their current status. When this was entered into evidence, Buddress continued by asking Jeans about his experience as a marine pilot and total hours of flying time. He was then asked about the average number of hours each pilot in VMF-422 had flown, to which he said, "About 130 hours." Buddress then inquired about how much experience the pilots had in long, over-water flights.

Captain Rex Jeans in 1944 while on Engebi in the Marshall Islands. (Photo courtesy Andrew Syrkin.)

This was one of the key points the board wanted to establish, and Jeans informed the officers that apart from himself, Hughes, and Rogers, none of the squadron had ever done any serious over-water navigation.

When asked to estimate Major MacLaughlin's total flight experience, Jeans told them it was about 1100 hours in all, with over a hundred in the F4U Corsair.

The questions covered their flight training at Santa Barbara, Hawaii, and Midway, and finally the day they arrived on Tarawa. Jeans detailed the briefings on the yacht and at Hawkins Field and what kind of navigational aids had been provided. He stated that he had been unimpressed with what they had been given, and that the radio ranges and frequencies were incorrect.

In response to further questions, he then told them how the flight was to proceed, and about the intended landing on Nanumea for refueling.

Buddress then asked about the weather reports, to which Jeans replied that MacLaughlin had intended to get the latest weather report just before takeoff. "He seemed satisfied with the weather," Jeans pointed out. He then added, "The only thing is that they told me that in the afternoon we could expect scattered showers and a line squall. The conditions, on my impression was that we would have scattered showers all over the horizon but nothing covering a large area like we ran into."

> Recorder: "From your observation of your squadron commander on both the evening before and the morning of the flight, would you say he was satisfied with the prospects of the flight?"

Jeans replied carefully, "That is taking in a lot of territory. There is the problem of the escort, problem of getting the correct weather. I think that he was satisfied with the weather but as far as the navigational facilities of our command, and problem of no escort, I don't think he was. I know for a fact that I certainly wasn't, and I think Captain Rogers and I were in accord."

Jeans had finally tossed the hot potato into the investigation.

> Recorder: "What was the major's attitude toward an escort for this flight?"
> Jeans: "The major was told that he would have no escort because they couldn't spare a plane from the operations that were then taking place to go with us, and that was the answer he gave Captain Rogers and myself."
> Recorder: "Who told the major that?"
> Jeans: "I do not know."
> Recorder: "How do you know the major was told that?"
> Jeans: "I don't know, I am merely quoting the major, but I had asked him at least three different times why we couldn't have an escort and I got the same answer each time."
> Recorder: "Do you know whether or not the major expressly asked for an escort?"

On this point, Jeans, who had not been present on the occasion when MacLaughlin had gone to Colonel Burke, could only reply with: "I couldn't say. He said that he had inquired and asked about getting one, but as far as saying specifically that he requested an escort and was denied, I can't say."

> Recorder: "Did you desire an escort for this flight?"
> Jeans: "I did."
> Recorder: "Did anyone else in the squadron ask for an escort?"
> Jeans: "Captain Rogers and I were together at the time that we asked the major if we could have an escort."
> Recorder: "Do you know what the major's attitude was toward making this flight without an escort?"

Jeans: "Apparently he was not too pleased about going without an escort, but as far as I know, it was the only indication that he gave."

Recorder: "How did you get the impression that the major was not too well pleased?"

Jeans: "That is pretty hard to say. I knew the major fairly well, but all in all, he was a fairly difficult man to figure out. But just by his actions the morning before we took off, he didn't appear to be too happy about the whole prospect."

This response was carefully given. Jeans was eager to point out that MacLaughlin was upset by the refusal of an escort, but military officers, particularly in the navy and marines, are careful to avoid inflammatory language.

Recorder: "Considering the weather that you encountered, do you think that you would have had any trouble staying with an escort?"

This was obviously meant in reference to Merritt's offhand comment that an escort would have been of no use once the squadron encountered the storm. But Jeans' flat reply shattered this.

Jeans: "No sir, I don't."

The questioning then turned to matters of the time before, during, and after entering the storm. This was the first time the members heard what VMF-422 had actually encountered. Jeans described the storm as they approached, and what it was like inside the eye wall. He related, in terms that were almost casual, the rain, wind, and total lack of visibility. Then he came to the point where MacLaughlin had made the two radical turns under the cloud deck, the fateful turns that had scattered the squadron. Although his statements are factual, there is no doubt that Captain Jeans was of two minds regarding his commander's actions. His descriptions convey that he felt MacLaughlin had done the best he could to protect his men, but did make some decisions that only contributed to the disaster.

Recorder: "Did you consider that the squadron commander's turn was intended to take you direct to Funafuti?"

Jeans: "No sir."

Recorder: "If, in your opinion, the major's radio was not functioning properly, is it not logical to assume he would turn the lead over to someone with a good radio?"

Jeans: "Yes sir."

Recorder. "In your narrative, after you had flown away from Nui for some minutes, you decided it was best to return to Nui. What was the reason for that decision rather than deciding to ride the range into Nanumea when you took the lead?"

Jeans: "One reason was that I was not oriented. I could hear the station at Nanumea but I did not know in which quadrant I was in. In order to have bracketed the beam, I would have had to [go back into] the storm."

Recorder: "After you reached Nui the second time, why didn't you fly into Nanumea from there?"

Jeans: "We never reached Nui the second time; it was our intention at least, if we still had enough gas to fly a direct course from Nui to Nanumea. We never reached Nui the second time."

Recorder: "I believe you stated in response to a prior question that, in your opinion, your trouble was by bad weather information that you had and by lack of an escort. Is it true that the weather information you had for the part of your flight from Tarawa to Nanumea was quite accurate?"

Jeans: "I think the weather information was accurate only in as far as it went. It didn't give the severity of the storm which we encountered."

Recorder: "Can you estimate the area over which this storm lay that you encountered?"

Jeans: "The area that the storm covered in my observation was as far as you could see on either side of our course. It was also too high to attempt to fly over. Inside of the storm, the rain came down in driving sheets."

Recorder: "Can you say with certainty whether or not, at the time you encountered that storm, you were beyond Nanumea coming from Tarawa?"

Jeans: "No, we were not beyond Nanumea, but about eighteen minutes this side of the island, which would be approximately sixty miles."

Captain Jeans was on the stand for over two hours and asked eighty-three questions. He was then asked if there was anything he wished to add to his testimony. He said he had nothing to add and after being warned not to discuss his testimony with anyone, was excused.

Captain Charley Hughes was called in next. Upon being sworn, Hughes took his seat. He was asked many of the same or similar questions as Jeans, but Hughes, not being the squadron executive officer, was less informed about some of the preflight preparations.

> Recorder: "Did you get any information as to radio aids to navigation?"
>
> Hughes: "We were given a sheet which gave the beam frequency at Nanumea, beam frequency at Funafuti with the leg headings into Nanumea, and no information other than the frequency on the Funafuti beam. Also we were given a list of frequencies to use at Nanumea and Funafuti, 6970."
>
> Recorder: "Were you satisfied with your weather information and navigational information prior to your take off?"
>
> Hughes: "No I wasn't satisfied, especially with no information on the Funafuti Beam. Also, we had assumed that the N quadrant in Nanumea and the north quadrant was where it should have been."

Hughes was saying that they had been given the radio range frequencies for Nanumea and Funafuti. Although they had the range legs or quadrants for Nanumea, the Funafuti range legs were missing, which as we have seen would have been of inestimable value to the lost squadron.

> Recorder: "Did you ask for an escort for this flight?"
>
> Hughes: "I didn't myself, but I told the major I thought it was a good idea."

He was then asked to describe the flight, including his attempts to get on the Nanumea radio range. With more descriptive language than Jeans used, Hughes told about entering the storm. When he related the sighting of Nui and Chris Lauesen's ditching, he concluded with, "Then [we] started flying in an erratic course. I became completely confused as to where the island we just passed was. I was still trying to keep with Major MacLaughlin and was rather far back by that time. The plane I was following had, I could see what looked like a "1." I found out it was a "4," Captain Jeans' plane. Then we started circling and climbing for altitude with the emergency IFF on. We started picking up "Rocky Base," which we didn't know [who it] was. At the time - we had not been given that call at all."

Hughes' testimony is not as clear and concise as Jeans', but it does contain several important details, including examples of the lack of correct radio call signs.

He also gave the board a good account of the mass ditching and how well Jeans had handled it. "Before we ditched [I] called "Rocky Base" and told them we were going down, and for God's sake, to get a bearing on us. I sent until the engine quit on the left tank, the main tank was already dry so with the few gallons on my right wing I circled and landed. It was just exactly 3:40 when I hit down in the water."

After only sixteen questions, Hughes was excused. Then the board called for First Lieutenant John Hansen. Hansen was sworn in and examined by the recorder. As the only VMF-422 pilot to actually reach the intended destination, he was of great interest to the investigation. The board wanted to know, if Hansen made it to Funafuti without an escort and with faulty navigational and weather data, why didn't the other twenty-two pilots do the same?

Buddress asked about MacLaughlin's actions as they approached the storm.

Hansen said, "At about 1215 we entered the storm. Just before, our major called and said that we would attempt to go over the storm, but immediately called back and belayed the order and said we would go into it."

This was the first time the board members learned of this sudden change in altitude as the squadron approached the storm. They had heard Captain Alan Campbell's statement the previous day about telling MacLaughlin to avoid trying to fly under a large rain squall, so this appeared to support his testimony.

Hansen also mentioned seeing an island shortly after coming out of the storm that he assumed to be Nanumea, but he chose to try for Funafuti and turned southeast to 115 degrees. While this is certainly true, it does raise more questions than it answers. It is possible Hansen, who died in 2013 before the author read the transcript, felt he had been mistaken. Perhaps he didn't think it was possible to land on the island under the storm. In any event, this is the only time he mentioned sighting this island.

The last question for Hansen concerned his experience in long-range over-water flights.

Hansen: "Only navigation problems but never on a beam. This is the first time I have ever been on a beam except for a link trainer."

Hansen was excused after eleven questions.

On the stand, First Lieutenant Robert Lehnert had a great deal to say about the flight and the storm. After detailing the breakup of the squadron and the sighting of Nui, Lehnert described his refusal to leave Lauesen behind, and his attempt to bail out close to him. He was then asked about the longest single-engine flight over water he had made prior to 25 January.

Lehnert: "One and a half hour to two hours."
Recorder: "Where was that?"
Lehnert: "Jacksonville or Santa Barbara."

Once again, the board excused the witness after only a few questions. After Lehnert, they called First Lieutenant Walter Wilson and First Lieutenant Jules Flood. As with the previous two witnesses, they were only asked about their personal recollections of the flight and the storm. Wilson's story must have generated some raised eyebrows, but his account of the more than two hours he spent wandering around before literally stumbling on Niutao only added more pages to the investigation transcript. The choice of John Hansen, Robert Lehnert, Walter Wilson, and Jules Flood may seem random, but it was quite shrewd. With those four witnesses, the board heard from the one man who managed to reach Funafuti, the man who had been the first to voluntarily leave the squadron after the first storm, the man who had crashed on Niutao, and one who had been in the main group and had also witnessed MacLaughlin's disappearance. However, by not spreading their net a bit wider, they missed the opportunity to question Mark Syrkin and Sterling Price, the only two living pilots who had witnessed General Merritt's verbal outburst at Burke on Tarawa, and prove that both Burke and Merritt had lied on the stand.

But another, larger matter was pressing on the board. The invasion of the Marshalls was imminent and many of the members had important roles in Operation Flintlock. This was likely a factor in expediting the investigation. Up to this time, the primary focus had been on how VMF-422 had been permitted to take off without clearance; however, the testimony of Jeans and Hughes was important in examining the next witness, Lieutenant Colonel John Payne, the USAAF commander on Nanumea. Payne had detailed information on the radar plot that tracked the lost marines after 1223 until 1530 on 25 January. What he told the board showed a marked lack of initiative on the part of the Nanumea air operations department, but it proved that again, the poor ground control on Tarawa was a reason for the disaster.

> Recorder: "When did you first know that this flight consisted of fighters?"
> Payne: "When they were over Nui south of us. I asked the Filter Center, who was in contact with them, to ask them specifically what they were and who they were. At that time, they were talking about jumping out and water landings at this island."
> Recorder: "When was communication established between Nanumea and the flight?"
> Payne: "Between 1341 and 1418, two-way communications were established between the island and the aircraft."
> Recorder: "What was the nature of the communications between Nanumea and the subject flight?"
> Payne: "The subject of the conversation was to have the airplanes go up and orbit in an effort to bring them on the radar screen."
> Recorder: "Was this done? Was the flight again brought on to the screen?"
> Payne: "No sir, the flights were not again brought on to the screen."

This revealed that Nanumea had been in voice contact for over an hour prior to the mass ditching but failed to convey their request to Jeans that the Corsairs had to be higher in order to establish a radar fix. By the time this request was sent out, the main formation was well south of Nui and far out of range.

The bomb group commander had more bombshells in store for the investigation.

> Recorder: "State the weather at the Nanumea base during the morning of 25 January with emphasis on ceiling and visibility."
> Payne: "It was clouding up in the morning and at ten o'clock [was] overcast, but no rain, and starting at 1037, rain. It rained all the way through up till five o'clock."
> Recorder: "Tell what the weather was at the Nanumea base during the afternoon in as much detail as you can?"
> Payne: "Hard intermittent rain, what appeared to me almost an instrumental condition during the early afternoon, and it cleared up later in the day."
> Recorder: "About what time did it commence clearing?"
> Payne: "Approximately at 1700."
> Recorder: "In your opinion, could airplanes approaching Nanumea

from noon until three o'clock on the twenty-fifth have made the field and landed safely?"

Payne: "Properly briefed and I think a carefully thought out plan for covering their own traffic with very low visibility probably would have brought all airplanes in."

Recorder: "At what time did the last radar plot of any of the flight show on the screen?"

Payne: "It was approximately three o'clock."

Recorder: "When was the last time that any radio communication emanating from any of the flight was heard at Nanumea?"

Payne: "Between three and three thirty."

Recorder: "What date and time did you get a departure report of [the] flight in question?"

Payne: "On 25 January, approximately eight hours after the airplanes had gone down."

Payne's last statement was the first testimony that confirmed that air operations at Tarawa had contributed to the disaster by failing to follow established rules for departing flights.

Payne was on the stand for the remainder of Monday and returned on Tuesday. In all, he was asked more than sixty questions. When he stepped off the stand, the board had learned a great deal about the last two hours of VMF-422.

This was originally considered the end of the investigation. The board deliberated and recorded its initial findings. Since they do not differ greatly from the final report, only a few points will be noted here.

1. "There is no doubt that the flight to Funafuti was ill-prepared. The order from the Commanding General, Fourth Marine Base Defense Aircraft Wing made no provision for an escort. The general considered an escort on flights such as this unnecessary and on a similar, previous flight so informed his operations officer who had requested one. The orders for this flight were not sent on to the island and Air Commander Tarawa, and what knowledge or information his Field Operations Officer had was merely what was gathered by observation and hearsay."

2. "That the principal cause for the loss was an error in judgment on the part of the squadron commander in leading his squadron into a heavy cloud bank which he could not see over, beneath, or around, when he had no late terminal weather information or specific information on that storm."

3. "That the responsibility for not recognizing the need for an escort for this flight rests upon the Commanding General, Fourth Marine Base Defense Aircraft Wing."

The members again deliberated and chose to reopen the investigation, recalling several witnesses. From this, we can assume they were not satisfied with the results so far. One major issue was the matter of how a fighter squadron was able to take off on a long, hazardous flight completely unknown to the Hawkins Field chain of command, so Captain Tate was recalled for further testimony.

Tate was shown the dispatch from Admiral Hoover dated 27 December. He was asked to identify and read the dispatch out loud.

> Tate: "The dispatch is as follows: From Commander Task Force Fifty-Seven. To AirCom Tarawa, Info AirCom Apamama and Makin. It is dated the twenty-seventh of December and it reads as follows: "Air Operations at Hawkins is a full time job for a senior operations officer acting for you. Will also now be required at Ella. Please fill these billets immediately and locate on or near the fields readily accessible. The Acorn and CASU Commanders are not acceptable in these jobs as having too many other duties. Would expect you to use Brewster at least temporarily."

The board then asked Tate if this was done. He replied with, "On arrival in this area prior to the receipt of the dispatch previously mentioned, I had detailed Major Brewster as air operations officer on the field and he accounted in that capacity from about the twenty-sixth of November until about a week before the receipt of this dispatch when I returned him to headquarters. However, on receipt of the aforementioned dispatch, I showed this dispatch to Major Brewster and told him to report back to Hawkins as Air Operations. Subsequently, and about the nineteenth of January, I began to note considerable discrepancies in the arrival and departures of various planes. Commander Wheelock and I agreed that the situation required a written order in order that this difficulty in keeping a record of planes cleared and arriving at the field be clarified; therefore, a directive was sent out on the twentieth delineating what we expected from the operations officers. In addition to this, Commander Wheelock called and discussed arrival and departure reports with the operations officers."

According to Tate, as late as 19 January it was still possible for flights to leave Hawkins Field without written orders. Tate stated that Commander Wheelock and Major Brewster had not maintained his initial orders, but even after he had issued a dispatch sent on 20 January, the needed changes in field and air operations were still not in effect. Therefore VMF-422 was able to leave Hawkins without written orders or even the knowledge of the air operations staff.

The board then inquired about Tate's 20 January order.

> Recorder: "Do you know whether or not the unsatisfactory conditions in your field operations department, which prompted you to issue your order of January 20, have been corrected since that date?"
>
> Tate: "They have not been corrected to my satisfaction, and the same conditions exist on practically every other field in the central pacific. We are sending repeated messages daily trying to check on various flights. I am also informed this condition exists at Pearl Harbor. I think this is due mainly to the nature of combat operations and inexperienced pilots."

With that statement, Tate blamed a shorthanded staff faced with too much work. But it will be remembered that Hoover had told him to fill the billets of air operations officer and base operations officers with new personnel whose sole duty was to those posts. But Tate had only shifted Brewster to the job on a temporary basis, and never followed up on permanently assigning new officers.

After Tate left the stand, Commander Wheelock was brought back in to give further testimony on his duties as base operations officer. While he did not drop any bombshells, it was obvious that Wheelock felt that the system in place at Hawkins Field as of 25 January was ineffectual for the increasing level of air traffic coming and going at Tarawa. He too pointed the finger at overworked staff. Major Brewster then took the stand again to describe his own memories of the operations between 20 and 25 January. After this, he was asked what he had done just prior to the departure of VMF-422. He stated that he had driven Major MacLaughlin to the field and dropped him off, then returned to the command post. Not once did he ever ask MacLaughlin if he or anyone had filed a flight plan for the Funafuti flight.

> Recorder: "Did you at any time advise Major MacLaughlin to formally or informally obtain a clearance for his flight?"

Brewster: "Not in so many words. The expression 'clearance' was not used in connection with airplane arrivals or departures at that time."

This was certainly splitting hairs on Brewster's part.

Recorder: "Did you obtain from Major MacLaughlin the call of his plane, the preparation of the flight, and the distance of the flight?"

Brewster: "I did not."

Recorder: "Did you make any effort to hold the planes of VMF-422 on the field until that information was obtained?"

Brewster: "I made no effort since they departed while I was away from the command post and I did not know that the information had not been obtained until subsequent check revealed this fact."

Recorder: "Did you, prior to January twenty-fifth, issue orders to tower operators that they would show a red light to planes about to take off unless they, the tower operators, had been informed that that plane was properly cleared?"

Brewster: "Yes."

Recorder: "Then the allowing of a green light to Major MacLaughlin was a violation of your order?"

Brewster: "That is right."

When Brewster left the stand, the board deliberated off the record for a time, after which Buddress made the following observation: "I believe it is clear to this board, both from the testimony of the witness himself and from his demeanor and attitude before the board, that Major Brewster is not sufficiently competent to be operations officer at Hawkins Field, and it is accordingly suggested that his removal as such should be recommended."

As to this, the record does not show what prompted this decision. Brewster's verbal responses did illustrate his lack of initiative. To a few questions, he was defensive and curt, but certainly no more than Merritt.

At last, the members interviewed Radioman Allison, the man who had shown MacLaughlin the green light. He confirmed that they had not needed written orders for that purpose, provided someone in the chain of command, in this case Lieutenant Seebury Waring, was informed of the departure. Allison also told the board that he had informed Lieutenant Sandlin in the command post that the flight had taken off and was bound for Funafuti. He admitted he had not been told that VMF-422 was first to stop at Nanumea.

At 1135 on Saturday, 5 February 1944, the Board of Inquiry finished hearing from witnesses. They had been at it since 27 January, having heard the testimony of twenty-three witnesses, generating over 140 pages of transcript, and entered seventeen documents into evidence. The board was ready to begin its deliberations the following day.

It is worth noting that of the twenty-three witnesses called, only one said that an escort for this type of flight was unnecessary and he did not feel, even after the disaster, that it had ever been needed. That single witness was Brigadier General Lewie G. Merritt.

The United States Navy officially announced the loss of VMF-422 on 1 February in a press release sent from Pearl Harbor.

NAVY DEPARTMENT
IMMEDIATE RELEASE
CINCPAC PRESS RELEASE NO. 248

"Twenty-two planes of a squadron of twenty-three Marine Corsair fighters failed to reach their destination on a routine flight from Gilbert islands to a base in the Ellice Islands on January 25 (West Longitude Date), where they ran into a severe local weather disturbance.

One plane reached base safely, one made a crash landing on another island in the Ellice group, and the remainder, as far as is known, landed at sea. Search operations were started immediately, and all but six of the pilots are safe. One body has been recovered and five of the pilots are missing. Their next of kin have been notified."

Nowhere in the release was the squadron number given nor were any of the missing men named. Moran's family in Depue, Illinois was told of his death. The families of MacLaughlin, Rogers, Aycrigg, Lauesen, and Thompson were informed that they were missing. According to War Department policy, they would be considered as missing in action for one year and then declared dead. So the families of five marine officers would have to wait a full year to learn the fate of their loved ones.

Coincidentally, on the day the board adjourned, an article appeared in the Joplin *Globe* reporting that Captain Cloyd R. Jeans was awarded the Distinguished Flying Cross for his action in supporting the marines at Guadalcanal. The reader may recall in Chapter Three, the fragmentary news story of Jeans helping to save some stranded marines. He was notified through official channels, which had to have caused him some amusement in light of what he'd just been through.

The board's actual deliberations, which lasted from 6 to 10 February were not recorded. Instead their findings, opinions, and recommendations were given to the reporter for typing and then read into the record. Lieutenant Commander Buddress began with a summary of VMF-422's history and training, leading up to their activities from their arrival on Tarawa to their takeoff the following day. This included MacLaughlin's meetings with Burke and the other officers, what information and preparation he had received, and the weather report. Buddress outlined the intended flight plan and radio frequencies, which he stated were outdated and incorrect.

VMF-422's flight to Nanumea was uneventful until the storm was sighted about 1215 hours, after which matters became almost totally unmanageable. He detailed the breakup of the squadron, the loss of several planes, and the attempt to return to Nui.

While describing the ditching and time in the rafts, he included how the Nanumea radar plot had tracked them and the subsequent failed attempts to establish contact. It is worth noting that the board had assembled as accurate a timeline of the event as is ever likely to exist, but even so, it was based on often contradictory testimony.

Buddress then outlined the command structure, policies, and procedures at Hawkins Field, including the manner in which VMF-422 was allowed to leave without authorization.

Although the findings were stated in dry, unbiased terms, some indications of what it deemed important were added. For instance, Buddress said, "Neither General Merritt nor Colonel Burke considered themselves responsible for preparations for the flight."

He continued, "Both General Merritt and Colonel Burke were under the impression that the squadron was well qualified for the flight, and that it had previously made long overwater flights, which was not true. Both assumed, and did not investigate or verify, the experience or qualifications of the squadron."

Then Buddress finished with:

"At no time was the Island Commander officially advised of the proposed flight, although the Island Operations Officer (Wheelock) and his assistant (Brewster) at Hawkins Field were aware that it was to be made and of the approximate time of take-off. The Island Operations Officer would have provided an escort had he known about the flight and considered the flight to be under his orders."

At that point, it was time to list the findings and recommendations. One by one, the board read into the record what it believed to be the reasons for the disaster. While a few dealt with technical matters, there are many observations that key personnel erred in or neglected their duties.

1. That the loss of VMF-422 was due to improper action by the leader, Major John S. MacLaughlin, after his squadron encountered bad weather.

2. That the squadron was inadequately trained for long overwater flights.

3. That the squadron was poorly prepared for the subject flight.

4. That the weather forecast furnished to the squadron's pilots before taking off was adequate and would not have been improved materially by later information.

5. That the departure of the flight from Hawkins Field was improperly reported, and that this seriously hampered efforts to help the squadron after it was in trouble.

6. That no clearance was required of the flight leader before his departure, and that this is to be laid to the fact that the operations organization at Hawkins Field was poorly and ineffectively administered.

7. That the Island and Air Commander, Tarawa, the Island Operations Officer Tarawa, and the Operations Officer, Hawkins Field are each and severally responsible for the situation described in paragraphs 5 and 6 above.

8. That an escort, or guide plane, would, in all probability, have prevented the disaster.

9. That an escort, or guide plane, should have been provided, and that the responsibility for not recognizing the need for one rests upon the Commanding General, Fourth Marine Base Defense Air Wing.

10. That the Commanding General, Fourth Marine Base Defense Aircraft Wing is responsible for not taking adequate measures to ascertain the training and degree of preparedness of the squadron for the movement which he ordered.

11. That the steps taken by the Air Commander Nanumea were ineffective in assisting the flight in reaching destination safely and indicated poor organization to cope with the emergency after it became known.

12. That the pilots who perished died in line of duty and not as a result of their own misconduct.

The findings, stated in plain language, were intended to convey exactly what the board found, no more, no less. From this, the reader can see that the board did consider Merritt to be culpable in his refusal to provide an escort and that such an escort would probably have been instrumental in preventing the loss. It is interesting that for the first time the word "disaster" was used to describe the scope of the tragedy.

Then the board listed its recommendations for possible actions. Unlike a civil or criminal court judge's rulings, these were not automatically done. The recommendations were just that; suggestions for what the members deemed should be done to prevent another such disaster, and disciplinary actions against specific officers.

1. That no action be taken against Major John S. MacLaughlin due to the fact that he is missing and probably has perished.

2. That a letter of severe reprimand be addressed to Brigadier General Lewie G. Merritt, USMC for:

(a) his failure properly to ascertain the preparedness of VMF-422 for the movement which he ordered;

(b) his failure to recognize the need for an escort, or guide plane;

(c) effectively preventing use of an escort.

3. That a letter of reprimand be addressed to Major T. O. Brewster, USMC, for failure to institute a forcible (sic) and efficient system of aircraft clearance and for failure otherwise properly to organize the operations department, Hawkins Field, Tarawa.

4. That letters of admonition be addressed to Captain J. R. Tate, USN, and Commander A. W. Wheelock, USN, for poor supervision and failure to take steps to see that the Island and Air Commander's order dated 20 January 1944 was effectively implemented.

5. That all higher echelons of command recognize the relative inexperience of new aircraft squadrons, the youth and lack of seasoning of pilots, and the specialized and accelerated training to which individual pilots and squadrons are exposed.

6. That all higher echelons of command assume an increased responsibility for conscientious supervision and direction of aircraft squadrons in, or about to be assigned to, combat areas in order that these new squadrons may receive the maximum benefit of available experienced guidance.

7. That an escort plane, piloted by personnel experienced in local conditions, and equipped with adequate navigation and communication facilities, be provided for all movements of aircraft such as that of VMF-422 from Tarawa to Funafuti.

8. That flights such as that of VMF-422 be carefully guarded in order that any unfavorable weather developments, terminal or on route, may be communicated to the guide plane without delay.

Signed on 10 February 1944.

Captain Scott E. Peck, US Navy, senior member (Commander, USS *Curtiss*)

Commander James C. Lang, US Navy, member

Lieutenant Colonel John W. Stage, US Marine Corps, member

Lieutenant Commander Elmer N. Buddress, US Navy Reserve, recorder.

It is interesting to note that Colonel Burke seemed to have escaped censure by the board, even though it considered him to be nearly as, if not equally as culpable as General Merritt for his failure to assure better preparation for the flight. More significantly, as noted in recommendations numbers five, six, seven, and eight, the board made it clear that it believed that better training was needed for new squadrons and that the Pacific commanders should be more aware of the relative inexperience of these new units. In a way, this alone was a watershed moment in the Pacific war. It shone a harsh light on something that had not been recognized before. It also meant, in effect, that the death of six marines would result in more effective training.

At this point, the Board of Inquiry into the loss of VMF-422 adjourned. Its recommendations would be sent up the line to Admiral Hoover and Admiral Pownall. From there, they would reach Pearl Harbor and Admiral Nimitz. At each level, the flag officers had some leeway in what they could do, such as accept or decline the board's recommendations or recommend further action or specific modifications. But they did not have the authority to make actual changes. Every amendment to the recommendations had to be sent to each senior commander and again be approved before their collective decision could be moved up the chain of command. This process often took months, with the memos and letters flying back and forth between Tarawa, Hawaii, and Washington, DC like so many white leaves in a gale. But for now, the board had done its job and could return to the business of fighting the war.

The first official response to the board's findings was sent by Admiral Hoover on 15 February. It reads as follows:

> From: Commander Aircraft, Central Pacific Force.
> To: The Judge Advocate General.
> Via: (1) Commander Air Force, Pacific Fleet, Rear Admiral C. A. Pownall
> (2) Commander in Chief, US Pacific Fleet, Admiral C. W. Nimitz
> Subj: Board of Investigation - Record of.
>
> 1. Forwarded.
> 2. The proceedings, findings of fact and opinions of the Board of Investigation in the attached case are approved.
> 3. The recommendations are in general approved. The matter of a Letter of Reprimand to Brigadier General L.G. Merritt, US Marine Corps is referred to the Commander in Chief US Pacific Fleet, in accordance with his verbal order to Commander Aircraft, Central Pacific Force.
> A Letter of Reprimand will be addressed to Major T. O. Brewster, US Marine Corps. Letters of Caution will be addressed to Captain J. R. Tate, US Navy, and Commander A. W. Wheelock, US Navy
> With respect to recommendation number seven, (7), a directive will be issued to this command requiring escort for fighters on long or hazardous flights over water. It is suggested that something of this nature be put out by higher authority.
> J. A. Hoover

This was only the beginning. For the next eight months, the report on VMF-422 would continue to be passed among the high-ranking navy brass.

A few days later, Admiral Charles Pownall, in a letter to Nimitz, had this to say:

"VMF-422 was one of the better trained squadrons that have thus far been transferred to a combat area by this command. The progress of training, particularly the average flying hours of the pilots and the time in type of plane operated, was higher than can be normally expected in wartime. The leader, Major MacLaughlin, was a well-seasoned fighter pilot, careful and conservative, an excellent navigator, and well experienced in beam flying. He had successfully led several formation flights of fighter planes from Floyd Bennett Field in New York to San Diego, California, during seasons of unfavorable weather. The fact that so many of the pilots were

Rear Admiral Charles Pownall felt strongly that General Merritt should have been court-martialed after the inquiry revealed his role in the disaster. (Official U.S. Navy photo.)

able to stay together under the foul weather conditions that prevailed indicates that a fairly high degree of training existed in the organization."

Pownall was setting the stage for his own observations and recommendations on the board's report. They would prove to be as controversial as the disaster itself.

But Mother Nature was not done with storms. As noted above, a huge typhoon tore apart Halsey's fleet in December 1944, and another disaster struck American aviators on 1 June of the following year. Boeing B-29 Superfortresses of the Twentieth Bomber Command in the Marianas were escorted to Osaka by 184 P-51 Mustangs of the Seventh Fighter Command based on Iwo Jima. Halfway to Japan, they encountered a massive weather front that extended to more than thirty thousand feet. Chaos ensued, and twenty-seven Mustangs fell into the churning sea. Twenty-five pilots were lost. As in the Flintlock Disaster fourteen months earlier the tragedy was wholly avoidable. It resulted in a Board of Inquiry attended by no less than Chief of the Air Force, General Henry "Hap" Arnold himself.

As for the surviving Flying Buccaneers, they were finally about to go to war.

CHAPTER 21

IN THE WAR AT LAST

The Marshall Islands, located more than two thousand miles southwest of Hawaii, consisted of hundreds of islands and coral reefs in scores of atolls over a vast area of the central Pacific. The four main atolls were laid out in a rough square with Kwajalein and Mele to the south, Maloelap and Wotje to the north, Jaluit to the southwest, and Majuro on the east. The Japanese had over eleven thousand troops and hundreds of shore defense and anti-aircraft guns, but little means of attacking the American ships as they appeared like a vast tsunami over the southern horizon as Operation Flintlock began.

The first planned phase was the attack and neutralization of Kwajalein and the twin islands of Roi and Namur

Kwajalein was a major staging area for Japanese surface warships and submarines, and hosted the largest air base in the region. After the Solomons fell in early 1943 and the subsequent capture of the Ellice and Gilbert Islands, the Imperial General Staff chose to draw in its remaining forces to the Marshalls and consolidate every combat asset they still possessed. The defense of the Marshalls was essential to protect Truk Lagoon, a vast anchorage in the Carolines. Truk's superb lagoon was an important Imperial Japanese Navy and merchant fleet base, but was already in Nimitz's crosshairs.

Before the main assault could begin it was necessary to also take the atoll at Majuro, 190 miles southeast of Kwajalein, in order to protect the US supply lines and establish an eastern air base. Majuro fell on 31 January without, as official sources maintain, a single American life lost.

Flintlock officially began with systematic air attacks by US Navy fighters and bombers to destroy the enemy air forces on the island. By 3 February, this had largely been accomplished. The massive air strikes against the Marshalls in Flintlock proved the utility of the fast carrier task group. In a few hours, Mitscher's carriers had done more to neutralize enemy naval, ground, and air forces than Hoover's land-based heavy and medium bomb groups had been able to accomplish in two weeks. On Roi alone they destroyed over one hundred planes in the air and on the ground. The navy lost twenty-seven fighters and twenty-two bombers from accidents and combat.

Admiral Masashi Kobayashi had been convinced the initial American assault would come from the east and attack Wotje and Maloelap, the easternmost atolls of the Marshalls. He had assembled most of his forces on these islands, but it was a lost cause.

Ten US Navy battleships, some new, others more than twenty years old, added their brawn to the weight of metal aimed at Kwajalein. The huge warships dominated the horizon like hulking gray castles of steel. For the first time, the battleship would play a decisive role in a major land assault. Among the half-dozen heavy cruisers assigned to the invasion was Spruance's flagship, USS *Indianapolis* (CA-35), which was destined to be sunk by the *I-68* in July 1945 after delivering the components of the first atom bomb to Tinian.

At zero hour, the battleships opened fire. Orange flame blossomed from dozens of fourteen-inch and sixteen-inch guns. A continuous roar like nothing heard on earth swept over the sea as towering fountains of gray and brown soil blasted into the sky over Kwajalein like hundred-foot stalagmites. Soon the island looked like the cratered surface of the moon.

The immense weight of shells and bombs that rained on Kwajalein, Maloelap, Roi, Namur, and Wotje prompted one wag aboard Admiral Turner's flagship to quip, "Never in the field of human conflict was so much thrown by so many at so few." Another witness was reported to have said after the battleships, cruisers, destroyers, and bombers had done their deadly work, "The entire island of Kwajalein looked as if it had been lifted up to twenty thousand feet and then dropped."

The Fourth Marine Division began landings on the northern islands of Ro and Namur, while the army's Seventh Infantry Division moved in to take Kwajalein. The Japanese had not been able to assemble a defense in depth because of the limited land area. They settled for massing their heavy guns on the seaward side of the islands, not realizing that the American landing craft could cross the reefs and assault the lagoon side.

It was estimated that the capture of the islands would take two weeks, but to the surprise of the planners, it was over in less than a week. The casualty figures told an accurate, if sterile, account of the operation's success. The 20,100 marines who attacked the northern islands of Roi and Namur suffered 195 killed and 545 wounded. Japanese losses were 3,472 killed out of 3,563.

On Kwajalein to the south, the army's 21,342 troops killed 4,398 enemy of the 5,012 engaged. Army losses were 177 killed and 1,037 wounded. Compared to Tarawa only two months before, Flintlock had been a cakewalk.

Author Herman Wouk, who had witnessed the assault while serving on a destroyer minesweeper wrote of Kwajalein in his best-selling novel, *The Caine Mutiny*. He described it as a classic, widely conceived and surgically executed operation. It was not known at the time that the Japanese high command had decided not to rescue, reinforce, or even support the Marshalls. The garrisons there were totally on their own and expected to die honorably for the emperor.

The original timetable laid out by Nimitz in December had stipulated at least a month of reorganization before beginning Operation Catchpole, the assault on Eniwetok and Engebi. But Spruance and his staff had their blood up and chose to start the assault on Eniwetok by first launching initial air strikes on Truk Lagoon in the Carolines and Saipan in the Marianas. This would remove any chance of the Japanese reinforcing the garrisons on Eniwetok. The Fifth Fleet's carriers bombed Truk on 16-17 February, leaving almost thirty ships on the bottom or beached. Over two hundred planes were destroyed and another one hundred damaged.

Eniwetok Atoll fell on 19 February, further consolidating the US hold on the Marshalls. Several Japanese island bases were still fully occupied and defended. These included Nauru, Wotje, Maloelap, and Jaluit. Their neutralization would be the job of the Marine Corps' fighters and bombers. They would never be assaulted or taken, being little more than targets for Spruance's ships to practice their gunnery. The marine fighters and bombers were tasked with the destruction of every enemy base, harbor, gun emplacement, supply dump, command post, ship, and aircraft in the Marshalls.

Meanwhile, the survivors of VMF-422 were assembled at Tarawa, where they were informed that they would be flown back to Funafuti. There they would be issued new Corsairs and replacement pilots from the rear echelon, which had finally arrived in the Gilberts. Once they were reorganized and refitted, they were to fly short ferry hops up the chain of islands back to Tarawa to begin their role in Operation Catchpole. It was ironic; after all they had been through, they were too late to participate in Flintlock.

The island of Engebi in Eniwetok Atoll, where VMF-422 was stationed after they had been reorganized. (Official U.S. Navy photo.)

The Joint Chiefs of Staff in the Pentagon sent a memo to the Pacific commanders regarding the Allies' next major objective. Nimitz was of the opinion that they should invade and take Truk Lagoon, then move west towards China. From there the next target would be the Philippines, just as Japan had done in 1941. However, General Henry H. "Hap" Arnold, chief of the air force felt the Marianas should be taken next. The three principal islands, Guam, Saipan, and Tinian were well-suited for the huge air bases that would be needed to support the hundreds of B-29 Superfortresses slated for the bombing campaign on the Japanese Home Islands. After the memo landed on the desk of Admiral Spruance, commander of the Fifth Fleet, he drafted a response to Admiral Nimitz. Spruance directed Admiral Pownall, his Commander, Air Force Pacific Fleet (ComAirPacFor) to personally deliver it to Nimitz in Pearl Harbor.

At this same time, the board's recommendations were being reviewed by Nimitz, so it is likely that he and Pownall took the time to discuss the findings.

Pownall's official 9 March memo to Nimitz listed his own observations and recommendations on the board's findings. In it, he stated that Merritt deserved more punishment than a mere official slap on the wrist.

"That predicated upon the testimony presented in this report the punishment recommended for Brigadier General Lewis (sic) G. Merritt, USMC, is considered inadequate. The evidence and the final opinions of the Board as expressed in opinions eight, nine, ten, and eleven, the loss of life and aircraft resulting would indicate that under the conditions existing, Brigadier General Merritt displayed serious error in judgment and leadership which cannot be condoned, particularly in one in his high office and position of responsibility. It is recommended that he be relieved from his command, tried by General Court Martial, or that his case be referred to the Major General Commandant for such actions as he may deem appropriate."

Pownall's opinions may have been influenced by the frustrating scandal over the lost TBF Avenger crew in August. With this sour memory still haunting him in the spring of 1944, the admiral may have felt particularly resentful of how easily General Merritt could escape with his skirts nice and clean despite the board's findings that he was largely responsible for the lives of six marines, not to mention twenty-two new planes.

This went up the chain of command to the Chief of Naval Operation, Admiral Ernest J. King at the Pentagon. While both Hoover and Pownall were willing to throw Merritt to the wolves, Pownall went one better in the same memo. "Although not contained in the Board's recommendations, it is evident that the organization and administration for the proper and adequate control of aircraft, on extended flights in the Central Pacific area, particularly at Tarawa was ambiguous, inadequate, and ineffectual in this instance. Particular reference is made to opinions four, five, six, and twelve of the Board's report. For this situation and the regrettable consequences attendant thereon, the administrative responsibility that such a condition did exist rests in the final analysis upon the Flag Officer commanding, Commander Aircraft, Central Pacific Force, Rear Admiral John H. Hoover, USN."

Hoover was probably stung by this last comment from his superior, but he had little to fear. He knew he could count on Nimitz's full support.

Chester Nimitz's backing of "Genial John," with whom he had a good personal relationship, never wavered. For instance, in early February the Commander in Chief had arrived in the Marshalls for consultations when he learned that the US Army Air Force bomb group commanders had long resented being under Hoover and petitioned to have themselves placed directly under CINCPAC, an unworkable chain of command if ever there was one. Nimitz chose to keep the USAAF bombers under Hoover.

Around this time Pownall wrote a letter directly to CNO King in which he suggested that Major MacLaughlin be cleared of all blame for the disaster.

Nimitz read over the last memos and added his own recommendations and changes, which were then seconded by both Hoover and Pownall. On 25 March, Nimitz had written his fifth endorsement of the board's findings. The full text is shown below.

5th Endorsement to:
ComAirCenPacFor, Conf.
Letter of 15 February 1944

From: Commander in Chief, U. S. Pacific Fleet and Pacific Ocean Areas.
To: Commander in Chief, United States Fleet (JAG)
Subj: Board of Investigation, forwarding Proceedings of.

1. Forwarded, inviting attention to Commander in Chief, U. S. Pacific Fleet and Pacific Ocean Areas, 4th Endorsement of 23 March 1944, Serial 00977 under which a copy of the Board of Investigation convened by CTF 57 on 27 January 1944 was forwarded.

2. The Inspector General, Pacific Fleet and Pacific Ocean Areas, has concluded that a further investigation of the loss of VMF-422 is warranted and a copy of that report is appended hereto, (Enclose A), and it will he noted that:

Brigadier General L. G. Merritt, USMC, Colonel L. T. Burke, USMC, Major T. O.

Brewster, USMCR, Captain J. R. Tate, USN, and Commander A. W. Wheelock, USN, were all given the opportunity to examine the testimony of the original Board, and were made defendants or interested parties in the recent Investigation.

3. Commander in Chief, US Pacific Fleet and Pacific Ocean areas, approves the action of ComAirCenPacFor in issuing a letter of reprimand to Major T. O. Brewster, USMCR, and letters of caution to Captain J. R. Tate, USN and Commander A. W. Wheelock, USN, all of whom were directly connected with the organization of Air Operations at Hawkins Field.

4. Commander in Chief, US Pacific Fleet and Pacific Ocean Areas, is also issuing a letter of reprimand to Brigadier General L. G. Merritt, USMC for his failure to advise proper authorities of the

orders of which he had issued to VMF-422, and for his announcement of a policy regarding escorts for fighter planes which failed
completely to take into consideration the experience or training of
fighter pilots. A letter of admonishment is also being issued to Colonel L. T. Burke, USMC for his actions in advising the Commander
of VMF-422 that an escort plane was not available when one had
been requested, and for his failure to advise the commander of the
4th Marine Base Defense Air Wing, or the Air Operations Office at
Hawkins Field or the Island Commander, Tarawa of the request for
an escort plane that was made to and refused by him.

5. Commander in Chief, US Pacific Fleet and Pacific Ocean Areas will issue a directive that whenever practicable, fighter planes
on long over water flights be provided with an escort plane whenever there is any question as to the ability of the fighter pilots to
make the flight unescorted.

6. No further action in this case is recommended.

C. W. Nimitz

For the first time, Colonel Burke was added to the list of officers
found to be liable for the disaster. Nimitz held nothing back in his
opinion that Burke had failed in his duty. Furthermore, CINCPAC
made it known that as far as he was concerned, no fighter planes
should fly long over water flights without an escort.

The following month King too endorsed the board's and Nimitz's
changes and forwarded his own letter to James Forrestal, Undersecretary of the navy in the Pentagon.

That was the navy's last salvo in the exchange of memos. From
that point on, the paper war was fought in the Pentagon and official
Washington.

As noted previously, Merritt was permitted to read the board's
findings and recommendations. Upon realizing his actions were being singled out as the primary cause of the loss of VMF-422, he
likely began a campaign to erase the stain on his record. Having
served on the staff of two Marine Corps commandants and spent
two years in the JAG office in Washington he had made many considerable political connections with influential South Carolina poli-
ticians, including Strom Thurmond, who had served in the state
General Assembly and would soon become governor, and George
Timmerman, Sr. As a US District Court judge in South Carolina,
Timmerman had his own influence in the White House. He had

been appointed by President Roosevelt in 1941 and served in the South Carolina House of Representatives from 1908 to 1920. To put it mildly, Merritt had powerful friends.

As a result, James Forrestal found himself with a hot potato in his lap. As a political appointee, Forrestal was subject to pressure from the White House, Congress, and the Senate. Likewise, he was sensitive to media criticism of the military, particularly on casualty figures. After the battle of Tarawa, the newspapers used words like "bloody" and "slaughter" to describe the fighting. The War Department censors were initially able to keep such inflammatory terms from reaching the public, but eventually they gave up. There was no doubt that Tarawa was a bloodbath. But when it came to the disaster that struck VMF-422, Forrestal was caught between the three antagonistic gods of political pragmatism, national security, and personal integrity. He had authorized the 2 February press release, but the official findings of the board were not to be made public until agreed upon by the CNO and Secretary of the Navy, Frank Knox.

This played right into Merritt's hands. As long as the board's recommendations were kept secret, he had free rein to carry out his campaign. For nearly six months, there was little progress on the matter.

The Flying Buccaneers were not to learn of any of this for several months. They were frustrated and angry at the loss of six of their number, including their commander, but at last they were going to war. Having to be flown back to Funafuti again, then fly back to Tarawa only deepened their resentment. Upon their arrival on a navy R4D at Funafuti, they were appalled to see what they had been told were to be "new" Corsairs. VMF-422, having suddenly found itself bereft of twenty-two planes could not be resupplied until a new shipment arrived from the States.

Syrkin commented, "We were told they were going to refurbish our squadron. But they didn't tell us that we were going to get hangar queens from other squadrons, who weren't going to give us the best planes that they had. We wound up with some pretty elderly airplanes. I had one of the first ones off the line. When we got up to Engebi, it was scrapped and used for spare parts."

The Buccaneers were frustrated at having to fly what amounted to antiques and "hangar queens," as Syrkin labeled them. The latter were planes that had more than their share of chronic mechanical faults and a tendency to spend most of their time in the maintenance hangars.

But as undesirable as their replacement Corsairs were, they had to accept them and in late February began ferrying them up the Gilberts to Tarawa. This had to be galling, but it paled in comparison to the first tragedy suffered by the squadron after the disaster.

First Lieutenant Ted Thurnau of Westwood, New Jersey had survived all alone in his raft for four days before being rescued by the *Welles.* On 27 February, flying one of the castoffs, he was off Syrkin's starboard wing on one of the short hops up the Gilbert Islands.

"We were landing at Apamama," Syrkin said in the 1998 video. "I looked over at Ted's plane and saw something alarming. I said, 'Hey Ted —' and he said, 'Don't even open your mouth, I see the indicator on the wing sticking up.' That meant the wing was not locked. When you lower the wings before takeoff, you pull this handle in the cockpit and see the indicator on the wings that shows they are down and locked. In his case the little indicator flap was up."

Thurnau, already lucky to have made it to Apamama without his wing folding in flight, was able to land. He told the ground crew to fix the wing before he had to make the next flight to Makin Island.

"The next morning Ted went out to the plane and saw that the indicator was down and that meant the wing was locked. We climbed in and took off. Then his wing folded and he was killed."

According to Lincoln, "Syrkin was so angry over Ted's death that if he could have found that ground crew he would have killed them."

In the squadron history, Wrenn states in dry terms: "On 28 February 1944, Lt. Thurnau was killed on takeoff at Apamama, Gilbert Islands. The left wing locking pin worked out of the locked position just as the Corsair was airborne. The aircraft was totally wrecked."

Rob Patterson of the Planes of Fame Air Museum explained that when the wing folded, a large chrome steel pin slid into place. It was actuated by a hydraulic plunger triggered by the wing coming down. "After the wing locks into place," he said, "a small door on top of the wing closes. Then the pilot has to pull the locking handle up, which then slides another pin into place, holding the first one. If the handle is not up, the big pin can slip out of position." Thurnau was too good a pilot not to make sure the handle was in the locked position, especially after his close call the previous day. It is more likely the Corsair, being old, had worn or faulty locking mechanisms and the pin slipped out, allowing the wing to fold up in flight. Thurnau died exactly one day short of a month after his

One of the prefabricated huts that the VMF-422 officers lived in during their time on Engebi. (Photo courtesy Andrew Syrkin.)

rescue. In a way, Ted Thurnau could be considered the seventh victim of the Flintlock Disaster. He was killed while flying an older Corsair issued after the mass ditching. If the squadron had been able to reach Funafuti as planned he would have been flying the new one. He would not be the last of the Flintlock survivors to die.

The ground echelon, along with the spare parts and tools had departed Hawaii on 27 January on board the *MS Island Mail* and the *SS Cape Isabel.* The original intention was that all the air and ground elements of VMF-422 would be on hand for operations when the Marshalls had been taken. When they had first arrived on 24 January, they were expected to be based on either Kwajalein or Majuro. But the delay caused by the disaster put them on the back burner, and so by the time they started receiving new airplanes and replacement pilots from the rear echelon, they were just in time to join the ground element on Engebi as part of Colonel Daly's MAG-22.

On 18 February, the first marines of VMF-422's ground element stepped on the coral sands of Engebi Island, but not without opposition. A Japanese sniper shot Staff Sergeant John Strubel as he climbed out of an LST.

Engebi is one of the northern islands of Eniwetok Atoll. Eniwetok itself was at the southern end of the fifty-mile-long lagoon. Nearby Perry Island had been a Japanese seaplane base. Now all three were in American hands. While the last elements of enemy

*Marine mechanics and ground crew repaired and serviced the Corsairs on
Engebi and Eniwetok. (Photo courtesy Andrew Syrkin.)*

defenders were eliminated by marine troops, the SeaBees and marine ground crew turned Engebi into a base for air operations. At
the same time, they built Stickell Field on Eniwetok with a 6,800-
foot runway. From there six squadrons of PB4Y-1 Liberators conducted patrols and bombing missions. The field had been named in
honor of Navy Cross recipient Lieutenant John H. Stickell, a pilot of
VB-108 who had died as a result of wounds sustained in a dangerous bombing mission to Jaluit Atoll in December 1943.

The base on Engebi was named, with a touch of humor, Wrig-
ley Field. Compounds for each of the squadrons were set up with
Quonset huts, mess hall, and dispensary and operations buildings.

Six replacement pilots were assigned to VMF-422's lead echelon.
Among them were First Lieutenants Donald K. Skillicorn of Morgan
Hill, California; John H. Stout, Jr. of Oklahoma City, Oklahoma;
Duane A. Dahquist of Hedley, Minnesota; and Second Lieutenants
Emerald E. Wolverton of Pueblo, Colorado and Raymond Schroeder
of Colby, Kansas. They joined the reconstituted lead echelon on 25
February, about the same time Wrenn received order No. F8-44
from the Fourth MBDAW that they were now to be part of MAG-22
under Colonel D. W. Torrey, who had taken over from Colonel Jim
Daly.

Although they were still under the Fourth MBDAW, they would
take their orders from Torrey. By 24 March, exactly two months after the squadron had landed on Hawkins Field, the last of the new

F4U-1Ds had arrived and VMF-422 was declared fully operational. They were placed in the rotation for combat assignment.

VMF-113 had been on the island since 20 February, and already flown several missions against nearby enemy air bases. At the end of March, they had flown down to Ponape in the Carolines and shot down nine Zeros and damaged three others.

The next day General Merritt flew up from Tarawa to congratulate Doc Everton for a successful mission. He brought a case of scotch whiskey for the pilots of VMF-113. Apparently, Merritt had chosen to forget Everton's insubordination on Tarawa over the demand for an escort.

This may or may not be indicative of Merritt's normal behavior, but he did this in full view of the survivors of the very squadron he failed to support. One can only guess at what they thought of such brazen behavior. In any case, as of 1 April, Merritt was still in command of the Fourth MBDAW.

· CHAPTER 22 ·

WHISTLING DEATH

After settling into the tents in Engebi's VMF-422 compound, the Flying Buccaneers were at last ready for combat. On 2 April, they got their chance. At the island's makeshift outdoor theater, the pilots were briefed on their first real combat assignment by Major Wrenn. "He told us about the island of Ponape in the Carolines," Hansen said. "We were pretty excited."

After briefing they went to retrieve their flight gear. Near the main Quonset hut was an area where there were bins for each pilot's gear. They retrieved their parachutes and flight gear. It was not surprising that the men who had lived through the disaster took more time to check out their survival equipment.

Eight Corsairs under Captain Jeans flew to Ponape to participate in the first of a series of strafing and bombing missions against Japanese airfields and defenses. They were the escort for USAAF B-25 Mitchell medium bombers. For the most part, the escort missions were simple in concept. They flew in at low altitude ahead of the B-25s to strafe and knock out the anti-aircraft guns. Each four-plane division moved in from out of the sun and raked the defenses. Each attack run was timed for the fighters to pull out just as the bombers arrived. The marines maintained radio silence for maximum surprise.

"I think our guns were bore-sighted to converge at about five hundred yards ahead," recalled Hansen. "We fired in short bursts to keep from overheating the guns, which reduced their accuracy."

As their .50 caliber shells tore through the Japanese guns and crews, they left behind long trails of smoke, dust, and destruction. Some AA gunners managed to shoot back and their 20mm tracers looked like long orange fingers reaching up to follow the darting Corsairs. Bigger guns left puffs and ribbons of black smoke over the island. Then the bombs began falling from the B-25s. Yellow and orange flashes erupted from the pale tan ground, white beaches, and among the thick green trees, creating a macabre artist's pallet of colors across the landscape.

Some fighter opposition was anticipated, but no Zeros came at the marines, much to the frustration of eager and aggressive pilots

*Bill Reardon was killed during a strafing run over Ponape
Island. (Photo courtesy Andrew Syrkin.)*

like Syrkin, Gunderson, Watson, and Lincoln. They were left with
strafing the airfields, installations, and targets of opportunity.

Syrkin strafed a Zero on the runway at Ponape on 4 April. The
plane wasn't even moving but it was a triumph to see the green-
painted fighter with its red "Meatballs" erupt into a pillar of orange
fire and black smoke.

Even though they felt elation for flying their first real combat
mission, it gave them far deeper satisfaction when they landed.
"We had made one of the longest single-engine fighter strikes of the
war," said Price with evident pride. "We did it and proved we could
have made it to Funafuti."

Each of the three flights participated in the three missions to
Ponape. But again fate struck the marines on 8 April when Bill
Reardon and his wingman, Lieutenant Donald Skillicorn were
strafing enemy AA batteries on Ponape. Skillicorn was hit in the
engine by ground fire as he came off the target. His engine began to
miss and smoke erupted from the cowling. He managed to ditch in
a bay on the northern coast of Ponape. Reardon stayed with him to
provide cover and saw Skillicorn climb out of the sinking F4U and

inflate his Mae West. But like others before him, he did not manage to retrieve his life raft.

Heavy clouds hampered Reardon's efforts to remain on station while Rex Jeans, the flight leader, called for the escort PBY to pick up Skillicorn. Reardon then turned back toward his patrol area and dived into a break in the clouds. But he was too low. His Corsair clipped the trees and crashed. It was not clear whether he had been hit by enemy fire or had lost his bearings in the heavy clouds.

Curly Lehnert, who was on the PBY that always accompanied the missions to Ponape, searched in vain for both men. Neither Skillicorn nor Reardon was found. Only an oil slick remained to mark the place where Skillicorn ditched.

With Reardon's death, one-third of the pilots who had taken off from Tarawa on 25 January were now gone.

Curly Lehnert had renewed his acquaintance with Andrew Jones of VMF-113 on Engebi. When asked if Jones had ever inquired about the disaster, Lehnert replied, "Not really. They all knew about it, but it was just not discussed."

"We didn't talk about it," said Hansen. "Some other pilots asked and even a few of the replacements wanted to know. It was just not something we wanted to remember."

Eventually the memories of the days under MacLaughlin were relegated to a quiet place in the back of their minds. The job before them was to help win the war.

Then in mid-April they were assigned to fly combat air patrol over Eniwetok, an uneventful and fruitless venture that accomplished little and satisfied no one.

"Day after day we flew patrol over the islands and never saw so much as a Japanese kite," said Hansen.

But the Japanese proved they could still be dangerous. On the night of 14 April, a flight of Mitsubishi G4M Betty bombers arrived from their base in the Carolines. Andrew Jones later wrote, "The second Japanese air attack on Engebi occurred shortly after midnight. The warning siren wailed and we piled out of our tents. A wispy orange thread of flame descended toward the horizon far off to the southwest. "That's the other team," someone yelled, "Let's get underground."

Jones and his fellow marines scrambled down into the slit trenches and foxholes while radar-equipped Corsair night fighters homed in on the dark bombers.

Engebi's anti-aircraft guns began hammering into the night.

The three harrowing days on the raft had forced Chick Whalen to pull himself from the flight roster. He too was a victim of the Flintlock Disaster.(Photo courtesy Andrew Syrkin.)

The Japanese bombers dropped no more bombs and less than an hour later the "all clear" siren howled. The marines climbed out of their holes. The Corsairs had shot down two more Betty bombers before the enemy had turned for home.

The Buccaneers said good-bye to one of the survivors in April. First Lieutenant Bob "Chick" Whalen had taken himself off the flight rotation. Jones, who had known Whalen at Jacksonville, said, "Abe Lincoln and I had been spending a lot of time trying to buck up Chick Whalen, who was still badly shaken by his near drowning in February. He'd flown two thousand ocean miles up from Funafuti and flown Engebi patrols since he'd arrived. Then he came over to our area to tell us he couldn't do it anymore."

"I can't handle it," said the man who had spent three days and nights naked and defenseless, battered in a storm-tossed rubber raft. His face was a mask of personal agony. "I just can't fly over water."

Jones said, "Chick had given his problem the best shot he had. He'd tried to beat it and he'd succeeded for a while, but now it had gotten the better of him."

Abe Lincoln, Whalen's fellow Bostonian tried to reassure him but to no avail.

Chick shook his head. "I can't do it," he murmured. He turned and walked back toward the 422 compound. We watched him go, the cocky little ball player with the swaggering strut, crooked smile, and ever-ready wise crack, scuffing the ground now, head down in heartrending defeat."

That afternoon, orders were cut for Whalen to return to the States. he could reasonably be considered another casualty of the disaster.

Their missions took a dramatic change in May. In order to make maximum use of the Corsair's capabilities, they were to become dive bombers. The F4Us usually carried three one-thousand-pound high-explosive general-purpose bombs. One was slung on the fuselage centerline and the others on the wing hardpoints. On a long-range mission, they substituted the center bomb for a 150-gallon drop tank. Interestingly, the B-25s carried a smaller bomb load but their range was far greater, and the F4Us had to be modified to serve as dive bombers. With the same Pacific Theater Yankee ingenuity that had turned the B-25 into a skip bomber, a chief ordnance man named George Garner designed a simple bomb rack out of leftover steel piping. The squadron engineers welded it and the contraption was tested by VMF-113 commander Doc Everton. Everton had flown dive bombers at Midway and knew the technique. He had a one-thousand-pound bomb slung on the new rack and made a steep dive on a section of the coral reef and hit it perfectly. The improvised rack was a success. A production line was set up and within a week, every Corsair in the two squadrons was turned into an impromptu dive bomber.

For the Corsairs, the technique of dive bombing wasn't as extreme as was used by the SBD Dauntless. The SBDs usually flew at fifteen thousand feet until they were within sight of the target. Then they nosed over in a seventy-eight-degree dive, nearly straight down, keeping the ship in sight through their bombsight crosshairs. This seemingly suicidal method had two advantages. First, it was very difficult for AA gunners or fighters to hit a steeply diving plane, and the kinetic energy built up in the dive was transmitted into the bomb itself, adding greatly to its penetrating power.

The SBD's unique perforated dive brakes were extended to slow the power dive, which could reach 350 knots, too fast for effective control. The dive brakes kept the dive speed down to about 250 knots. At between 2,000 and 1,200 feet, they released the bomb and pulled up, curving away from the anticipated blast radius. A moving ship was a very hard target to hit, but as was seen at

Midway, the Dauntlesses tore the heart out of Admiral Nagumo's carrier fleet.

For the Corsairs, which had no dive brakes and were most often going for stationary land targets, the dive was started at about 15,000 feet and at a shallower angle. Still, the speed could reach to four hundred knots so the pilots extended the landing gear.

This led to one of the Corsair's most famous nicknames. The three-hundred-knot slipstream entered the two oil cooler intakes on the leading edges of the wing roots, creating a high-pitched whistling noise. The pilots could not hear this, but those on the ground, the Japanese, did. There is a legend that the Japanese called the F4U "Whistling Death," but there is little evidence that this is true. It was more likely the name was of American or Australian origin. In any event, there is little doubt that the enemy troops who heard that eerie shriek coming from the sky recognized it for what it was: death.

After dropping their bombs, the marines raised the landing gear and flew away at low altitude, turning and twisting to throw off the AA gunner's aim.

In the 1980 interview, Hansen said, "Coming off the target at low altitude, the gunners aimed horizontally so we jinked up and down. At higher altitudes, we jinked back and forth because they were aiming from underneath us."

"Those tracers looked like big orange balls being thrown right at me," recalled Lehnert. "Sometimes the flak was so thick it was like a damned spider web all around us."

Some planes were hit and the pilots, with the others flying close by in a protective cocoon, nursed it back to base. "That was when the ground crew and mechanics really did a great job," said Syrkin. "They performed miracles I still can't believe. Day after day they kept those planes flying and us alive."

Future astronaut John Glenn, who was at that time headed towards Pearl Harbor from California with VMF-155, wrote about his arrival on Majuro. Even though he was based on a different island and did not enter combat until May, his descriptions of life on a marine fighter base in the Marshalls offers an excellent account of what the men of VMF-422 found on Engebi in March. He related setting up Quonset huts they built themselves from kits. Each was set up on sawed-off palm tree logs and accommodated twelve to fifteen men. The mess and sanitary facilities were part kit and part innovation from whatever was available, like palm tree trunks, boards, fuel drums, and bomb crates. Beds were the usual wood-and-canvas folding camp cots, but the marines made them more comfortable by cutting strips from Corsair inner tubes and weaving them across the frames.

They subsisted on canned and boxed rations, but were woefully short on fresh meat or fruit. Spam was never in short supply and the cooks became very innovative in creating different dishes to relieve the monotony. Spam loaf, Spam stew, Spam patties, and Spam in gravy were daily fare. Glenn said that if he survived the war, he would never eat Vienna sausage again.

One thing that was in abundance was fish, which they caught on hook and line, or as some innovative marines learned, by tossing hand grenades into the lagoon. The resulting explosions always brought up dead and stunned fish, ready for the grill.

When not flying, they swam, wrote letters, or played volleyball and baseball. Weekly movies were projected onto a large white sheet hung between two palm trees, while the marines sat on log benches. They usually wore ponchos and pith helmets to ward off the frequent, but brief rain showers. The rain helped to supplement the fresh water ration, which was brought in by ship. Several fifty-five-gallon drums were cut in half as large troughs to catch the rainwater and served for washing and shaving.

Glenn said, with tongue-in-cheek humor, that the greatest danger when not flying was from sunburn and falling coconuts. Millions of tiny black flies, attracted by the open latrines, got into everything, including the food. As the weather grew hotter, sleeping with a mosquito net over one's face became the norm. Only improved sanitation facilities ended the nuisance.

As the weather grew extremely hot and humid, it was very hard to keep clean. Laundry was primitive. There was nothing like a real washing machine. Glenn described a sort of automatic washing machine powered by a windmill, as was seen in the movie of Rogers & Hammerstein's *South Pacific*. They used salt water detergent. It worked, but the khaki uniforms would never have passed inspection. Often they tied the clothing to a coral reef outcropping and let the surf wash them clean. Then they were hung up so the frequent rains washed the salt out. It was simple, but it worked well enough.

Every week they eagerly awaited letters from home. Chick Whalen, who had been sent home in the spring had promised to call and write their wives, girlfriends, and families. Since the survivors had been directed not to write home about the disaster, Whalen's calls were the first time their loved ones learned the full story of the ill-fated flight to Funafuti.

Day after day the Buccaneers bombed airfields and AA batteries, communication posts, and underground fuel dumps on Wotje. For the latter, they carried five-hundred-pound bombs with long needle-like steel noses that penetrated the concrete and detonated underground. When the bomb found its mark, a towering orange and black fireball laced with chunks of concrete erupted into the sky. "That was very satisfying to see," Hansen said.

On 28 May, they flew thirty-one individual strikes, or sorties, to Wotje, and after five more days had completed more than ninety.

Not every pilot flew on every mission, though. Often Red Flight flew one mission, then came back to be replaced by Gold. Then Green Flight went. This way they avoided what was euphemistically called a "furball" of dozens of planes streaking back and forth over a particular target. "I flew one bombing mission in the morning and then Jules Flood took my plane for an afternoon mission," said Lehnert. "We alternated and everybody got a shot. The planes were maintained or repaired while we were on the ground."

On the evening of 6 June, the marines gathered at the theater to hear the radio broadcasts of the Invasion of Normandy. Being almost exactly halfway around the world and nearly twelve hours ahead, they first heard about D-day at 1900 hours. They listened with rapt attention as the greatest air, ground, navy, and amphibious operation in history drove into occupied France. "We listened intently to what was happening in Europe," recalled Hansen. "It was exciting, but we felt kind of left out."

The Japanese on Wotje claimed the life of one of the pilots on 7 July. First Lieutenant Donald Stout, Jr. was shot down as he was making strafing runs on the airfield. His last radio transmission was brief but chilling. "I'm hit. My whole leading edge of my right wing is ripped open. I haven't much control of the plane."

When last seen he was at two hundred feet altitude. The area was searched that night and the following morning without finding Stout.

The bombing and strafing raids continued nearly every day. A month later, another of the replacement pilots was killed. Kansas-born Second Lieutenant Raymond Schroeder died on 4 August in a crash as he attempted to take off on a weather recon flight. Schroeder's plane crashed into two parked F4Us.

The Grim Reaper was still not done with the Flying Buccaneers. Three days later, Second Lieutenant Emerald Wolverton of Colorado was killed after he pulled out of a steep dive after a bomb run on Taroa in Maloelap Atoll. He may have been hit by AA fire, but it is also possible he partially blacked out from the sharp pull-out. He crashed into the lagoon near the pier on the northwest coast of the island.

Just over a week later, First Lieutenant Duane A. Dahquist died when he crashed on landing at Stickell Field on Eniwetok after returning from an early-morning weather flight.

Five men had been lost in as many months.

The base commander, Colonel Daniel Torrey and Major Wrenn kept up their morale with concerts, baseball games, and movies. Curly Lehnert organized boxing matches between squadrons. According to some accounts, but not verified, one was to be between the ever-adversarial Syrkin and Gunderson. "I think we were supposed to have it, but I can't remember if it ever happened."

The fight of the century notwithstanding, there was entertainment in the War Zone. The prototypical comedian Bob Hope was working his way across the Central Pacific on his USO "Pineapple Tour," or the "Malaria Circuit," as he called it. He had landed at Mullinix Field on Tarawa at the end of July, then flew to Kwajalein and Majuro. When he saw the devastated islands, he joked, "Why didn't you let the Japs keep it?" Eniwetok was the next stop. With Hope was the beautiful singer Frances Langford, who sang a smoky contralto rendition of Hope's signature song "Thanks for the Memories."

Hollywood wasn't through with the Marshalls. Jack Benny arrived on his own USO tour on 6 September. More than six thousand sailors, marines, army soldiers, and airmen cheered as the famous comedian and his troupe entertained them. Syrkin admitted he never took his eyes off curvaceous blonde actress Carole Landis's legs.

On 9 September, VMF-422 was designated the Flying Buccaneers. They had been using the name from the beginning but now it was official. Major Wrenn called all the offices and men together and unrolled a large panel of white canvas. On it was a color cartoon painting of a pirate complete with eye patch astride a Corsair. Across the bottom were the words "VMF-422—The Flying Buccaneers." He explained that Walt Disney Studios had a special art department that created unit emblems and airplane nose art.

The squadron at Mille Island in 1944. (Photo courtesy Andrew Syrkin.)

"We were thrilled to see that painting," said Lehnert. "I still re-member how we all posed for a squadron photo in front of one of the Corsairs."

That same day, James Forrestal, now the Secretary of the Navy after the death of Frank Knox, received the agreed-upon recom-mendations of the Board of Inquiry.

From: Chief of Naval Operations.
To: Secretary of the Navy.
Subj: Board of Investigation – Flight and subsequent loss of planes and personnel of 422nd MarFightRon; convened by ComTaskFor -57, Aircraft, CenPacFor, PacFlt, 26 January 1944.

Forwarded, recommending approval
Approve: Oct. 5, 1944
J. Forrestal
Secretary of the Navy

The final endorsement was signed on 8 October. Admiral King concurred. This was the last official word on the subject of VMF-422.

All the air operations on Engebi were transferred to the larger base on Eniwetok on 16 September. In the squadron history, Wrenn wrote of this period. "Alternating with its sister squadron, VMF-113, our squadron participated in precision-like strikes against

Wotje, Mille, and Jaluit Atolls, all Japanese-held Marshall island bases. Two weeks out of the month, VMF-422 would stage through Roi and attack these enemy positions."

The bombing attacks turned in a new direction when shipments of 1,500 lb. napalm bombs arrived. These looked like drop tanks but were filled with jellied gasoline and an igniting fuze. Dropping the napalm bombs was less dangerous to the pilots as they did not detonate in sprays of hot shrapnel, but the sight of what they did to Japanese bases, buildings, and troops was not something that a man could look upon without a feeling of horror and shame.

"Those things were terrible," said Lehnert. "They burned everything to a crisp. I never felt good about using them."

Later that month, a special visitor arrived on Eniwetok. Charles Lindbergh, the most famous aviator in the world, and a hero to most of the marines since their childhood, was on an unofficial tour of Pacific army, navy, and marine air bases. The man who had been the first to fly the Atlantic in 1927 had spent months talking to and flying with army air force pilots, offering his expertise to help them in extending the range of and bomb load of their fighters. He was there unofficially, the result of his pre-war outspoken isolationist views against Roosevelt's policies. He was flying as a "technical representative," but at great risk. If he were captured by the Japanese, he would be a man without a country. His khaki uniform bore no rank or unit insignia. He didn't even wear pilot's wings. In June, he joined the US Army's 475th Fighter Group, known as "Satan's Angels," who flew the famed P-38 Lightning in New Guinea. The army pilots knew full well that Lindbergh knew how to get the most out of a gallon of gas. He taught the pilots how to extend the maximum range of the Lightning by almost three hundred miles by running on a lean mixture, raising manifold pressure and lowering revolutions per minute. It was a major boost to the P-38's capabilities.

On a mission out of New Guinea on 28 July, he shot down a Mitsubishi Ki-51 "Sonya" light bomber in a head-on encounter.

As he worked his way north and east, he began meeting the marines in the Solomons, the Gilberts, and Marshalls. In his role as an evaluation pilot for Chance-Vought, he had shown the F4U was capable of carrying a staggering four thousand pounds of bombs, an unheard-of load for a single-engine fighter. Lindbergh was as eager to test the Corsair's capability as to increase the hitting power of an attack.

Lindbergh's arrival on Eniwetok took the base by surprise.

Tex Watson, still considered the best pilot in the squadron, was in the officer's mess tent. "Some of us had given the mess boys a

The famous aviator Charles Lindbergh visited Eniwetok in September 1944. He flew three missions with VMF-422. (Author's collection.)

ride in a two-seater," he said. "They wanted to treat us to a steak dinner. They told us to be there at a certain time. And we were sittin' there enjoyin' a steak when this civilian walks in. He walks over to us and said, 'I understand you fellows are fighter pilots, and the cooks over there say you're the greatest.' So I said, 'Well, we're workin' on that.' He goes over and gets a tray of food and sits down. I didn't know who he was so I introduced myself. Then he puts out his hand and says, 'I'm Charles Lindbergh.' Boy that was the most embarrassing moment in all my life."

Syrkin, who had seen Lindbergh waving at him in 1927 said, "He was a wonderful man. He played volleyball with us, talked flying, just a great pilot."

Ken Gunderson recalled his first meeting with the legendary airman. "He was a very humble man, not like I expected."

Lindbergh, still boyish at forty-two years of age, managed to join in a few combat missions with his fellow aviators. He flew at least three missions with Curly as division leader to Wotje Island, dropping bombs and strafing ground installations. Lindbergh showed them how they could carry extremely heavy bomb loads on the Corsair by increasing the length of their takeoff and moving from side to side down the runway.

Price related his memories of the flyer's first bombing mission with marines. "All of us went out to the flight line and checked out our planes. We just made sure it had two wings, a propeller, and a tail. Boom, got in. Lindbergh didn't do it that way. He went over every single inch of that airplane. He took forty-five minutes before he climbed in. We flew to Wotje and made our runs; he didn't hit a thing. He missed the whole island with his bombs. When we got back, he asked us, 'How'd you fellows do that?' So we explained our technique and the next day we went back, and he put it right in there. Quick learner."

Syrkin scoffed at this. "I've heard that some pilots said he couldn't hit the island. That's a crock of baloney. He was a great man, great pilot. I was proud to fly with him."

Curiously, Lindbergh's visit was not mentioned in the official history, but did appear in virtually every pilot's flight log.

After flying fifty combat missions all over the Pacific, Charles Lindbergh returned home. He later stated that he considered the F4U Corsair the "best navy fighter built during the war."

But the Holy Grail of all fighter pilots continued to elude the Buccaneers. "Not one of us had shot down a Japanese fighter," said Lehnert. "They were just not up there. Every enemy plane we hit was on the ground. I heard Breeze Syrkin got some, but I also heard that he called them kills, which means an air-to-air victory."

Syrkin's flight log listed the Japanese planes he destroyed on the ground:

3 September 1944. Zeke, Wotje, confirmed
18 October 1944. Zeke, Ponape, confirmed
22 November 1944. Mitzu, Ponape, confirmed
9 December 1944. Kate, Ponape, confirmed

Syrkin uses the official US Navy code name for the Zero, the "Zeke." Counting the first Zero on Ponape in April, this brought his score to five.

This was typical for the most aggressive pilots of VMF-422, but it wasn't as good as shooting down a Zero in combat.

The marines continued to bomb and strafe Ponape, Wotje, and other islands, effectively neutralizing the stubborn enemy resistance in the Marshalls and Carolines. But from radio broadcasts, rumors, and briefings, it was apparent the war had moved on.

The Marshall Islands, which only a few months earlier had been the focus of the largest naval and amphibious force ever assembled in the Pacific was now a relatively quiet backwater.

Farther north the three main islands of the Marianas, Saipan, Guam, and Tinian, had fallen. It was a costly battle. Despite

Corsairs of the Fourth MBDAW on a bombing mission over the Marshalls in 1944. (Official U.S. Marine Corps photo.)

meticulous planning, American casualties were shockingly high, proof that the Japanese determination to fight to the last was still strong. Two huge carrier fleets came to death blows in the Philippine Sea, giving birth to the legendary "Marianas Turkey Shoot," in which navy fighter pilots scoured the skies of Japanese Army and Navy aircraft, but VMF-422 saw none of this.

"I remember wondering if we'd been forgotten," said Lehnert. "After all our training and what we went through, we never really got into the leading edge of the war. It left us where we were."

They flew more strikes to Ponape in November and early December totaling 117 sorties. Being 372 nautical miles from Eniwetok, the Ponape missions took three hours each way. It had usually been a practice to have a PBY flying patrol nearby to pick up downed pilots, but in the days prior to Flintlock, strike missions were rarely escorted. Admiral Nimitz's directives changed that in the spring of 1944. All long-range flights by single-engine planes were accompanied by a patrol plane, regardless of the objective. That was why, on the later Ponape missions, VMF-422 had a Lockheed PV-1 hovering nearby like a watchful mother.

John Glenn wrote of two bombing missions from Tarawa to the enemy-held phosphate mines at Nauru, which was nearly four hundred miles to the southwest. Since the flight was over open ocean

The big Christmas party of 1944 was also the last hurrah for the departing pilots of VMF-422. (Photo courtesy Andrew Syrkin.)

without any island landmarks, they were escorted by a Lockheed PV Ventura all the way to the target and back.

In a way, this was the true legacy VMF-422 left behind as their tour drew to a close.

On Christmas day there were no missions. After the December supply shipment had been unloaded, the cooks and stewards traded and bartered with other bases to put together a special Christmas feast. They mimeographed a type written Christmas banquet menu which listed foods the marines had hardly remembered even existed.

Roast turkey and baked ham, giblet gravy, buttered peas, cranberry sauce, sweet and sour pickles, fruit cake, and salted nuts.

The marines were able to cut loose, feasting, drinking, singing, and toasting.

"We drank a toast to Mac and the others we lost," said Hansen. "It was a great time. I think I got sick on all that rich food. The mess boys did a terrific job."

The feast also marked the swan song for the original officers and enlisted men of VMF-422. On 28 December 1944, twenty-one new officers and forty-five enlisted men arrived to replace the personnel who had served fifteen months of overseas duty.

Turkey and all the trimmings were scrounged by the mess cooks to make up this sumptuous menu. This became a treasured keepsake for the departing pilots. (Courtesy Andrew Syrkin.)

After a round of handshakes, hugs, and promises to pass on messages to the wives and families of the ones still staying, the men who had survived the January disaster boarded a transport to return to Pearl Harbor.

"We were going home," said Hansen. "It was great, but still kind of hard to leave the others behind."

Two days later they were back on Oahu. According to Hansen, the first thing the returnees noticed after entering the Ford Island administration building was the clean, neatly pressed khaki uniforms of the staff. "We were all wearing our best uniforms, but after nearly a year of rain, sweat, humidity, salt water, laundry, and normal wear and tear, we looked like a bunch of derelicts."

After enduring medical checkups and reams of paperwork, the Flying Buccaneers went into Honolulu where they all had haircuts and shaves and bought new uniforms and souvenirs of Hawaii for their families. Some, like Watson and Lincoln, went straight for the nightclubs and bars.

"I wondered if Breeze was going to head for that night club and find that reporter," Lehnert said with a laugh. "I don't remember if he did, but I would not have been surprised."

In the first week of January, it was time to leave Hawaii. Some were taking a flight back to San Diego, while a few would fly to San Francisco. Their role in the war had not been a large one, but they had all done their duty and never failed to carry out a combat assignment. There were few regrets, except that fifteen of them were never going home.

The Flying Buccaneers were soon scattered all over the country on leave. Gunderson went home to his wife in Milwaukee, Price flew directly to St. Louis, Jeans joined his family in Joplin, and Hughes took his leave in Oklahoma. Hansen stepped off a train in Iowa to be greeted by a crowd of family and friends. Among them was Mary Shreffler, soon to be his wife. Watson was back in Texas, Lincoln in Boston, and Jake Wilson returned to Mississippi where he may have told the truth about his time on Niutao.

Syrkin and Lehnert headed for New York City, where they spent a month trying to get the mold and sand out of their pores. But as Lehnert stated, it was not as easy to leave the war behind. "For a time it felt great to be home. But you know, it's kind of hard to let go. I spent a lot of time listening to the radio and reading the paper, keeping up with what was happening in the Pacific. I kept hoping to see the squadron mentioned, but it never was. I called Mac's wife and parents. I was glad to hear that most of the fellows had also done so. Poor Naomi, to be widowed so young. Mac's son never got to know his father. I met him years later and told him what a great guy Mac was." Lehnert, still feeling guilt for not being able to save Chris Lauesen, wrote the grieving parents and related the entire story of the disaster.

Likewise, Syrkin wrote to the parents of his friend, Tiger Moran.

The Navy Department officially declared Major John S. MacLaughlin, Jr. dead on 25 January 1945. He was posthumously promoted to the rank of Lieutenant Colonel. Also declared dead were Captain John Rogers and First Lieutenants Bill Aycrigg, Earl Thompson, and Christian Lauesen. It was closure of a sort for the families, but not for the survivors, who continued to reflect on the tragedy. "At least Mac wasn't held responsible," said Syrkin. "He was a good man and I'm glad the marines saw fit to promote him."

In the squadron history, Major Elmer Wrenn wrote of his predecessor, Major MacLaughlin: "It was ironic that the Major's main recreational interest, the sea, should claim him as its victim. His interest in the welfare and comfort of each officer and enlisted man knew no bounds. His loss was keenly felt by all."

By May 1945, the war had entered a new and terrible phase. Saipan and Iwo Jima had proved that the Japanese, despite having almost no navy left and only a shell of an air force, was still a determined and ruthless foe. They fought to the death and contested every square foot of soil, and their fanaticism only increased as the Americans drove closer to the Home Islands.

A new threat, the Kamikaze suicide planes, posed a deadly menace to the invasion fleets. VMF-422's replacement pilots were interdicting the Kamikazes that threw themselves against the vast juggernaut arrayed around Okinawa. Marine pilots were at last fighting over the fleet while the United States Navy flew strikes against the island defenses.

The coordinated cooperation between the navy and marines that Alfred Cunningham, Ben Smith, and William McIlvain had envisioned back in the 1920s had finally become a reality.

VMF-422's replacement pilots were credited with nine kills. Okinawa was the last major island objective before the "Big One," the invasion of Japan. Although no official word was issued, the ever-active grapevine had it coming in late 1945. If the bloody battles that had preceded it were any indication, the invasion could cost over a million lives on both sides.

General Curtis E. LeMay's Twentieth Bomber Command B-29s were flattening Japanese cities day and night, while Admiral Charles Lockwood's submarines scoured the oceans clear of Japanese shipping. New fighters were streaming off the line, including a hot new Grumman predator called the F8F Bearcat. Corsairs, now part of the regular carrier inventory, were tearing Kamikazes out of the sky and proving to be superb ground-attack planes.

Lehnert and Syrkin were both posted to MCAS El Toro south of Los Angeles. Other former VMF-422 pilots were sent to Jacksonville, Cherry Point, or Santa Barbara. With dozens of new squadrons being formed and reconsolidated, they saw their chance to get into real combat.

That summer, as the former Buccaneers were training with their new squadrons, the atomic bombs on Hiroshima and Nagasaki sounded the death knell of Imperial Japan's conquest of the Pacific. The war was over.

CHAPTER 23

HOME ARE THE HUNTERS

Syrkin was at MCAS El Toro on 14 August going over paperwork for his new squadron when he heard of the Japanese surrender. That night he and Lehnert, the only two former VMF-422 pilots at El Toro, celebrated the hard-won victory. It had been a costly war for the Flying Buccaneers. Counting the Farrell-Drake crash at Midway, ten lead echelon pilots had died and five replacement pilots were killed during their time in the Marshalls, bringing the death toll to fifteen, more than a third of the forty in the squadron. This was an unusually high ratio even for squadrons that had seen action in the Solomons or Okinawa. The author found only one other marine fighter squadron to have suffered greater losses. That was VMF-221 at Midway.

Over drinks, Syrkin and Lehnert discussed what they would do next. Both chose to stay in the marines and fly. Lehnert intended to go back to college. Syrkin would stay in the reserves for now. "I figured I was too old to play professional baseball," he said with a wry grin. "So I stayed in. I liked being a marine aviator."

Serving in the reserves and stationed at NAS New York (now Floyd Bennett Field) on Long Island, Syrkin met Marilyn Fried, the daughter of a wealthy member of the New York Stock Exchange. While he enjoyed attending parties at country clubs and other society functions, he admitted he felt out of place in the rarified atmosphere of Long Island's Gold Coast. He and Marilyn, known as Lynn, were married at the prestigious Woodmere Country Club on June 2, 1946. Her father, Albert Fried, tried to persuade his son-in-law to leave the Marine Corps and join him on Wall Street, but Breeze Syrkin was still committed to the marines and flying. Their first child, a son named Andrew, was born in Hewlett, New York in April 1948.

With the defeat of Nazi fascism and Japanese imperialism, America returned to a peacetime footing.

The War Department began cancelling defense contracts and decommissioning army, navy, and air force units. They mercilessly cut the size of the military. With the stroke of a pen, more planes, ships, tanks, and trucks were destroyed than Hitler, Mussolini, and Tojo had in four years of war. Units with proud names ceased to exist. Thousands of venerable warplanes were exiled to the Arizona desert, forgotten and abandoned. Hundreds were sold to serve in the air forces of other nations. Warships were decommissioned and mothballed for the next time they would be called upon to save American democracy.

VMF-422 was not spared. It was deactivated at MCAS Cherry Point, North Carolina on 7 April 1947, just three years and four months after it had been formed at El Toro. An era had ended. The tragedy of the Flintlock Disaster was soon forgotten by all but those who had lived through it.

As the 1950s began, the world entered the Cold War. A new enemy, international Communism, dominated the headlines. When Syrkin's daughter Wendy was born in August 1950, the media was beginning to focus on a faraway place in Asia called Korea.

Japan, the former enemy homeland, became a staging base for the Korean War. Syrkin, Watson, Lincoln, Lehnert, Hansen, and other former Buccaneers were recalled to active duty. Syrkin was assigned to the famous VMF-211 which flew Corsairs more advanced and powerful than the ones he'd used in World War Two. He was promoted to captain and assigned as the squadron executive officer.

"My father-in-law was adamant that I not go to Korea and even offered to fix it for me, but it was no use." Captain Mark W. Syrkin, USMCR, Executive Officer of Marine Fighter Squadron 211 was eager to get back into combat. Leaving his wife and children in Hewlett, he deployed to Korea on board the carrier USS *Coral Sea* (CV-43). They flew bombing and ground attack missions against North Korean targets in support of marines during some of the heaviest fighting in the war. It was real fighting as Syrkin had never seen it in 1944. The other former Buccaneers were also either flying missions over Korea or back in the states testing new aircraft.

For the first time, the air was filled with the sound of jet planes. The jet age had begun and little by little, the great but now-antiquated propeller planes of the Second World War were being left behind. Syrkin in particular loved the big gull-winged F4U, but he wanted to get into the "Blowjobs" as the sleek new jets were euphemistically called. Then the air wing commander announced that VMF-211 was going to change over to fly the hot new Grumman F9F Panther jet.

With little fanfare and even less preparation, they were soon flying the tiny Panther, a straight-winged tricycle landing gear fighter.

On his first flight from the marine air base in Japan, Syrkin thrilled at the feeling of pure, raw power and speed. The little Panther handled like a race car. "Jules Flood would have loved to fly it," he said.

VMF-211 again deployed to Korea on its second tour, flying more air strikes against Communist positions.

Curly Lehnert had also gone on to fly Panthers with VMF-115. The two old Buccaneers met in Japan for drinks and dinner. Curly had married a girl named Doris whom he'd met while stationed at Quantico, Virginia. John Hansen was his best man.

Then fate intervened for Syrkin. During a high-speed dive and pull-out after an attack run, he felt a strange ripping sensation in his belly. The flight surgeon told him he was bleeding internally. He was the victim of the high stresses from jet speeds. He underwent surgery and several weeks of recovery, but his combat days were over, and Breeze was put on limited flight status.

Back in New York while at Floyd Bennett Field on Long Island, he kept in touch with many of his buddies from VMF-422. They wrote one another and exchanged Christmas cards. When two or more former Buccaneers found themselves in the same city they got together over lunch, dinner, or drinks and talked about the old days.

"I never passed up the chance when a duty assignment put me close enough to an old buddy to check out an SNJ to go and see him."

In an effort to pass the torch, Syrkin told his son Andy the story so the boy would grow up knowing the names of the men who died. He took young Andy to the field and let him sit in a Corsair and even taxied around with the wide-eyed boy in his lap. It was totally against regulations but Syrkin reckoned he wasn't a candidate for a Good Conduct Medal anyway.

Then Syrkin heard that the F4U Corsair was being retired. The ones that hadn't been scrapped were slated for shipment to a place in Kingman, Arizona. The reign of the best piston-engine fighter-bomber ever built was finally coming to an end.

He had to fly it one more time. On 21 April 1953, almost exactly ten years after climbing into his first Corsair at NAS San Diego, Syrkin signed out FG-1D Corsair, Bureau No. 92489 at Floyd Bennett Field on Long Island. The FG-1D was a late-war variant of the Corsair built by Goodyear with the more powerful and efficient R-2800-8W water-injection engine. But outwardly, it looked almost exactly like the ones he'd flown from the fall of 1943 to the end of the war.

After doing a preflight check, he climbed onto the starboard wing and into the cockpit. He was the last man to call himself sentimental, but knowing that this would be his last ride in the venerable warplane, Syrkin took his time and relished the feeling of being in the last of the breed. He had also developed, as he said later, a tendency to be extra careful about his survival gear and radios, a common trait among the Flintlock survivors.

With a roar of pure, unbridled power, the engine came to life and Syrkin steered to the end of the runway. He was not on a tiny island far out in the vast Pacific, he was on Long Island, New York, only a few miles from where he'd grown up.

Receiving clearance, he advanced the throttle and streamed into the clear sky headed out over the Atlantic Ocean.

For three hours, the marine pilot reveled in the sheer joy of freedom, speed, and power. He opened the throttle to maximum and streaked over the water at four hundred knots as fishing boat crews watched in awe.

"I put that Corsair through every maneuver I remembered," he told his son years later. "I climbed to thirty thousand feet far out over the ocean until the coast was totally gone. It was a real thrill."

But all too soon it was over. Captain Mark "Breeze" Syrkin, USMCR, erstwhile of VMF-422, landed the last Corsair he would ever fly.

The survivors of the disaster never turned down an interview or a chance to tell their story. Even enlisted men of the ground crews like Leon Furgatch, Larry Myles, Eddie Walsh, Jack Brouse, and Howard Markwardt got involved. Furgatch began collecting every document, letter, and memo he could find. He asked the survivors to write about their experiences and even managed to acquire a copy of the board's findings. He was not, however, able to obtain a transcript of the investigation or the exhibits.

For the most part, the Buccaneers had put the war behind them and moved on. But there was a dark cloud on the horizon that refused to go away.

General Merritt, upon returning to the states in the spring of 1944, was put in command of the Ninth MAW at MCAS Cherry Point. From September to January, he commanded the entire air station. He received a second star and retired from the marines as a major general in the summer of 1947. Ironically his retirement took place at MCAS Cherry Point, where, only a few months earlier, VMF-422 had ceased to exist.

The author attempted to obtain Merritt's personnel file through the Freedom of Information Act, but as of this writing, was not successful. However, an official at the JAG office in Washington, who wished to remain anonymous stated that "it was unlikely you will ever be able to see those files. The letter of reprimand, not a chance."

What follows is pure speculation. General Merritt never again had a combat command, but he had received a second star. The date of his promotion is not recorded, which in itself is odd, but his retirement followed. A promotion followed by a retirement is often called a "tombstone promotion," and in some cases, is the result of an arrangement between the officer and the Pentagon. It was not unheard-of for an officer with a brilliant career – and skeleton in his closet – to be asked to leave the service to avoid embarrassment. There is no way to ascertain this in Merritt's case, but the reader may draw their own conclusion.

In an attempt to dig deeper into the layers of bureaucratic dust that has collected over the past seven decades, the author researched Merritt's postwar life and career and located a biography entitled: "Major General Lewie G. Merritt, Marine Corps Aviation Pioneer, Citadel Class of 1917," written jointly by Lieutenant Colonel Frederick J. Whittle, USMC (Retired), Citadel Class of 1980, and Lieutenant Colonel Andrew D. Kullberg, USAF (Retired), Citadel Class of 1983.

The biography is very detailed, up to a point. It covers his family history as far back as the Civil War. His service in the Dominican Republic and France during the First World War are described, as was his work in organizing marine air wings prior to 1942. Yet at this point there is a curious gap.

According to Whittle and Kullberg, the last combat campaign Merritt participated in was the Solomons, overseeing marine air operations from a tent. This duty ended in 1944. However, the Solomons Campaign was over by the spring of 1943, then followed by the invasion of the Gilberts. Guadalcanal is listed as the end of his wartime experience. Nowhere in the 2,640-word biography is there any mention of Operation Galvanic, Tarawa, the Marshall Islands, Operation Flintlock, or VMF-422. The entire investigation and subsequent findings, and the letter of reprimand were absent. While the bulk of the document is thorough, it reads as though a large portion was omitted. Bearing in mind that it was written by two officers who had both graduated from the Citadel in the 1980s, it is interesting that such a sizable gap appears in Merritt's history.

Lewie Merritt after his promotion to Major General. (Photo courtesy The Citadel.)

It is not a small omission, and considering that the Flintlock Disaster was the subject of Pentagon-level interest, a very intriguing one.

After the war, he was invited by President Truman to serve on the Strategic Bombing Survey, a detailed study of US bombing and its effects on the Japanese military. The biography went on to say that Merritt's wisdom in military aviation was unsurpassed and recognized at the highest levels, but the ambitious southern general did not stop there.

In 1949, he was appointed the first director of the South Carolina Legislative Council by Governor Strom Thurmond. In this post, he exercised considerable political, legal, and legislative power while drafting bills and organizing laws for South Carolina. Furthermore, Merritt was chosen by Lieutenant Governor George Timmerman, Jr. Citadel Class of 1937, to serve as campaign manager in his successful run for Governor.

The former general practiced law in Columbia, South Carolina until his death in 1974. He was buried with full honors at Arlington

National Cemetery. Even after his death, his legacy of ambition did not wither. On 15 September 1975, the airfield at MCAS Beaufort, South Carolina was renamed Merritt Field.

There can be little doubt that Merritt had successfully managed to erase the stain on his record. Merritt never publicly acknowledged his role in the loss of VMF-422, nor did he ever express his condolences to the families of the men who died under his command.

As for the other officers named in the boards' recommendations, Captain Jackson R. Tate retired from the United States Navy as a rear admiral and died in 1978. The author was unable to find any pertinent postwar information on Brewster or Wheelock. In Tate's case, the letter of caution did not hurt his military career.

But according to research by VMF-422 historian Leon Furgatch, Colonel Lawrence Burke had temporarily commanded the Ninth MAW at MCAS Cherry Point from February to May 1945. He retired from the marines after the war and became a school teacher at Pensacola Junior College. There is no evidence that Merritt ever made any attempt to clear the name of his former operations officer.

Rear Admiral Charles Pownall was appointed military governor of Guam in 1946. He retired in 1948 and died in 1975. Rear Admiral John Hoover spent the rest of the war overseeing the construction of air bases from the Marshalls to Okinawa. He was appointed head of the Board of Inquiry that investigated Admiral Halsey's actions during the disastrous typhoon of December 1944. He died at Bethesda Naval Hospital in 1970.

The years have taken their toll on the veterans of the Second World War. The survivors of VMF-422 were no different. As of this writing, only one is still alive, colonel Robert "Curly" Lehnert.

Lehnert earned his law degree at George Washington University in 1953. He and his wife Doris had two sons and a daughter.

When Lehnert retired from the marines at the rank of colonel in January 1973, he became a Colorado State Assistant Attorney General. He held that position until 1988.

In addition to the Navy and Marine Corps Commendation Medal he received for his efforts to save Chris Lauesen, he also earned seven Air Medals, three Distinguished Flying Crosses, and the Legion of Merit. He still has the citation, signed by Admiral Nimitz himself.

After being elected president of the VMF-422 Association of Veterans, he arranged reunions and was often interviewed by magazines and newspapers. He and Doris now live in Denver.

United States Pacific Fleet

Flagship of the Commander-in-Chief

In the name of the President of the United States,
the Commander in Chief, United States Pacific Fleet,
takes pleasure in presenting the NAVY and MARINE CORPS
MEDAL to

FIRST LIEUTENANT ROBERT C. LEHNERT
UNITED STATES MARINE CORPS RESERVE

for service as set forth in the following

CITATION:

"For heroism while participating in an aerial flight
as section leader of a Marine Fighting Squadron engaged
in a ferrying operation between Tarawa, Gilbert Islands
and Nanumea, Ellice Islands on 25 January 1944. When
engine trouble forced his wingman to make a water landing in a severe hurricane, he volunteered to leave the
rest of the formation and circle the pilot until aid arrived. Atmospheric disturbances made it impossible for
him to contact the nearby base of Nanumea. Though it became obvious that there was no prospect of rescue facilities that day, he continued in flight over the distressed
pilot until his fuel supply was practically exhausted.
Since the man in the water depended on a life jacket only,
he parachuted from his plane to share his own life raft
with him. Although the other pilot was lost, he kept a-
float for fifty-six hours, being rescued by a patrol plane
on 27 January 1944. His courageous conduct and skillful
use of his aircraft were in keeping with the highest traditions of the United States Naval Service."

C. W. NIMITZ,
Fleet Admiral, U.S. Navy.

Temporary Citation

*The citation for the Navy and Marine Corps Commendation Medal,
signed by Admiral Nimitz, was awarded to Robert Lehnert for his effort
to rescue Chris Lauesen. (Photo courtesy Colonel Robert Lehnert.)*

Captain Cloyd Rex Jeans, who had been given the Distinguished
Flying Cross for his role in the rescue of the marines at Guadalcanal in 1942 was recognized for his actions to keep his pilots alive
after the ditching. The citation reads "Cloyd R. Jeans, United States
Marine Corps, was awarded the Legion of Merit for exceptionally
meritorious conduct in the performance of outstanding services to
the Government of the United States in the Pacific Theater of Operations on 25 January 1944." He and his wife Patricia divorced in
1961. The last reunion he attended was in July 1982.

Ken Gunderson left the marines and became a police officer in Los Angeles until he retired in 1966. He later went to work for Douglas Aircraft. He and his wife Verna had one daughter, Sandy. They lived in Los Angeles, Orange County, and Hemet, California. After Verna's death, he moved back to Wisconsin. He bought a hunting lodge in Colorado and spent much of his free time hunting and fishing. Until his death of pneumonia in July 2015 he was still an avid, if somewhat slower, athlete.

Colonel John Hansen retired from the marines in June 1973. He returned to Florida with his wife Mary and their four children. As active and athletic as ever, he took up a career as an international tennis official. He was active in tennis until the age of 87.

"I was in the marines for thirty years and played professional tennis for the same length of time," he said. "I preferred the tennis." Hansen's daughter Heidi said the marine base tennis courts in Da Nang, Vietnam had been named Hansen Courts in his honor.

Hansen died in 2013 during the early research for this book.

John "Abe" Lincoln retired to Rockland, Maine, after a sterling marine career as a test pilot and combat veteran. He earned two more DFCs in addition to the one he had been awarded for flying in the war. He died in 2008.

Sterling "Shou" Price left the marines and became a sales manager for a hydraulics company in Missouri. He was married to a local girl named Lois and remained active with the VMF-422 Association for the rest of his life and never passed up an opportunity to say publicly that he felt General Merritt should have been court-martialed and shot. Price passed away in the mid-1990s.

Walter "Jake" Wilson, considered the luckiest guy in the squadron, went home to Mississippi and married his sweetheart. He played the trombone in a jazz band on weekends.

Charley Hughes retired from the marines after the war and moved to Seattle to work as an aeronautical engineer for Boeing.

Robert "Chick" Whalen had voluntarily grounded himself after the disaster. He went on to be a scout for the Philadelphia Phillies, but the ordeal of three days in the raft had taken its toll on him and he spent much of the rest of his life at the bottom of a bottle. Like Captain Charley Hughes and Jake Wilson, he died in the 1980s.

George Davidson, the PBY pilot, retired as a lieutenant commander after twenty-four years. He returned to Florida and became purchasing director for Reynolds, Smith & Hills of Jacksonville, a facilities and infrastructure consulting firm. Davidson died in 2014.

*John Hansen after returning home from the Pacific. He
married Mary Shreffler and stayed in the Marine Corps.
(Photo courtesy Heidi Hansen.)*

Major Royce "Tex" Watson, the most colorful and skilled pilot
in VMF-422, married his girlfriend Mary. He flew fighter-bombers
during the Korean Conflict where he was awarded the Korean Service Medal, The United Nations Medal, and The National Defense
Service Medal. Tex continued to serve in various staff and command posts until his retirement from active duty in 1965. During
his military career, he flew over 5700 flight hours in thirty-one different types of aircraft, including jets and helicopters. Watson died
in January 2011 in Texas.

Jules Flood, who was the most skilled at working with engines,
remained in the marine reserves. He married and had a son and

daughter. He continued to fly as a private and charter pilot. Flood died in 1956.

As for Mark "Breeze" Syrkin, he had earned, in addition to his World War II Victory and Korean War medals, two Air Medals, the Distinguished Flying Cross, and the American Campaign, Asiatic Pacific, and European Occupation ribbons. "But the Good Conduct Medal," Andy Syrkin said with a laugh. "Not my dad."

Breeze Syrkin retired from the marines at the rank of major and moved from Ohio to Charlotte, North Carolina. He was, to the rest of his days an active and earnest member of the Flying Buccaneers and always paid sincere respect to the unsung heroes of the war, the mechanics and ground crew.

Andy Syrkin took up the reins of keeping the squadron's dwindling list of survivors in touch with one another. He became the official squadron historian. After his father's mental and physical health deteriorated in the late 1990s, Andy brought him home to Columbus, Ohio to live with him until the old marine veteran died on 4 March 2000. He was laid to rest with full military honors at Arlington, in Section Fifty-Nine, Grave 2003-3.

In April 2000, the mayor of the city of Charlotte, in recognition of one of its revered Second World War veterans, proclaimed April 22, 2000 to be Major Mark W. Syrkin Day. The proclamation reads in part,

> "*Whereas*, Major Mark W. Syrkin, USMCR, served this country faithfully and became a highly decorated World War II and Korean War combat fighter pilot who was awarded the Distinguished Flying Cross and Air Medal; and
>
> *Whereas*, Major Syrkin had the vision to honor all who faithfully served their country in war and in peacetime; and
>
> *Whereas*, the Charlotte City Council voted unanimously to change the name of the Monument of Valor to the Major Mark W. Syrkin Memorial:
>
> *Now*, therefore, I Patrick McCrory, Mayor of Charlotte do hereby proclaim April 22, 2000 as
>
> Major Mark W. Syrkin Day."

One can't help but wonder what Breeze would have thought of that. The monument is now in the "Hallowed Ground" area of the Charlotte Convention Center.

The author was not able to learn the fates of Robert K. Wilson, Bob Scott, Don Walker, or Caleb Smick, the man who was the first since Jesus to walk on water.

Rex Jeans and Breeze Syrkin at the 1982 reunion. (Photo courtesy Andrew Syrkin.)

The biggest squadron reunion was held in 1990 in Santa Barbara, near the old air station, where today a monument lists all the marine squadrons from MCAS Santa Barbara that served in the war. Pilots and ground crew, file clerks, and mess cooks gathered to refight the war and remember old friends. The reunions were spirited affairs, full of raucous stories and heartfelt memories. "There wasn't as much drinking as in the old days," said Lehnert with a twisted grin. "Too bad."

In 1991, the VMF-422 reunion had a special guest. George Davidson had not kept in touch with the Buccaneers, even though he had been awarded the Navy and Marine Commendation Medal for his heroic rescue of thirteen of its pilots. "When we said our goodbyes on Funafuti," he said in in 1998 video interview, "that was the last I saw of those guys until 1991 when I got a call from California and asked if I'd like to come to a reunion."

The assembled Buccaneers watched Davidson come in with his wife, Barbara.

"When I got there, there was a whole bunch of people, I didn't know who they were. But I recognized Syrkin. When I walked in they all said, 'Is he a marine?' Then one man said, 'No he's not a marine, but if it weren't for him none of us would be here.'"

A wave of applause and cheering ensued and Davidson found himself the guest of honor. Andy Syrkin, then forty-four, went up to thank the man who had saved his father's life. "If you hadn't saved my dad I wouldn't be here today."

Davidson was unanimously voted as an honorary Buccaneer and marine, and thereafter invited to every squadron reunion.

As the years passed, the number of attendees dropped. Andy continued to arrange them even after his father's death. For the 2005 event he had an F4U Corsair fly over so the old veterans could see it just once more. "What a thrill it was to watch that Corsair fly over us," recalled Lehnert. "It felt really good. I missed flying them."

But the story does not quite end here. The day after returning home from Arlington, Andy Syrkin stood looking at the shelves full of his father's papers and war memorabilia. He flipped through the old flight logs, photos, letters, reports and, personal papers. He had known about the disaster since he was a boy, but his father's passing had given him a reason to learn more.

The flight logs listed every plane his father had flown since 1942. One entry boldly stated "25 Jan. F4U,B/N #55883, 6.0 hours. Tarawa to Funafuti. Encountered storm, lost at sea 53 hrs. Picked up by PBY-5A."

Andy read through pages and pages of entries, looking for something, but not sure if it even existed. "I wrote down the serial and tail numbers of every Corsair he flew," Andy recalled. "I wanted to find out if any of my dad's Corsairs were still around."

He spent hours searching on the internet through listings of airworthy warplanes before he struck pay dirt. FG-1D #92489, which his father had flown from Floyd Bennett Field on 21 April 1953, was owned by Frank Arrufat, a retired TWA pilot who had purchased it from El Salvador. The plane had been in the inventory of the Escuadrilla 2 of the Escuadrón Caza y Bombardeo of the Salvadoran Air Force from 1957 to 1976. Arrufat had spent years restoring the Corsair, and then turned it over to John Lane, owner of the American Airpower Museum in Jerome, Idaho.

"I called Lane and tried to tell him that my dad had flown the Corsair, but he didn't even give me the time of day. I got back to him and said I could fax my dad's flight log page. He agreed, and after realizing I was telling the truth and not some nut job trying to wrangle a free ride, invited me to Idaho to see the Corsair."

Andrew Syrkin next to the last Corsair his father ever flew back in 1953. (Photo courtesy Andrew Syrkin.)

The day he went to Idaho in 2008 was a watershed moment for Andy Syrkin. He stared at the last Corsair his father had ever flown. "I touched it and realized my dad had done the same thing in 1953. It felt kind of weird but I was very glad to do it. In a way, I was actually touching his history."

The Corsair, named "Whistling Death," is now part of the collection of the Texas Flying Legends Museum in Houston. In 2010, it won the Grand Champion World War II Restoration Award at Oshkosh AirVenture, a very high honor and one of which Breeze would have been proud.

Today, the Flintlock Disaster has been relegated to a tiny paragraph in the pages of history. This is not where it should remain. It was the worst non-combat loss to a marine squadron in the entire war. Yet in the more than seven decades since, only a few magazine and newspaper articles, and two independent documentaries, have been produced to tell the story. What happened to VMF-422 was a completely avoidable tragedy. In the final analysis, the manner in which the marines were readied for the flight and the subsequent failure to prevent it from taking off can only be described in that term so beloved of American military, "snafu." The root of the blame can certainly be placed at the feet of General Merritt, but Colonel Burke was nearly as culpable. While it can be assumed that he was cowed into not pressing for an escort, his real failure was in taking full control of VMF-422's entire stay on the island. He never once brought the base operations structure into his plans. If Burke had inquired into the procedure for clearing a flight with Wheelock, Brewster, or Waring, one of them would have asked, "Did you file a flight plan with Air Operations?" That would lead to the further question of the escort, which, as in the case of VMF-113, would be provided through the island commander independent of Merritt. Thus the story of the Flying Buccaneers would have had a far different and happier ending. Six young men would not have suffered lonely and desperate deaths in the empty ocean, and this book need never have been written.

In his 1980 oral history for the Navy Department, Colonel John Hansen was asked by the interviewer, "You received a letter of commendation, but it was labeled secret. Why?"

Hansen replied, "This whole thing just plain wasn't announced. It wasn't one of the things you go around and tell about. Not at that time." With a conspiratorial chuckle, he ended the interview.

THE MYSTERIES
OF THE
FLINTLOCK DISASTER

History is almost never "chiseled in stone." It is an ever-shifting foundation that constantly hides and reveals the past under its fluid surface. Even as time adds layers of dust to obscure the secrets, the work of researchers sifts the sands of the ages. In some cases, new information is found by sheer chance, such as when a person finds a hidden treasure trove of forgotten letters and documents in their attic. But there are always imponderables, always perplexing mysteries. Why didn't Captain Lord of the liner *SS Californian* investigate the strange ship that was seen firing distress rockets on that cold April night in 1912? Did Mary Surratt know more about the plot to assassinate Lincoln? Was John F. Kennedy accidentally shot by one of his Secret Service agents who was responding to the shots from the book depository? Did President Roosevelt really know the Japanese were about to attack Pearl Harbor? Some of these questions can never be answered. It is up to the historians to dig into the past and learn more.

The Flintlock Disaster has more than its share of ironies and enigmas. This book has touched on some in the text, but refrained from examining them in detail until now. The author has been very fortunate to have obtained several documents, letters, and transcripts that shed some light on the disaster. In addition, being able to view the events of January 1944 from the perspective of 20/20 historical hindsight, there is a great deal of supporting information that can help fill in some of the missing puzzle pieces.

Who was Nanumea tracking on radar?

One of the many mysteries that surround the odyssey of VMF-422 concerns the many isolated and scattered radar contacts plotted on the Nanumea radar screens. By using the plot report, Board of Investigation exhibits ten through twelve, it is possible to make some educated guesses. But added to this has to be the storm's effects. As stated earlier, a large, fully developed Pacific cyclone is a powerful force. If we assume the eye wall, or main vortex, of the cyclone was about 150 miles in diameter, which is slightly below average, it should have covered an area roughly one-third of the distance between Nanumea and Funafuti, 376 miles to the south-southeast. South Pacific cyclones move east and revolve in a clockwise direction. If we further assume winds speeds of 150 knots, and that its northern edge crossed over or close to Nanumea, starting at 1030 hours (based on Colonel Payne's testimony), then we have a basis for determining how the Flying Buccaneers ended up strewn all over the Central Pacific. The documents do not provide any means of identifying individual IFF signals, so there is virtually no way to track each plane from one minute to the next. Even by using a chart and noting every radar contact by time and location, the result is little more than a seemingly random spattering of dots and tracks.

We will start from the point where Nanumea first detected approaching planes.

1. At 1229 hours, the first radar contact was plotted at 000 degrees, range nineteen miles. The contacts moved southeast until 1240, when the plot showed them to be east of the island. We know that between 1215 and 1237, VMF-422 was in the storm, first at about two thousand feet, descending until they broke out from the cloud deck at less than two hundred feet. At that point, they were probably no longer seen on the radar screen. This is supported by the next entry, which stated that by 1255, the plot went blank after the planes disappeared into what was known as a "null." Nulls were "blind spots" in radar coverage, sometimes caused by weather or obscuring land features.

2. Around 1240 - 1245, Major MacLaughlin made his first radical course change from 135 degrees and headed northeast. This unannounced maneuver created havoc, splitting the already ragged formation. Rogers led Wilson, Hansen, and Walker up and away, while Moran, fourth in line in Jeans' Green Flight, tried to stay with his leader as Green crossed over Gold. Thompson, on MacLaughlin's wing, managed to stay with his leader in the first turn. The second turn, about three minutes later caused more chaos. MacLaughlin returned to 135 degrees. By 1250, the squadron had broken up into one large and one small group with at least two single planes by themselves.

3. At 1258, the first Emergency IFF was picked up at 075, range forty-five miles.

4. Ten minutes later, another IFF was plotted. This shows conclusively that the formation had broken up. Instead of all the planes being southeast, at least two were just north of east.

5. At 1311 hours the report shows the IFF plots "turned Bogey," which is to say they were designated as unknown.

6. At 1323, they both faded from the screen.

7. The radar operators had been busy, as at 1317 another "Bogey" was picked up at 055 degrees, fifty-three miles. Two minutes later, it faded out at 050 degrees, fifty-two miles. This contact was almost exactly to the northeast. The bearing change showed it was headed north when it faded out.

8. When the next Bogey appeared at 1320, it was at 072 degrees, range thirty-two miles, and then it too faded at 1322 hours. There appears to have been two, possibly three individual planes on the plot between 1307 and 1322 hours. They were all, more or less, northeast of Nanumea, and within seventy miles. As will be discussed later, one was certainly Jake Wilson. But the other two, it is hard to say. Hansen was already climbing to get out of the storm. Rogers and Moran, who lost contact at the same time, had been heading east or northeast. Thompson, who disappeared after the second turn, could have been headed anywhere within a ninety-degree arc.

9. Another IFF came on at 1330 and assumed to be the same plane. Three minutes passed when another Emergency IFF came on the screen at 090 degrees, sixty-three miles. It too faded at 1341 hours, seventy-three miles away at 095 degrees.

From this point on, the radar screens showed no solid contacts. Intermittent radio reception meant that as few as two or three planes could have triggered all the separate IFF contacts. But as we know, by that time, the main formation of VMF-422 was far to the south, desperately blundering about in the storm, looking for Nui. So the question is: whose planes and IFF signals had triggered all those radar plots? Logically it could only be Rogers and his band of orphans. Even though they broke from the formation around 1235 when the squadron was already far south of Nanumea, they turned up on the radar plot to the northeast of the island. In other words, they actually flew over or close to Nanumea in their desperate attempts to find open sky. This illustrates how capricious fate could be. Looking first at Hansen, Wilson, and Moran, consider that they all lost contact with the formation at about the same time and place, each found themselves all alone in the storm, and each stayed in the air for at least two hours, looking for safety. Each one found an island. The three islands were separated by 370 miles. Two of the pilots were very lucky, while the third died from a cruel twist of fate.

How did Hansen escape the storm?

John Hansen followed Rogers up into the storm ceiling at 1235. At about thirteen thousand feet, he found himself all alone. Understandably unwilling to go back down in the storm, Hansen sought a way clear of it. That presented itself around 1330 hours, when he cleared the eye wall. After receiving the Funafuti radio range from Jeans via Walker, he turned south, and found his goal at 1430.

There can be no disputing that John Hansen was freakishly lucky. It is not possible to say for certain where he emerged from the wall of cloud at 1330, but he was probably within 180 miles of Funafuti. Since he landed at 1430, he had to have come out of the storm less than two hundred miles from the island.

The vagaries of wind within the revolving storm pushed him south and east from where he was separated from the rest of the squadron.

Do any of the radar plots match Hansen's location? The answer is, probably not. Without exception, every one of the single IFF signals and radar fixes was either east or northeast of Nanumea, and the range was never more than seventy-three miles. By 1341, Hansen was well away from the storm and hell bent for Funafuti.

How did Jake Wilson end up on Niutao?

Of all the Buccaneers, it is the tale of Walter "Jake" Wilson that generates the most awe and envy. He flew around blindly in the storm for over two hours, lost and alone, and managed to stumble on the only island inhabited by friendly natives whose pretty girls were literally throwing themselves at him.

But how did he end up there? First we have to assume a few things based on his testimony, given a few days after the disaster. He said he had already followed Captain Rogers up and away from the others after the wild maneuvering under the storm. They climbed and he lost sight of Hansen and the others between five thousand and thirteen thousand feet.

"When I knew I was lost I [turned my fuel mixture] to manual lean and was using 1300 turns and I ran my wing tanks for thirty-five minutes, and still had a little bit of gas left, and switched to my right-wing tank, ran it dry, switched [back] to my left. Couldn't find any this way. I had to do something so I started climbing. Climbed to sixteen thousand feet and still wasn't out, there was still a big overcast. It was layers thick. I was trying to find a ship or island, tried to see something. It was so cloudy I couldn't see anything. I turned on my IFF, tried to find the Funafuti beam but couldn't do it and I could hear Captain Jeans every now and then saying something to the boys. I heard the major two or three times but his [voice] was kind of garbled. I couldn't hear him very well. I came back down."

"I first thought about flying a reciprocal course and try to get back up to Tarawa or some of these chains of islands. I flew that for about fifteen minutes. The storm was getting worse, turned around and flew 149 until my gasoline was about ready to give out. I kept calling Captain Jeans or Captain Hughes but they couldn't receive me. Lieutenant Walker received me and I asked them what course they were flying. He didn't tell me they were lost also. He called back and said, 'Wilson, fly 156,' and I said, 'Thank you,' and I flew 156 for a long time, I burned all the gasoline in both wing tanks, switched to my main tank. I had approximately eighty gallons in my main tank. At that time I tried to burn it as dry as I could. I never did get out of the storm. I was in it all the time I was flying along about one hundred feet [at] approximately 150 knots. Saw this island; it looked like a shadow of a cloud on the water and the storm was so bad I let down close to the water. The storm was so bad I almost ran into the palm trees."

All in all, a remarkable story. His testimony to the board is erratic and disjointed. For example, he mentioned running his left-wing tank nearly dry, switching to the other wing and ran it dry, and then went back to the left, and there was no fuel in it. Yet later he mentions using all the fuel in his wing tanks again. If we assume he was stating facts but the sequence was in error or distorted, then we have something to work with. Again this is theory, but taken as a whole, may help us to understand how he turned out to be, as Syrkin called him "the luckiest son-of-a-bitch in the squadron."

Wilson was flying roughly northeast when he followed Rogers back up into the storm at 1240 hours. He climbed to sixteen thousand feet and turned on his IFF. From that altitude, the IFF would stand out clearly. The Emergency IFF seen on Nanumea's radar at 1308 was plotted at 070 or 075 degrees, forty-five miles, or just north of east of the island.

If this is the case, we can place Jake Wilson, at shortly after 1300 hours, about twenty miles north-northwest of Niutao. Ironically, from his altitude of sixteen thousand feet, both islands, eighty-four miles apart, would have been visible, but according to Colonel Payne, they were under the storm.

Wilson said he heard Jeans and MacLaughlin on the radio, and the time would be close to when the two officers were discussing the island they had seen, and that MacLaughlin had caught the Funafuti radio range. Wilson, probably in an effort to get closer to the others, lowered his altitude. At about this same time Nanumea lost the IFF signal. Again this fits. Then Wilson said he considered taking a reciprocal heading, turning 180 degrees back the way they'd come and head to Tarawa or one of the chain of islands they had passed. The fact that he considered such a radical move is a good indicator of his state of mind.

He turned to 329 degrees for fifteen minutes. This is slightly west of north. His progress against the wind was greatly impeded. Even at 180 knots, fifteen minutes may have gained him twenty miles of actual distance covered. He said the storm was getting worse, so he then turned to 149 degrees, or 31 degrees east of due south "until my gasoline was about ready to give out."

At this point he was well south of Niutao, rapidly widening the distance with every minute. It was close to 1345 hours. He was actually headed more or less, straight at Funafuti. His altitude was one hundred feet at 150 knots and he never did get out of the storm, which explains why Nanumea no longer had his IFF on the screens.

Wilson mentioned that his radio calls were picked up by Walker, but there was no mention of this in other survivor accounts. Walker told him to fly 156 degrees which was seven degrees closer to due south. "I flew this for a long time until I burned all the gas in my two wing tanks. I had approximately eighty gallons in my main tank."

His last two courses, 149 and 156 were almost due south. If we accept that he began north of Niutao two hours before, he would have ended up more than two hundred miles south of the island. It is likely that this is when he made that reciprocal turn. And if this is when he flew for thirty-five minutes on his left-wing tank, then ran the other one dry, and at last went to the eighty gallons in his main tank, he had retraced the route north. Headed directly into the leading edge of the cyclone, he was forced to the east. The reciprocal of 156 is 324 degrees. An eastward push aimed him directly at Niutao.

It sounds more complicated than it was. Basically, Wilson flew over or past Nanumea, wandered in confusion entirely around Niutao, then headed south where he heard the others on the radio. Then thinking better of it, he turned north until he ended up over the island.

This is only one scenario that could put Jake Wilson's Corsair over a three-mile wide island in the middle of a major cyclone after three hours of aimless wandering. Freakishly good luck? Perhaps. But Divine Intervention may have played a role. Jake Wilson, the stout Southern Baptist was about to have his faith tested in a way he never imagined. But he was certainly very lucky.

What happened to Captain John Rogers?

His story is an enigma, since, other than a brief radio call, nothing is known of his actions from the point where he left the main formation. Rogers led Gold Flight, with Hansen, Jake Wilson, and Don Walker following. After MacLaughlin's first turn, he led his division up into the storm. This was an impulsive act, but in view of the wild, chaotic maneuverings of twenty-three Corsairs moving back and forth at 180 knots, an entirely reasonable one. Walker was able to rejoin the others, but Wilson and Hansen lost contact. Where did Rogers go, and in what direction?

He did make brief radio contact with Nanumea sometime around the time Moran was acting as go-between for Jeans and the island. His single transmission was laced with urgency, "For God's sake, can't anyone hear me?" Almost certainly, Rogers was one of the pilots to turn on his Emergency IFF, but when he did this can only be guessed.

At 1317, a Bogey was picked up at 055 degrees, fifty-three miles. Two minutes later it faded out at 050 degrees, fifty-two miles. If this was Rogers, he was almost exactly to the northeast. The bearing change showed he was headed north when it faded out, but to have been heard over the radio, he had to have turned back at some point. Again, we can only guess. All we know is that Captain John Rogers was never seen again.

Where did Earl Thompson go?

First Lieutenant Earl Thompson, as Red Two, was wingman to MacLaughlin. As wingman, he was to literally "follow the leader" in formation and combat maneuvers. A wingman was the eyes in the back of the leader's head, and never flew his own plane, but let his leader fly it, by following his every move.

Thompson was slightly behind and to the right of MacLaughlin all the way down from Tarawa. When they entered the storm, he kept his leader in sight, ready to react to any sudden maneuver or change. Under normal conditions, a squadron leader would announce his intentions, but in the heat of combat or when radio communication was impractical, hand signals were used. Thompson stayed with MacLaughlin all the way down until they broke free of the cloud deck. When MacLaughlin made the first turn to port, Thompson was still with him. But when the second turn to starboard was finished, he was gone. All that is known is that when the squadron reformed upon emerging from the first stormfront, Thompson was no longer there.

MacLaughlin almost certainly made a radio call to turn ninety degrees to port, but no one heard it. About three minutes later, MacLaughlin turned to starboard back onto the original course.

Did Thompson follow him? No one knows, but we can speculate. It was easier for a wingman to follow a turn to port than to starboard, because the port turn had the wingman on the outside, whereas starboard had him on the inside. In a sudden unexpected turn to starboard, the wingman had to fall back slightly to keep from plowing into the leader's plane as it passed in front of him. That may be when Thompson lost contact. But there is another possibility. Chris Lauesen had engine trouble in the storm. Their Pratt & Whitney R-2800 radial engines were marvels of technology, but they were being forced to run with huge amounts of water being swallowed by the intakes. Under normal conditions, the engines could handle some water, but these were not normal conditions. Thompson's engine may have been running rough or cutting out. This is only guesswork, but if his engine lost power at a critical moment at less than two hundred feet, he would have gone down in the raging tempest completely unnoticed by anyone. Without power, his plane plowed like a runaway train into the towering waves. In seconds, his Corsair carried him into the cold embrace of the uncaring sea.

This may explain why, unlike Hansen, Wilson, Moran, and even Rogers, Thompson never made radio contact with anyone. He could have been the first to die.

What happened to Major MacLaughlin?

Major John S. MacLaughlin's disappearance has been the subject of much debate among historians who have studied the disaster. Some maintain that he simply gave up after realizing he had failed his men and that they were all going to die as a result of his orders. It is worth keeping in mind that not one surviving pilot agreed with this opinion. "He was a great leader and friend," said Hansen firmly. "He had a lovely young wife and baby back home. I know he would never have given up."

The author spoke with Bobbie MacLaughlin, the widow of John S. MacLaughlin, III. Her husband had died a few months before this book was begun, but she said that everything that she had heard about her dead father-in-law from her mother-in-law was that he was a devoted husband and father. He would not throw his life away.

All evidence shows that MacLaughlin was a conscientious officer who looked out for his men. He took extra pains to make them into the best marine fighter squadron in the corps. He even took them snorkeling off the California coast, and at Midway, to help them become better swimmers. A true leader of men, he always went first in training, including the ditching practice at Pearl Harbor. The fact that he seemed to put extra emphasis on ditching and swimming has prompted some critics to say MacLaughlin was more concerned with training his men to survive after a ditching than to get them to their destination. This is absurd. Any good commander will try to cover every possible contingency and prepare for the worst. This is borne out by the fact that of the twenty pilots who did ditch or bail out over the ocean, seventeen survived. Lauesen and Aycrigg had not been able to get into their rafts, while Moran died in the Nui surf of a broken neck.

If MacLaughlin fell short in any aspect of the training he provided for his men, it was in the area of long-range over-water navigation. But that was a common failing in the navy and marines at the time, as stated in the boards' findings.

While MacLaughlin was not the kind of man to crack under pressure, it cannot be denied, even by his defenders, that he was faced with the imminent destruction of his first command. He made the two radical course changes that had caused chaos among the pilots and resulted in the disappearance of Rogers, Thompson, and Moran. He made the decision to bypass Nui and continue on to Funafuti. A conscientious officer like MacLaughlin would take the loss of so many of his men very hard. He had been close to them from the first day at MCAS Santa Barbara.

One of the survivors voiced the opinion that perhaps MacLaughlin had also suffered a casualty to his radio just as Watson had. He may have been completely focused on fixing the problem and was not able to respond. This does not explain his failure to react to Lincoln's vigorous attempts to get his attention by "waving, waggling my wings, and even firing my guns."

MacLaughlin had been trying to find Funafuti. He caught the radio range at about the time they had spotted Nui. Funafuti was close enough to reach. When he lost the beam, it must have been heartbreaking. The fact that he willingly allowed Jeans to lead the squadron back to Nui indicates that he was in full command of his senses. However, when they were unable to find Nui, he resumed his determined efforts to catch the radio range again. He can't be blamed for grasping for the last thread of hope.

Lincoln also said, "He had a hand on his earphones. "It looked like he was trying to hear something and just stared straight ahead."

The radio dials and controls were located on the right console, and required that the pilot look down to change frequencies or adjust reception. He was holding the earphones to his head in an effort to cut out as much external noise as possible to hear. Also, Lincoln was on MacLaughlin's starboard side, meaning that the hand that the major had pressed to his headset was the right hand. Therefore his left hand was on the control stick. He would not have been able to key the transmitter switch, which was on the throttle handle to his left. This could explain why he did not respond to Jeans' course change. He was listening on either the Funafuti or Nanumea radio range frequencies. So, at the very time Lincoln was trying to get the squadron commander's attention, he might very well have been completely focused on a faint intermittent "dash-dot" from some distant island.

The details of his loss will never be known. He was lost and alone in the storm, ran out of fuel and crashed into the cold sea. He, like Rogers and Thompson, literally flew into oblivion.

Why didn't the investigation know the truth about Merritt?

Another matter, not so much a mystery as a curious twist of fate, may be of interest. The Board of Inquiry only called six of the seventeen surviving pilots to testify. We can assume the board believed to call all seventeen would needlessly stretch out the investigation when they all had more important duties. Admittedly, the board chose carefully. They called Captains Jeans and Hughes and Lieutenants Lehnert, Wilson, Hansen, and Flood. With Jeans and Hughes, they had the senior surviving officers, Lehnert was witness to Lauesen's death, Hansen was the only pilot to reach Funafuti, Wilson made it to Niutao, and Flood was presumably a representative of the pilots in the mass ditching. With six men, all the bases were covered.

Yet the board missed a chance that might have changed the entire character of the investigation. None of the men called to testify had witnessed MacLaughlin's request for an escort at 0925 on 25 January, when Merritt shouted at Burke to "get the hell out," after refusing to allow an escort to be sent on the flight.

The only surviving pilots who saw this were Syrkin and Price. Rogers, Moran, Aycrigg, Thompson, or Lauesen might also have witnessed it, but we will never know. MacLaughlin, also among the fallen, did not have his day in court.

When the board questioned Jeans and Hughes, they learned that MacLaughlin had been disturbed that there would be no escort, and that Jeans, Hughes, and the now-dead Rogers had pressed him to make a formal request for one. This was what Syrkin and Price had seen. They both spoke of it in later years, and wrote of it in letters and articles.

Curiously, none of the pilots called to testify mentioned hearing about this even when asked to speak freely. They had been on rafts with Syrkin and Price, two of the most outspoken men in the squadron for more than seventy hours, then on Funafuti, and on the plane back to Tarawa. It is absurd to think that these two men, who for the rest of their lives railed that General Merritt had caused the deaths of six good men would keep their silence, even if told to do so by Major Wrenn.

It would only have taken one of the witnesses to say, "I did not personally see Major MacLaughlin request an escort, but I believe Lieutenant Syrkin and Lieutenant Price did."

If this had come out, the board would have good reason to call both pilots to the stand and hear the full story. Obviously, both Burke and Merritt had lied under oath and would be recalled and questioned further. Merritt, being the canny former JAG attorney would certainly have denied or sidestepped the issue, but Burke was another matter. Clearly more of a loyal, but uninspired, officer than an efficient one, he might well have folded under rigorous questioning. Then the entire matter would have come to light that both he and Merritt knew MacLaughlin had formally requested an escort and was refused.

Admiral Pownall's wish that Merritt be court-martialed would have come true. A Pyrrhic victory perhaps, but victory nonetheless.

Why Syrkin and Price did not tell their buddies what they had seen or if they had, why none of those called to the stand related it, no one can say. Yet, it is only another of the peculiar aspects of the Flintlock Disaster. One factor may be the American mindset of that period. Today, the post-Baby Boomer generations have become cynical and distrustful of the government and in particular, the military, artifacts of Watergate and the Vietnam War. But back during the Second World War, Americans were more trusting in the government. Conspiracy theories and cover-ups were virtually unheard of and not even considered. American military personnel accepted the word and decisions of those in authority. For that reason, Syrkin and Price may have acknowledged the board's findings as a *fait accompli* and let it go at that, whatever their personal feelings. We may never know.

What if?

What's a mystery without a paradox? Paradoxes are a favorite subject for historians, a kind of "What if?" The odyssey of VMF-422 contains at least one paradox. If one or both of two things had happened, there would have been no Flintlock Disaster. Consider that if Colonel Burke had prevailed in sending VMF-422 off on the afternoon of 24 January, they would have reached Nanumea nearly eighteen hours ahead of the cyclone. In that case, they may have spent the night on the island and continued to Funafuti in the morning. If Colonel Payne felt that the approaching storm warranted an escort, the marines would have been provided one.

The other "What if?" is even simpler. If Burke had done as he should have, the flight would have come to the attention of the Hawkins Field hierarchy, and Major Brewster or Commander Wheelock would have provided an escort. What would the escort plane have done when the cyclone was first seen? The logical assumption is that they would have directed VMF-422 to fly southeast to avoid the storm while they made contact with Nanumea. Then they would have brought the Corsairs in just as the storm was reaching its peak on the island. A day or two later, with the cyclone well past, the marines would have continued on to their destination, none the worse for wear. Neither of those events occurred, and the rest is history.

AIRCRAFT AND SQUADRON DESIGNATIONS

The system used by the Navy and Marines to designate aircraft types and squadrons is often confusing. In many cases the Army Air Force and Navy flew the exact same planes, but used completely different conventions to identify them. For instance, the Army's North American AT-6 Texan, stood for Advanced Trainer #6. To the Navy it was the SNJ, for "Scout-Trainer-North American." The Navy used a system with the aircraft type, then the manufacturer's code. The F4F stood for Fighter Number 4, Grumman, and F4U meant Fighter Number 4, Vought. For obscure reasons, Grumman's code was "F" while "G" stood for Goodyear. "N" meant Naval Aircraft Factory, not North American, whose code was "J."

To further confuse the matter, some aircraft were built under license by a different manufacturer, such as the Grumman TBF Avenger torpedo bomber being built by General Motors. GM-built TBFs were known as the TBM.

Below is a listing of aircraft codes and type, followed by the codes for the manufacturer. I hope this will help the reader understand how it works. For example, the Catalina PBY-5A comes from PB: Patrol Bomber, Y: Consolidated, 5A: Number Five, Variant A.

CODE	AIRCRAFT TYPE
B	Bomber
F	Fighter
FB	Fighter Bomber (after 1944) Later A: Atack
H	Rotary-wing (Helicopters)
J	Utility
M	Marine
N	Night (Fighter or Bomber)
O	Observation/Reconnaissance

CODE	AIRCRAFT TYPE
P	Patrol
PB	Patrol Bomber
R	Transport
SB	Scout/Dive Bomber
SN	Trainer
T	Torpedo Bomber
V	Heavier-than-air (fixed wing)
Z	Lighter-than-air (Dirigibles and Blimps

CODE	MANUFACTURER
A	Brewster
B	Boeing
C	Curtiss
D	Douglas
F	Grumman
G	Goodyear
J	North American
L	Bell
M	General Motors
N	Naval Aircraft Factory
O	Lockheed
P	Piper
S	Stearman
T	Northrop
U	Chance Vought
V	Lockheed Vega
Y	Consolidated Vultee (Later Convair)

GLOSSARY

AA: Anti-aircraft gun, or Anti-aircraft artillery (AAA)

Air Group: The fighter, bomber and scout squadrons assigned to an aircraft carrier

BB: Battleship

Bogie or Bogey: Slang term for unidentified radar contact

CA: Heavy Cruiser

Call Sign: Call name for a base or unit for use in open radio communications

CAP: Carrier or Combat Air Patrol

CASU: Combat Area Service Unit

CENCATS: Central Pacific Combat Air Transport Service

CINCPAC: Commander, U.S. Pacific Fleet (Nimitz)

COMSUBPAC: Commander, Submarines, Pacific (Lockwood)

COMAIRPACFOR: Commander, Air Forces, Pacific Fleet (Pownall)

COMAIRCENTPAC: Commander, Air Forces, Central Pacific (Hoover)

CPTP: Civilian Pilot Training Program

CQT: Carrier Qualification Training

CV: Aircraft Carrier

CVE: Escort Carrier

DD: Destroyer

Degree: 1/360th of a circle

Ditch: To crash-land a plane in the water

Division: The four-plane portion in a Flight

Echelon: A portion of a squadron roster. i.e. Ground or Flight Echelon. Also can refer to Lead and Rear Echelon

Echelon Formation: A diagonal "ladder' formation, Right echelon, all planes follow to right and behind the squadron leader

Element: The two-plane portion of a division with one leader and one wingman. Sometimes called a Section.

FMF: Fleet Marine Force

Flight: An eight-plane element of a squadron, usually under the command of a Captain

Flight Deck: The open deck of an aircraft carrier used for flight operations

Hangar Deck: The deck below the Flight Deck of a carrier, used for storage, transport, maintenance and repair of aircraft

Hood: Cockpit canopy

IFF: Identify, Friend or Foe

IFR: Instrument Flight Rules

JAG: Judge Advocate General

Kc: Kilocycles (now Kz for Kilohertz)

Knot: Unit of speed used for both aircraft and ships, as well as meteorology. A knot is approximately 1.15 miles per hour.

LCVP: Landing Craft, Vehicle, Personnel, also known as Higgins Boat

Leader: The command position of a flight, division or element in formation

LFR: Low Frequency Radio Range

LSO: Landing Signal Officer. Also known as "Paddles"

Mae West: Standard issue Navy life preserver, named for the busty Hollywood actress

MAG: Marine Air Group, consisting of as many as six squadrons

MarFightRon: Marine Fighter Squadron

MAW: Marine Air Wing, consisting of three to four MAGs

MBDAW: Marine Base Defense Air Wing

MCAS: Marine Corps Air Station

Mission: Term used for a squadron or air group's flight, route, and objective

NAB: Naval Amphibious Base

NAS: Naval Air Station

Nautical mile: Unit of distance for maritime and military use, approximately 6,070 feet or 1.15 statute miles.

NAVCAD: Naval Aviation Cadet

NAWS: Naval Air Weapons Station

NCO: Non-commissioned officer, i.e. sergeant

NRAB: Naval Reserve Air Base

NTB: Naval Training Base

P.A.: Public-Address System

Plane Captain. A flight deck crew posting on an aircraft carrier who assists the pilot as well as to oversee the movement of the aircraft.

Port: Left side or to the left

Range Leg: Also called a Quadrant, a 90-degree segment of the LFR beam

Radio Range: See LFR

Ready Room: A room assigned to a squadron on a carrier, used for briefings

Revetment: Area for parking an aircraft on a base, usually protected by concrete or sandbags

Section or Element: the two planes in a Division, one leader and a wingman

Six: Slang term for the six o'clock position behind another aircraft in combat

Sortie: A single flight by a single plane

Squadron: A full unit of pilots and aircraft, usually forty in all

Starboard: Right side or to the right

TF: Task Force, assembled for a specific campaign

TG: Task Group, or a specialized portion of a Task Force

UCMJ: Uniform Code of Military Justice

Very Flare Pistol: Launcher named for manufacturer, Very, sometimes spelled Verey

VF: Navy Fighter Squadron

VFB: Navy Fighter-Bomber Squadron

VFR: Visual Flight Rules

VMF: Marine Fighter Squadron

VMJ: Marine Utility Squadron

VMO: Marine Observation Squadron

VMSB: Marine Scout/Dive Bomber Squadron

VP: Navy Patrol Squadron

Wardroom: Officers' off-duty room, also used for meals and meetings

Wingman: Follows an element leader in flight (see Leader)

• ACKNOWLEDGMENTS •

Now that the story has been told...

It may be of interest to the reader, but is of little real importance, that I am legally blind. I lost my sight through a hereditary disorder back in the 1990s, which led to the end of my illustration and graphics career. I turned to writing full time. Rather than colors, words became my media and instead of canvas, the computer screen was my work surface. Always a voracious reader, I turned to audio books, and with the help of advanced talking software and scanners, I found few real obstacles in my writing. Those were either nullified or reduced by the generous support of my family, friends, and professional associates. In a way, being blind has given me both an advantage and an insight that mere sight could never hope to accomplish.

The way this book came to be written is an odyssey in itself. It began with yet another book. As an aviation historian, my interests had centered primarily on pre-jet age military aviation. My articles have been published in more than a dozen aviation and military history magazines and my interest in classic film gave rise to my second book. *Flying on Film – A Century of Aviation in the Movies, 1912 - 2012.* I was invited to do a presentation and book signing for the Quiet Birdmen Fort Worth Hangar in early 2013. The QB is a raucous bunch of pilots and aviators, so during the course of the evening, several came over and buttonholed me with ideas for a magazine article or book. Well, on that night, a big, ebullient man named Dan Brouse walked up and handed me a beer. A good start, even though I already had one in my hand. Then he asked me if I had heard about The Flintlock Disaster. I admitted I had not. Between drinks, the Texan told me the story, and I found it very intriguing. What was most surprising was that even with all my reading and research into the Pacific air war, I had never heard of the disaster that struck VMF-422 in 1944.

Dan asked for my card. Back in San Diego, I received a DVD and letter in the mail from his father Jack, who had been a ground crew sergeant in the squadron. The note simply read, "Call me after you've watched this."

The DVD was a professionally produced documentary entitled "The Flintlock Disaster." I was completely captivated by the tale of VMF-422. An hour later I called Jack.

"Well, what y'all think?" he asked me. "Interested?"
"That's putting it mildly," I said. "How do I find any of the survivors?"
"No problem," he said in his drawl. "Y'all got a pen?"

That was where my personal odyssey into the past really began. As the history of the events that took place near the islands of Nanumea, Nui, Tarawa, and Funafuti from 25 to 29 January 1944 unfolded, my fascination increased. I had stumbled on the Holy Grail of all historians, to relate a long-forgotten or concealed event of the Second World War. It was remarkable that this had never been generally known. Other than a few sporadic stories in some publications and the single documentary—which the survivors of the disaster paid for—being shown on some local PBS stations, the drama of the Flying Buccaneers had never been publicized.

When I had enough to go on, I pitched the story to my editors and waited. Carl von Wodtke of *Aviation History* magazine bit the hook and I was off and running, but even after the article was published in the January 2015 issue of *Aviation History*, I wasn't satisfied. I wanted to keep the momentum going, and that meant a full-length book. That simple decision affected my life more than I could ever have imagined.

Learning the story and making it into a workable manuscript was like assembling a five-thousand-piece jigsaw puzzle in which I had never seen the picture. To make it even more challenging, I didn't know how many pieces were missing, and the rest were scattered among a dozen people across the country. A few critical pieces were hidden in the files of the Navy JAG office in Washington, and I wasn't sure if I'd ever see them.

This book is the result of three years of work, cold coffee, fingernails, and a sheer pigheaded determination to write the best book I could. I owe a lot to many, many special people. I am deeply indebted to Jim Knapp and Dan Brouse, Quiet Birdmen, Ft. Worth Hangar for starting me on this path, although I admit to occasionally swearing at them under my breath.

I began my search with Andy Syrkin, the son of Major Mark W. Syrkin. Andy generously provided me with an entire library of documents, letters, diaries, interviews, photos, and videos he had collected over the years. As the official historian of VMF-422, he helped fill in many of the missing pieces of the seventy-year-old puzzle by relating personal recollections of his father and the other surviving members of the squadron.

I am deeply grateful to survivor Colonel Robert Lehnert, who spent hour after hour on the phone to help a non-aviator understand just how the Marines did it back in 1944. The late First Lieutenant Ken Gunderson and Colonel John Hansen also provided the most valuable commodity to a historian, personal memories. We all owe much to the late Sergeant Leon Furgatch, who had begun the long personal struggle to tell the story of the Buccaneers and carried the torch to his dying day.

Also my thanks to Heidi Hansen, daughter of John Hansen; Sandy Lynde, daughter of Ken Gunderson; Jackie MacLaughlin, daughter-in-law of Major John MacLaughlin; and Barbara Davidson, widow of PBY Catalina pilot George Davidson, for help in telling me about some of their memories of the men of VMF-422 and VP-53.

To marine sergeants Larry Myles, Howard Markwardt, and Jack Brouse for relating the world of the squadron's ground crew. Gary Edmisten was a valuable resource on the destroyer USS *Hobby,* the ship that rescued fourteen of the VMF-422 survivors.

Much of my research took me far beyond the history of a marine fighter squadron. For that I owe a great deal to Commander Chuck Sweeney, USN, President of the Distinguished Flying Cross Society for his never-failing support in helping me find the right person to talk to at the right time. The DFCS is a national organization of holders of the Distinguished Flying Cross, the nation's highest award for aviators. Through the DFCS I had a lively talk with Lieutenant Colonel Dean Caswell, USMC, the last surviving Second World War marine ace, for relating his experiences during training and life at MCAS Santa Barbara. The DFCS also helped me make friends with P-51 double ace Colonel Spiro "Steve" Pisanos, USAF, for generously relating the life and career of a fighter pilot. Steve passed away in June 2016, just as this manuscript was nearing completion.

No words can convey my gratitude to one of my veteran friends, the late Captain Wallace S. "Griff" Griffin, USN, who was my first interview on the subject of naval aviation and helped me understand what it meant to be an aviator. Commander Dean "Diz" Laird, USN, Hellcat ace, career navy aviator and friend, gave me a detailed account of how the United States Navy did their job back in the Second World War.

To my editor friends, Budd Davison at *Flight Journal,* Carl von Wodtke at *Aviation History,* and Jim Busha at *EAA Warbirds,* and others who have published my writings, thank you for believing in me.

I did have some real fun while working on this book. For that I am indebted to Rob Patterson, pilot, Planes of Fame Air Museum, for helping me understand what it was like to fly the Corsair. With his help I understood where things were and how they worked. After studying the few written accounts of the Flintlock Disaster, I realized no one had ever truly understood what VMF-422 had flown into. In that regard, I conferred with experts on Pacific typhoons to comprehend how these massive storms are born and behave, and even more important, what it is like inside a raging typhoon. Therefore, I offer my sincere gratitude to Professor Gary Barnes, PhD, Chairman, Department of Atmospheric Science at the University of Hawaii. Without his enthusiastic assistance and information, I would never have made it out alive.

Richard Gillespie of The International Group for Historical Aircraft Recovery (TIGHAR) talked with me for hours on the topic of storms and lost airplanes. TIGHAR is arguably the most famous organization involved in finding and solving some of the world's most enduring missing aircraft mysteries, including Amelia Earhart.

I also owe a great deal to the staff and researchers at the San Diego Air & Space Museum Library, the Flying Leathernecks Air Museum at MCAS Miramar, the National Naval Aviation Museum at NAS Pensacola, Florida, and Planes of Fame Air Museum in Chino, California. And the same to the late Colonel Carl Lawson, USMC, librarian and researcher at the National Naval Aviation Museum for providing a wealth of data on marine air operations, tactics, and equipment. To Richard Niedner, aircraft restorer at the National Museum of the Marine Corps in Quantico, Virginia for helping me dig out those hard to find contacts and sources, especially museum archivist Kara Newcomer, who went far afield to find rare images of Marine Corps aviation.

A special thanks to Fred Trapnell, Jr. and Dana Trapnell Tibbitts, the son and granddaughter of Admiral Fred "Trap" Trapnell for sending me a copy of their book "Harnessing the Sky," and sharing stories of the career of the man who literally "sold the US Navy on the Corsair." To Commander David Bruhn, author and historian, for sending me valuable information on the eyes of the fleet, the seaplane squadrons, and tenders.

Also to Lieutenant Colonel Jay Cibler, USMC, Vice Chairman, Flying Leathernecks Air Museum. Colonel Cibler is a career aviator and combat veteran who read the manuscript and strongly endorsed it to Major General Robert Butcher, USMC, Chairman of the

Flying Leathernecks Air Museum. General Butcher wrote the foreword. Both of these senior marine officers agreed "This is a story that needed to be told."

Some of my personal friends were unflagging in their support and assistance. These include Robert E. Johnston, Management Consultant at the San Diego Air & Space Museum and retired aerospace industry executive, who eagerly read and edited the manuscript. Ellie Hodge, a warm and sincere lady who loved my aviation stories. Pam Gay, librarian at the SDASM for being so sweet and supportive. Chief Warrant Officer Barry Stemler, Aviation Chief Ordnance man, who read the manuscript with such enthusiasm that I made him part of the inner circle. Don Ramm, the computer genius who generously kept my hard drive driving and the bytes biting. Without him, I'd have had to write this book like Fred Flintstone with a slate and chisel.

Special thanks and praise go to my friend and ardent supporter, Linda Stull, who never stopped being an airplane buff while she encouraged me on this project. Without Linda's help, this book would never have been written.

My editor at Sunbury Press, Erika Hodges was the perfect person to proofread the manuscript to assure that it conformed to the Holy Bible of writing, the Chicago Manual of Style. Although we did not agree on every point, I am grateful that she took extra pains to make sure the finished book was the best it could be. I look forward to working with her on my next book.

I found an ally in Linda Alvers, who processed my FOIA request to the right people, the willing and sincere staff at the Judge Advocate General's Office at the Washington Navy Yard. Particular thanks to Jennifer Zeldis, who processed my request for the VMF-422 inquiry documents so fast I was sure she couldn't possibly be working for the government.

I am honored to thank Colonel Walter J. Boyne, USAF, former curator of the National Air and Space Museum in Washington, DC and one of the foremost military aviation historians in the country, for reading my manuscript and agreeing to write a few blurbs for publicity. To me, it was akin to a high school physics student getting an "A" from Albert Einstein.

And most of all, to my beloved wife Jane, whose support, love, and even more important, patience gave me the perfect environment to create this book. It was hard for her, having to endure my hours, days, months, and years of research and writing. She was the Rock of Gibraltar I could lean on. I could not have done it without her. My deepest love to Jane for never failing to believe in me, no matter what.

To all those above and so many more, my sincere and earnest gratitude.

Mark Carlson, San Diego, California
August 2017

• SELECTED BIBLIOGRAPHY AND SOURCES •

OFFICIAL DOCUMENTS

Allied Order of Battle, Operation Flintlock. Department of the Navy.
Allied Order of Battle, Operation Galvanic. Department of the Navy.
Cushman, R. Major General, USMC (1962) *A Brief History of Marine Corps Aviation.* Marine Corps Historical Reference Series. Department of the Navy.
Naval Board of Investigation. Marine Fighter Squadron 422, 1944 27 January – 10 February 1944. Transcripts and Exhibits, official correspondence. Office of the Navy Judge Advocate General.
Naval Heritage and History Collection. NHHC, A History of Marine Corps Aviation, Volume 5.. Washington, DC.
PROCEDURES APPLICABLE TO COURTS AND BOARDS OF INQUIRY JAGINST 5830.1A. Office of the Navy Judge Advocate General. Washington Navy Yard, Washington DC.
Transcript of Interview of Colonel John Hansen USMC Retired, 4 October, 1980. Neal R. Gross, Transcriber. Department of the Navy.
Wrenn, E. Major, USMC, *Official History, VMF-422, January 1943 to January 1945.* Department of the Navy.

ARTICLES

Carlson, M. "The Marines' Lost Squadron." *Aviation History Magazine,* January 2015.
Carlson, M. "Top Ten Most Influential Allied Warplanes of WWII: #9 The PBY Catalina." *EAA Warbirds Magazine,* July 2013.
Emmett, M. W. "The Mystery of VMF-422." *Leathernecks Magazine* (date unknown).
Furgatch, L. "The Flintlock Disaster." King, J. *A Tale of Heroes.*
Stepzinski T. *Clay County Veterans in Documentary.* May 2013.
Syrkin, M. "The Flintlock Disaster." *Sea Classics,* October 2005 (Published posthumously).

BOOKS

Bergerud, E. (2000) *Fire in the Sky: The Air War in the South Pacific.* Westview Press, Boulder, CO.

Boone, G. (1994) *Whistling Death: The Test Pilot's Story of the F4U Corsair.* Schiffler, New York.

Bruhn, D. (2016) *Eyes of the Fleet: The U.S. Navy's Seaplane Tenders and Patrol Aircraft in World War II.* Heritage Books, Berwyn Heights, MD.

Carlson, M. (2012) *Flying on Film – A Century of Aviation in the Movies, 1912 – 2012.* Bear Manor Media, Duncan, OK.

Caswell, D. (2010) *My Taking Flight - A Life Story of My Love of Flying.* Austin, TX. Used with permission.

Drury, B. (2008) *Halsey's Typhoon.* Atlantic Monthly Press New York.

Glenn, J. (1999) *John Glenn, A Memoir.* Bantam Books, New York, NY.

Horikoshi, J. (1956) *Zero!* E.P. Dutton & Co, New York.

Hoyt, E. (2000 *How they Won the War in the Pacific.* Lyons Press, New York.

Johnston, R. (1948) *Follow Me! The Story of the Second Marine Division in World War II.* Random House New York, NY.

Jones, A. (1995) *the Corsair Years.* Turner Publishing, Paducah, KY.

Lord, W. (1957 *Day of Infamy.* Harper, New York, NY.

———. (1967) *Incredible Victory.* Harper, New York, NY.

Morison, Samuel Eliot. 1948. *History of United States Naval Operations in World War II, Volume VII: Aleutians, Gilberts, and Marshalls, June 1942 – April 1944.* Little, Brown, and Company, Boston.

Mrazek, R. (2008) *A Dawn Like Thunder – The True Story of Torpedo Squadron Eight.* Little, Brown, and Co, New York, NY.

Perrett, G. (1993) *Winged Victory, The Army Air Forces in World War II.* Random House New York, NY.

Prange, G. (1981) *At Dawn We Slept.* McGraw-Hill, New York NY.

———. (1988) *December 7, 1941.* McGraw-Hill, New York NY.

———. (1983 *Miracle at Midway.* Penguin Books, New York, NY.

Sherrod, R. (1987*) Marine Corps Aviation in WWII.* Duell, Sloan & Pearce, New York, NY.

———. (1973) *Tarawa: The Story of a Battle.* Duell, Sloan & Pearce, New York, NY.

Stanton, D. (2001) *In Harm's Way, the sinking of the* USS *Indianapolis.* H. Holt, New York.

Tillman, B. (1997) *Vought F4U Corsair.* Warbird Tech Books Vol. 4, Specialty Press.

Trapnell F. & Tibbets, D. (2015) *Harnessing the Sky: Frederick Trapnell, the U.S. Navy's Aviation Pioneer.* Naval Institute Press, Annapolis, MD.

ARCHIVAL SOURCES

Department of Atmospheric Science, University of Hawaii, Honolulu, Hawaii
Distinguished Flying Cross Society, Lindbergh Chapter, San Diego, California
Flying Leathernecks Museum, MCAS Miramar, San Diego, California
Museum of the Pacific, Pearl Harbor, Oahu
National Museum of Naval Aviation, NAS Pensacola, Florida
National Museum of the United States Marine Corps, Quantico, Virginia
Navy and Marine Corps Association
Navy Judge Advocate General, Washington Navy Yard, Washington DC
Pearl Harbor Survivors Association, Chapter 3, San Diego, California
Planes of Fame Air Museum, Chino, California
San Diego Air & Space Museum, San Diego, California
Santa Barbara Historical Society, Santa Barbara, California
The Pacific War Online Encyclopedia
USS *Midway* Aircraft Carrier Museum, San Diego, California

· INDEX ·

Page numbers in *Italics* denotes photographs.

MARK CARLSON is an aviation historian and the author of two other books.

Legally blind, he is the author of "Confessions of a Guide Dog – The Blonde Leading the Blind." The book has won three national awards and been reviewed in several national magazines.

His second book "Flying on Film – A Century of Aviation in the Movies 1912 - 2012" won two awards and been reviewed in six national magazines.

A member of several aviation, maritime, historical and veteran organizations, Carlson has been a contributing writer for over a dozen national magazines. His articles run the gamut of topics of aviation, military history, classic film and television, humor and essays. He started by writing stories about his first Guide Dog, Musket and later, about his work at the San Diego Air & Space Museum. This led to more articles in major aviation and military history magazines and then to his books. An award-winning club president in Toastmasters International, he is a respected public speaker on historical topics. He is an ardent student of history and never passes up the opportunity to meet and interview veterans about their experiences. This trait is what led to this book. "History is my passion and vocation," he says with sincerity. "I take my responsibilities as a writer of history very seriously." Carlson freely gives much credit to his network of family, friends and associates, all of whom have been ardent supporters of his work.

Although blind, he makes extensive use of advance computer software to work and write. He travels and works with his second Guide Dog, Saffron, a female Yellow Labrador retriever. Never one to take it slow, he is always working on his next book and several other projects. He lives in San Marcos, California with his wife, Jane.

Made in the USA
Columbia, SC
01 July 2020